CW00520305

ISBN 978-0-282-31837-6
PIBN 10847308

# LIVY.

TRANSLATED BY

GEORGE BAKER, A.M.

IN FIVE VOLUMES.

VOL. IV.

NEW-YORK:

PUBLISHED BY HARPER & BROTHERS,

NO. 82 CLIFF-STREET

1836.

# CONTENTS
OF
# THE FOURTH VOLUME.

# HISTORY OF ROME.

## ARGUMENTS.

### BOOK XXXI.

Renewal of the war with Philip, king of Macedon.—Successes of Publius Sulpicius, consul, who had the conduct of that war.—The Abydenians, besieged by Philip, put themselves to death, together with their wives and children.—Lucius Furius, pretor, defeats the Insubrian Gauls who had revolted; and Hamilcar, who stirred up the insurrection, is slain, with thirty-five thousand men.—Further operations of Sulpicius, Attalus, and the Rhodians, against Philip.

### BOOK XXXII.

Successes of Titus Quintius Flamininus against Philip; and of his brother Lucius, with the fleet, assisted by Attalus and the Rhodians.—Treaty of friendship with the Achæans.—Conspiracy of the slaves discovered and suppressed.—The number of the pretors augmented to six.—Defeat of the Insubrian Gauls by Cornelius Cethegus.—Treaty of friendship with Nabis, tyrant of Lacedæmon.—Capture of several cities in Macedonia.

### BOOK XXXIII.

Titus Quintius Flamininus, proconsul, gains a decisive victory over Philip at Cynoscephalæ.—Caius Sempronius Tuditanus, pretor, cut off by the Celtiberians.—Death of Attalus at Pergamus.—Peace granted to Philip, and liberty to Greece.—Lucius Furius Purpureo and Marcus Claudius Marcellus, consuls, subdue the Boian and Insubrian Gauls.—Triumph of Marcellus.—Hannibal, alarmed at an embassy from Rome concerning him, flies to Antiochus, king of Syria, who was preparing to make war on the Romans.

A 2

## BOOK XXXIV.

The Oppian law, respecting the dress of the women, after much debate repealed, notwithstanding it was strenuously supported by Marcus Porcius Cato, consul.—The consul's successes in Spain.—Titus Quintius Flamininus finishes the war with the Lacedæmonians and the tyrant Nabis; makes peace with them, and restores liberty to Argos.—Separate seats at the public games for the first time appointed for the senators.—Colonies sent forth.—Marcus Porcius Cato triumphs on account of his successes in Spain.—Further successes in Spain against the Boians and Insubrian Gauls.—Titus Quintius Flamininus, having subdued Philip, king of Macedonia, and Nabis, the Lacedæmonian tyrant, and restored all Greece to freedom, triumphs for three days.—Carthaginian ambassadors bring intelligence of the hostile designs of Antiochus and Hannibal.

## BOOK XXXV.

Publius Scipio Africanus sent ambassador to Antiochus; has a conversation with Hannibal at Ephesus.—Preparations of the Romans for war with Antiochus.—Nabis, the tyrant of Lacedæmon, instigated by the Ætolians, makes war on the Achæans; is put to death by a party of the Ætolians.—The Ætolians, violating the treaty of friendship with the Romans, invite Antiochus, who comes with a small force into Greece, and, in conjunction with them, takes several towns, and the whole island of Eubœa.—The Achæans declare war against Antiochus and the Ætolians.

## BOOK XXXVI.

Manius Acilius Glabrio, consul, aided by King Philip, defeats Antiochus at Thermopylæ, and drives him out of Greece; reduces the Ætolians to sue for peace.—Publius Cornelius Scipio Nasica reduces the Boian Gauls to submission.—Sea fight between the Roman fleet and that of Antiochus, in which the Romans are victorious.

## BOOK XXXVII.

Lucius Cornelius Scipio, consul, accompanied by his brother, Publius Scipio Africanus, sent into Asia against Antiochus; the first Roman who ever led an army thither.—Æmilius Regillus, aided by the Rhodians, defeats Antiochus' fleet at Myonnesus.—The son of Scipio Africanus, taken prisoner by Antiochus, is sent back to his father.—Marcus Acilius Glabrio, having driven Antiochus out of Greece, triumphs over him and the Ætolians.—Lucius Cornelius Scipio, assisted by Eumenes, king of Pergamus, vanquishes Antiochus; grants him peace on condition of his evacuating all the countries on the hither side of Mount Taurus.—Lands and cities given to Eumenes, to requite his assistance in the conquest of Antiochus; also to the Rhodians on the like account.—A new colony established called the Bononian.—Æmilius Regillus triumphs on account of his naval victory.—Lucius Cornelius Scipio obtains the surname of Asiaticus.

## BOOK XXXVIII.

Marcus Fulvius, consul, receives the surrender of Ambracia, in Epirus; subdues Cephalenia; grants peace to the Ætolians.—His colleague, Manlius, subdues the Gallogræcians, Tolistoboians, Tectosagians, and Trocmians.—A census held, in which the number of Roman citizens is found to amount to two hundred and fifty-eight thousand three hundred and twenty-eight.—Treaty of friendship with Ariarathes, king of Cappadocia.—Manlius triumphs over the Gallogræcians.—Scipio Africanus, prosecuted by the plebeian tribunes on a charge of embezzling the public money, goes into a voluntary exile at Liternum.—Whether he died there or at Rome is uncertain, monuments to his memory being erected in both places.—Scipio Asiaticus, charged with the like crime, convicted, and ordered to prison, is enlarged by Tiberius Sempronius Gracchus, hitherto at enmity with him.—His property being found unequal to the discharge of his fine, his friends raise it by contribution among themselves, which he refuses.

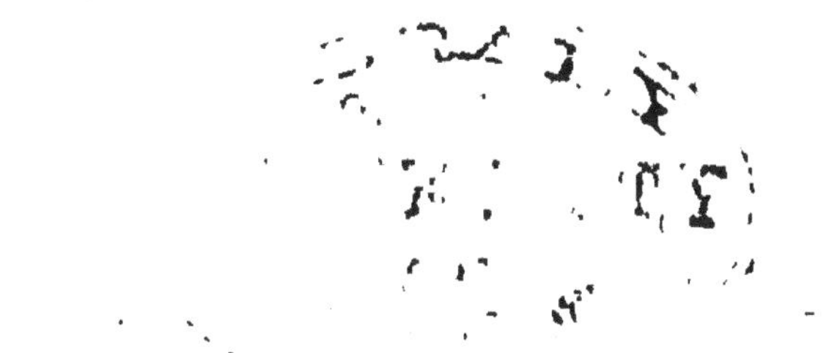

# HISTORY OF ROME.

## BOOK XXXI.

CHAP. 1. I FEEL a degree of pleasure in having come to the end of the Punic war, as if myself had borne a share of the toil and danger: for though it ill becomes a person, who has ventured to promise an entire history of all the Roman affairs, to be fatigued by any particular parts of so extensive a work; yet when I reflect that sixty-three years, (for so many there are from the first Punic war to the end of the second,) have filled up as many volumes for me, as the four hundred and eighty-seven years, from the building of the city to the consulate of Appius Claudius, who first made war on the Carthaginians, I plainly perceive that, like those who are tempted by the shallows near the shore to walk into the sea, the farther I advance, I am carried into the greater depth and abyss, as it were; and that my work rather increases on my hands than diminishes, as I expected it would, by the first parts being completed. The peace with Carthage was quickly followed by a war with Macedonia: a war, not to be compared with the former, indeed, either in danger, or in the abilities of the commanders, or the valour of the soldiers; but rather more remarkable with regard to the renown of their former kings, the ancient fame of that nation, and the vast extent of their empire, which formerly comprehended a large part of Europe, and the greater part of Asia. The contest with Philip, which had begun about ten years before, had been intermitted for the three last years, the Ætolians having been the occasion both of the commencement and of the cessation of hostilities. The Romans being now disengaged from all employment, and being incensed against Philip, on account both of his infringing the peace with regard to the Ætolians, and the other allies in those parts, and also on account of his having lately sent aid of men and money into Africa to Hannibal and the Carthaginians, were excited to a renewal of the war by the entreaties of the Athenians, whose country he had ravaged, and shut up the inhabitants within the walls of the city.

2. About the same time ambassadors arrived both from King Attalus, and from the Rhodians, with information that the Macedonian was tampering with the states of Asia. To these embassies an answer was given, that the senate would give attention to the affairs of Asia. The determination with regard to the making war on him was left open to the consuls, who were then in their provinces. In the mean time, three ambassadors were sent to Ptolemy, king of Egypt, namely, Caius Claudius Nero, Marcus Æmilius Lepidus, and Publius Sempronius Tuditanus, to announce their conquest of Hannibal and the Carthaginians; to give thanks to the king for his faithful adherence to his engagements in the time of their distress, when even the nearest allies of the Romans abandoned them; and to request that, if they should be compelled by ill treatment to break with Philip, he would preserve the same disposition towards the Roman people. In Gaul, about this time, the consul, Publius Ælius, having heard that, before his arrival, the Boians had made inroads on the territories of the allies, levied two occasional legions on account of this disturbance; and adding to them four cohorts from his own army, ordered Caius Oppius, the prefect, to march with this tumultuary band through Umbria, (which is called the Sappinian district,) and to invade the territories of the Boians; leading his own troops thither openly, over the mountains which lay in the way. Oppius, on entering the same, for some time committed depredations with good success and safety. But afterward, having pitched on a place near a fort called Mutilum, convenient enough for cutting down the corn which was now ripe, and setting out, without having acquired a knowledge of the country, and without establishing armed posts of sufficient strength to protect those who were unarmed and intent on their work, he was suddenly surrounded, together with his foragers, and attacked by the Gauls. On this, even those who were furnished with weapons, struck with dismay, betook themselves to flight. Seven thousand men, dispersed through the corn fields, were put to the sword, among whom was the commander himself, Caius Oppius. The rest were driven in confusion into the camp; from whence, in consequence of a resolution there formed, they set out on the following night, without any particular commander; and, leaving behind a great part of their baggage, made their way through woods almost impassable to the consul, who returned to Rome without having performed any thing in his province worth notice, except that he ravaged the lands of the Boians, and made a treaty with the Ingaunian Ligurians.

3. The first time he assembled the senate, it was unani-

mously ordered that he should propose no other business before that which related to Philip, and the complaints of the allies; it was of course immediately taken into consideration, and in full meeting decreed that Publius Ælius, consul, should send such person as he might think proper, vested with command to receive the fleet which Cneius Octavius was bringing home from Sicily, and pass over to Macedonia. Accordingly, Marcus Valerius Lævinus, propretor, was sent; and, receiving thirty-eight ships from Cneius Octavius, near Vibo, he sailed to Macedonia, where, being met by Marcus Aurelius, the ambassador, and informed what numerous forces and what large fleets the king had prepared, and how busily he was employed in prevailing on divers states to join him, applying to some in person, to others by agents, not only through all the cities of the continent, but even in the islands. Lævinus was convinced from this that the war required vigorous exertions on the side of the Romans; for, should they be dilatory, Philip might be encouraged to attempt an enterprise like to that which had been formerly undertaken by Pyrrhus, who possessed not such large dominions. He therefore desired Aurelius to convey this intelligence, by letter, to the consuls and to the senate.

4. Towards the end of this year the senate, taking into consideration the lands to be given to the veteran soldiers, who under the conduct and auspices of Publius Scipio had finished the war in Africa, decreed that Marcus Tunius, pretor of the city, should, if he thought proper, appoint ten commissioners to survey and distribute among them that part of the Samnite and Apulian lands which was the property of the Roman people. For this purpose were appointed, Publius Servilius, Quintus Cæcilius Metellus, Caius and Marcus Servilius, both surnamed Geminus, Lucius and Aulus Hostilius Cato, Publius Villius Tappulus, Marcus Fulvius Flaccus, Publius Ælius Pætus, and Quintus Flaminius. At the same time Publius Ælius presiding at the election of consuls, Publius Sulpicius Galba and Caius Aurelius Cotta were elected. Then were chosen pretors, Quintus Minucius Rufus, Lucius Furius Purpureo, Quintus Fulvius Gillo, Cneius Sergius Plancus. The Roman stage-games were exhibited, in a sumptuous and elegant manner, by the curule ediles, Lucius Valerius Flaccus and Lucius Quintius Flaminius, and repeated for two days; and a vast quantity of corn, which Scipio had sent from Africa, was distributed by them to the people, with strict impartiality and general satisfaction, at the rate of four asses a peck. The plebeian games were thrice repeated entire by the plebeian ediles, Lucius Apustius Fullo and Quintus

Minucius Rufus; the latter of whom was, from the edileship, elected pretor. There was also a feast of Jove on occasion of the games.

5. In the year five hundred and fifty-two from the building of the city, [A. U. C. 552. B. C. 200,] Publius Sulpicius Galba and Caius Aurelius being consuls, within a few months after the conclusion of the peace with the Carthaginians, war began against King Philip. This was the first business introduced by the consul, Publius Sulpicius, on the ides of March, the day on which, in those times, the consuls entered into office; and the senate decreed that the consuls should perform sacrifices with the greater victims to such gods as they should judge proper, with prayers to this purpose:—that "the business which the senate and people of Rome had then under deliberation, concerning the state, and the entering on a new war, might be attended with success and prosperity to the Roman people, the allies, and the Latine confederacy;" and that, after the sacrifices and prayers, they should consult the senate on the state of public affairs and the provinces. At this time, very opportunely for promoting a war, the letters were brought from Marcus Aurelius, the ambassador, and Marcus Valerius Lævinus, propretor. An embassy likewise arrived from the Athenians, to acquaint them that the king was approaching their frontiers, and that in a short time not only their lands, but their city also, must fall into his hands, unless they received aid from the Romans. When the consuls had made their report that the sacrifices had been duly performed, and that the gods had accepted their prayers; that the aruspices had declared that the entrails showed good omens, and that enlargement of territory, victory, and triumph, were portended, the letters of Valerius and Aurelius were read, and audience given to the ambassadors of the Athenians. After which a decree of the senate was passed, that thanks should be given to their allies, because, though long solicited, they had not been prevailed on, even by dread of a siege, to depart from their engagements. With regard to sending assistance to them, they resolved that an answer should be given as soon as the consuls should have cast lots for the provinces, and when the consul to whose lot Macedonia fell should have proposed to the people to declare war against Philip, king of the Macedonians.

6. The province of Macedonia fell by lot to Publius Sulpicius; and he proposed to the people to declare, "that they chose and ordered, that on account of the injuries and hostilities committed against the allies of the Roman people, war should be proclaimed against King Philip and the Macedonians under his government." The province of Italy

fell to the lot of the other consul, Aurelius. The pretors then cast lots: to Cneius Sergius Plancus fell the city jurisdiction; to Quintus Fulvius Gillo, Sicily; to Quintus Minucius Rufus, Bruttium; and to Lucius Furius Purpureo, Gaul. At the first meeting of the people, the proposal concerning the Macedonian war was rejected by almost all the tribes. This was occasioned partly by the people's own inclinations, who, wearied by the length and severity of the late war, longed to be freed from toils and dangers; and partly by Quintus Bæbius, tribune of the people, who, pursuing the old practice of criminating the patricians, charged them with multiplying wars one after another, so that the people could never enjoy peace. This proceeding gave great offence to the patricians, and the tribune was severely reprehended in the senate, where all earnestly recommended it to the consul to call a new assembly for passing the proposal; to rebuke the backwardness of the people; and to prove to them how highly detrimental and dishonourable it would be to decline engaging in that war.

7. The consul having assembled the people in the field of Mars, before he called on the centuries to give their votes, required their attention, and addressed them thus:—"Citizens, you seem to me not to understand that the question before you is not whether you choose to have peace or war; for Philip, having already commenced hostilities with a formidable force, both on land and sea, allows you not that option. The question is, whether you choose to transport your legions to Macedonia, or to suffer the enemy to come into Italy? How important the difference is between these two cases, if you knew it not before, you have sufficiently learned in the late Punic war: for who entertains a doubt, but if, when the Saguntines were besieged, and implored our protection, we had assisted them with vigour, as our fathers did the Mamertines, we should have averted the whole weight of the war on Spain; which, by our dilatory proceedings, we suffered to our extreme loss to fall on Italy? Nor does it admit a doubt, that what confined this same Philip in Macedonia, (after he had entered into an engagement with Hannibal, by ambassadors and letters, to cross over into Italy,) was, our sending Lævinus with a fleet to carry the war home to him. And what we did at that time, when we had Hannibal to contend with in Italy, do we hesitate to do now, after Hannibal has been expelled Italy, and the Carthaginians subdued? Suppose for an instant that we allow the king to experience the same inactivity on our part, while he is taking Athens, as Hannibal found while he was taking Saguntum: it will not be in the fifth month, as the Carthaginian came from Saguntum, but on the fifth day after

the Macedonian sets sail from Corinth, that he will arrive in Italy. Perhaps you may not consider Philip as equal to Hannibal, or the Macedonians to the Carthaginians: certainly, however, you will allow him equal to Pyrrhus. Equal, do I say? what a vast superiority has the one man over the other—the one nation over the other! Epirus ever was, and is at this day, deemed but an inconsiderable accession to the kingdom of Macedonia. Philip has the entire Peloponnesus under his dominion; even Argos itself, not more celebrated for its ancient glory than for the death of Pyrrhus. Now compare our situation. How much more flourishing was Italy when Pyrrhus attacked it! How much greater its strength, possessing so many commanders, so many armies, which the Punic war afterward consumed! Yet was he able to give it a violent shock, and advanced victorious almost to the gates of Rome: and not the Tarentines only, and the inhabitants of that tract of Italy which they call the greater Greece, whom you may suppose to have been led by the similarity of language and name, but the Lucanian, the Bruttian, and the Samnite, revolted from us. Do you believe that these would continue quiet and faithful if Philip should come over to Italy, because they continued faithful afterward, and during the Punic war? Be assured those states will never fail to revolt from us, except when there is no one to whom they can go over. If you had disapproved of a Roman army passing into Africa, you would this day have had Hannibal and the Carthaginians to contend with in Italy. Let Macedonia, rather than Italy, be the seat of war. Let the cities and lands of the enemy be wasted with fire and sword. We have already found, by experience, that our arms are more powerful and more successful abroad than at home. Go, and give your voices with the blessing of the gods; and what the senate have voted, do you ratify by your order. This resolution is recommended to you, not only by your consul, but even by the immortal gods themselves; who, when I offered sacrifice, and prayed that the issue of this war might be happy and prosperous to me and to the senate, to you and the allies and Latine confederates, granted every omen of success and happiness."

8. After this speech of Sulpicius, being sent to give their votes, they declared for the war as he had proposed. On which, in pursuance of a decree of the senate, a supplication for three days was proclaimed by the consuls; and prayers were offered to the gods at all the shrines, that the war which the people had ordered against Philip might be attended with success and prosperity. The consul Sulpicius, inquiring of the heralds whether they would direct the declaration of the war against King Philip to be made to himself in person, or

whether it would be sufficient to publish it in the nearest garrison within the frontiers of his kingdom, they answered that either would do. The consul received authority from the senate to send any person whom he thought proper, not being a senator, as ambassador, to denounce war against the king. They then proceeded to arrange the armies for the consuls and pretors. The consuls were ordered to levy two legions, and to disband the veteran troops. Sulpicius, to whom the management of this new and highly important war had been decreed, was allowed permission to carry with him as many volunteers as he could procure out of the army which Publius Scipio had brought home from Africa; but he was not empowered to compel any veteran soldier to attend him. They ordered that the consul should give to the pretors, Lucius Furius Purpureo and Quintus Minucius Rufus, five thousand of the allies of the Latine confederacy; with which forces they should hold, one, the province of Gaul, the other, Bruttium. Quintus Fulvius Gillo was ordered, in like manner, to select out of the army which Publius Ælius, late consul, had commanded, such as had been the shortest time in the service, until he also made up five thousand of the allies and Latine confederates, for guarding his province of Sicily. To Marcus Valerius Falto, who, during the former year, had held the province of Campania, as pretor, the command was continued for a year; in order that he might go over in quality of propretor to Sardinia, and choose out of the army there five thousand of the allies of the Latine confederacy, who also had been the shortest time in the service. The consuls were at the same time ordered to levy two legions for the city, which might be sent wherever occasion should require; as there were many states in Italy infected with an attachment to the Carthaginians, which they had formed during the war, and in consequence, swelling with resentment. The state was to employ during that year six Roman legions.

9. In the midst of the preparations for war, ambassadors came from King Ptolemy, with the following message:—That "the Athenians had petitioned the king for aid against Philip; but that although they were their common allies, yet the king would not, without the direction of the Roman people, send either fleet or army into Greece, for the purpose of defending or attacking any person: that he would remain quiet in his kingdom, if the Romans were at leisure to protect their allies; or, if more agreeable to them to be at rest, would himself send such aid as should effectually secure Athens against Philip." Thanks were returned to the king by the senate, and this answer:—that "it was the intention of the Roman people to protect their allies: that if

they should have occasion for any assistance towards carrying on the war, they would acquaint the king; and that they were fully sensible that, in the power of his kingdom, their state had a sure and faithful resource." Presents were then, by order of the senate, sent to the ambassadors, of five thousand asses* to each. While the consuls were employed in levying troops, and making other necessary preparations, the people, prone to religious observances, especially at the beginning of new wars, after supplications had been already performed, and prayers offered up at all the shrines, lest any thing should be omitted that had ever been practised, ordered that the consul who was to have the province of Macedonia should vow games, and a present to Jove. Licinius, the chief pontiff, occasioned some delay in the performance of it, alleging that "he could not properly frame the vow, unless the money to discharge it were specified: for as the sum to be named could not be applied to the uses of the war, it should be immediately set apart, and not to be intermixed with other money; and that, unless this were done, the vow could not be fulfilled." Although the objection, and the person who proposed it, were both of weight, yet the consul was ordered to consult the college of pontiffs, whether a vow could not be undertaken without specifying the amount to discharge it? The pontiffs determined that it could; and that it would be even more in order to do it in that way. The consul, therefore, repeating after the chief pontiff, made the vow in the same words in which those made for five years of safety used to be expressed; only that he engaged to perform the games, and make the offerings, at such expense as the senate should direct by their vote, at the time when the vow was to be put in act. Before this the great games, so often vowed, were constantly rated at a certain expense: this was the first time that the sum was not specified.

10. While every one's attention was turned to the Macedonian war, and at a time when people apprehended nothing less, a sudden account was brought of an inroad made by the Gauls. The Insubrians, Cænomanians, and Boians, having been joined by the Salyans, Ilvatians, and other Ligurian states, and putting themselves under the command of Hamilcar, a Carthaginian, who, having been in the army of Hasdrubal, had remained in those parts, had fallen on Placentia; and, after plundering the city, and in their rage burning a great part of it, leaving scarcely two thousand men among the flames and ruins, passed the Po, and advanced to plunder Cremona. The news of the calamity, which

* 16*l*. 2*s*. 1*d*.

had fallen on a city in their neighbourhood, having reached thither, the inhabitants had time to shut their gates, and place guards on the walls, that they might at least try the event of a siege, and send messengers to the Roman pretor. Lucius Furius Purpureo, who had then the command of the province, had, in pursuance of the decree of the senate, disbanded the army, excepting five thousand of the allies and Latine confederates, and had halted with these troops in the nearest district of the province about Ariminum. He immediately informed the senate, by letter, of the subsisting tumult: that, "of the two colonies which had escaped the general wreck in the dreadful storm of the Punic war, one was taken and sacked by the present enemy, and the other besieged. Nor was his army capable of affording sufficient protection to the distressed colonists, unless he chose to expose five thousand allies to be slaughtered by forty thousand invaders, (for so many there were in arms;) and by such a loss, on his side, to augment their courage, already elated on having destroyed one Roman colony."

11. On reading this letter, it was decreed, that the consul Aurelius should order the army which he had appointed to assemble on a certain day in Etruria, to attend him on the same day at Ariminum; and should either go in person, if the public business would permit, to suppress the tumult of the Gauls, or write to the pretor Lucius Furius, that, as soon as the legions from Etruria came to him, he should send five thousand of the allies to guard that place in the mean time, and should himself proceed to relieve the colony from the siege. It was also decreed, that ambassadors should be sent to Carthage, and also into Numidia to Masinissa; to Carthage, to tell that people that "their countryman, Hamilcar, having been left in Gaul, (either with a part of the army formerly commanded by Hasdrubal, or with that of Mago—they did not with certainty know which,) was waging war, contrary to the treaty: that he had raised forces from among the Gauls and Ligurians, and persuaded them to take arms against Rome: that, if they chose a continuance of peace, they must recall him, and give him up to the Roman people." They were ordered at the same time to tell them, that "all the deserters had not been produced; that a great part of them were said to appear openly in Carthage, who ought to be sought after, and surrendered, according to the treaty." This was the message they were to deliver to the Carthaginians. To Masinissa they were charged with congratulation, on his "having not only recovered the kingdom of his father, but enlarged it by the acquisition of the most flourishing parts of Syphax's territories." They were ordered also to acquaint him, that "the

Romans had entered into a war against Philip, because he had given aid to the Carthaginians, while, by the injuries which he offered to the allies of the Roman people, he had obliged them to send fleets and armies into Greece, at a time when the flames of war spread over all Italy; and that by thus making them separate their forces, had been the principal cause of their being so late in passing over to Africa; and to request him to send some Numidian horsemen to assist in that war." Ample presents were given them to be carried to the king; vases of gold and silver, a purple robe, and a tunic adorned with palms of purple, an ivory sceptre, and a robe of state, with a curule chair. They were also directed to assure him, that if he deemed any thing farther requisite to confirm and enlarge his kingdom, the Roman people, in return for his good services, would exert their utmost zeal to effect it. At this time, too, the senate was addressed by ambassadors from Vermina, son of Syphax, apologizing for his mistaken conduct, on account of his youth and want of judgment, and throwing all the blame on the deceitful policy of the Carthaginians; adding, that, as Masinissa had from an enemy become a friend to the Romans, so Vermina would also use his best endeavours that he should not be outdone in offices of friendship to the Roman people, either by Masinissa or by any other; and requesting that he might receive from the senate the title of king, friend, and ally." The answer given to these ambassadors was, that "not only his father Syphax, from a friend and ally, had on a sudden, without any reason, become an enemy to the Roman people, but that he himself had made his first essay of manhood in bearing arms against them. He must therefore sue to the Roman people for peace before he could expect to be acknowledged king, ally, and friend; that it was the practice of that people to bestow the honour of such title in return for great services performed by kings toward them: that the Roman ambassadors would soon be in Africa, to whom the senate would give instructions to regulate conditions of peace with Vermina, as he should submit the terms entirely to the will of the Roman people; and that, if he wished that any thing should be added, left out, or altered, he must make a second application to the senate." The ambassadors sent to Africa on those affairs were Caius Terentius Varro, Publius Lucretius, and Cneius Octavius, each of whom had a quinquereme assigned him.

12. A letter was then read in the senate from Quintus Minucius, the pretor, who held the province of Bruttium, that "the money had been privately carried off by night out of the treasury of Proserpine at Locri; and that there were no traces which could direct to the discovery of the guilty

persons." The senate was highly incensed at finding that the practice of sacrilege continued, and that even the fate of Pleminius, an example so recent and so conspicuous both of the guilt and of the punishment, did not deter from it. They ordered the consul, Cneius Aurilius, to signify to the pretor in Bruttium, that "it was the pleasure of the senate that an inquiry be made concerning the robbery of the treasury, according to the method used by Marcus Pomponius, pretor, three years before; that the money which could be discovered should be restored, and any deficiency be made up; and that, if he thought proper, atonements should be made for the purpose of expiating the violation of the temple, in the manner formerly prescribed by the pontiffs." At the same time also, accounts were brought of many prodigies happening in several places. It was said, that in Lucania the sky had been seen in a blaze; that at Privernum, in clear weather, the sun had been of a red colour during a whole day; that at Lanuvium, in the temple of Juno Sospita, a very loud bustling noise had been heard in the night. Besides, monstrous births of animals were related to have occurred in many places: in the country of the Sabines an infant was born whose sex could not be distinguished; and another was found sixteen years old, whose sex also was doubtful. At Frusino, a lamb was born with a swine's head; at Sinuessa, a pig with a human head; and in Lucania, in the land belonging to the state, a foal with five feet. All these were considered as horrid and abominable, and as if Nature were straying from her course in confounding the different species. Above all, the people were particularly shocked at the hermaphrodites, which were ordered to be immediately thrown into the sea, as had been lately done with a production of the same monstrous kind, in the consulate of Caius Claudius and Marcus Livius. Not satisfied with this, they ordered the decemvirs to inspect the books in regard of that prodigy; and the decemvirs, from the books, directed the same religious ceremonies which had been performed on an occasion of the same kind. They ordered, besides, a hymn to be sung through the city by thrice nine virgins, and an offering to be made to imperial Juno. The consul, Caius Aurelius, took care that all these matters were performed according to the direction of the decemvirs. The hymn was composed by Publius Licinius Tegula, as a similar one had been, in the memory of their fathers, by Livius.

13. All religious scruples were fully removed by expiations: at Locri, too, the affair of the sacrilege had been thoroughly investigated by Quintus Minucius, and the money replaced in the treasury out of the effects of the guilty. When the consuls wished to set out to their provinces, a num-

ber of private persons, to whom the third payment became due that year, of the money which they had lent to the public in the consulate of Marcus Valerius and Marcus Claudius, applied to the senate. The consuls, however, having declared that the treasury being scarcely sufficient for the exigences of a new war, in which a great fleet and great armies must be employed, there were no means of paying them at present. The senate could not avoid being affected by their complaints, in which they alleged, that "if the state intended to use, for the purpose of the Macedonian war, the money which had been lent for the Punic war, as one war constantly arose after another, what would be the issue, but that, in return for their kind assistance to the public, their property would be confiscated, as if they had been guilty of some crime?" The demands of the private creditors being equitable, and the state being in no capacity of discharging the debt, they determined to pursue a middle course between equity and convenience; and accordingly they decreed, that "whereas many of them mentioned that lands were frequently exposed to sale, and that they themselves wished to become purchasers; they should therefore have liberty to purchase any belonging to the public, and which lay within fifty miles of the city. That the consuls should make a valuation of these, and impose on each acre a quit-rent of one *as*, as an acknowledgment that the land was the property of the public, in order that when the people should become able to pay, if any one chose rather to have the money than the land, he might restore it." The private creditors accepted the terms with joy; and that land was called Trientius and Tabulius, because it was given in lieu of the third part of their money.

14. Publius Sulpicius, after making his vows in the capitol, set out from the city in his robes of war, attended by his lictor, and arrived at Brundusium; where, having formed into legions the veteran soldiers of the African army who were willing to follow him, and chosen his number of ships out of the fleet of the late consul, Cornelius, he set sail, and next day arrived in Macedonia. There he was met by ambassadors from the Athenians, intreating him to relieve their city from the siege. Immediately Caius Claudius Centho was despatched to Athens, with twenty ships of war, and a small body of land forces; for it was not the king himself who carried on the siege of Athens; he was at that time intently occupied in besieging Abydus, after having tried his strength at sea against Attalus, and against the Rhodians, without meeting success in either engagement. But, besides the natural presumptuousness of his temper, he acquired confidence from a treaty which he had formed with Anti-

ochus, king of Syria, in which they had divided the wealth of Egypt between them; an object which, on hearing of the death of Ptolemy, they were both eager to secure. As to the Athenians, they had entangled themselves in a war with Philip on too trifling an occasion, and at a time when they retained nothing of their ancient dignity but pride. During the celebration of the mysteries, two young men of Acarnania, who were not initiated, unapprized of its being an offence against religion, entered the temple of Ceres along with the rest of the crowd; their discourse quickly betrayed them, by their asking questions which discovered their ignorance; whereon, being carried before the president of the temple, although it was evident that they went in through mistake, yet they were put to death, as if for a heinous crime. The Acarnanian nation made complaint to Philip of this barbarous and hostile act, and prevailed on him to grant them some aid of Macedonian soldiers, and to allow them to make war on the Athenians. At first this army, after ravaging the lands of Attica with fire and sword, retired to Acarnania with booty of all kinds. This was the first provocation to hostilities. The Athenians afterwards, on their side, entered into a regular war, and proclaimed it by order of the state; for king Attalus and the Rhodians, having come to Ægina in pursuit of Philip, who was retiring to Macedonia, the king crossed over to Piræus, for the purpose of renewing and strengthening the alliance between him and the Athenians. On entering the city he was received by the whole inhabitants, who poured forth with their wives and children to meet him; by the priests, with their emblems of religion; and in a manner by the gods themselves, called forth from their abodes.

15. Immediately the people were summoned to an assembly, that the king might treat with them in person on such subjects as he chose; but afterwards it was judged more suitable to his dignity to explain his sentiments in writing, than, being present, to be forced to blush, either at the recital of his extraordinary favours to the state, or at the immoderate applause of the multitude, which would overwhelm his modesty with acclamations and other signs of approbation. In the letter which he sent, and which was read to the assembly, was contained, first, a recapitulation of the several acts of kindness which he had shown to the Athenian state, as his ally; then, of the actions which he had performed against Philip; and lastly, an exhortation to "enter immediately on the war, while they had him, (Attalus,) the Rhodians, and the Romans also, to assist them:" not omitting to warn them, that, "if they were backward now, they would hereafter wish in vain for the opportunity which they ne-

glected." They then gave audience to the ambassadors of the Rhodians, to whom they were under a recent obligation for having retaken and sent home four of their ships of war, which had been lately seized by the Macedonians. War was determined on against Philip with universal consent. Unbounded honours were conferred on king Attalus, and then on the Rhodians. At that time mention was made of adding a tribe, which they were to call Attalis, to the ten ancient tribes; the Rhodian state was presented with a golden crown, as an acknowledgment of its bravery, and the inhabitants with the freedom of Athens, in like manner as Rhodes had formerly honoured that people. After this, king Attalus returned to Ægina, where his fleet lay. From Ægina the Rhodians sailed to Cia, and thence to Rhodes, steering their course among the islands, all of which they brought to join in the alliance, except Andros, Paros, and Cythnus, which were held by Macedonian garrisons. Attalus, having sent messengers to Ætolia, and expecting ambassadors from thence, was detained at Ægina for some time in a state of inaction; failing also in his endeavours to excite the Ætolians to arms, for they were rejoiced at having made peace with Macedon on any terms. Had Attalus and the Rhodians pressed Philip vigorously, they might have acquired the illustrious title of the deliverers of Greece; but by suffering him to pass over again into Hellespontus, and to strengthen himself by seizing the advantageous posts in Greece, they increased the difficulties of the war, and yielded up to the Romans the glory of having conducted and finished it.

16. Philip acted with a spirit more becoming a king; for, though he had found himself unequal to the forces of Attalus and the Rhodians, yet he was not dismayed, even by the prospect of an approaching war with the Romans. Sending Philocles, one of his generals, with two thousand foot and two hundred horse to ravage the lands of the Athenians, he gave the command of his fleet to Heraclides, with orders to sail to Maronea, and marched thither himself by land, with two thousand foot lightly equipped, and two hundred horse. Maronea he took at the first assault; and afterwards, with a good deal of trouble, got possession of Ænus, which was at last betrayed to him by Ganymede, who commanded there for Ptolemy. He then seized on other forts, Cypselus, Doriscos, and Serrheus; and, advancing from thence to the Chersonesus, received Elæus and Alopeconnesus, which were surrendered by the inhabitants. Callipolis also and Madytos were given up to him, with several forts of but little consequence. The people of Abydus shut their gates against him, not suffering even his ambassadors to enter the

place. The siege of this city detained Philip a long time; and it might have been relieved, if Attalus and the Rhodians had acted with any vigour. The king sent only three hundred men for a garrison, and the Rhodians one quadrireme from their fleet, although it was lying idle at Tenedos: and afterwards, when the besieged could with difficulty hold out any longer, Attalus, going over in person, did nothing more than show them some hope of relief being near, giving not any real assistance to these his allies either by land or sea.

17. At first the people of Abydus, by means of engines placed along the walls, not only prevented the approaches by land, but annoyed the enemy's ships in their station. Afterwards a part of the wall being thrown down, and the assailants having penetrated by mines to an inner wall, which had been hastily raised to oppose their entrance, the besieged sent ambassadors to the king to treat of terms of capitulation. They demanded permission to send away the Rhodian quadrireme, with the crew and the troops of Attalus in the garrison; and that they themselves might depart from the city, each with one suit of apparel; but Philip's answer afforded no hopes of accommodation, unless they surrendered at discretion. When this was reported by their ambassadors, it so exasperated them, rousing at the same time their indignation and despair, that, seized with the same kind of fury which had possessed the Saguntines, they ordered all the matrons to be shut up in the temple of Diana, and the free-born youths and virgins, and even the infants with their nurses, in the place of exercise; the gold and silver to be carried into the forum; their valuable garments to be put on board the Rhodian ship, and another from Cyzicum, which lay in the harbour; the priests and victims to be brought, and altars to be erected in the midst. There they appointed a select number, who, as soon as they should see the army of their friends cut off in defending the breach, were instantly to slay their wives and children; to throw into the sea the gold, silver, and apparel, that was on board the ships, and to set fire to the buildings, public and private: and to the performance of this deed they were bound by an oath, the priests repeating before them the verses of execration. Those who were of an age capable of fighting then swore to continue the battle till they fell, unless victorious. These, regardful of the gods by whom they had sworn, maintained their ground with such obstinacy, that although the night would soon have put a stop to the fight, yet the king, terrified by their fury, first drew off his forces. The chief inhabitants, to whom the more shocking part of the plan had been given in charge, seeing that few survived

the battle, and that these were exhausted by fatigue and wounds, sent the priests (having their heads bound with the fillets of suppliants) at the dawn of the next day to surrender the city to Philip.

18. Before the surrender, one of the Roman ambassadors who had been sent to Alexandria, Marcus Æmilius, being the youngest of them, in pursuance of a resolution which the three had jointly formed, on hearing of the present siege, came to Philip, and complained of his having made war on Attalus and the Rhodians; and particularly of the attack on Abydus, in which he was then employed: and on Philip's saying that he had been forced into the war by Attalus and the Rhodians commencing hostilities against him,—"Did the people of Abydus, too," said he, "commence hostilities against you?" To him, who was unaccustomed to hear truth, this language seemed too arrogant to be used to a king, and he answered,—"Your youth, the beauty of your form, and, above all, the name of Roman, render you too presumptuous. However, my first desire is, that you would observe the treaties, and continue in peace with me; but if you begin an attack, I am, on my part, determined to prove that the kingdom and name of the Macedonians is not less formidable in war than that of the Romans." Having dismissed the ambassadors in this manner, Philip got possession of the gold and silver which had been thrown together in a heap, but was disappointed of his booty with respect to prisoners; for such violent phrensy had seized the multitude, that, on a sudden, taking up a persuasion that they were guilty of treachery towards those who had fallen in the battle, and upbraiding one another with perjury, especially the priests, who would surrender alive to the enemy those persons whom they themselves had devoted, they all at once ran different ways to put their wives and children to death; and then they put an end to their own lives by every possible method. The king, astonished at their madness, restrained the violence of his soldiers, and said, "that he would allow the people of Abydus three days to die in;" and, during this space, the vanquished perpetrated more deeds of cruelty on themselves, than the enraged conquerors would have committed; nor did any one of them come into the enemy's hands alive, except such as were in chains, or under some other insuperable restraint. Philip, leaving a garrison in Abydus, returned to his kingdom; and, just when he had been encouraged by the destruction of the people of Abydus, to proceed in the war against Rome, as Hannibal had been by the destruction of Saguntum, he was met by couriers, with intelligence that the consul was already in Epirus, and

had drawn his land forces to Apollonia, and his fleet to Corcyra, into winter quarters.

19. In the mean time the ambassadors who had been sent into Africa, on the affair of Hamilcar, the leader of the Gallic army, received from the Carthaginians this answer: that "it was not in their power to do more than to inflict on him the punishment of exile, and to confiscate his effects; that they had delivered up all the deserters and fugitives, whom, on a diligent inquiry, they had been able to discover, and would send ambassadors to Rome, to satisfy the senate on that head." They sent two hundred thousand measures of wheat to Rome, and the same quantity to the army in Macedonia. From thence the ambassadors proceeded into Numidia, to the kings; delivered to Masinissa the presents and the message according to their instructions, and out of two thousand Numidian horsemen which he offered, accepted one thousand. Masinissa superintended in person the embarkation of these, and sent them, with two hundred thousand measures of wheat, and the same quantity of barley, into Macedonia. The third commission which they had to execute was with Vermina. He advanced to meet them as far as the utmost limits of his kingdom, and left it to themselves to prescribe such conditions of peace as they thought proper, declaring that "he should consider any peace with the Roman people as just and advantageous." The terms were then settled, and he was ordered to send ambassadors to Rome to procure a ratification of the treaty.

20. About the same time Lucius Cornelius Lentulus, proconsul, came home from Spain; and having laid before the senate an account of his brave and successful conduct, during the course of many years, demanded that he might be allowed to enter the city in triumph. The senate, on this, gave their opinion, that, "his services were, indeed, deserving of a triumph; but that they had no precedent left them by their ancestors, of any person enjoying a triumph, who was not, at the time of performing the service on account of which he claimed that honour, either dictator, consul, or pretor; that he had held the province of Spain in quality of proconsul, and not of consul or pretor." They determined however that he might enter the city in ovation. Against this Tiberius Sempronius Longus, tribune of the people, protested, alleging, that such proceedings would be no less unprecedented, and contrary to the practice of their ancestors, than the other; but overcome at length by the unanimous desire of the senate, the tribune withdrew his opposition, and Lucius Lentulus entered the city in ovation. He carried to the treasury forty-four thousand pounds weight of silver, and two thousand four hundred pounds weight of

gold. To each of the soldiers he distributed of the spoil, one hundred and twenty assés.*

21. The consular army had by this time removed from Arretium to Ariminum, and the five thousand Latine confederates had gone from Gaul into Etruria. Lucius Furius therefore advanced from Ariminum, by forced marches, against the Gauls, who were then besieging Cremona, and pitched his camp at the distance of one mile and a half from the enemy. Furius had an excellent opportunity of striking an important blow, had he, without halting, led his troops directly to attack their camp; they were scattered and dispersed through the country, and the guard which they had left was very insufficient; but he was apprehensive that his men were too much fatigued by their hasty march. The Gauls, recalled from the fields by the shouts of their party, returned to the camp without seizing the booty within their reach, and, next day, marched out to offer battle; the Roman did not decline the combat, but had scarcely time to make the necessary dispositions, so rapidly did the enemy advance to the fight. The right brigade (for he had the troops of the allies divided into brigades) was placed in the first line, the two Roman legions in reserve. Marcus Furius was at the head of the right brigade, Marcus Cæcilius of the legions, and Lucius Valerius Flaccus of the cavalry: these were all lieutenants-general. Two other lieutenants-general, Cneius Lætorius and Publius Titinius, the pretor kept near himself, that with their assistance, he might observe, and take proper measures against any sudden attack. At first, the Gauls, bending their whole force to one point, were in hopes of being able to overwhelm, and trample under foot, the right brigade, which was in the van; but not succeeding, they endeavoured to turn round the flanks, and to surround their enemy's line, which, considering the multitude of their forces, and the small number of the others, seemed easy to be done. On observing this, the pretor, in order to extend his own line, brought up the two legions from the reserve, and placed them on the right and left of the brigade which was engaged in the van; vowing a temple to Jupiter, if he should on that day prove victorious. To Lucius Valerius he gave orders to make the horsemen of the two legions on one flank, and the cavalry of the allies on the other, charge the wings of the enemy, and not suffer them to come round to his rear. At the same time, observing that the centre of their line was weakened, from having extended the wings, he directed his men to make an attack there in close order, and to break through their ranks. The wings were routed

* 7*s*. 9*d*.

by the cavalry, and, at the same time, the centre by the foot. Being worsted in all parts with great slaughter, the Gauls quickly turned their backs, and fled to their camp in hurry and confusion. The cavalry pursued them; and the legions coming up in a short time after, assaulted the camp, from whence there did not escape so many as six thousand men. There were slain and taken above thirty-five thousand, with eighty standards, and above two hundred Gallic wagons laden with booty of all kinds. Hamilcar, the Carthaginian general, fell that day, and three distinguished generals of the Gauls. The prisoners taken at Placentia, to the number of two thousand free men, were restored to the colony.

22. This was an important victory, and caused great joy at Rome. On receipt of the pretor's letter, a supplication for three days was decreed. In that battle there fell of the Romans and allies two thousand, most of them in the right brigade, against which, in the first onset, the most violent efforts of the enemy had been directed. Although the pretor had brought the war almost to a conclusion, yet the consul, Cneius Aurelius, having finished the business which required his attendance at Rome, set out for Gaul, and received the victorious army from the pretor. The other consul arriving in his province towards the end of autumn, passed the winter in the neighbourhood of Apollonia. Caius Claudius, and the Roman triremes which had been sent to Athens from the fleet that was laid up at Corcyra, as was mentioned above, arriving at Piræus, greatly revived the hopes of their allies, who were beginning to give way to despair. Their arrival not only put a stop to the inroads by land, which used to be made from Corinth through Megara, but so terrified the pirates from Chalcis, who had been accustomed to infest both the Athenian sea and coast, that they dared not venture round the promontory of Sunium, nor even trust themselves out of the straits of the Euripus. In addition to these came three quadriremes from Rhodes, the Athenians having three open ships, which they had equipped for the protection of their lands on the coast. While Claudius thought, that if he were able with his fleet to give security to the Athenians, it was as much as could be expected at present, fortune threw in his way an opportunity of accomplishing an enterprise of greater moment.

23. Some exiles driven from Chalcis, by ill-treatment received from the king's party, brought intelligence that the place might be taken without even a contest; for the Macedonians, being under no immediate apprehension from an enemy, were straying idly about the country; and the townsmen, depending on the Macedonian garrison, neglected the guard of the city. Claudius, in consequence of this, set out,

and though he arrived at Sunium early enough to have sailed forward to the entrance of the strait of Eubœa, yet fearing that, on doubling the promontory, he might be descried by the enemy, he lay by with the fleet until night. As soon as it grew dark he began to move, and favoured by a calm, arrived at Chalcis a little before day; and then, approaching the city, on a side where it was thinly inhabited, with a small party of soldiers, and by means of scaling ladders, he got possession of the nearest tower, and the wall on each side. Finding in some places the guards asleep, and other parts left without any watch, they advanced to the more populous parts of the town, and having slain the sentinels, and broke open a gate, they gave an entrance to the main body of the troops. These immediately spread themselves through all parts of the city, and increased the tumult by setting fire to the buildings round the forum, by which means both the granaries belonging to the king, and his armory, with a vast store of machines and engines, were reduced to ashes. Then commenced a general slaughter of those who fled, as well as of those who made resistance; and after having either put to the sword or driven out every one who was of an age fit to bear arms, (Sopater also, the Acarnanian, who commanded the garrison, being slain,) they first collected all the spoils in the forum, and then carried it on board the ships. The prison, too, was forced open by the Rhodians, and those whom Philip had shut up there were set at liberty. They next pulled down and mutilated the statues of the king; and then, on a signal being given for a retreat, re-embarked and returned to Piræus, from whence they had set out. If there had been a sufficient number of Roman soldiers to have kept possession of Chalcis, without stripping Athens of a proper garrison, that city and the command of the Euripus would have been a most important advantage at the commencement of the war; for as the pass of Thermopylæ is the principal barrier of Greece by land, so is the strait of the Euripus by sea.

24. Philip was then at Demetrias, and as soon as the news arrived there of the calamity which had befallen the city of his allies, although it was too late to carry assistance to those who were already ruined, yet anxious to accomplish what was next to assistance, revenge, he set out instantly with five thousand foot, lightly equipped, and three hundred horse. With a speed almost equal to that of racing, he hastened to Chalcis, not doubting but that he should be able to surprise the Romans. Finding himself disappointed, and that his coming answered no other end than to give him a melancholy view of the smoking ruins of that friendly city, (so few being left, that they were scarcely sufficient to bury those

who had fallen by the sword of the enemy,) with the same rapid haste which he had used in coming, he crossed the Euripus by the bridge, and led his troops through Bœotia to Athens, in hopes that a similar attempt might be attended by a similar issue: and he would have succeeded, had not a scout, (one of those whom the Greeks call day-runners,* because they run through a journey of great length in one day,) descrying from his post of observation the king's army in its march, set out at midnight, and arrived before them at Athens. The same sleep, and the same negligence, prevailed there which had proved the ruin of Chalcis a few days before. Roused, however, by the alarming intelligence, the pretor of the Athenians, and Dioxippus, commander of a cohort of mercenary auxiliaries, called the soldiers together in the forum, and ordered the trumpets to sound an alarm from the citadel, that all might be informed of the approach of the enemy. On which the people ran from all quarters to the gates, and afterward to the walls. In a few hours after, and still some time before day, Philip approached the city, and observing a great number of lights, and hearing the noise of the men hurrying to and fro, as usual on such an alarm, he halted his troops, and ordered them to sit down and take some rest; resolving to use open force, since his design of surprise had not succeeded. Accordingly he advanced on the side of Dipylos, or the double gate, which being the principal entrance of the city, is somewhat larger and wider than the rest. Both within and without the streets are wide, so that the townsmen could form their troops from the forum to the gate, while on the outside, a road of about a mile in length, leading to the school of the academy, afforded open room to the foot and horse of the enemy. The Athenians, who had formed their troops within the gate, marched out with Attalus's garrison, and the cohort of Dioxippus, along that road. This Philip observed, and thinking that he had the enemy in his power, and might now satisfy his revenge in their destruction, and which he had long wished for, (being more incensed against them than any of the Grecian states,) he exhorted his men to keep their eyes on him during the fight, and to take notice, that wherever the king was, there the standards and the army ought to be. He then spurred on his horse, animated not only with resentment, but with a desire of gaining honour, reckoning it a glorious opportunity of displaying his prowess in the view of an immense crowd which covered the walls, many of them for the purpose of beholding the engagement. Advancing far before the line, and with a small body of horse,

* Hemerodromoi.

rushing into the midst of the enemy, he inspired his men with great ardour, and the Athenians with terror. Having wounded many with his own hand, both in close fight and with missive weapons, and driven them back within the gate, he still pursued them closely; and having made greater slaughter among them while embarrassed in the narrow pass, rash as the attempt was, he yet retired unmolested; because those who were in the towers withheld their weapons lest they should hit their friends who were mingled in confusion among their enemies. The Athenians, after this, confining their troops within the walls, Philip sounded a retreat, and pitched his camp at Cynosarges, a temple of Hercules, and a school surrounded by a grove. But Cynosarges, and Lycæum, and whatever was sacred or pleasant in the neighbourhood of the city, he burned to the ground, and levelled not only the houses, but sepulchres, paying no regard, in the violence of his rage, to any privilege either of men or gods.

25. Next day, the gates having at first been shut, and afterward suddenly thrown open, in consequence of a body of Attalus's troops from Ægina, and the Romans from Piræus, having entered the city, the king removed his camp to the distance of about three miles. From thence he proceeded to Eleusis, in hopes of surprising the temple, and a fort which overlooks and surrounds it; but, finding that the guards were attentive, and that the fleet was coming from Piræus to support them, he laid aside the design, and led his troops, first to Megara, and then to Corinth; where, on hearing that the council of the Achæans was then sitting at Argos, he went and joined the assembly, to the surprise of that people. They were at the time employed in forming measures for a war against Nabis, tyrant of the Lacedæmonians; who (observing, on the command being transferred from Philopœmen to Cycliades, a general much inferior to him, that the confederates of the Achæans were falling off) had renewed the war, and besides ravaging the territories of his neighbours, was become formidable even to the cities. While they were deliberating what number of men should be raised out of each of the states to oppose this enemy, Philip promised that he would relieve them from all anxiety, as far as concerned Nabis and the Lacedæmonians; and that he would not only secure the lands of their allies from devastation, but transfer the whole terror of the war on Laconia itself, by leading his army thither instantly. This discourse being received with general approbation, he added: "It is but reasonable, however, that while I am employed in protecting your property by my arms, my own should not be exposed without defence; therefore, if you think proper,

provide such a number of troops as will be sufficient to secure Orcus, Chalcis, and Corinth; that my affairs, being in a state of safety behind me, I may proceed, without distraction, to attack Nabis and the Lacedæmonians." The Achæans were not ignorant of the tendency of these kind promises, and his offer of assistance against the Lacedæmonians, and that his view was to draw the Achæan youth out of Peloponnesus as hostages, that he might have it in his power to embroil the nation in a war with the Romans. Cycliades, pretor, thinking that it would answer no purpose to expose his scheme by argument, said nothing more than that it was not allowable, according to the laws of the Achæans, to take any matter into consideration except that on which they had been called together; and the decree for levying an army against Nabis being passed, he dismissed the assembly, after having presided in it with much resolution and public spirit, although, until that day, he had been reckoned a partisan of the king. Philip, grievously disappointed, after having collected a few voluntary soldiers, returned to Corinth, and from thence into the territories of Athens.

26. While Philip was in Achaia, Philocles, one of the generals, marching from Eubœa with two thousand Thracians and Macedonians, intending to lay waste the territories of the Athenians, crossed the forest of Cithæron opposite to Eleusis. Despatching half of his troops to make depredations in all parts of the country, he lay concealed with the remainder in a place convenient for an ambush; in order that if any attack should be made from the fort at Eleusis on his men employed in plundering, he might suddenly fall on the enemy unawares, and while they were in disorder. His stratagem did not escape discovery: wherefore, calling back the soldiers, who had gone different ways in pursuit of booty, and drawing them up in order, he advanced to assault the fort at Eleusis; but being repulsed from thence with many wounds, he joined Philip on his return from Achaia, who was also induced to a similar attempt: but the Roman ships coming from Piræus, and a body of forces being thrown into the fort, he was compelled to relinquish the design. On this the king, dividing his army, sent Philocles with one part to Athens, and went himself with the other to Piræus; that while his general, by advancing to the walls and threatening an assault, should keep the Athenians within the city, he might be able to make himself master of the harbour, which he supposed would be left with only a slight garrison. But he found the attack of Piræus no less difficult than that of Eleusis, the same persons acting in its defence. He therefore hastily

led his troops to Athens, and being repulsed by a sudden sally of both foot and horse, who engaged him in the narrow ground, enclosed by the half-ruined wall, which, with two arms, joins Piræus to Athens, he laid aside the scheme of attacking the city, and, dividing his forces again with Philocles, set out to complete the devastation of the country. As, in his former ravages, he had employed himself in levelling the sepulchres round the city, so now, not to leave any thing unviolated, he ordered the temples of the gods, of which they had one consecrated in every village, to be demolished and burned. The country of Attica afforded ample matter for the exercise of this barbarous rage; for it was highly embellished with works of that kind, having plenty of marble, and abounding with artists of exquisite ingenuity. Nor was he satisfied with merely destroying the temples themselves, and overthrowing the images, but he ordered even the stones to be broken, lest, remaining whole, they should give a degree of grandeur to the ruins; and then, his rage not being satiated, but no object remaining on which it could be exercised, he retired into Bœotia, without having performed in Greece any thing else worth mention.

27. The consul, Sulpicius, who was at that time encamped on the river Apsus, between Apollonia and Dyrrachium, having ordered Lucius Apustius, lieutenant-general, thither, sent him with part of the forces to lay waste the enemy's country. Apustius, after ravaging the frontiers of Macedonia, and having, at the first assault, taken the forts of Corragos, Gerrunios, and Orgessos, came to Antipatria, a city situated in a narrow vale; where, at first inviting the leading men to a conference, he endeavoured to prevail on them to put themselves under the protection of the Romans; but finding that from confidence in the size, fortification, and situation of their city, they paid no regard to his discourse, he attacked the place by force of arms, and took it by assault: then, putting all the young men to the sword, and giving up the entire spoil to his soldiers, he razed the walls, and burned the buildings. This proceeding spread such terror, that Codrion, a strong and well fortified town, surrendered to the Romans without a struggle. Leaving a garrison there, he took Ilion by force, a name better known than the town, on account of that of the same denomination in Asia. As the lieutenant-general was returning to the consul with a great quantity of spoil, Athenagoras, one of the king's generals, falling on his rear, in its passage over a river, threw it into disorder. On hearing the shouting and tumult, Apustius rode back in full speed, ordered the troops to face about, and drew them up in order, with the baggage in the centre. The king's troops could not support the onset of the Roman

soldiers: so that many of them were slain, and more made prisoners. The lieutenant-general, having brought back the army without loss to the consul, was ordered to return immediately to the fleet.

28. The war commencing thus brilliantly with this successful expedition, several petty kings and princes, whose dominions bordered on Macedonia, came to the Roman camp: Pleuratus, son of Scerdilædus and Amynander, king of the Athamanians; and from the Dardanians, Bato, son of Longarus. This Longarus had in his own quarrel supported a war against Demetrius, father of Philip. To their offers of aid, the consul answered, that he would make use of the assistance of the Dardanians and of Pleuratus, when he should lead his troops into Macedonia. To Amynander he allotted the part of exciting the Ætolians to war. To the ambassadors of Attalus (for they also had come at the same time) he gave directions that the king should wait at Ægina, where he wintered, for the arrival of the Roman fleet; and when joined by that, he should, as before, harass Philip by such enterprises as he could undertake by sea. To the Rhodians, also, an embassy was sent, to engage them to contribute their share towards carrying on the war. Nor was Philip, who had by this time arrived in Macedonia, remiss in his preparations for the campaign. He sent his son Perseus, then very young, with part of his forces to block up the pass near Pelagonia, appointing persons out of the number of his friends to attend him, and direct his unexperienced age. Sciathus and Peparethus, no inconsiderable cities, he demolished, fearing they might fall a prey to the enemy's fleet; despatching at the same time ambassadors to the Ætolians, lest that restless nation might change sides on the arrival of the Romans.

29. The assembly of the Ætolians, which they call Panætolium, was to meet on a certain day. In order to be present at this, the king's ambassadors hastened their journey, and Lucius Furius Purpureo also arrived, being sent in like capacity by the consul, Ambassadors from Athens, likewise, came to this assembly. The Macedonians were first heard, as with them the latest treaty had been made; and they declared that "as no change of circumstances had occurred, they had nothing new to introduce; for the same reasons which had induced the Ætolians to make peace with Philip, after experiencing the unprofitableness of an alliance with the Romans, should engage them to preserve it, now that it was established. Do you rather choose," said one of the ambassadors, "to imitate the inconsistency, or levity, shall I call it, of the Romans, who ordered this answer to be given to your ambassadors at Rome: 'Why, Ætoli-

ans, do you apply to us, when, without our approbation, you have made peace with Philip?' Yet these same people now require that you should, in conjunction with them, wage war against Philip. Formerly, too, it was pretended that they took arms on your account, and in your defence, against Philip: now they do not allow you to continue at peace with him. To assist Messana, they first embarked for Sicily; and a second time to vindicate the liberty of Syracuse, oppressed by the Carthaginians. Both Messana and Syracuse, and all Sicily, they hold in their own possession, and have reduced it into a tributary province under their axes and rods. You imagine, perhaps, that in the same manner as you hold an assembly at Naupactus, according to your own laws, under magistrates of your own appointment, at liberty to choose allies and enemies, and to have peace or war at your own option, so the assembly of the states of Sicily is summoned to Syracuse, or Messana, or Lilybæum. No; a Roman pretor presides at the meeting; at his command they assemble; they behold him, attended by his lictors, seated on a lofty throne, issuing his haughty edicts. His rods are ready for their backs, his axes for their necks, and every year they are allotted a different master. Neither ought they, nor can they wonder at this, when they see all the cities of Italy bending under the same yoke,—Rhegium, Tarentum, Capua, not to mention those in their own neighbourhood, out of the ruins of which their city of Rome grew into power. Capua indeed subsists, the grave and monument of the Campanian people, who were either cut off or driven into banishment; the mutilated carcass of a city, without senate, without commons, without magistrates; a sort of prodigy, the leaving which to be inhabited in this manner showed more cruelty than if it had been razed to the ground. If foreigners who are separated from us to a greater distance by their language, manners, and laws, than by the length of sea and land, are allowed to get footing here, it is madness to hope that any thing will continue in its present state. Does your liberty appear to be in any degree of danger from the government of Philip, who at a time when he was justly incensed, demanded nothing more of you than peace; and at present requires no more than the observance of the peace which he agreed to? Accustom foreign legions to these countries, and receive the yoke; too late and in vain will you look for an alliance with Philip, when you will have become a property of the Romans. Trifling causes occasionally unite and disunite the Ætolians, Acarnanians, and Macedonians, men speaking the same language. With foreigners, with barbarians, all Greeks have, and ever will have, eternal war; because they are enemies by nature, which is always the same, and not from causes which change with the times. I conclude my discourse with the same argument with which I began. Three years since, the same persons, assembled in this same place, determined on peace with the same Philip, contrary to the inclinations of the same Romans, who now wish that the peace should be broken, after it has been adjusted and ratified. In the subject of your deliberation fortune has made no change; why you should make any, I do not see."

30. Next after the Macedonians, with the consent and at the desire of the Romans, the Athenians were introduced; who, having suffered grievously, could with the greater justice inveigh against the cruelty and inhumanity of the king. They represented in a deplorable light the miserable devastation and ruin of their country; adding, that "they did not complain on account of having, from an enemy, suffered hostile treatment; for there were certain rights of war, according to which, as it was just to act, so it was just to endure. Their crops being burned, their houses demolished, their men and cattle carried off as spoil, were to be considered rather as misfortunes to the sufferer, than as ill treatment. But of this they had good reason to complain, that he who called the Romans foreigners and barbarians, had so atrociously violated, himself, all rights both divine and human, as, in his former inroad, to have waged an impious war against the infernal gods, in the latter, against those above. That every sepulchre and monument within their country was demolished, the graves torn open, and the bones left uncovered. There had been several temples, which, in former times, when their ancestors dwelt in the country in their separate districts, had been consecrated in each of their little forts and villages, and which, even after they were incorporated into one city, they did not neglect or forsake. Every one of these sacred edifices had Philip destroyed by fire, and left the images of the gods lying scorched and mutilated among the prostrated pillars of the temples. Such as he had rendered the country of Attica, formerly opulent, and adorned with improvements, such, if he were suffered, would he render Ætolia and every part of Greece. That Athens, also, would have been reduced to the same ruinous state, if the Romans had not come to its relief: for he had shown the same wicked rage against the gods, who are the guardians of the city, and Minerva, who presides over the citadel; the same against the temple of Ceres at Eleusis; the same against Jupiter and Minerva at Piræus. In a word, having been repelled by force of arms, not only from their temples, but even from their walls, he had vented his fury on those sacred edifices, which had no defence but in

the respect due to religion. They therefore entreated and besought the Ætolians, that, compassionating the Athenians, and following the guidance of the gods, and, under them, of the Romans, who, next to the gods, possessed the greatest power, they would take part in the war."

31. The Roman ambassador then addressed them to this purport: "The Macedonians first, and afterward the Athenians, have obliged me to change entirely the method of my discourse: for, on the one hand, the Macedonians, by introducing charges against the Romans, when I had come prepared to make complaint of the injuries committed by Philip against so many cities in alliance with us, have obliged me to think of defence rather than accusation; and, on the other hand, after the relation given by the Athenians of his inhuman and impious crimes against the gods both celestial and infernal, what room is there left for me or any other to make any addition to the charge? You are to suppose that the same complaints are made by the Cianians, Abydenians, Æneans, Maronites, Thasians, Parians, Samians, Larissenians, Messenians, on the side of Achaia; and complaints, still heavier and more grievous, by those whom he had it more in his power to injure: for as to those proceedings which he censures in us, if they are not found highly meritorious, let them not be defended. He has objected to us, Rhegium, and Capua, and Syracuse. As to Rhegium, during the war with Pyrrhus, a legion which, at the earnest request of the Rhegians themselves, we had sent thither as a garrison, wickedly possessed themselves of the city which they had been sent to defend. Did we then approve of that deed? or did we exert the force of our arms against that guilty legion, until we reduced them under our power, and then, after making them give satisfaction to the allies, by their stripes and the loss of their heads, restore to the Rhegians their city, their lands, and all their effects, together with their liberty and laws? To the Syracusans, when oppressed, (and, to add to the indignity, by foreign tyrants,) we lent assistance; and after enduring great fatigues in carrying on the siege of so strong a city, both by land and sea, for almost three years, (although the Syracusans themselves chose to continue in slavery to the tyrants, rather than to trust to us,) yet, becoming masters of the place, and by exertion of the same force setting it at liberty, we restored it to the inhabitants. At the same time, we do not deny that Sicily is our province, and that the states which sided with the Carthaginians, and, in conjunction with them, waged war against us, pay us tribute and taxes; on the contrary, we wish that you and all nations should know, that the condition of each is such as it has deserved at our hands:

and ought we to repent of the punishment inflicted on the Campanians, of which even they themselves cannot complain? These men, after we had on their account carried on war against the Samnites for near seventy years, with great loss on our side; had united them to ourselves, first by treaty, and then by intermarriages, and the consequent affinities; and lastly, by admitting them to a participation of the rights of our state, yet, in the time of our adversity, were the first of all the states of Italy which revolted to Hannibal, after basely putting our garrison to death, and afterward, through resentment at being besieged by us, sent Hannibal to attack Rome. If neither their city nor one man of them had been left remaining, who could take offence, or consider them as treated with more severity than they had deserved? From consciousness of guilt, greater numbers of them perished by their own hands than by the punishments inflicted by us. And while from the rest we took away the town and the lands, still we left them a place to dwell in, we suffered the city which partook not of the guilt to stand uninjured; so that there is not visible this day any trace of its having been besieged or taken. But why do I speak of Capua, when even to vanquished Carthage we granted peace and liberty? The greatest danger is, that by our too great readiness to pardon such, we may encourage others to try the fortune of war against us. Let so much suffice in our defence, and against Philip, whose domestic crimes, whose parricides and murders of his relations and friends, and whose lust, more disgraceful to human nature, if possible, than his cruelty, you, as being nearer to Macedonia, are better acquainted with. As to what concerns you, Ætolians, we entered into a war with Philip on your account: you made peace with him without consulting us. Perhaps you will say, that while we were occupied in the Punic war, you were constrained by fear to accept terms of pacification from him who possessed superior power; and that on our side, pressed by more urgent affairs, we suspended our operations in a war which you had laid aside. At present, as we, having, by the favour of the gods, brought the Punic war to a conclusion, have fallen on Macedonia with the whole weight of our power, so you have an opportunity offered you of regaining a place in our friendship and alliance, unless you choose to perish with Philip, rather than to conquer with the Romans."

32. After this discourse of the ambassadors, the inclinations of all leaning towards the Romans, Damocritus, pretor of the Ætolians, (who, it was reported, had received money from the king,) without seeming to favour either party, said, that "in consultations wherein the public safety was deeply

interested, nothing was so injurious as haste. That repentance, indeed, generally followed, and that quickly, but yet too late and unavailing; because designs carried on with precipitation could not be recalled, nor matters brought back to their original state. The time however for determining the point under consideration, which, for his part, he thought should not be too early, might yet immediately be fixed in this manner. As it had been provided by the laws, that no determination should be made concerning peace or war, except in the Panætolic or Pylaic councils; let them immediately pass a decree, that the pretor, when he chooses to treat of either, may have full authority to summon a council; and that whatever shall be then debated and decreed, shall be, to all intents and purposes, legal and valid, as if it had been transacted in the Panætolic or Pylaic assembly. And thus dismissing the ambassadors, without coming to any resolution, he said, "that therein he acted most prudently for the interest of the state; for the Ætolians would have it in their power to join in alliance with whichever of the parties should be more successful in the war." Nothing farther was done in the assembly.

33. Meanwhile Philip was making vigorous preparations for carrying on the war both by sea and land. His naval forces he drew together at Demetrias in Thessaly; supposing that Attalus, and the Roman fleet, would move from Ægina in the beginning of the spring. He gave the command of the fleet and of the sea-coast to Heraclides, to whom he had formerly intrusted it. The equipment of the land-forces he took care of in person; and thought that he had deprived the Romans of two powerful auxiliaries, the Ætolians on the one side, and the Dardanians on the other, by making his son Perseus block up the pass at Pelagonia. The consul was employed, not in preparations, but in the operations of war. He led his army through the country of the Dassaretians, leaving the corn untouched which he had brought from his winter-quarters, for the fields afforded supplies sufficient for the consumption of the troops. The towns and villages surrendered to him, some through inclination, others through fear; some were taken by assault, others were found deserted, the barbarians flying to the neighbouring mountains. He fixed a standing camp at Lycus near the river Beous, and from thence sent to bring in corn from the magazines of the Dassaretians. Philip saw the whole country filled with consternation, and not knowing the designs of the consul, he sent a party of horse to discover his route. Sulpicius was in the same state of uncertainty; he knew that the king had moved from his winter-quarters, but in what direction he had proceeded, he knew

not: he also had sent horsemen to gain intelligence. These two parties having set out from opposite quarters, after wandering a long time among the Dassaretians, through unknown roads, fell at length into the same road. Neither doubted, as soon as the noise of men and horses was heard at a distance, that an enemy approached: therefore before they came within sight of each other, they got their arms in readiness, and the moment they met, both hastened eagerly to engage. As they happened to be nearly equal in number and valour, being picked men on both sides, they fought during several hours with vigour, until fatigue, both of men and horses, put an end to the fight, without deciding the victory. Of the Macedonians, there fell forty horsemen; of the Romans, thirty-five. Still, however, neither party was able to carry back any certain information in what quarter the camp of his enemy lay. But this was soon made known to them by deserters; of whom, either through restlessness, or the prospect of reward, a sufficient number are found, in every war, to discover the affairs of the contending parties.

34. Philip, judging that it would tend considerably towards conciliating the affections of his men, and induce them to face danger more readily on his account, if he bestowed some pains on the burial of the horsemen, who fell in that expedition, ordered them to be conveyed into the camp, in order that all might be spectators of the honours paid them at their funeral. Nothing is so uncertain or so difficult to form a judgment of, as the minds of the multitude. The very measures which seem calculated to increase their alacrity, in exertions of every sort, often inspire them with fear and timidity. Accordingly those, who, being always accustomed to fight with Greeks and Illyrians, had only seen wounds made with javelins and arrows, seldom even by lances, came to behold bodies dismembered by the Spanish sword, some with their arms lopped off, or, the neck entirely cut through, heads severed from the trunk, and the bowels laid open, with other shocking circumstances which the present warfare had wrought: they therefore perceived, with horror, against what weapons and what men they were to fight. Even the king himself was seized with apprehensions, having never yet engaged the Romans in a regular battle. Wherefore, recalling his son, and the guard posted at the pass of Pelagonia, in order to strengthen his army by the addition of those troops, he thereby opened a passage into Macedonia for Pleuratus and the Dardanians. Then, taking deserters for guides, he marched towards the enemy with twenty thousand foot, and four thousand horse, and, at the distance of somewhat more than two hundred paces from the Roman camp, and near Ithacus, he fortified a hill with

a trench and rampart. From this place, taking a view of the Roman station in the valley beneath, he is said to have been struck with admiration, both at the general appearance of the camp, and the regular disposition of each particular part, distinguished by the order of the tents, and the intervals of the passages, and to have declared that, certainly, that was not a camp of barbarians. For two days, the consul and the king, each waiting for the other's making some attempt, kept their troops within the ramparts. On the third day the Roman led out all his forces and offered battle.

35. But the king, not daring to risk so hastily a general engagement, sent four hundred Trallians, who are a tribe of the Illyrians, as we have said in another place, and three hundred Cretans; adding to this body of infantry an equal number of horse, under the command of Athenagoras, one of his nobles honoured with the purple, to make an attack on the enemy's cavalry. When these troops arrived within a little more than five hundred paces, the Romans sent out the light infantry, and two cohorts of horse, that both cavalry and infantry might be equal in number to the Macedonians. The king's troops expected that the method of fighting would be such as they had been accustomed to; that the horsemen, pursuing and retreating alternately, would at one time use their weapons, at another time turn their backs; that the agility of the Illyrians would be serviceable for excursions and sudden attacks, and that the Cretans might discharge their arrows as they advanced eagerly to the charge: but this plan of fighting was entirely disconcerted by the manner in which the Romans made their onset, which was not more brisk than it was obstinate; for the light infantry, as if in a general line of battle, after discharging their javelins, carried on a close fight with their swords; and the horsemen, when they had once made a charge, stopping their horses, fought, some on horseback, while others dismounted and intermixed themselves with the foot. By this means neither were the king's cavalry, who were unaccustomed to a steady fight, a match for the others; nor were the infantry, who were unacquainted with any other mode of fighting but that of skirmishing and irregular attacks, and were besides but half covered with the kind of harness which they used, at all equal to the Roman infantry, who carried a sword and buckler, and were furnished with proper armour, both to defend themselves and to annoy the enemy: nor did they sustain the combat, but fled to their camp, trusting entirely to their speed for safety.

36. After an interval of one day, the king, resolving to make an attack with all his cavalry and light-armed infantry, had, during the night, placed in ambush, in a conve-

nient place between the two camps, a body of targeteers, whom they call peltastæ, and given orders to Athenagoras and the cavalry, if they found they had the advantage in the open fight, to pursue their success; if not, that they should retreat leisurely, and by that means draw on the enemy to the place where the ambush lay. The cavalry accordingly did retreat; but the officers of the body of targeteers, by bringing forward their men before the time, and not waiting for the signal, as they ought, lost an opportunity of performing considerable service. The Romans having gained the victory in open fight, and also escaped the danger of the ambuscade, retired to their camp. Next day the consul marched out with all his forces, and offered battle, placing his elephants (which had been taken in the Punic war) in the front of the foremost battalions, and which was the first time that the Romans made use of those creatures in the field. Finding that the king kept himself quiet behind his intrenchments, he advanced close up to them, upbraiding him with cowardice; and as, notwithstanding, he still declined an engagement, the consul, considering how dangerous foraging must be while the camps lay so near each other, where the soldiers, dispersed through the country, were liable to be suddenly attacked by the horse, removed his camp to a place called Octolophus, distant about eight miles, where he could forage with more safety. While the Romans were collecting corn in the adjacent fields, the king kept his men within the trenches, in order to increase both the negligence and confidence of the enemy. But, when he saw them scattered, he set out with all his cavalry, and the auxiliary Cretans; and marching with such speed that the swiftest footmen could, by running, but just keep up with the horse, he took post between the camp of the Romans and their foragers. Then, dividing the forces, he sent one part of them in quest of the marauders, with orders to give no quarter; with the other, he himself halted, and placed guards on the roads through which he supposed the enemy would fly back to their camp. The slaughter and flight of the provisioning party had continued for some time on all sides, and no intelligence of the misfortune had yet reached the Roman camp, because those who fled towards the camp fell in with the guards which the king had stationed to intercept them, and greater numbers were slain by those who were placed in the roads than by those who had been sent out to attack them. At length a few affected their escape through the midst of the enemy's posts, but were so filled with terror, that they excited a general consternation in the camp, without being able to give any certain account of what was going on.

37. The consul, ordering the cavalry to carry aid to those who were in danger, in the best manner they could, drew out the legions from the camp, and led them in order of battle towards the enemy. The cavalry, taking different ways through the fields, missed the road, being deceived by the various shouts raised in several quarters. Some of them met with the enemy, and battles began in many places at once. The hottest part of the action was at the station where the king commanded; for the guard there was, in numbers both of horse and foot, almost a complete army; and, as they were posted on the middle road, the greatest number of the Romans fell in with them. The Macedonians had also the advantage in this, that the king himself was present to encourage them; and the Cretan auxiliaries, fighting in good order, and in a state of preparation, against troops disordered and irregular, wounded many at a distance, where no such danger was apprehended. If they had acted with prudence in the pursuit, they would have secured an advantage of great importance, not only in regard to the glory of the present contest, but to the general interest of the war; but, greedy of slaughter, and following with too much eagerness, they fell in with the advanced cohorts of the Romans under the military tribunes. The horsemen who were flying, as soon as they saw the ensigns of their friends, faced about against the enemy, now in disorder; so that in a moment's time the fortune of the battle was changed, those now turning their backs who had lately been the pursuers. Many were slain in close fight, many in the pursuit; nor was it by the sword alone that they perished; several being driven into morasses, were, together with their horses, swallowed up in the deep mud. The king himself was in danger; for his horse falling, in consequence of a wound, threw him headlong to the ground, and he very narrowly escaped being overpowered before he could recover his feet. He owed his safety to a trooper, who instantly leaped from his horse, on which he mounted the affrighted king; himself, as he could not run so fast as to keep up with the horsemen, was slain by the enemy, who had collected about the place where Philip fell. The king, in his desperate flight, rode about among the morasses, some of which were easily passed, and others not; at length, when most men despaired of his ever returning, he arrived in safety at his camp. Two hundred Macedonian horsemen perished in that action; about one hundred were taken: eighty horses, richly caparisoned, were led off the field; at the same time the spoils of arms were also carried off.

38. Some have found fault with the king, as guilty of rashness on that day; and with the consul as not having

pushed with spirit the advantage which he had gained: for Philip, they say, on his part, ought to have avoided coming to action, knowing that in a few days the enemy, having exhausted all the adjacent country, must be reduced to the extremity of want; and that the consul, after having routed the Macedonian cavalry and light infantry, and nearly taken the king himself, ought to have led on his troops directly to the enemy's camp, where, dismayed as they were, they could have made no stand, and that he might have finished the war in a moment's time. This, like most other matters, was easier in speculation than in practice: for if the king had brought his infantry into the engagement, then, indeed, during the tumult, and while vanquished and struck with dismay, they fled from the field into their intrenchments, (and even continued their flight from thence on seeing the victorious enemy mounting the ramparts,) the king's camp might have fallen into the Roman's possession. But as the infantry had remained in the camp, fresh and free from fatigue, with outposts before the gates, and guards properly disposed, what would he have gained in having imitated the rashness of which the king had just now been guilty, by pursuing the routed horse? On the other side, the king's first plan of an attack on the foragers, while dispersed through the fields, was not injudicious, could he have satisfied himself with a moderate degree of success: and it is the less surprising that he should have made a trial of fortune, as there was a report that Pleuratus and the Dardanians had marched with very numerous forces, and had already passed into Macedonia; so that, if he should be surrounded on all sides, there was reason to think that the Roman might put an end to the war without stirring from his seat. Philip, however, considered, that after his cavalry had been defeated in two engagements, he could with much less safety continue in the same post; accordingly, wishing to remove from thence, and at the same time to keep the enemy in ignorance of his design, he sent a herald to the consul a little before sunset, to demand a truce for the purpose of burying the horsemen; and thus imposing on him, he began his march in silence, about the second watch, leaving a number of fires in all parts of his camp.

39. The consul had already retired to take refreshment, when he was told that the herald had arrived, and on what business: he gave him no other answer than that he should be admitted to an audience early the next morning: by which means Philip gained what he wanted, the length of that night and part of the following day, during which he might march his troops beyond the enemy's reach. He directed his route towards the mountains, a road which he knew the

Romans, with their heavy baggage, would not attempt. The consul, having at the first light dismissed the herald, with a grant of a truce, in a short time after discovered that the enemy had gone off; but not knowing what course to take in pursuit of them, he remained in the same camp for several days, which he employed in collecting forage. He then marched to Stubera, and brought thither, from Pelagonia, the corn that was in the fields. From thence he advanced to Pellina, not having yet discovered to what quarter the Macedonian had bent his course. Philip having at first fixed his camp at Bryanium, marched thence through cross roads, and gave a sudden alarm to the enemy. The Romans, on this, removed from Pellina, and pitched their camp near the river Osphagus. The king also sat down at a small distance, forming his intrenchment on the bank of the river Erigonus. Having there received certain information that the Romans intended to proceed to Eordæa, he marched away before them, in order to take possession of the defiles, and prevent the enemy from making their way, where the roads are confined to narrow straits. There, with much labour, he fortified some places with a rampart, others with a trench, others with stones heaped up, instead of walls, others with trees laid across, according as the situation required, or as materials lay convenient; and thus a road, in its own nature difficult, he rendered, as he imagined, impregnable by the works which he drew across every pass. The adjoining ground being mostly covered with woods, was exceedingly incommodious to the phalanx of the Macedonians, which is of no manner of use except when they extend their very long spears before their shields, forming as it were a pallisade; to perform which they require an open plain. The Thracians, too, were embarrassed by their lances, which also are of great length, and were entangled among the branches that stood in their way on every side. The body of Cretans alone was not unserviceable; and yet even these, though in case of an attack made on them, they could to good purpose discharge their arrows against the horses or riders, where they were open to a wound, yet against the Roman shields they could do nothing, because they had neither strength sufficient to pierce through them, nor was there any part exposed at which they could aim. Perceiving, therefore, that kind of weapon to be useless, they annoyed the enemy with stones, which lay in plenty in all parts of the valley: the strokes made by these on their shields, with greater noise than injury, for a short time retarded the advance of the Romans; but quickly learning to despise these weapons also, some closing their shields in form of a tortoise, forced their way through the enemy in front; others having, by a short circuit, gained the summit of the hill, dislodged the dismayed Macedonians from their guards and posts, and even slew the greater part of them, the difficulties of the ground preventing their escape.

40. Thus with less opposition than they had expected to meet, they passed the defiles, and came to Eordæa; then, having laid waste the whole country, the consul withdrew into Elimea. From thence he made an irruption into Orestis, and laid siege to the city Celetrum, situated in a peninsula: a lake surrounds the walls; and there is but one entrance from the main land along a narrow isthmus. Relying on their situation, the townsmen at first shut the gates, and refused to submit; but afterward, when they saw the troops in motion, and advancing under cover of their closed shields, and the isthmus, covered by the enemy marching in, their courage failed them, and they surrendered without hazarding a struggle. From Celetrum he advanced into the country of the Dassaretians, took the city Pelium by storm, carried off the slaves with the rest of the spoil, and discharging the freemen without ransom, restored the city to them, after placing a strong garrison in it, for it lay very convenient for making inroads into Macedonia. Having thus carried devastation through the enemy's country, the consul led back his forces into those parts which were already reduced to obedience near Apollonia, from whence, at the beginning of the campaign, he had set out to begin his operations. Philip's attention had been drawn to other quarters by the Ætolians, Athamanians, and Dardanians: so many were the wars that started up on different sides of him. Against the Dardanians, who were now retiring out of Macedonia, he sent Athenagoras with the light infantry and the greater part of the cavalry, and ordered him to hang on their rear as they retreated; and, by cutting off their hindmost troops, make them more cautious for the future of leading out their armies from home. As to the Ætolians, Damocritus, their pretor, the same who at Naupactum had persuaded them to defer passing a decree concerning the war, had in the next meeting roused them to arms, after hearing of the battle between the cavalry at Octolophus; the irruption of the Dardanians and of Pleuratus, with the Illyrians, into Macedonia; of the arrival of the Roman fleet, too, at Oreus; and that Macedonia, besides being beset on all sides by so many nations, was in danger of being invested by sea also.

41. These reasons had brought back Damocritus and the Ætolians to the interest of the Romans. Marching out, therefore, in conjunction with Amynander, king of the Athamanians, they laid siege to Cercinium. The inhabi-

tants here had shut their gates, whether of their own choice or by compulsion is unknown, as they had a garrison of the king's troops. However, in a few days, Cercinium was taken and burned; and after great slaughter had been made, those who survived, both free men and slaves, were carried off amongst other spoil. This caused such terror, as made all those who dwelt round the lake Bœbius abandon their cities, and fly to the mountains; and the Ætolians not finding booty, turned away from thence, and proceeded into Perrhæbia. There they took Cyretiæ by storm, and sacked it without mercy. The inhabitants of Mallœa, making a voluntary submission, were received into alliance. From Perrhæbia, Amynander advised to march to Gomphi, because that city lies close to Athamania, and there was reason to think that it might be reduced without any great difficulty. But the Ætolians, for the sake of plunder, directed their march to the rich plains of Thessaly, Amynander following, though he did not approve either of their careless method of carrying on their depredations, or of their pitching their camp in any place where chance directed, without choice, and without taking any care to fortify it. Therefore, lest their rashness and negligence might be the cause of some misfortune to himself and his troops, when he saw them forming their camp in low grounds, under the city Phecadus, he took possession, with his own troops, of an eminence about five hundred paces distant, which could be rendered secure by a slight fortification. The Ætolians seemed to have fogotten that they were in an enemy's country, excepting that they continued to plunder, some straggling in small parties without arms, others spending whole days and nights in drinking and sleeping in the camp, neglecting even to fix guards, when Philip unexpectedly came on them. His approach being announced by those who had fled out of the fields in a fright, threw Damocritus and the rest of the officers into great confusion. It happened to be mid-day, and when most of the men, after a hearty meal, lay fast asleep. Their officers roused them, however, as fast as possible; ordered them to take arms; despatched some to recall those who were straggling through the fields in search of plunder; and so violent was their hurry, that many of the horsemen went out without their swords, and but few of them put on their corslets. After marching out in this precipitate manner, (the whole horse and foot not amounting to six hundred,) they met the king's cavalry, superior in number, in spirit, and in arms. They were therefore routed at the first charge; and, having scarcely attempted resistance, returned to the camp in shameful flight. Several were slain; and some taken, having been cut off from the main body of the runaways.

42. Philip, when his troops had advanced almost to the rampart, ordered a retreat to be sounded, because both men and horses were fatigued, not so much by the action, as by the length of their march, and the extraordinary celerity with which they had made it. He therefore despatched the horsemen by troops, and the companies of light infantry in turn, for water; after which they took refreshment. The rest he kept on guard, under arms, waiting for the main body of the infantry, which had marched with less expedition, on account of the weight of their armour. As soon as these arrived, they also were ordered to fix their standards, and, laying down their arms before them, to take food in haste; sending two, or at most three, out of each company to provide water. In the mean time the cavalry and light infantry stood in order, and ready, in case the enemy should make any motion. The Ætolians, as if resolved to defend their fortifications, (the multitude which had been scattered about the fields having, by this time, returned to the camp,) posted bodies of armed men at the gates, and on the rampart, and from this safe situation looked with a degree of confidence on the enemy, as long as they continued quiet. But, as soon as the troops of the Macedonians began to move, and to advance to the rampart, in order of battle, and ready for an assault they all quickly abandoned their posts, and fled through the opposite part of the camp, to the eminence where the Athamanians were stationed. During their flight in this confusion many of the Ætolians were slain, and many made prisoners. Philip doubted not that, had there been daylight enough remaining, he should have been able to make himself master of the camp of the Athamanians also; but the day being spent in the fight, and in plundering the camp afterward, he sat down under the eminence, in the adjacent plain, determined to attack the enemy at the first dawn. But the Ætolians, under the same apprehensions which had made them desert their camp, dispersed, and fled during the following night. Amynander was of the greatest service; for, by his directions, the Athamanians, who were acquainted with the roads, conducted them into Ætolia, whilst the Macedonians pursued them over the highest mountains through unknown paths. In this disorderly flight a few, missing their way, fell into the hands of the Macedonian horsemen, whom Philip, at the first light, on seeing the eminence abandoned, had sent to infest them on their march.

43. About the same time also, Athenagoras, one of the king's generals, overtaking the Dardanians in their retreat

homeward, at first threw their rear into disorder: but these unexpectedly facing about, and forming their line, the fight became like a regular engagement. When the Dardanians began again to advance, the Macedonian cavalry and light infantry harassed those who had no troops of that kind to aid them, and were, besides, burdened with unwieldy arms. The ground too favoured the assailants: very few were slain, but many wounded; none were taken, because they rarely quit their ranks, but both fight and retreat in a close body. Thus Philip, having checked the proceedings of those two nations by these well-timed expeditions, gained reparation for the damages sustained from the operations of the Romans; the enterprise being as spirited as the issue was successful. An accidental occurrence lessened the number of his enemies on the side of Ætolia. Scopas, a man of considerable influence in his own country, having been sent from Alexandria by King Ptolemy, with a great sum of gold, hired and carried away to Egypt, six thousand foot and some horse; nor would he have suffered one of the young Ætolians to remain at home had not Damocritus, (it is not easy to say, whether out of zeal for the good of the nation, or out of opposition to Scopas, for not having secured his interest by presents,) by sometimes reminding them of the war with which they were threatened, at other times, of the solitary state in which their country would be left, detained some of them. Such were the actions of the Romans and of Philip during that summer.

44. In the beginning of the same summer the fleet under Lucius Apustius, lieutenant-general, setting sail from Corcyra, and passing by Malea, formed a junction with King Attalus, off Scyllæum, which lies in the district of Hermione. The Athenian state, which had for a long time, through fear, restrained their animosity against Philip within some bounds, assuming confidence from the support now afforded them, gave full scope to it without any reserve. There are never wanting in that city orators, who are ready on every occasion to inflame the people; a kind of men, who, in all free states, and more particularly in that of Athens, where eloquence flourishes in the highest degree, are maintained by the favour of the multitude. These immediately proposed a decree, and the commons passed it, that "all the statues and images of Philip, with their inscriptions, and likewise those of all his ancestors of both sexes, should be removed and defaced; that the festival days, solemnities, and priests, which had been instituted in honour of him or them, should all be abolished; and that even the ground where any such statue had been set up, and inscribed with his name, should be held abominable."

And it was resolved that, "for the future, nothing which ought to be erected or dedicated in a place of purity should be there erected; and that the public priests, as often as they should pray for the people of Athens, for their allies, armies, and fleets, so often should they utter curses and execrations against Philip, his offspring, his kingdom, his forces by sea and land, and the whole race and name of the Macedonians." It was added to the decree, that "if any person in future should make any proposal tending to throw disgrace and ignominy on Philip, the people of Athens would ratify it in its fullest extent; if, on the contrary, any one should, by word or deed, endeavour to lessen his ignominy, or to do him honour, that whoever slew such person should be justified in so doing." Lastly, a clause was annexed, that "all the decrees, formerly passed against the Pisistratidæ, should be in full force against Philip." Thus the Athenians waged war against Philip with writings and with words, in which alone their power consists.

45. Attalus and the Romans having, from Hermione, proceeded first to Piræus, and stayed there a few days, after being loaded with decrees of the Athenians, (in which the honours paid to their allies were as extravagant as the expressions of their resentment against their enemy had been,) sailed to Andros, and, coming to an anchor in the harbour called Gaureleos, sent persons to sound the inclinations of the townsmen, whether they chose voluntarily to surrender, rather than run the hazard of an assault. On their answering that they were not at their own disposal, the citadel being possessed by the king's troops, Attalus and the Roman lieutenant-general, landing their forces, with every thing requisite for attacking towns, made their approaches to the city on different sides. The Roman engines and arms, which they had never seen before, together with the spirit of the soldiers, so briskly approaching the walls, were particularly terrifying to the Greeks, insomuch, that they immediately fled into the citadel, leaving the city in the power of the enemy. After holding out for two days in the citadel, relying more on the strength of the place than on their arms, on the third both they and the garrison capitulated, on condition of their being transported to Delium in Bœotia, and being each of them allowed a single suit of apparel. The island was yielded up by the Romans to King Attalus; the spoil, and the ornaments of the city, they themselves carried off. Attalus, desirous that the island, of which he had got possession, might not be quite deserted, persuaded almost all the Macedonians, and several of the Andrians, to remain there; and, in some time after, those who, according to the capitulation, had been transported to Delium, were induced

to return from thence by the promises made them by the king, in which they were disposed the more readily to confide, by the ardent affection which they felt for their native country. From Andros the combined army passed over to Cythnus: there they spent several days to no purpose, in attempting to get possession of the city; when, at length, finding it scarcely worth the trouble, they departed. At Prasiæ, a place on the main land of Attica, twenty barks of the Issæans joined the Roman fleet. These were sent to ravage the lands of the Carystians, the rest of the fleet lying at Geræstus, a noted harbour in Eubœa, until their return from Carystus: on which, setting sail together, and steering their course through the open sea, until they passed by Scyrus, they arrived at the island of Icus. Being detained there for a few days by a violent northerly wind, as soon as it abated, they passed over to Sciathus, a city which had been lately plundered and desolated by Philip. The soldiers, spreading themselves over the country, brought back to the ships corn and many other kinds of provisions. Plunder there was none, nor had the Greeks deserved to be plundered. Directing their course to Cassandrea, they first came to Mendis, a village on the coast of that state; and, intending from thence to double the promontory, and bring round the fleet to the very walls of the city, they were near being buried in the waves by a furious storm. However, after being dispersed, and a great part of the ships having lost their rigging, they escaped on shore. This storm at sea was an omen of the kind of success which they were to meet on land; for, after collecting their vessels together, and landing their forces, having made an assault on the city, they were repulsed with considerable loss, there being a strong garrison of the king's troops in the place. Being thus obliged to retreat without accomplishing their design, they passed over to Canastrum in Pallene, and from thence, doubling the promontory of Torona, conducted the fleet to Acanthus. There they first laid waste the country, then stormed the city itself, and plundered it. They proceeded no farther, for their ships were now heavily laden with booty, but went back to Sciathus, and from Sciathus to Eubœa, whence they had first set out.

46. Leaving the fleet there, they entered the Malian bay with ten light ships, in order to confer with the Ætolians on the method of conducting the war. Sipyrrhicus, the Ætolian, was at the head of the embassy that came to Heraclea, to hold a consultation with the king and the Roman lieutenant-general. They demanded of Attalus that, in pursuance of the treaty, he should supply them with one thousand soldiers, which number he had engaged for on condition of

their taking part in the war against Philip. This was refused to the Ætolians, because on their part they had formerly showed themselves unwilling to march out to ravage Macedonia, at a time when Philip, being employed near Pergamus in destroying by fire every thing sacred and profane, they might have compelled him to retire from thence, in order to preserve his own territories. Thus, instead of aid, the Ætolians were dismissed with hopes, the Romans making them large promises. Apustius and Attalus returned to their ships, where they began to concert measures for the siege of Oreus. This city was well secured by fortifications; and also, since the attempt formerly made on it, by a strong garrison. After the taking of Andros, the combined fleet had been joined by twenty Rhodian ships, all decked vessels, under the command of Agesimbrotus. This squadron they sent to cruise off Zelasium, a promontory of Isthmia, very conveniently situate beyond Demetrias, in order that, if the ships of the Macedonians should attempt to come out, they might be at hand to oppose them. Heraclides, the king's admiral, kept his fleet there, rather with a view of laying hold of any advantage which the negligence of the enemy might afford him, than with a design of employing open force. The Romans and King Attalus carried on their attacks against Oreus on different sides; the Romans against the citadel next to the sea, the king's troops against the lower part of the town, lying between the two citadels, where the city is also divided by a wall. As their posts were different, so were their methods of attack: the Romans made their approaches by means of covered galleries, some carried by men, others moving on wheels, applying also the ram to the walls; the king's troops, by throwing in weapons with the balista, catapulta, and every other kind of engine. They cast stones also of immense weight, formed mines, and made use of every expedient, which, on trial, had been found useful in the former siege. On the other side, the Macedonian garrison, in the town and the citadels, was not only more numerous than on the former occasion, but exerted themselves with greater spirit, in consequence of the reprimands which they had received from the king for their former misconduct, and also from remembrance both of his threats and promises with regard to their future behaviour; so that there was very little hope of its being speedily taken. The lieutenant-general thought that, in the mean time, some other business might be accomplished; wherefore, leaving such a number of men as seemed sufficient to finish the works, he passed over to the nearest part of the continent, and, arriving unexpectedly, made himself master of Larissa, except the citadel,—not that celebrated city in Thessaly, but another, which they call Cremaste. Attalus also surprised Ægeleos, where nothing was less apprehended than such an enterprise, during the siege of another city. The works at Oreus had now begun to take effect, while the garrison within were almost spent with unremitted toil, (keeping watch both by day and night,) and also with wounds. Part of the wall, being loosened by the strokes of the ram, had fallen down in many places; and the Romans, during the night, broke into the citadel through the breach which lay over the harbour. Attalus, likewise, at the first light, on a signal given from the citadel by the Romans, assaulted the city on his side, where great part of the walls had been levelled; on which the garrison and townsmen fled into the other citadel, and even that they surrendered in two days after. The city fell to the king, the prisoners to the Romans.

47. The autumnal equinox now approached, and the Eubœan gulf, called Cœla, is reckoned dangerous by mariners. Choosing therefore to remove thence before the winter storms came on, they returned to Piræus, from whence they had set out for the campaign. Apustius, leaving there thirty ships, sailed by Malea to Corcyra. The king was delayed during the celebration of the mysteries of Ceres, immediately after which he also retired into Asia, sending home Agesimbrotus and the Rhodians. Such, during that summer, were the proceedings by sea and land of the Roman consul and lieutenant-general, aided by Attalus and the Rhodians, against Philip and his allies. The other consul, Caius Aurelius, on coming into his province, and finding the war there already brought to a conclusion, did not dissemble his resentment against the pretor for having proceeded to action in his absence; wherefore, sending him away to Etruria, he led on the legions into the enemy's country, where their operations, having no other object than booty, produced more of it than glory. Lucius Furius, finding nothing in Etruria that could give him employment, and at the same time fired with ambition of obtaining a triumph for his success against the Gauls, which he knew would be more easily accomplished in the absence of the consul, who envied and was enraged against him, came to Rome unexpectedly, and called a meeting of the senate in the temple of Bellona: where, after making a recital of the services which he had performed, he demanded to be allowed to enter the city in triumph.

48. A great part of the senate, induced by their regard for him, and the importance of his services, showed an inclination to grant his request. The elder part refused to agree to such grant, both "because the army, with which he had acted, belonged to another; and because he had left his prov-

ince through an ambitious desire of snatching that opportunity of procuring a triumph,—a conduct altogether unprecedented." The senators of consular rank particularly insisted that "he ought to have waited for the consul; for that he might, by pitching his camp near the city, and thereby securing the colony without coming to an engagement, have protracted the affair until his arrival; and that, what the pretor had not done, the senate ought to do; they should wait for the consul. After hearing the business discussed by the consul and pretor in their presence, they would be able, on better grounds, to form a judgment on the case." Great part were of opinion that they ought to consider nothing but the service performed, and whether he had performed it while in office, and under his own auspices: for, "when of two colonies, which had been opposed, as barriers, to restrain the tumultuous inroads of the Gauls, one had been already sacked and burned, the flames being ready to spread (as if from an adjoining house) to the other, which lay so near, what ought the pretor to have done? If it was improper to enter on any action without the consul, then the senate had acted wrong in giving the army to the pretor; because, if they chose that the business should be performed, not under the pretor's auspices, but the consul's, they might have limited the decree in such a manner, that not the pretor, but the consul, should have the management of it: or else the consul had acted wrong, who after ordering the army to remove from Etruria into Gaul, did not meet it at Ariminum, in order to be present at operations, which were not allowed to be performed without him. But the exigences of war do not wait for the delays and procrastinations of commanders; and battles must be sometimes fought, not because commanders choose it, but because the enemy compels it. The fight itself, and the issue of the fight, is what ought to be regarded now. The enemy were routed and slain, their camp taken and plundered, the colony relieved from a siege, the prisoners taken from the other colony recovered and restored to their friends, and an end put to the war in one battle. And not only men rejoiced at this victory, but the immortal gods also had supplications paid to them for the space of three days, on account of the business of the state having been wisely and successfully, not rashly and unfortunately, conducted by Lucius Furius, pretor. Besides, the Gallic wars were, by some fatality, destined to the Furian family."

49. By means of discourses of this kind, made by him and his friends, the interest of the pretor, who was present, prevailed over the respect due to the dignity of the absent consul, and the majority decreed a triumph to Lucius Furius.

Lucius Furius, pretor, during his office triumphed over the Gauls. He carried into the treasury three hundred and twenty thousand asses,* and one hundred and seventy thousand pounds' weight of silver. There were neither any prisoners led before his chariot, nor spoils carried before him, nor did any soldiers follow him. It appeared that every thing except the victory belonged to the consul. Publius Scipio then celebrated in a magnificent manner the games which he had vowed when consul in Africa; and with respect to the lands for his soldiers, it was decreed that whatever number of years each of them had served in Spain or in Africa, he should for every year receive two acres; and that ten commissioners should make the distribution. Three commissioners were then appointed to fill up the number of colonists at Venusia, because the strength of that colony had been reduced in the war with Hannibal: Caius Terrentius Varro, Titus Quintius Flamininus, Publius Cornelius, son of Cneius Scipio, were the commissioners who enrolled the colonists for Venusia. During the same year, Caius Cornelius Cethegus, who in the quality of proconsul commanded in Spain, routed a numerous army of the enemy in the territory of Sedeta; in which battle it is said that fifteen thousand Spaniards were slain, and seventy-eight military standards taken. The consul Caius Aurelius, on returning from his province to Rome, to hold the elections, made heavy complaints, not on the subject on which they had supposed he would, that the senate had not waited for his coming, nor allowed him an opportunity of arguing the matter with the pretor; but, that "the senate had decreed a triumph in such a manner, without hearing the report of any one of those who were present at the operations of the war, except the person who was to enjoy the triumph: that their ancestors had made it a rule that the lieutenants-general, the military tribunes, the centurions, and even the soldiers, should be present at the same; for this reason, that the reality of his exploits, to whom so high an honour was paid, might be publicly ascertained. Now, of that army which fought with the Gauls, had any one soldier, or even a soldier's servant, been present, of whom the senate could inquire concerning the truth or falsehood of the pretor's narrative? He then appointed a day for the elections, at which were chosen consuls, Lucius Cornelius Lentulus and Publius Villius Tappulus. The pretors were then appointed, Lucius Quintius Flamininus, Lucius Valerius Flaccus, Lucius Villius Tappulus, and Cneus Bæbius Tamphilus.

50. During that year provisions were remarkably cheap. The curule ediles, Marcus Claudius Marcellus and Sextus

* 1033*l.* 6*s.* 8*d.*

Ælius Pætus, distributed among the people a vast quantity of corn brought from Africa, at the rate of two asses a peck. They also celebrated the Roman games in a magnificent manner, repeating them a second day; and erected in the treasury five brazen statues out of the money paid as fines. The plebeian games were thrice repeated entire, by the ediles, Lucius Terentius Massa, and Cneius Bæbius Tamphilus, who was elected pretor. There were also funeral games exhibited that year in the forum for the space of four days, on occasion of the death of Marcus Valerius Lævinus, by his sons Publius and Marcus, who gave also a show of gladiators, in which twenty-five pairs fought. Marcus Aurelius Cotta, one of the ten commissioners for keeping the books of the Sibyl, died, and Manius Acilius Glabrio was substituted in his room. It happened that both the curule ediles, lately chosen, were persons who could not immediately undertake the office: for Caius Cornelius Cethegus was absent when he was elected, being then commander in Spain; and Caius Valerius Flaccus, who was present, being flamen Dialis, could not take the oath of observing the laws; and no person was allowed to hold any office longer than five days without taking the oath. Flaccus petitioned to be excused from complying with the law, on which the senate decreed, that if the edile produced a person approved of by the consuls, who would take the oath for him, the consuls, if they thought proper, should make application to the tribunes, that it might be proposed to the people. Lucius Valerius Flaccus, pretor elect, was produced to swear for his brother. The tribunes proposed to the commons, and the commons ordered, that this should be as effectual as if the edile himself had sworn. With regard to the other edile, likewise, an order of the commons was made. On the tribunes putting the question, what two persons they chose should go and take the command of the armies in Spain, in order that Caius Cornelius, curule edile, might come home to execute his office, and that Lucius Manlius Acidinus might leave that province, where he had continued many years, the commons ordered Cneius Cornelius Lentulus and Lucius Stertinius, proconsuls, to command in Spain.

---

## BOOK XXXII.

Chap. 1. The consuls and pretors entering into office on the ides of March, [A. U. C. 553. B. C. 199,] cast lots for the provinces. Italy fell to Lucius Cornelius Lentulus, Macedonia to Publius Villius. Of the pretors, the city jurisdiction fell to Lucius Quintius, Ariminum to Cneius Bæbius, Sicily to Lucius Valerius, Sardinia to Lucius Villius. The consul, Lentulus, was ordered to levy new legions; Villius to receive the army from Publius Sulpicius; and, to complete its number, power was given him to raise as many men as he thought proper. To the pretor Bæbius were decreed the legions which Caius Aurelius, late consul, had commanded, with directions that he should keep them in their present situation until the consul should come with the new army to supply their place; and that on his arriving in Gaul, all the soldiers who had served out their time should be sent home, except five thousand of the allies, which would be sufficient to protect the province round Ariminum. The command was continued to the pretors of the former year; to Cneius Sergius, that he might superintend the distribution of land to the soldiers, who had served for many years in Spain, Sicily, and Sardinia; to Quintus Minucius, that he might finish the inquiries concerning the conspiracies in Bruttium, which, while pretor, he had managed with care and fidelity. That he should also send to Locri, to suffer punishment, those who had been convicted of sacrilege, and who were then in chains at Rome; taking care at the same time, that whatever had been carried away from the temple of Proserpine should be replaced, and proper atonements made. The Latine festival was repeated in pursuance of a decree of the pontiffs, because ambassadors from Ardea had complained to the senate, that during the said solemnity they had not been supplied with meat as usual. From Suessa an account was brought, that two of the gates, and the wall between them, were struck with lightning. Messengers from Formiæ related that the temple of Jupiter was also struck by lightning; from Ostia, likewise, news came of the like accident having happened to the temple of Jupiter there; it was said, too, that the temples of Apollo and Sancus, at Veliternum, were struck in like manner; and that in the temple of Hercules, hair grew on the statue. A letter was received from Quintus Minucius, propretor, from Bruttium, that a foal had been born with five feet, and three chickens with three feet each. Afterward a letter was brought from Macedonia, from Publius Sulpicius, proconsul, in which, among other matters, it was mentioned, that a laurel tree had sprung up on the poop of a ship of war. On occasion of the former prodigies, the senate had voted, that the consuls should offer sacrifices with the greater victims, to such gods as they thought proper. On account of the last prodigy, alone, the aruspices were called before the senate, and in pursuance of their answer, the people were ordered by proclamation to perform a supplication for one day, and worship was solemnized at all the shrines.

2. This year the Carthaginians brought to Rome the first payment of the silver imposed on them as a tribute; and the questors having reported that it was not of the proper standard, and that on the assay it wanted a fourth part, they borrowed money at Rome, and made up the deficiency. On their requesting that the senate would be pleased to order their hostages to be restored to them, a hundred were given up, with assurances in regard to the rest, if they continued to observe the treaty. They then further requested, that the remaining hostages might be removed from Norba, where they were ill accommodated, to some other place, and they were permitted to remove to Signia and Ferentinum. The request of the people of Gades was likewise complied with; that a governor should not be sent to their city; being contrary to their stipulation with Lucius Marcius Septimus, when they came under the protection of the Roman people. Deputies from Narnia, complaining that they had not their due number of settlers, and that several who were not of their community had crept in among them, and assumed the privileges of colonists, Lucius Cornelius, consul, was ordered to appoint three commissioners to adjust these matters. The three appointed were Publius and Sextus Ælius, both surnamed Pætus; and Caius Cornelius Lentulus. The favour granted to the Narnians, of filling up their number of colonists, was refused to the people of Cossa, who applied for it.

3. The consuls, having finished the business that was to be done at Rome, set out for their provinces. Publius Villius, on coming into Macedonia, found the soldiers in a violent mutiny, signs of which had appeared some time before. There were two thousand concerned in it. These troops, after Hannibal was vanquished, had been transported from Africa to Sicily, and in about a year after, into Macedonia, as volunteers: they denied, however, that this was done with their consent, affirming that "they had been put on board the ships by the tribunes, contrary to their remonstrances; but, in what manner soever they had become engaged in that service, whether by compulsion or not, the time of it was now expired, and it was reasonable that some end should be put to their toils. For many years they had not seen Italy, but had grown old under arms in Sicily, Africa, and Macedonia; they were now, in short, worn out with labour and fatigue, and had lost the best part of their blood by the many wounds which they had received." The

consul told them, that "the grounds on which they demanded their discharge appeared to him to be reasonable, if the demand had been made in a moderate manner; but that neither on that, nor on any other grounds, could mutiny ever be justified. Wherefore, if they were contented to adhere to their standards, and obey orders, he would write to the senate concerning their release; and that what they desired would more easily be obtained by modest behaviour than by turbulence."

4. At this time, Philip was pushing on the siege of Thaumaci, with the utmost vigour, by means of mounds and engines, and was ready to bring up the ram to the walls, when he was obliged to relinquish the undertaking by the sudden arrival of the Ætolians, who, under the command of Archidamus, having made their way into the town between the posts of the Macedonians, never ceased, day or night, making continual sallies, sometimes against the guards, sometimes against the works. They were at the same time favoured by the nature of the place; for Thaumaci stands near the road from Thermopylæ, and the Malian bay, through Lamia, on a lofty eminence, hanging immediately over the narrow pass called Cæle. After passing through the craggy grounds of Thessaly, the roads are rendered intricate by the windings of the valleys, and on the near approach to the city, such an immense plain opens at once to view, like a vast sea, that the eye can scarcely reach the bounds of the expanse beneath. From this surprising prospect it was called Thaumaci. The city itself is secured, not only by the height of its situation, but by its standing on a rock, from the sides of which, all round, the projecting parts had been pared off. In consequence of these difficulties, and the prize not appearing sufficient to recompense so much toil and danger, Philip desisted from the attempt. The winter also was approaching; he therefore retired from thence, and led back his troops into winter-quarters in Macedonia.

5. There, while others, glad of any interval of rest, consigned both body and mind to repose, Philip, in proportion as the season of the year had relieved him from the incessant fatigues of marching and fighting, found his care and anxiety increase the more, when he turned his thoughts towards the general issue of the war. He dreaded, not only his enemies, who pressed him hard by land and sea, but also the dispositions, sometimes of his allies, at others of his own subjects. The former, he thought, might be induced, by hopes of friendship with the Romans, to change sides, and the Macedonians themselves be seized with a desire of innovation. Wherefore he despatched ambassa-

dors to the Achæans, both to require their oath, (for it had been made an article of their agreement that they should take an oath of fidelity to Philip every year,) and at the same time to restore to them Orchomenes, Heræa, and Triphylia. To the Megalopolitans he delivered up Aliphera; which city, they insisted, had never belonged to Triphylia, but ought to be restored to them, having been one of those that were incorporated by the council of the Arcadians for the founding of Megalopolis. These measures had the desired effect of strengthening his connexion with the Achæans. The affections of the Macedonians he conciliated by his treatment of Heraclides: for finding that, from having countenanced this man, he had incurred the general displeasure of his subjects, he charged him with a number of crimes, and threw him into chains, to the great joy of the people. In his preparations for war, he exerted the most vigorous efforts; exercised both the Macedonian and mercenary troops in arms, and in the beginning of spring sent Athenagoras, with all the foreign auxiliaries and light troops, through Epirus into Chaonia, to seize the pass at Antigonia, which the Greeks called Stena. He followed, in a few days, with the heavy troops; and having viewed every situation in the country, he judged that the most advantageous post for fortifying himself was on the river Aous. This river runs in a narrow vale, between two mountains, one of which the natives call the river Asnaus, affording a passage of very little breadth along the bank. He ordered Athenagoras, with the light infantry, to take possession of Asnaus, and to fortify it. His own camp he pitched on Æropus. Those places where the rocks were steep, were defended by guards of a few soldiers only; the less secure he strengthened, some with trenches, some with ramparts, and others with towers. A great number of engines, also, were disposed in proper places, that, by means of weapons thrown from these, they might keep the enemy at a distance. The royal pavilion was pitched on the outside of the rampart, on the most conspicuous eminence, in order, by this show of confidence, to dishearten the foe, and raise the hopes of his own men.

6. The consul received intelligence from Charopus of Epirus, that the king, with his army, had posted himself in this pass. As soon therefore as the spring began to open, he left Corcyra, where he had passed the winter, and, sailing over to the continent, led on his army. When he came within about five miles of the king's camp, leaving the legions in a strong post, he went forward in person with some light troops to view the nature of the country; and, on the day following, held a council, in order to determine whether

he should, notwithstanding the great labour and danger to be encountered, attempt a passage through the defiles occupied by the enemy, or lead round his forces by the same road through which Sulpicius had penetrated into Macedonia the year before. The deliberations on this question had lasted several days, when news arrived that Titus Quintius had been elected consul; that he had obtained, by lot, Macedonia as his province; and that, hastening his journey, he had already come over to Corcyra. Valerius Antias says that Villius marched into the defile, and that, as he could not proceed straight forward, because every pass was occupied by the king, he followed the course of a valley, through the middle of which the river Aous flows, and having hastily constructed a bridge, passed over to the bank, where the king lay, and fought a battle with him; that the king was routed, and driven out of his camp; that twelve thousand Macedonians were killed, and two thousand two hundred taken, together with a hundred and thirty-two military standards, and two hundred and thirty horses. He adds, that during the battle a temple was vowed to Jupiter in case of success. The other historians, both Greek and Latin, (all those at least whose accounts I have read,) affirm, that nothing memorable was done by Villius, and that Titus Quintius the consul, who succeeded him, found that no progress whatever had been made in the business of the war.

7. During the time of these transactions in Macedonia, the other consul, Lucius Lentulus, who had stayed at Rome, held an assembly for the election of censors. Out of many illustrious men who stood candidates, were chosen Publius Cornelius Scipio Africanus and Publius Ælius Pætus. These, acting together in perfect harmony, read the list of the senate without passing a censure on any one member: they also let to farm the port-duties at Capua, and those at the fort of Puteoli, situate where the city now stands; enrolling for this latter place three hundred colonists, that being the number fixed by the senate: they also sold the lands of Capua, which lie at the foot of Mount Tifata. About the same time Lucius Manlius Acidinus, on his return from Spain, was hindered from entering the city in ovation by Marcus Portius Læca, plebeian tribune, notwithstanding he had obtained permission of the senate: coming then into the city in a private character, he conveyed to the treasury one thousand two hundred pounds weight of silver, and about thirty pounds weight of gold. During this year Cneius Bæbius Tamphilus, who had succeeded to the government of the province of Gaul, in the room of Caius Aurelius, consul of the year preceding, having, without proper caution, entered the territories of the Insubrian Gauls, was, with almost

the whole of his army, attacked at disadvantage and overthrown. He lost above six thousand six hundred men,—a severe blow from an enemy who had for some time ceased to be considered as being formidable. This event called away the consul, Lucius Lentulus, from the city; who, arriving in the province, which was in general confusion, and taking the command of the army, which he found dispirited by its defeat, severely reprimanded the pretor, and ordered him to quit the province, and return to Rome. Neither did the consul himself perform any considerable service, being called home to preside at the elections, which were obstructed by Marcus Fulvius and Manius Curius, plebeian tribunes, who wished to hinder Titus Quintius Flamininus from standing candidate for the consulship, after passing through the office of questor. They alleged that "the edileship and pretorship were now held in contempt, and that the nobility did not make their way to the consulship through the regular gradations of offices; but, passing over the intermediate steps, pushed at once from the lowest to the highest." From a dispute in the field of Mars, the affair was brought before the senate, where it was voted "that when a person sued for any post, which by the laws he was permitted to hold, the people had the right of choosing whoever they thought proper." To this decision of the senate the tribunes submitted, and thereon Sextus Ælius Pætus and Titus Quintius Flamininus were elected. Then was held the election of pretors. The persons chosen were Lucius Cornelius Merula, Marcus Claudius Marcellus, Marcus Porcius Cato, and Caius Helvius, who had been plebeian ediles. These repeated the plebeian games, and, on occasion of the games, celebrated a feast of Jupiter. The curule ediles, also, Caius Valerius Flaccus, who was flamen of Jupiter, and Caius Cornelius Cethegus, celebrated the Roman games with great magnificence. Servius and Caius Sulpicius Galba, pontiffs, died this year: in their room, in the college, were substituted Marcus Æmilius Lepidus and Cneius Cornelius Scipio.

8. The new consuls, Sextus Ælius Pætus and Titus Quintius Flamininus, on assuming the administration, [A. U. C. 554. B. C. 198.] convened the senate in the capitol, and the fathers decreed, that "the consuls should settle between themselves, or cast lots, for the provinces Macedonia and Italy. That he to whom Macedonia fell should enlist, as a supplement to the legions, three thousand Roman footmen, and three hundred horse; and also five thousand footmen, and five hundred horsemen, of the Latine confederates." The army assigned to the other consul was to consist entirely of new-raised men. Lucius Lentulus, consul of the preceding year, was continued in command, and was ordered

not to depart from the province, nor to remove the old army, until the consul should arrive with the new legions. The consuls cast lots for the provinces, and Italy fell to Ælius, Macedonia to Quintius. Of the pretors, the lots gave to Lucius Cornelius Merula the city jurisdiction; to Marcus Claudius, Sicily; to Marcus Porcius, Sardinia; and to Caius Helvius, Gaul. The levying of troops was then begun; for besides the consular armies, they had been ordered also to enlist men for the pretors: for Marcellus, in Sicily, four thousand foot and three hundred horse of the Latine confederates; for Cato, in Sardinia, three thousand foot and two hundred horse of the same country; with directions that both these pretors, on their arrival in their provinces, should disband the veterans, both foot and horse. The consuls then introduced to the senate ambassadors from king Attalus. These, after representing that their king gave every assistance to the Roman arms on land and sea, with his fleet and all his forces, and had hitherto executed with zeal and alacrity every order of the consuls, added, that "they feared it would not be in his power to continue so to do, as he was much embarrassed by Antiochus, who had invaded his kingdom when the sea and land forces, which might have defended it, were removed to a distance. That Attalus therefore entreated the conscript fathers, if they chose to employ his army and navy in the Macedonian war, then to send a body of forces to protect his territories; or if that were not agreeable, to allow him to go home for that purpose, with his fleet and troops." The following answer was ordered to be given to the ambassadors; that "the senate retained a due sense of Attalus's friendship, in aiding the Roman commanders with his fleet and other forces. That they would neither send succours to Attalus against Antiochus, the ally and friend of the Roman people, nor would they detain the troops which he had sent to their assistance, to his inconvenience. That it was ever a constant rule with the Roman people to use the aid of others, so far only as was agreeable to the will of those who gave it; and even to leave those who were so inclined at full liberty to determine when that assistance should commence, and when it should cease. That they would send ambassadors to Antiochus, to represent to him that Attalus, with his fleet and army, were at the present employed by the Roman people against Philip, their common enemy; and that they would request Antiochus to leave the dominions of Attalus unmolested, and to refrain from all hostilities; for that it was much to be wished that kings, who were allies and friends to the Roman people, should maintain friendship between themselves also."

9. When the consul Titus Quintius had finished the levies, in making which he chose principally such as had served in Spain or Africa, that is, soldiers of approved courage, and when hastening to set forward to his province, he was delayed by reports of prodigies, and the expiations of them necessary to be performed. There had been struck by lightning the public road at Veii, a temple of Jupiter at Lanuvium, a temple of Hercules at Ardea, with a wall and towers at Capua; also the edifice which is called Alba. At Arretium the sky appeared as on fire; at Velitræ the earth, to the extent of three acres, sunk down so as to form a vast chasm. From Suessa Aurunca an account was brought of a lamb born with two heads; from Sinuessa, of a swine with a human head. On occasion of these ill omens, a supplication of one day's continuance was performed; the consuls employed themselves diligently in the worship of the gods, and as soon as these were appeased set out for their provinces. Ælius, accompanied by Caius Helvius, pretor, went into Gaul, where he put under the command of the pretor the army which he received from Lucius Lentulus, and which he ought to have disbanded, intending to carry on his own operations with the new troops which he had brought with him; but he effected nothing worth recording The other consul, Titus Quintius, setting sail from Brundusium earlier than had been usual with former consuls, reached Corcyra, with eight thousand foot and eight hundred horse. From this place he passed over, in a quinquereme, to the nearest part of Epirus, and proceeded by long journeys to the Roman camp. Here he dismissed Villius; and waiting a few days, until the forces from Corcyra should come up and join him, held a council, to determine whether he should endeavour to force his way straight forward through the camp of the enemy; or whether, without attempting an enterprise of so great difficulty and danger, he should not rather take a circuitous and safe road, so as to penetrate into Macedonia by the country of the Dassaretians and Lycus. The latter plan would have been adopted, had he not feared that, in removing to a greater distance from the sea, the enemy might slip out of his hands; and that if the king should resolve to secure himself in the woods and wilds, as he had done before, the summer might be spun out without any thing being effected. It was therefore determined, be the event what it might, to attack the enemy in their present post, disadvantageous as it would seem to an assailant. But it was easier to resolve on this measure than to devise any safe or certain method of accomplishing it.

10. Forty days were passed in view of the enemy, without making any kind of effort. Hence Philip conceived hopes

of bringing about a treaty of peace, through the mediation of the people of Epirus; and a council, which was held for the purpose, having appointed Pausanias the pretor, and Alexander the master of the horse, as negotiators, they brought the consul and the king to a conference, on the banks of the river Aous, where the channel was narrowest. The sum of the consul's demands was, that the king should withdraw his troops from the territories of the several states; that to those whose lands and cities he had plundered he should restore such of their effects as could be found; and that the value of the rest should be estimated by a fair arbitration. Philip answered, that "the cases of the several states differed widely from each other: that such as he himself had seized on he would set at liberty; but he would not divest himself of the hereditary and just possessions which had been conveyed down to him from his ancestors. If those, with whom hostilities had been carried on, complained of any losses in the war, he was ready to submit the matter to the arbitration of any state with whom both parties were at peace." To this the consul replied, that "the business required neither judge nor arbitrator: for who did not see clearly that every injurious consequence of the war was to be imputed to the first aggressor? And in this case Philip, unprovoked by any, had first commenced hostilities against all." When they next began to treat of those nations which were to be set at liberty, the consul named, first, the Thessalians; on which the king indignantly exclaimed, "What harsher terms, Titus Quintius, could you impose on me, if I were vanquished?" With these words he retired hastily from the conference; and they were prevented only by the river, which separated them, from assaulting each other with missile weapons. On the following day many skirmishes took place between parties sallying from the outposts, in a plain sufficiently wide for the purpose. Afterward the king's troops drew back into narrow and rocky places, whither the Romans, keenly eager for fighting, penetrated also. These had in their favour order and military discipline, while their arms were of a kind well calculated for pressing close on the Macedonians, who had indeed the advantage of ground, with balistas and catapultas disposed on almost every rock as on walls. After many wounds given and received on both sides, and numbers being slain, as in a regular engagement, darkness put an end to the fight.

11. While matters were in this state, a herdsman, sent by Charopus, prince of the Epirots, was brought to the consul. He said, that "being accustomed to feed his herd in the forest, then occupied by the king's camp, he knew every winding and path in the neighbouring mountains; and that,

if the consul thought proper to send some troops with him, he would lead them by a road, neither dangerous nor difficult, to a spot over the enemy's head." Charopus sent a message to the Roman, to give just so much credit to this man's account as should still leave every thing in his own power, and as little as possible in that of the other. Though the consul rather wished than dared to give the intelligence full belief, and though his emotions of joy were strongly checked by fear, yet being moved by the confidence due to Charopus, he resolved to put to trial the favourable offer. In order to prevent all suspicion of the matter, during the two following days he carried on attacks against the enemy without intermission, drawing out troops against them in every quarter, and sending up fresh men to relieve the wearied. Then, selecting four thousand foot and three hundred horse, he put them under the command of a military tribune, with directions to advance the horse as far as the nature of the ground allowed; and when they came to places impassable to cavalry, then to post them in some plain; that the infantry should proceed by the road which the guide would show; and that when, according to his promise, they arrived on the height over the enemy's head, then they should give a signal by smoke, but raise no shout, until the tribune should have reason to think that, in consequence of the signal received from him, the battle was begun. He ordered that the troops should march by night, (the moon shining through the whole of it,) and employ the day in taking food and rest. The most liberal promises were made to the guide, provided he fulfilled his engagement; he bound him nevertheless, and delivered him to the tribune. Having thus sent off this detachment, the Roman general exerted redoubled vigour in every part to make himself master of the posts of the enemy.

12. On the third day the Roman party made the signal by smoke to notify that they had gained possession of the eminence to which they had been directed; and then the consul, dividing his forces into three parts, marched up with the main strength of his army through a valley in the middle, and made the wings on right and left advance to the camp of the enemy. Nor did these betray any want of spirit, but came out briskly to meet him. The Roman soldiers, in the ardour of their courage, long maintained the fight on the outside of their works, for they had no small superiority in bravery, in skill, and in the nature of their arms; but when the king's troops, after many of them were wounded and slain, retreated into places secured either by intrenchments or situation, the danger reverted on the Romans, who pushed forward inconsiderately, into disadvantageous grounds

and defiles, out of which a retreat was difficult. Nor would they have extricated themselves without suffering for their rashness, had not the Macedonians first, by a shout heard in their rear, and then by an attack begun on that quarter, been utterly dismayed and confounded at the unthought-of danger. Some betook themselves to a hasty flight; some keeping their stand, rather because they could find no way for flight, than that they possessed spirit to support the engagement, were cut off by the Romans, who pressed them hard both on front and rear. Their army might have been entirely destroyed had the victors continued their pursuit of the fugitives; but the cavalry were obstructed by the narrowness of the passes and the ruggedness of the ground; and the infantry by the weight of their armour. The king at first fled with precipitation, and without looking behind him; but afterward, when he had proceeded as far as five miles, he began, from recollecting the unevenness of the road, to suspect (what was really the case) that the enemy could not follow him; and halting, he despatched his attendants through all the hills and valleys to collect the stragglers together. His loss was not more than two thousand men. The rest of his army coming to one spot, as if they had followed some signal, marched off in a compact body towards Thessaly. The Romans after having pursued the enemy as far as they could with safety, killing such as they overtook, and despoiling the slain, seized and plundered the king's camp; to which, even when there were no troops to oppose them, they could not easily make their way. The following night they were lodged within their own trenches.

13. Next day the consul pursued the enemy through the same defiles, following the course of the river as it winds through the valleys. The king came first to the camp of Pyrrhus, a place so called in Triphylia, a district of Melotis; and on the following day, by a very long march, his fears urging him on, he reached Mount Lingos. This ridge of mountains belongs to Epirus, and stretches along between Macedonia and Thessaly; the side next to Thessaly faces the east, that next to Macedonia the north. These hills are thickly clad with woods, and on their summits have open plains and springs of water. Here Philip remained encamped for several days, being unable to determine whether he should continue his retreat until he arrived in his own dominions, or whether he might venture back into Thessaly. At length he resolved to direct his route into Thessaly; and going by the shortest roads to Tricca, he made hasty excursions from thence to all the cities within his reach. The inhabitants who were able to accompany

him he carried away from their habitations, and burned the towns, allowing the owners to take with them such of their effects as they were able to carry; the rest became the prey of the soldiers; nor was there any kind of cruelty which they could have suffered from an enemy that they did not suffer from these their confederates. The infliction of such hardships was irksome to Philip, even while he authorized it; but as the country was soon to become the property of the foe, he wished to rescue out of it their persons at least. In this manner were ravaged the towns of Phacium, Iresia, Euhydrium, Eretria, and Palæphatus. On his coming to Pheræ the gates were shut against him, and as it would necessarily occasion a considerable delay, if he attempted to take it by force, and as he could not spare time, he dropped the design, and crossed over the mountains into Macedonia; for he had received intelligence that the Ætolians too were marching towards him. These, on hearing of the battle fought on the banks of the river Aous, first laid waste the nearest tracts round Sperchia, and Long Come, as it is called, and then, passing over into Thessaly, got possession of Cymine and Angea at the first assault. From Metropolis they were repulsed by the inhabitants, who, while a part of their army was plundering the country, assembled in a body to defend the city. Afterward, making an attempt on Callithere, they were attacked by the townsmen in a like manner; but withstood their onset with more steadiness, drove back into the town the party which had sallied, and content with that success, as they had scarcely any prospect of taking the place by storm, retired. They then took by assault and sacked the towns of Theuma and Calathas. Achorræ they gained by surrender. Xyniæ, through similar apprehensions, was abandoned by the inhabitants. These having forsaken their homes, and going together in a body, fell in with a party of Athamanians employed in protecting their foragers; all of whom, an irregular and unarmed multitude, incapable of any resistance, were put to the sword by the troops. The deserted town of Xyniæ was plundered. The Ætolians then took Cyphara, a fort conveniently situated on the confines of Dolopia. All this the Ætolians performed within the space of a few days.

14. Amynander and the Athamanians, when they heard of the victory obtained by the Romans, continued not inactive. Amynander, having little confidence in his own troops, requested aid from the consul; and then advancing towards Gomphi, he stormed on his march a place called Pheca, situated between that town and the narrow pass which separates Thessaly from Athamania. He then attacked Gomphi, and though the inhabitants defended it for several

days with the utmost vigour, yet, as soon as he had raised the scaling-ladders to the walls, the same apprehensions which had operated on others, made them capitulate. This capture of Gomphi spread the greatest consternation among the Thessalians: their fortresses of Argenta, Pherinus, Thimarus, Lisinæ, Stimon, and Lampsus, surrendered, one after another, with several other garrisons equally inconsiderable. While the Athamanians and Ætolians, delivered from fear of the Macedonians, converted to their own profit the fruits of another's victory, and Thessaly, ravaged by three armies at once, knew not which to believe its foe or its friend, the consul marched on, through the pass which the enemy's flight had left open, into the country of Epirus. Though he well knew which party the Epirots, excepting their prince Charopus, were disposed to favour, yet as he saw that even from the motive of atoning for past behaviour, they obeyed his orders with diligence, he regulated his treatment of them by the standard of their present rather than of their former temper, and by this readiness to pardon, conciliated their affection for the future. Then, sending orders to Corcyra, for the transport ships to come into the Ambrician bay, he advanced by moderate marches, and on the fourth day pitched his camp on Mount Cercetius. Hither he ordered Amynander to come with his auxiliary troops; not so much because he wanted such addition of his forces, as with design to use them as guides into Thessaly. With the same purpose, many volunteers of the Epirots also were admitted into the corps of auxiliaries.

15. Of the cities of Thessaly, the first which he attacked was Phaleria. The garrison here consisted of two thousand Macedonians, who made at first a most vigorous resistance, availing themselves, to the utmost, of every advantage that their arms and works could afford. The assault was carried on without intermission or relaxation, either by day or by night, because the consul thought that it would have a powerful effect on the spirits of the rest of the Thessalians, if the first who made trial of the Roman strength were unable to withstand it; and this at the same time subdued the obstinacy of the Macedonians. On the reduction of Phaleria, deputies came from Metropolis and Piera, surrendering those cities. To them, on their petition, pardon was granted: Phaleria was sacked, and burned. He then proceeded to Æginium; but finding this place so circumstanced that, even with a moderate garrison, it was safe, after discharging a few weapons against the nearest advanced guard, he directed his march towards the territory of Gomphi; and thence, into the plains of Thessaly. His army was now in want of every thing, because he had spared

the lands of the Epirots; he therefore despatched messengers to learn whether the transports had reached Leuças and the Ambracian bay; sending the cohorts, in turn, to Ambracia for corn. Now the road from Gomphi to Ambracia, although difficult and embarrassed, is very short; so that in a few days provisions were brought up from the sea in abundance. He then marched to Atrax, which is about ten miles from Larissa, on the river Peneus. The inhabitants came originally from Perrhæbia. The Thessalians here were not in the least alarmed at the first coming of the Romans; and Philip, although he durst not himself advance into Thessaly, yet keeping his station in the vale of Tempe, whenever any place was attempted by the enemy, he sent up reinforcements as occasion required.

16. About the time that Quintius first pitched his camp opposite to Philip's, and at the entrance of Epirus, Lucius, the consul's brother, whom the Senate had commissioned both to the naval command and to the government of the coast, sailed over with two quinqueremes to Corcyra; and when he learned that the fleet had departed thence, thinking any delay improper, he followed, and overtook it at the island of Zama. Here he dismissed Lucius Apustius, in whose room he had been appointed, and then proceeded to Malea, but at a slow rate, being obliged, for the most part, to tow the vessels which accompanied him with provisions. From Malea, after ordering the rest to follow with all possible expedition, himself, with three light quinqueremes, hastened forward to the Piræus, and took under his command the ships left there by Lucius Apustius, lieutenant-general, for the protection of Athens. At the same time two fleets set sail from Asia; one of twenty-four quinqueremes, under King Attalus; the other belonging to the Rhodians, consisting of twenty decked ships, and commanded by Agesimbrotus. These fleets, joining near the island of Andros, sailed for Eubœa, to reach which place they had only to cross a narrow channel. They first ravaged the lands belonging to Carystus; but, judging that city too strong, in consequence of a reinforcement hastily sent from Chalcis, they bent their course to Eretria. Lucius Quintius also, on hearing of the arrival of King Attalus, came thither with the ships which had lain at the Piræus, having left orders that his own ships should, as they arrived, follow him to Eubœa. The siege of Eretria was now pushed forward with the utmost vigour; for the three combined fleets carried machines and engines of all sorts, for the demolition of towns, and the adjacent country offered abundance of timber for the construction of new works. At the beginning the townsmen defended themselves with a good degree of

spirit; afterward, when they felt the effects of fatigue, a great many being likewise wounded, and a part of the wall demolished by the enemy's works, they became disposed to capitulate. But they had a garrison of Macedonians, of whom they stood in no less dread than of the Romans; and Philocles, the king's general, sent frequent messages from Chalcis, that he would bring them succour in due time, if they could hold out the siege. The hope of this, in conjunction with their fears, obliged them to protract the time longer than was consistent either with their wishes or their strength. However, having learned soon after that Philocles had been repulsed in the attempt, and forced to fly back in disorder to Chalcis, they instantly sent deputies to Attalus to beg pardon and protection. While intent on the prospect of peace, they remitted their diligence in the duties of war, and kept armed guards in that quarter only where the breach had been made in the wall, neglecting all the rest; Quintius made an assault by night on the side where it was least apprehended, and carried the town by scalade. The townsmen, with their wives and children, fled into the citadel, but soon after surrendered themselves prisoners. The quantity of money, of gold and silver taken, was not great. Of statues and pictures, the works of ancient artists, and other ornaments of that kind, a greater number was found than could be expected, either from the size of the city, or its opulence in other particulars.

17. The design on Carystus was then resumed, and the fleets sailed thither; on which the whole body of the inhabitants, before the troops were disembarked, deserted the city, and fled into the citadel, whence they sent deputies to beg protection from the Roman general. To the townspeople life and liberty were immediately granted; and it was ordered that the Macedonians should pay a ransom of three hundred drachmas* a head, deliver up their arms, and quit the country. After being thus ransomed, they were transported, unarmed, to Bœotia. The combined fleets having, in the space of a few days, taken these two important cities of Eubœa, sailed round Sunium, a promontory of Attica, and steered their course to Cenchrea, the grand mart of the Corinthians. In the mean time the consul found the siege of Atrax more tedious than he had imagined, the enemy making an unexpected resistance. He had supposed that the whole of the trouble would be in demolishing the wall, and that if he could once open a passage for his soldiers into the city, the consequence would then be, the flight and slaughter of the enemy, as usually happens on the capture of towns. But when, on a breach being made in the wall

* 9l. 13s. 9d.

by the rams, and when the soldiers, by mounting over the ruins, had entered the place, this proved only the beginning, as it were, of an unusual and fresh labour: for the Macedonians in garrison, who were both chosen men and many in number, supposing that they would be entitled to extraordinary honour if they should maintain the defence of the city by means of arms and courage, rather than by the help of walls, formed themselves in a compact body, strengthening their line by an uncommon number of files in depth. These, when they saw the Romans entering by the breaches, drove them back, so that they were entangled among the rubbish, and with difficulty could effect a retreat. This gave the consul great uneasiness; for he considered such a disgrace, not merely as it retarded the reduction of a single city, but as likely to affect materially the whole process of the war, which in general depends much on the influence of events in themselves unimportant. Having therefore cleared the ground about the half-ruined wall, he brought up a tower of extraordinary height, consisting of many stories, and which carried a great number of soldiers. He likewise sent up the cohorts in strong bodies one after another, to force their way if possible through the wedge of the Macedonians, which is called a phalanx. But in such a confined space (for the wall was thrown down to no great extent) the enemy had the advantage, both in the kind of weapons which they used and in the manner of fighting. When the Macedonians, in close array, stretched out before them their long spears against the target fence which was formed by the close position of their antagonists' shields, and when the Romans, after discharging their javelins without effect, drew their swords, these could neither press on to a closer combat, nor cut off the heads of the spears; and if they did cut or break off any, the shaft being sharp at the part where it was broken, filled up its place among the points of those which were unbroken, in a kind of palisade. Beside this, the parts of the wall still standing, covered safely the flanks of the Macedonians, who were not obliged, either in retreating or in advancing to an attack, to pass through a long space, which generally occasions disorder in the ranks. An accidental circumstance also helped to confirm their courage; for as the tower was moved along a bank not sufficiently compacted, one of the wheels sinking into a rut, made the tower lean in such a manner that it appeared to the enemy as if falling, and threw the soldiers posted on it into consternation and affright.

18. As none of his attempts met any success, the consul was very unwilling to allow the difference between the two kinds of soldiery and their weapons to be manifested in such

trials; at the same time, he could neither see any prospect of reducing the place speedily, nor any means of subsisting in winter, at such a distance from the sea, and in a country desolated by the calamities of war. He therefore raised the siege; and as, along the whole coast of Acarnania and Ætolia, there was no port capable of containing all the transports that brought supplies to the army, nor any place which afforded lodgings to the legions, he pitched on Anticyra, in Phocis, on the Corinthian gulf, as most commodiously situated for his purpose. There the legions would be at no great distance from Thessaly, and the places belonging to the enemy; while they would have in front Peloponnesus, separated from them by a narrow sea; on their rear, Ætolia and Acarnania; and on their sides, Locris and Bœotia. Phanotea in Phocis he took without difficulty, at the first assault. The siege of Anticyra gave him not much delay. Then Ambrysis and Hyampolis were taken. Daulis, being situated on a lofty eminence, could not be reduced either by scalade or works: he therefore provoked the garrison by missile weapons to make sallies from out the town. Then by flying at one time, pursuing at another, and engaging in slight skirmishes, he led them into such a degree of carelessness, and such a contempt of him, that at length the Romans, mixing with them as they ran back, entered by the gates, and stormed the town. Six other fortresses in Phocis, of little consequence, came into his hands, through fear rather than by force of arms. Elatia shut its gates, and the inhabitants seemed determined not to admit within their walls either the army or the general of the Romans, unless compelled by force.

19. While the consul was employed in the siege of Elatia, a prospect opened to him of effecting a business of much more importance; of being able to prevail on the Achæans to renounce their alliance with Philip, and attach themselves to the Romans. Cycliades, the head of the faction that favoured the interest of Philip, they had now banished; and Aristænus, who wished for a union between his countrymen and the Romans, was pretor. The Roman fleet, with Attalus and the Rhodians, lay at Cenchrea, and were preparing to lay siege to Corinth with their whole combined force. The consul therefore judged it prudent that, before they entered on that affair, ambassadors should be sent to the Achæan state, with assurances that if they came over from the king to the side of the Romans, the latter would consign Corinth to them, and annex it to the old confederacy of their nation. Accordingly, by the consul's direction, ambassadors were sent to the Achæans, by his brother Lucius Quintius, by Attalus, and by the Rhodians and Athenians—a general

assembly being summoned to meet at Sicyon to give them audience. Now the minds of the Achæans laboured with a complication of difficulties. They feared the Lacedæmonians, their constant and inveterate enemies; they dreaded the arms of the Romans; they were under obligations to the Macedonians, for services both of ancient and of recent date; but the king himself, on account of his perfidy and cruelty, they looked on with jealous fear, and not judging from the behaviour which he then assumed for the time, they knew that, on the conclusion of the war, they should find him a more tyrannic master. So that every one of them was not only at a loss what opinion he should support in the senate of his own particular state, or in the general diets of the nation; but, even when they deliberated within themselves, they could not with any certainty determine what they ought to wish, or what to prefer. Such was the unsettled state of mind of the members of the assembly when the ambassadors were introduced to audience. The Roman ambassador, Lucius Calpurnius, spoke first; next, the ambassadors of King Attalus; after them, those of the Rhodians; and then Philip's. The Athenians were heard the last, that they might refute the discourses of the Macedonians. These inveighed against the king with the greatest acrimony of any, for no others had suffered from him so many and so severe hardships. So great a number of speeches succeeding each other, took up the whole of the day; and about sunset the council was adjourned.

20. Next day the council met again; and when the magistrates, according to the custom of the Greeks, gave leave, by their herald, to any person who chose to deliver his sentiments, not one stood forth; but they sat a long time, looking on each other in silence. It was no wonder that men, revolving in their minds matters of such contradictory natures, and who found themselves puzzled and confounded, should be involved in additional perplexity by the speeches continued through the whole preceding day; in which the difficulties, on all sides, were brought into view, and stated in their full force. At length Aristænus, the pretor of the Achæans, not to dismiss the council without any business being introduced, said: "Achæans, where are now those violent disputes, in which, at your feasts and meetings, whenever mention was made of Philip and the Romans, you scarcely refrained from blows? Now, in a general assembly, summoned on that single business, when you have heard the arguments of the ambassadors on both sides, when the magistrates demand your opinions, when the herald calls you to declare your sentiments, you are struck dumb. Although your concern for the common safety be insufficient for

determining the matter, cannot the party zeal which has attached you to one side or the other extort a word from any one of you? especially when none is so blind as not to perceive that the time for declaring and recommending what each either wishes or thinks most advisable, must be at the present moment; that is, before we make any decree. When a decree shall be once passed, every man, even such as at first may have disapproved the measure, must then support it as good and salutary." These persuasions of the pretor, so far from prevailing on any one person to declare his opinion, did not excite in all that numerous assembly, collected out of so many states, so much as a murmur or a whisper.

21. Then the pretor, Aristænus, proceeded thus:—"Chiefs of Achæa, you are not more at a loss what advice to give than you are for words to deliver it in; but every one is unwilling to promote the interest of the public at the risk of danger to himself. Were I in a private character, perhaps I too should be silent; but as pretor, it is my duty to declare that I see evidently, either that the ambassadors ought to have been refused an audience of the council, or that they ought not to be dismissed from it without an answer. Yet how can I give them an answer, unless by a decree of yours? And, since not one of you who have been called to this assembly either chooses or dares to make known his sentiments, let us examine (as if they were opinions proposed to our consideration) the speeches of the ambassadors delivered yesterday; supposing, for a moment, the speakers not to have required what was useful to themselves, but to have recommended what they thought most conducive to our advantage. The Romans, the Rhodians, and Attalus, request an alliance and friendship with us; and they demand to be assisted in the war which they are now engaged in against Philip. Philip reminds us of our league with him, and of the obligation of our oath: he requires only that we declare ourselves on his side; and says he will be satisfied if we do not intermeddle in the operations of the war. Who is there so short-sighted as not to perceive the reason why those, who are not yet our allies, require more than he who is? This arises not from modesty in Philip, nor from the want of it in the Romans. The Achæan harbours show what it is, which, while it bestows confidence to requisitions on one side, precludes it on the other. We see nothing belonging to Philip but his ambassador; the Roman fleet lies at Cenchrea, exhibiting to our view the spoils of the cities of Eubœa. We behold the consul and his legions, at the distance of a small tract of sea, overrunning Phocis and Locris. You were surprised at Philip's ambassador, Cleomedon, showing such diffidence yesterday in his application to us to take

arms on the side of the king against the Romans. But if we, in pursuance of the same treaty and oath, the obligation of which he inculcated on us, were to ask of him that Philip should protect us, both from Nabis and his Lacedæmonians, and also from the Romans, he would be utterly unable to find, not only a force for the purpose, but even an answer to return. As much so, in truth, as was Philip himself, who endeavoured, by promises of waging war against Nabis, to draw away our youth into Eubœa: but finding that we would neither decree such assistance to him, nor choose to be embroiled with Rome, forgot that alliance on which he now lays such stress, and left us to the Lacedæmonians to be spoiled and plundered. Besides, to me the arguments of Cleomedon appeared utterly inconsistent. He made light of the war with the Romans; and asserted, that the issue of it would be similar to that of the former which they waged against Philip. If such be the case, why does he, at a distance, solicit our assistance, rather than come hither in person, and defend us, his old allies, both from Nabis and from the Romans? Us, do I say? Why, then, has he suffered Eretria and Carystus to be taken? Why so many cities of Thessaly? Why Locris and Phocis? Why does he at present suffer Elatia to be besieged? Did he, either through compulsion, or fear, or choice, quit the straits of Epirus, and those impregnable fastnesses on the river Aous: and why, abandoning the possession of the pass, did he retire into his own kingdom? If, of his own will, he gave up so many allies to the ravages of the enemy, what objection can he make to these allies, after his example, taking care of themselves? If through fear, he ought to pardon the like fear in us; if his retreat was in consequence of a defeat, let me ask you, Cleomedon, shall we Achæans be able to withstand the Roman arms, which you Macedonians have not withstood? Are we to give credit to your assertion, that the Romans do not employ, in the present war, greater forces or greater strength than they did in the former, or are we to regard the real facts? In the first instance, they aided the Ætolians with a fleet; they sent not to the war either a consul as commander, or a consular army. The maritime cities of Philip's allies were in terror and confusion; but the inland places so secure against the Roman arms, that Philip ravaged the country of the Ætolians, while they in vain implored succour from those arms. Whereas, in the present case, the Romans, after bringing to a final conclusion the Punic war, which, raging for sixteen years in the bowels, as it were, of Italy, had given them abundance of trouble, sent not auxiliaries to the Ætolians in their quarrels, but, being themselves principals, made a hostile invasion on Macedonia with land and sea forces at once. Their third consul is now pushing forward the war with the utmost vigour. Sulpicius, engaging the king within the territory of Macedonia itself, routed and utterly defeated him; and afterward despoiled the most opulent part of his kingdom. Then, again, when he was in possession of the strait of Epirus, where, from the nature of the ground, his fortifications, and the strength of his army, he thought himself secure, Quintius drove him out of his camp; pursued him, as he fled into Thessaly; and, almost in the view of Philip himself, stormed the royal garrisons and the cities of his allies. Supposing that there were no truth in what the Athenian ambassadors mentioned yesterday respecting the cruelty, avarice, and lust of the king; supposing the crimes committed in the country of Attica against the gods, celestial and infernal, concerned us not at all; that we had less to complain of than what the people of Cius and Abydos, who are far distant from us, have endured: let us, then, if you please, forget even our own wounds; let the murders and ravages committed at Messena, and in the heart of Peloponnesus, the killing of his host Garitenes, at Cyparissia, in the midst of a feast, in contempt of laws divine and human; the murder of the two Aratuses of Sicyon, father and son, though he was wont to call the unfortunate old man his parent; his carrying away the son's wife into Macedonia for the gratification of his vicious appetites, and all his violations of virgins and matrons;—let all these, I say, be forgotten; let all be consigned to oblivion. Let us suppose our business were not with Philip, through dread of whose cruelty you are all thus struck dumb; for what other cause could keep you silent, when you have been summoned to a council? Let us imagine that we are treating with Antigonus, a prince of the greatest mildness and equity, to whose kindness we have all been highly indebted; would he require us to perform what at the time was impossible? Peloponnesus is a peninsula, united to the continent by a narrow isthmus, particularly exposed and open to the attacks of naval armaments. Now, if a hundred decked ships, and fifty lighter open ones, and thirty Issean barks, shall begin to lay waste our coasts, and attack the cities which stand exposed, almost on the very shore,—shall we then retreat into the inland towns, as if we were not afflicted with an intestine war, though in truth it is rankling in our very bowels? When Nabis and the Lacedæmonians by land, and the Roman fleet by sea, shall press us, where must I implore the support due from the king's alliance; where the succours of the Macedonians? Shall we ourselves, with our own arms, defend, against the Roman forces, the cities that will be attacked? Truly, in the former war, we defended Dymæ excellently well! The calamities of others afford us abundant examples; let us not seek to render ourselves an example to the rest. Do not, because the Romans voluntarily desire your friendship, contemn that which you ought to have prayed for, nay, laboured with all your might to obtain. But it is insinuated that they are impelled by fear, in a country to which they are strangers; and that, wishing to shelter themselves under your assistance, they have recourse to your alliance, in the hope of being admitted into your harbours, and of there finding supplies of provisions. Now, at sea, they are absolute masters, and instantly reduce to subjection every place at which they land. What they request they have power to enforce. Because they wish to treat you with tenderness, they do not allow you to take steps that must lead you to ruin. Cleomedon lately pointed out, as the middle and safest way, to maintain a neutrality; but that is not a middle way; it is no way: for, besides the necessity of either embracing or rejecting the Roman alliance, what other consequence can ensue from such conduct than that, while we show no steady attachment to either side, as if we waited the event with design to adapt our counsels to fortune, we shall become the prey of the conqueror? Contemn not, then, when it is offered to your acceptance, what you ought to have solicited with your warmest prayers. The free option between the two, which you have this day, you will not always have. The same opportunity will not last long, nor will it frequently recur. You have long wished to deliver yourselves out of the hands of Philip, although you have not dared to make the attempt. Those have now crossed the sea, with large fleets and armies, who are able to set you at liberty, without any trouble or danger to yourselves. If you reject such allies, the soundness of your understandings may be called in question: but you must, unavoidably, have to deal with them, either as friends or foes."

22. This speech of the pretor was followed by a general murmur; some declaring their approbation, and others sharply rebuking those who did so. And now, not only individuals, but whole states engaged in altercation; and at length the magistrates, called demiurguses, who are ten in number, took up the dispute with as much warmth as the multitude. Five of them declared that they would propose the question concerning an alliance with Rome, and would take the votes on it; while five insisted that there was a law, by which the magistrates were prohibited from proposing, and the council from decreeing, any thing injurious to the alliance with Philip. This day also was spent in contention, and there remained now but one day more of the

regular time of sitting; for, according to the rule, the decree must be passed on the third day; and as that approached, the zeal of the parties was kindled into such a flame, that scarcely did parents refrain from offering violence to their own sons. There was present a man of Pallene, named Rhisiasus, whose son Memnon was a demiurgus, and was of that party which opposed the reading of the decree and taking the votes. This man, for a long time, entreated his son to allow the Achæans to take proper measures for their common safety, and not, by his obstinacy, to bring ruin on the whole nation; but, finding that his entreaties had no effect, he swore that he would treat him, not as a son, but as an enemy, and would put him to death with his own hand. By these threats he forced him, next day, to join the party that voted for the question being proposed. These, having now become the majority, proposed the question accordingly, while almost every one of the states, openly approving the measure, showed plainly on which side they would vote. Whereon the Dymæans, Megalopolitans, with several of the Argives, rose up and withdrew from the council; which step excited neither wonder nor disapprobation: for when, in the memory of their grandfathers, the Megalopolitans had been expelled their country by the Lacedæmonians, Antigonus had reinstated them in their native residence; and, at a later period, when Dymæ was taken and sacked by the Roman troops, Philip ordered that the inhabitants, wherever they were in servitude, should be ransomed, and not only restored to them their liberty, but their country. As to the Argives, besides believing that the royal family of Macedonia derived its origin from them, the greater part were attached to Philip by personal acts of kindness and familiar friendship. For these reasons, when the council appeared disposed to order an alliance to be concluded with Rome, they withdrew; and their secession was readily excused, in consideration of the many and recent obligations by which they were bound to the king of Macedon.

23. The rest of the Achæan states, on their opinions being demanded, ratified, by an immediate decree, the alliance with Attalus and the Rhodians. That with the Romans, as it could not be perfected without an order from the people, they deferred until such time as they could hear from Rome. For the present it was resolved, that three ambassadors should be sent to Lucius Quintius; and that the whole force of the Achæans should be brought up to Corinth, which city Quintius, after taking Cenchrea, was then besieging. The Achæans accordingly pitched their camp opposite to the gate that leads to Sicyon. The Romans made their ap-

proaches on the side of the city which faces Cenchreæ; Attalus having drawn his army across the isthmus, towards Lechæum, the port on the opposite sea. At first they did not push forward their operations with any great degree of vigour, because they had hopes of a dissension breaking out between the townsmen and the king's troops: but afterward, learning that they all co-operated with unanimity; that the Macedonians exerted themselves as if in defence of their native country; and that the Corinthians submitted to the orders of Androsthenes, commander of the garrison, as if he were their countryman, elected by their own suffrages, and invested with legal authority,—the assailants had no other hopes but in force, arms, and their works. They therefore brought up their mounds to the walls, though by very difficult approaches. On that side where the Romans attacked, their ram demolished a considerable part of the wall; and the Macedonians having run together to defend the place, thus stripped of its works, a furious conflict ensued. At first, by reason of the enemy's superiority in number, the Romans were quickly repulsed; but being joined by the auxiliary troops of Attalus and the Achæans, they restored the fight to an equality; so that there was no doubt of their easily driving the Macedonians and Greeks from their ground, but that there were in the town a great multitude of Italian deserters; some of whom, having been in Hannibal's army, had, through fear of being punished by the Romans, followed Philip; others, having been sailors, had lately quitted the fleets, in hopes of more honourable employment: despair of safety, therefore, in case of the Romans getting the better, inflamed these to a degree which might rather be called madness than courage. Opposite to Sicyon is the promontory of Juno Acræa, as she is called, stretching out into the main, the passage to Corinth being about seven miles. To this place Philocles, one of the king's generals, led, through Bœotia, fifteen hundred soldiers; and there were barks from Corinth ready to take these troops on board, and carry them over to Lechæum. Attalus, on this, advised to burn the works, and raise the siege immediately. Quintius was inclined to persevere in the attempt. However, when he saw the king's troops posted at all the gates, and that the sallies of the besieged could not easily be withstood, he came over to the opinion of Attalus. Thus baffled in their design, they dismissed the Achæans, and returned to their ships. Attalus steered to Piræus, the Romans to Corcyra.

24. While the naval forces were thus employed, the consul, having encamped before Elatia, in Phocis, first endeavoured, by conferring with the principal inhabitants, to

bring them over, and by their means to effect his purpose; but on their answering that they had nothing in their power, because the king's troops were more numerous and stronger than the townsmen, he assaulted the city on all sides at once with arms and engines. A battering ram shattered a part of the wall that reached from one tower to another, and this falling with a prodigious noise and crash, left much of the town exposed. On this a Roman cohort made an assault through the breach, while at the same time the townsmen, quitting their several posts, ran together from all parts to the endangered place. Others of the Romans climbed over the ruins of the wall, and brought up scaling ladders to the parts that were standing. As the conflict attracted the eyes and attention of the enemy to one particular spot, the walls were scaled in several places, by which means the soldiers easily entered the town. The noise and tumult which ensued so terrified the enemy, that quitting the place which they had crowded together to defend, they all fled in panic to the citadel, accompanied by the unarmed multitude. The consul having thus become master of the town, gave it up to be plundered, and then sent a messenger into the citadel, offering the king's troops their lives, on condition of their laying down their arms and departing. To the Elatians he offered their liberty; which terms being agreed to, in a few days after he got possession of the citadel.

25. In consequence of Philocles, the king's general, coming into Achaia, not only Corinth was delivered from the siege, but the city of Argos was betrayed into his hands by some of the principal inhabitants, after they had first sounded the minds of the populace. They had a custom, that, on the first day of assembly, their pretors, for the omen's sake, should pronounce the names Jupiter, Apollo, and Hercules; in addition to which, a rule had been made, that along with these they should join the name of King Philip. After the conclusion of the alliance with the Romans, the herald omitted so to honour him; on which a murmur spread through the multitude, and they soon became clamorous, calling out for the name of Philip, and insisting that the respect, due by law, should be paid as before; which at length being complied with, universal approbation ensued. On the encouragement afforded by this favourable disposition, Philocles was invited, who seized in the night a strong post called Larissa, seated on a hill which overhangs the city, and in which he placed a garrison. At the dawn of day, however, and as he was proceeding in order of battle to the forum, at the foot of the hill he was met by a line of troops, drawn up to oppose him. This was a body of Achæ-

ans, lately posted there, consisting of about five hundred young men, selected out of all the states. Their commander was Ænesidemus, of Dymæ. The king's general sent a person to recommend to them to evacuate the city, because they were not a match for the townsmen alone, who favoured the cause of Philip; much less when these were joined by the Macedonians, whom even the Romans had not withstood at Corinth. This at first had no effect, either on the commander, or his men: and when they, soon after, perceived the Argives also in arms, coming, in a great body, from the opposite side, and threatening them with destruction, they yet seemed determined to run every hazard, if their leader would persevere. But Ænesidemus, unwilling that the flower of the Achæan youth should be lost, together with the city, made terms with Philocles, that they should have liberty to retire, while himself remained armed with a few of his dependants, and without even stirring from his station. To a person sent by Philocles to inquire what he meant, he only answered, standing with his shield held out before him, "that he meant to die in arms in defence of the city intrusted to his charge." Philocles then ordered some Thracians to throw their javelins at him and his attendants; and they were, every man of them, slain. Thus, notwithstanding the alliance concluded by the Achæans with the Romans, two of their cities, and those of the greatest consequence, Argos and Corinth, were still in the hands of Philip. Such were the services performed in that campaign by the land and sea forces of Rome employed in Greece.

26. In Gaul, the consul Sextus Ælius did nothing worth mention, though he had two armies in the province; one, which he had retained under their standards, although it ought to have been disbanded; and of this, which had served under Lucius Cornelius, proconsul, he had given the command to Caius Helvius, the pretor: the other he had brought with him. He spent nearly the whole summer in compelling the people of Cremona and Placentia to return to their colonies, from whence they had been driven to various places by the calamities of war. While Gaul, beyond expectation, remained quiet through the whole year, an insurrection of the slaves was very near taking place in the neighbourhood of the city. The hostages given by the Carthaginians, were kept in custody at Setia: as they were the children of the principal families, they were attended by a great multitude of slaves; to this number many were added, in consequence of the late African war, and by the Setians themselves having bought, from among the spoil, several of those which had been captured. Having conspired together, they sent some of their number to engage in the

cause their fellows of the country round Setia, with those at Norba and Circeii. When every thing was fully prepared, they determined, during the games, which were soon to be solemnized at the first-mentioned place, to attack the people while intent on the show, and, putting them to death, to make themselves masters of the city in the sudden confusion; and then to seize on Norba and Circeii. Information of this atrocious plot was brought to Rome, to Lucius Cornelius Merula, the city pretor. Two slaves came to him before day, and disclosed the whole proceedings and intentions of the conspirators. The pretor, ordering them to be guarded in his own house, summoned a meeting of the senate; and having laid before them the information of the discoverers, he was ordered to go himself to the spot, and examine into, and crush the conspiracy. Setting out, accordingly, with five lieutenants-general, he compelled such as he found in the country to take the military oath, to arm, and follow him. Having by this tumultuary kind of levy armed about two thousand men, before it was possible to guess his destination he came to Setia. There the leaders of the conspiracy were instantly apprehended; on which the remainder fled from the city; but parties were sent through the country to search them out. The services of the two who made the discovery, and of one free person employed, were highly meritorious. The senate ordered a present to the latter of a hundred thousand asses;* to the slaves, twenty-five thousand asses† each, and their freedom. The price was paid to their owners out of the treasury. Not long after, intelligence was received, that others, out of the remaining spirit of the conspiracy, had formed a design of seizing Præneste. The pretor, Lucius Cornelius, went thither, and inflicted punishment on near five hundred persons concerned in that wicked scheme. The public were under apprehensions that the Carthaginian hostages and prisoners fomented these plots: watches were, therefore, kept at Rome in all the streets, which the inferior magistrates were ordered to go round and inspect; while the triumvirs of the prison, called the Quarry, were to keep a stricter guard than usual. Circular letters were also sent by the pretor to all the Latine states, directing that the hostages should be confined within doors, and not at any time allowed the liberty of going into public; and that the prisoners should be kept bound with fetters, of not less than ten pounds weight, and confined in the common jail.

27. In this year ambassadors from King Attalus made an offering, in the capitol, of a golden crown of two hundred

* 322*l*. 18*s*. 4.  † 80*l*. 14*s*. 7*d*.

and fifty-six pounds weight, and returned thanks to the senate, because Antiochus, complying with the requisitions of the Romans, had withdrawn his troops out of Attalus's territories. During this summer two hundred horsemen, ten elephants, and two hundred thousand pecks of wheat, were furnished by King Masinissa to the army in Greece. From Sicily also, and Sardinia, large supplies of provisions were sent with clothing for the troops. Sicily was then governed by Marcus Marcellus, Sardinia by Marcus Porcius Cato, a man of acknowledged integrity and purity of conduct, but deemed too severe in punishing usury. He drove the usurers entirely out of the island; and restricted or abolished the contributions, usually paid by the allies, for maintaining the dignity of the pretors. The consul, Sextus Ælius, coming home from Gaul to Rome to hold the elections, elected consuls, Caius Cornelius Cethegus and Quintus Minucius Rufus. Two days after was held the election of pretors; and this year, for the first time, six pretors were appointed, in consequence of the increase of the provinces, and the extension of the bounds of the empire. The persons elected were Lucius Manlius Vulso, Caius Sempronius Tuditanus, Marcus Sergius Silus, Marcus Helvius, Marcus Minucius Rufus, and Lucius Atilius. Of these Sempronius and Helvius were at the time plebeian ediles. The curule ediles were Quintus Minucius Thermus, and Tiberius Sempronius Longus. The Roman games were four times repeated during this year.

28. When the new consuls, Caius Cornelius and Quintus Minucius, entered into office, [A. U. C. 555. B. C. 197,] the chief business was the adjusting of the provinces of the consuls and pretors. Those of the pretors were the first settled, because that could be done by the lots. The city jurisdiction fell to Sergius; the foreign to Minucius; Atilius obtained Sardinia; Manlius, Sicily; Sempronius, the Hither Spain, and Helvius, the Farther. When the consuls were preparing to cast lots for Italy and Macedonia, Lucius Oppius and Quintus Fulvius, plebeian tribunes, objected to their proceeding, alleging that "Macedonia was a very distant province, and that the principal cause which had hitherto retarded the progress of the war was that, when it was scarcely entered on, and just at the commencement of operations, the former consul was always recalled. This was the fourth year since the declaration of war against Macedonia. The greater part of one year Sulpicius spent in seeking the king and his army; Villius, on the point of engaging the enemy, was recalled. Quintius was detained at Rome, for the greater part of his year, by business respecting religion; nevertheless, he had so conducted affairs,

that had he come earlier into the province, or had the cold season been at a greater distance, he might have put an end to hostilities. He was then just going into winter-quarters; but, by all accounts, he had brought the war into such a state, that if he were not prevented by a successor, there was a reasonable prospect of being able to put an end to it in the course of the ensuing summer." By such arguments the tribunes so far prevailed, that the consuls declared that "they would abide by the directions of the senate, if the cavillers would agree to do the same." Both parties having, accordingly, referred the determination entirely to those magistrates, a decree was passed, appointing the two consuls to the government of the province of Italy. Titus Quintius was continued in command, until a successor should be found. To each two legions were decreed; and they were ordered with these to carry on the war with the Cisalpine Gauls, who had revolted from the Romans. A reinforcement of five thousand foot and three hundred horse was ordered to be sent into Macedonia to Quintius, together with three thousand seamen. Lucius Quintius Flamininus was continued in the command of the fleet. To each of the pretors, for the two Spains, were granted eight thousand foot, of the allies and Latines, and four hundred horse; and they were ordered to discharge the veteran troops in their provinces, and also to fix the bounds which should divide the hither from the farther province. Two additional lieutenants-general were sent to the army in Macedonia, Publius Sulpicius and Publius Villius, who had been consuls in that province.

29. It was thought necessary that before the consuls and pretors went abroad, some prodigies should be expiated: for the temples of Vulcan and Summanus,* at Rome, and a wall and a gate at Fregellæ, had been struck by lightning. At Frusino, during the night, a light like day shone out. At Asculum, a lamb was born with two heads and five feet. At Formiæ, two wolves entering the town tore several persons who fell in their way; and, at Rome, a wolf made its way, not only into the city, but into the capitol. Caius Acilius, plebeian tribune, caused an order to be passed that five colonies should be led out to the sea-coast; two to the mouths of the rivers Vulturnus and Liternus; one to Puteoli, and one to the fort of Salernum. To these was added Buxentum. To each colony three hundred families were ordered to be sent. The commissioners appointed to make the settlements, who were to hold the office for three years, were Marcus Servilius Geminus, Quintus Minucius Thermus,

* Pluto, Summus Manium.

and Tiberius Sempronius Longus. As soon as the levies, and such other business, religious and civil, as required their personal attendance, was finished, the consuls set out for Gaul. Cornelius took the direct road towards the Insubrians, who were then in arms, and had been joined by the Cænomanians. Quintus Minucius turned his route to the left side of Italy, and leading away his army to the lower sea, to Genoa, opened the campaign with an invasion of Liguria. Two towns, Clastidium and Litubium, both belonging to the Ligurians, and two states of the same nation, Celela and Cerdicium, surrendered to him. And now, all the states on this side of the Po, except the Boians among the Gauls, and the Ilvatians among the Ligurians, were reduced to submission: no less, it is said, than fifteen towns and twenty thousand men. He then led his legions into the territory of the Boians.

30. The Boian army had, not very long before, crossed the Po, and joined the Insubrians and Cænomanians; for, having heard that the consuls intended to act with their forces united, they wished to increase their own strength by this junction. But when information reached them that one of the consuls was ravaging the country of the Boians, a dispute instantly arose. The Boians demanded that all, in conjunction, should carry succour to those who were attacked; while the Insubrians positively refused to leave their country defenceless. In consequence of this dissension, the armies separated; the Boians went to defend their own territory, and the Insubrians, with the Cænomanians, encamped on the banks of the river Mincius. About five miles below this spot the consul Cornelius pitched his camp close to the same river. Sending emissaries hence into the villages of the Cænomanians, and Brixia, the capital of their tribe, he learned with certainty that their young men had taken arms without the approbation of the elders; and that the Cænomanians had not joined in the revolt of the Insubrians by any authority from the state. On which he invited to him the principal of the natives, and endeavoured to contrive and concert with them the means of inducing the younger Cænomanians to forsake the party of the Insubrians; and either to march away and return home, or to come over to the side of the Romans. This he was not able to effect; but so far, he received solemn assurances that, in case of a battle, they would either stand inactive, or, should any occasion offer, would even assist the Romans. The Insubrians knew not that such an agreement had been concluded, but they harboured in their minds some kind of suspicion that the fidelity of their confederates was wavering. Wherefore, in forming their troops for battle, not daring to

intrust either wing to them, lest, if they should treacherously give ground, they might cause a total defeat, they placed them in reserve behind the line. At the beginning of the fight the consul vowed a temple to Juno Sospita, provided the enemy should on that day be routed, and driven from the field; on which the soldiers raised a shout, declaring, that they would ensure to their commander the completion of his vow, and at the same time attacked the enemy. The Insubrians did not stand even the first onset. Some writers affirm that the Cænomanians, falling on their rear, during the heat of the engagement, caused as much disorder there as prevailed in their front: and that, thus assailed on both sides, thirty-five thousand of them were slain, five thousand seven hundred taken prisoners, among whom was Hamilcar, a Carthaginian general, the original cause of the war; and that a hundred and thirty military standards, and above two hundred wagons, were taken. On this, the towns, which had joined in the revolt, surrendered to the Romans.

31. The other consul, Minucius, had at first spread his troops through the territories of the Boians, committing violent depredations everywhere; but afterward, when that people left the Insubrians, and came home to defend their own property, he kept his men within their camp, expecting to come to an engagement with the enemy. Nor would the Boians have declined a battle if their spirits had not been depressed, by hearing of the defeat of the Insubrians. This so deeply affected them, that, deserting their commander and their camp, they dispersed themselves through the several towns, each wishing to take care of his own effects. Thus they obliged the enemy to alter their mode of carrying on the war: for, no longer hoping to decide the matter by a single battle, he began again to lay waste the lands, burn the houses, and storm the villages. At this time Clastidium was burned, and the legions were led thence against the Ilvatian Ligurians, who alone refused to submit. That state also, on learning that the Insubrians had been defeated in battle, and the Boians so terrified that they had not dared to risk an engagement, made a submission. Letters from the consuls, containing accounts of their successes, came from Gaul to Rome at the same time. Marcus Sergius, city pretor, read them in the senate, and afterward, by direction of the Fathers, in an assembly of the people; on which a supplication, of four days' continuance, was decreed.—By this time winter had begun.

32. During the winter, while Titus Quintius, after the reduction of Elatia, had his troops cantoned in Phocis and Locris, a violent dissension broke out at Opus. One faction invited to their assistance the Ætolians, who were nearest at

hand; the other the Romans. The Ætolians arrived first; but the other party, which was the more powerful, refused them admittance, and, despatching a courier to the Roman general, held the citadel until he arrived. The citadel was possessed by a garrison belonging to the king, and they could not be prevailed on to give it up, either by the threats of the people of Opus, or by the commands of the Roman consul. What prevented their being immediately attacked was the arrival of an envoy from the king, to solicit the appointing of a time and place for a conference. This request was readily complied with; not that Quintius did not wish to see war concluded under his own auspices, partly by arms, and partly by negotiation: for he knew not yet whether one of the new consuls would be sent to take the government in his room, or whether he should be continued in the command; a point which he had charged his friends and relations to labour with all their might. But he thought that a conference would answer this purpose: that it would put it in his power to give matters a turn towards war, in case he remained in the province, or towards peace, if he were to be removed. They chose for the meeting a part of the sea-shore, in the Malian gulf, near Nicæa. Thither Philip came from Demetrias, with five barks and one ship of war: he was accompanied by some principal Macedonians, and an Achæan exile, named Cycliades, a man of considerable note. With the Roman general were King Amynander, Dionysidorus, ambassador from King Attalus, Agesimbrotus, commander of the Rhodian fleet, Phæneas, pretor of the Ætolians, and two Achæans, Aristænus and Xenophon. Attended by these, the Roman general advanced to the brink of the shore, and the king came forward to the prow of his vessel, as it lay at anchor; when the former said, "If you will come on the shore we shall converse with greater ease." This the king refused; and on Quintius asking him, "Whom do you fear?" With the haughty spirit of royalty, he replied, "Fear I have none, but of the immortal gods: but I have no confidence in the faith of those whom I see about you, and least of all in the Ætolians."—"That danger," said the Roman, "is equal in all cases; when men confer with an enemy, no confidence subsists."—"But, Titus Quintius," replied the king, "if treachery be intended, the prizes of perfidy are not equal: Philip and Phæneas. For it will not be so difficult for the Ætolians to find another pretor, as for the Macedonians to find another king in my place."—Silence then ensued.

33. The Roman expected that he who solicited the conference, should open it; and the king thought that he who was to prescribe, not he who received terms of peace, ought

to begin the conference. At length the Roman said that "his discourse should be very simple; for he would only mention those articles, without which no pacification could be admitted. These were that the king should withdraw his garrisons from all the cities of Greece. That he should deliver up to the allies of the Roman people the prisoners and deserters; should restore to the Romans those places in Illyricum of which he had possessed himself by force, since the peace concluded in Epirus; and to Ptolemy, king of Egypt, the cities which he had seized since the death of Ptolemy Philopater. These were the terms which he required, on behalf of himself and the Roman people: but it was proper that the demands of the allies also should be heard. The ambassador of King Attalus demanded "restitution of the ships and prisoners taken in the sea-fight at Cius: and that Nicephorium, and the temple of Venus, which Philip had pillaged and defaced, should be put in a state of thorough repair." The Rhodians laid claim to Peræa, a tract on the continent, lying opposite to their island, which from early times had been under their jurisdiction; and they required that "the garrisons should be withdrawn from Tassus, Bargylii, and Euroma, and from Sestus and Abydos on the Hellespont; that Perinthus should be restored to the Byzantians, in right of their ancient title; and that all the seaport towns and harbours of Asia should be free." The Achæans asserted their right to Corinth and Argos. Phæneas nearly repeated the demands made by the Romans, that the troops should withdraw out of Greece, and the Ætolians be put in possession of the cities which had formerly been under their dominion. He was followed by Alexander, a man of eminence among this people, and, considering his country, not uneloquent. He said that "he had long kept silence, not because he expected that any business would be effected in that conference, but because he was unwilling to interrupt any of the allies in their discourse." He asserted that "Philip had neither treated of peace with sincerity, nor waged war with courage, at any time: that in negotiating he was insidious and fraudulent: while in war he never fought on equal ground, nor engaged in regular battles; but, skulking about, burned and pillaged towns, and, when likely to be vanquished, destroyed the prizes of victory. But not in that manner did the ancient kings of Macedon behave: they decided the fate of the war in the field, and spared the towns as far as they were able, in order to possess the more opulent empire. For, what sort of conduct was it to destroy the objects, for the possession of which the contest was waged, and thereby leave nothing to himself but fighting? Philip had, in the last year, desolated more cities of his allies in Thessaly than all the enemies that Thessaly ever had. On the Ætolians themselves he had made greater depredations, when he was in alliance with them, than since he became their enemy. He had seized on Lysimachia, after dislodging the pretor and garrison of the Ætolians. Cius also, a city belonging to their government, he razed from the foundation. With the same injustice, he held possession of Thebes in Phthiotis, of Echinus, Larissa, and Pharsalus."

34. Philip, provoked by this discourse of Alexander, pushed his ship nearer to the land, that he might be the better heard, and began to speak with much violence, particularly against the Ætolians. But Phæneas, interrupting him, said that "the business depended not on words; he must either conquer in war, or submit to his superiors."—"That, indeed, is evident," said Philip, "even to the blind," sneering at Phæneas, who had a disorder in his eyes; for he was naturally fonder of such pleasantries than became a king; and even in the midst of serious business, he indulged a turn to ridicule farther than was decent. He then expressed great indignation at the "Ætolians assuming as much importance as the Romans, and insisting on his evacuating Greece; people who knew not even its boundaries: for, of Ætolia itself, a large proportion, consisting of the Agræans, Apodeotians, and Amphilochians, was no part of Greece. Have they just ground of complaint against me, for not refraining from war with their allies, when themselves, from the earliest period, follow, as an established rule, the practice of suffering their young men to carry arms against those allies, withholding only the public authority of the state; while very frequently contending armies have Ætolian auxiliaries on both sides? I did not seize on Cius by force, but assisted my friend and ally, Prusias, who was besieging it, and Lysimachia I rescued from the Thracians. But since necessity diverted my attention from the guarding of it to this present war, the Thracians have possession of it. So much for the Ætolians. To Attalus and the Rhodians I in justice owe nothing; for not to me, but to themselves, is the commencement of hostilities to be attributed. However, out of respect to the Romans, I will restore Peræ to the Rhodians, and to Attalus his ships, and such prisoners as can be found. As to what concerns Nicephorium, and the temple of Venus, what other answer can I make to those who require their restoration, than what I should make in case of woods and groves cut down; that, as the only way of restoring them, I will take on myself the trouble and expense of planting, since it is thought fit that, between kings, such kinds of demands should be made and answered?" The

last part of his speech was directed to the Achæans, wherein he enumerated, first, the kindnesses of Antigonus; then, his own towards their nation, desiring them to consider the decrees themselves had passed concerning him, which comprehended every kind of honour, divine and human; and to these he added their late decree, by which they had confirmed the resolution of deserting him. He inveighed bitterly against their perfidy, but told them that nevertheless he would give them back Argos. "With regard to Corinth, he would consult with the Roman general; and would, at the same time, inquire from him, whether he demanded only that he, Philip, should evacuate those cities which, being captured by himself, were held by the right of war; or those, also, which he had received from his ancestors."

35. The Achæans and Ætolians were preparing to answer, but, as the sun was near setting, the conference was adjourned to the next day; and Philip returned to his station whence he came, the Romans and allies to their camp. On the following day, Quintius repaired to Nicæa, which was the place agreed on, at the appointed time; but neither Philip nor any message from him, came for several hours. At length, when they begun to despair of his coming, his ships suddenly appeared. He said that "the terms enjoined were so severe and humiliating that, not knowing what to determine, he had spent the day in deliberation." But the general opinion was, that he had purposely delayed the business, that the Achæans and Ætolians might not have time to answer him: and this opinion he himself confirmed, by desiring, in order to avoid altercation, and to bring the affair to some conclusion, that the others should retire, and leave him to converse with the Roman general: for some time, this was not admitted, lest the allies should appear to be excluded from the conference. Afterward, on his persisting in his desire, the Roman general, with the consent of all, taking with him Appius Claudius, a military tribune, advanced to the brink of the coast, and the rest retired. The king, with the two persons whom he had brough the day before, came on shore, where they conversed a considerable time in private. What account of their proceedings Philip gave to his people is not well known: what Quintius told the allies was, "that Philip was willing to cede to the Romans the whole coast of Illyricum, and to give up the deserters and prisoners, if there were any. That he consented to restore to Attalus his ships, and the seamen taken with them; and to the Rhodians the tract which they call Peræa. That he refused to evacuate Iassus and Bargylii. To the Ætolians he was ready to restore Pharsalus and Larissa; Thebes he would keep: and that he would give back to the

Achæans the possession, not only of Argos, but of Corinth also." This arrangement pleased none of the parties; neither those to whom the concessions were to be made, nor those to whom they were refused; "for on that plan," they said, "more would be lost than gained; nor could the grounds of contention ever be removed but by his utterly evacuating every part of Greece."

36. These expressions, delivered with eagerness and vehemence by every one in the assembly, reached the ears of Philip, though he stood at a distance. He therefore requested of Quintius that the whole business might be deferred until the next day; and then he would, positively, either prevail on the allies to accede to his proposals, or suffer himself to be prevailed on to accede to theirs. The shore at Thronium was appointed for their meeting, and all the parties assembled there early. Philip began with entreating Quintius, and all who were present, not to harbour such sentiments as must tend to obstruct a pacification; and then desired time while he could send ambassadors to Rome, to the senate, declaring that "he would either obtain a peace on the terms mentioned, or would accept whatever terms the senate should prescribe." None approved of this: they said, he only sought a delay, and leisure to collect his strength. But Quintius observed, "that such an objection would have been well founded, if it were then summer and a season fit for action: as matters stood, and the winter being just at hand, nothing would be lost by allowing him time to send ambassadors: for, without the authority of the senate, no agreement which they might conclude with the king would be valid; and besides, they would by this means have an opportunity, while the winter itself would necessarily cause a suspension of arms, to learn what terms were likely to be approved by the senate." The other chiefs of the allies came over to this opinion; and a cessation of hostilities for two months being granted, they resolved that each of their states should send an ambassador with the necessary information to the senate, and in order that it should not be deceived by the misrepresentations of Philip. To the above contention was added an article, that all the king's troops should be immediately withdrawn from Phocis and Locris. With the ambassadors of the allies Quintius sent Amynander, king of Athamania; and, to add a degree of splendour to the embassy, a deputation from himself, composed of Quintus Fabius, the son of his wife's sister, Quintus Fulvius, and Appius Claudius.

37. On their arrival at Rome, the ambassadors of the allies were admitted to audience before those of the king. Their discourse, in general, was filled up with invectives

against Philip. What produced the greatest effect on the minds of the senate was, that, by pointing out the relative situations of the lands and seas in that part of the world, they made it manifest to every one that if the king held Demetrias in Thessaly, Chalcis in Eubœa, and Corinth in Achaia, Greece could not be free; and they added, that Philip himself, with not more insolence than truth, used to call these the fetters of Greece. The king's ambassadors were then introduced, and, when they were beginning a long harangue, they were stopped by a short question, "Whether he was willing to yield up the three above-mentioned cities?" They answered, that "they had received no specific instructions on that head:" on which they were dismissed, without having made any progress towards a peace. Full authority was given to Quintius to determine every thing relative to war and peace. As this demonstrated clearly that the senate were not weary of the war, so he who was more earnestly desirous of conquest than of peace, never afterward consented to a conference with Philip; and even gave him notice that he would not admit any embassy from him, unless it came with information that his troops were retiring from Greece.

38. Philip now perceived that he must decide the matter by arms, and collect his strength about him from all quarters. Being particularly uneasy in respect to the cities of Achaia, a country so distant from him, and also of Argos, even more, indeed, than of Corinth, he resolved, as the most advisable method, to put the former into the hands of Nabis, tyrant of Lacedæmon, in trust as it were, on the terms, that if he should prove successful in the war, Nabis should redeliver it to him; if any misfortune should happen, he should keep it himself. Accordingly, he wrote to Philocles, who had the command in Corinth and Argos, to have a meeting with the tyrant. Philocles, besides coming with a valuable present, added to that pledge of future friendship between the king and the tyrant, that it was Philip's wish to unite his daughters in marriage with the sons of Nabis. The tyrant at first refused to receive the city on any other terms than that of being invited by a decree of the Argives themselves: but afterward, hearing that in a full assembly they had treated his name not only with scorn, but even with abhorrence, he thought he had now a sufficient excuse for plundering them, and he accordingly desired Philip to give him possession of the place. Nabis was admitted into the city in the night, without the privity of any of the inhabitants, and, at the first light, seized on the higher parts of it, and shut the gates. A few of the principal people having made their escape during the first confusion, the properties

of all who were absent were seized as booty; those who were present were stripped of their gold and silver, and loaded with exorbitant contributions. Such as paid these readily were discharged without personal insult and laceration of their bodies; but such as were suspected of hiding or reserving any of their effects, were mangled and tortured like slaves. He then summoned an assembly, in which he proposed the passing of two laws; one for an abolition of debts, the other for a distribution of the land, in shares, to each man—two firebrands in the hands of the enemies of government, for inflaming the populace against the higher ranks.

39. The tyrant, when he had the city of Argos in his power, never considering from whom, or on what conditions, he had received it, sent ambassadors to Elatia, to Quintius, and to Attalus, in his winter-quarters at Ægina, to tell them that "he was in possession of Argos; and that if Quintius would come hither and consult with him, he had no doubt but that every thing might be adjusted between them." Quintius, glad of an opportunity of depriving Philip of that stronghold, along with the rest, consented to come: accordingly, sending a message to Attalus to leave Ægina, and meet him at Sicyon, he set sail from Anticyra with ten quinqueremes, which his brother Lucius Quintius happened to bring a little before from his winter station at Corcyra, and passed over to Sicyon. Attalus was there before him, who, representing that the tyrant ought to come to the Roman general, not the general to the tyrant, brought Quintius over to his opinion, which was, that he should not enter the city of Argos. Not far from it, however, was a place called Mycenica; and there the parties agreed to meet. Quintius came with his brother and a few military tribunes; Attalus, with his royal retinue; and Nicostratus, the pretor of the Achæans, with a few of the auxiliary officers: and they there found Nabis waiting with his whole army. He advanced, armed and attended by his guards, almost to the middle of the interjacent plain; Quintius, unarmed, with his brother and two military tribunes; the king was accompanied by one of his nobles, and the pretor of the Achæans, unarmed likewise. The tyrant, when he saw the king and the Roman general unarmed, opened the conference, with apologizing for having come to the meeting armed himself, and surrounded with armed men. "He had no apprehensions," he said, "from them; but only from the Argive exiles." When they then began to treat of the terms on which friendship was to be established between them, the Roman made two demands: one, that the Lacedæmonian should conclude a peace with the Achæans; the other, that

he should send him aid against Philip. He promised the aid required; but, instead of a peace with the Achæans, a cessation of hostilities was obtained, to last until the war with Philip should be ended.

40. A debate concerning the Argives also, was set on foot by King Attalus, who charged Nabis with holding their city by force, which was put into his hands by the treachery of Philocles; while Nabis insisted, that he had been invited by the Argives themselves to afford them protection. The king required a general assembly of the Argives to be convened, that the truth of that matter might be known. To this the tyrant did not object; but the king alleged that the Lacedæmonian troops ought to be withdrawn from the city, in order to render the assembly free; and that the people should be left at liberty to declare their real sentiments. This was refused, and the debate produced no effect. To the Roman general six hundred Cretans were given by Nabis, who agreed with the pretor of the Achæans to a cessation of arms for four months, and then the conference broke up. Quintius proceeded to Corinth, advancing to the gates with the cohort of Cretans, in order to show Philocles, the governor of the city, that the tyrant had deserted the cause of Philip. Philocles came out to confer with the Roman general; and, on the latter exhorting him to change sides immediately, and surrender the city, he answered in such a manner as showed an inclination rather to defer, than to refuse the matter. From Corinth, Quintius sailed over to Anticyra, and sent his brother thence to sound the disposition of the people of Acarnania. Attalus went from Argos to Sicyon. Here, on one side, the state added new honours to those formerly paid to the king; and on the other, the king, besides having on a former occasion redeemed for them, at a vast expense, a piece of land sacred to Apollo, unwilling to pass by the city of his friends and allies without a token of munificence, made them a present of ten talents of silver,* and ten thousand bushels of corn, and then returned to Cenchreæ to his fleet. Nabis, leaving a strong garrison at Argos, returned to Lacedæmon; and, as he himself had pillaged the men, he sent his wife to Argos to pillage the women. She invited to her house, sometimes singly, and sometimes in numbers, all the females of distinction who were related to each other; and partly by fair speeches, partly by threats, stripped them not only of their gold, but, at last, even of their garments, and every article of dress.

* 1937*l.* 10*s.*

# BOOK XXXIII.

CHAP. 1. SUCH were the occurrences of the winter. In the bginning of spring Quintius urged Attalus to join him, which he did at Elatia; and being anxious to bring under his authority the nation of the Bœotians, who had hitherto been wavering and irresolute, he marched through Phocis, and pitched his camp at the distance of five miles from Thebes, the capital of Bœotia. Next day, attended by one company of soldiers, and by Attalus, together with the ambassadors, who had come to him in great numbers from all quarters, he proceeded towards the city, having ordered the spearmen of two legions, being two thousand men, to follow him at the distance of a mile. About midway Antiphilus, pretor of the Bœotians, met him: the rest of the people stood on the walls, watching the arrival of the king and the Roman general. Few arms and few soldiers appeared—the hollow roads and the valleys concealing from view the spearmen, who followed at a distance. When Quintius drew near the city he slackened his pace, as if with intention to salute the multitude, who came out to meet him; but the real motive of his delaying was, that the spearmen might come up. The townsmen pushed forward, in a crowd, before the lictors, not perceiving the band of soldiers, who were following them close, until they arrived at the general's quarters. Then, supposing the city betrayed and taken, through the treachery of Antiphilus, their pretor, they were all struck with astonishment and dismay. It was now evident that no room was left to the Bœotians for a free discussion of measures in the assembly, which was summoned for the following day. However, they concealed their grief, which it would have been both vain and unsafe to have discovered.

2. When the assembly met, Attalus first rose to speak; and he began his discourse with a recital of the kindnesses conferred by his ancestors and himself on the Greeks in general, and on the Bœotians in particular. But, being now too old and infirm to bear the exertion of speaking in public, he lost his voice, and fell; and for some time, while they were carrying him to his apartments, (for he was deprived of the use of one half of his limbs,) the proceedings of the assembly were stopped. Then Aristænus spoke on the part of the Achæans, and was listened to with the greater attention, because he recommended to the Bœotians no other measures than those which he had recommended to the Achæans. A few words were added by Quintius, extolling the good faith rather than the arms and power of the Ro-

mans. A resolution was then proposed, by Dicæarchus of Platæa, for forming a treaty of friendship with the Roman people, which was read; and no one daring to offer any opposition, it passed by the suffrages of all the states of Bœotia. When the assembly broke up, Quintius made no longer stay at Thebes than the sudden misfortune of Attalus made necessary. When he found that the force of the disorder had not brought the king's life into any immediate danger, but had only occasioned a weakness in his limbs, he left him there, to use the necessary means for recovery, and went back to Elatia. Having now brought the Bœotians, as formerly the Achæans, to join in the confederacy, while all places were in a state of tranquillity and safety, he bent his thought and attention towards Philip, and the remaining business of the war.

3. Philip, on his part, as his ambassadors had brought no hopes of peace from Rome, resolved, as soon as spring began, to levy soldiers through every town in his dominions: but he found a great scarcity of young men; for successive wars, through several generations, had very much exhausted the Macedonians; and, even in the course of his own reign, great numbers had fallen, in the naval engagements with the Rhodians and Attalus, and in those on land with the Romans. Mere youths, therefore, from the age of sixteen, were enlisted; and even those who had served out their time, provided they had any remains of strength, were recalled to their standards. Having, by these means, filled up the numbers of his army, about the vernal equinox he drew together all his forces to Dius: he encamped them there in a fixed post; and, exercising the soldiers every day, waited for the enemy. About the same time Quintius left Elatia, and came by Thronium and Scarphea to Thermopylæ. There he held an assembly of the Ætolians, which had been summoned to meet at Heraclea, to determine what number of men they should send to assist the Romans. On the third day, having learned the determination of the allies, he proceeded from Heraclea to Xyniæ; and, pitching his camp on the confines between the Ænians and Thessalians, waited for the Ætolian auxiliaries. The Ætolians occasioned no delay. Two thousand foot and four hundred horse, under the command of Phæneas, speedily joined him; and then Quintius, to show plainly what he had waited for, immediately decamped. On passing into the country of Phthiotis, he was joined by five hundred Cretans of Gortynium, whose commander was Cydates, with three hundred Apollonians, armed nearly in the same manner; and, not long after, by Amynander, with one thousand two hundred Athamanian foot.

4. Philip, being informed of the departure of the Romans from Elatia, and considering that, on the approaching contest, his kingdom was at hazard, thought it advisable to make an encouraging speech to his soldiers; in which, after he had expatiated on many topics often insisted on before, respecting the virtues of their ancestors, and the military fame of the Macedonians, he touched particularly on two things, which at the time threw the greatest damp on their spirits, laying great stress on such as might revive their courage, and give them some degree of confidence. To the defeat suffered at the river Aous, where the phalanx of the Macedonians was thrown into consternation and disorder, he opposed the repulse given by main force to the Romans at Atrax: and even with respect to the former case, when they had not maintained possession of the pass leading into Epirus, he said, "the first fault was to be imputed to those who had been negligent in keeping the guards; and the second, to the light infantry and mercenaries in the time of the engagement; but that, as to the phalanx of the Macedonians, it had stood firm on that occasion, and would for ever remain invincible, on equal ground, and in regular fight." This body consisted of sixteen thousand men, the prime strength of the army and of the kingdom. Besides these, he had two thousand targeteers, called peltastæ; of Thracians and Illyrians, of the tribe called Trallians, the like number of two thousand; and of hired auxiliaries, collected out of various nations, about one thousand; and two thousand horse. With this force the king waited for the enemy. The Romans had nearly an equal number; in cavalry they had a superiority, by the addition of the Ætolians.

5. Quintius, marching to Thebes in Phthiotis, sat down before it; and having received encouragement to hope that the city would be betrayed to him by Timon, a leading man in the state, he came up close to the walls with only a small number of cavalry and some light infantry. So entirely were his expectations disappointed, that he was not only obliged to maintain a fight with the enemy, who sallied out against him, but would have been in extreme danger, had not both infantry and cavalry been called out hastily from the camp, and come up in time. Not meeting with that success which his too sanguine hopes had led him to expect, he desisted from any farther attempt on the city at present. He had received certain information of the king being in Thessaly; but as he had not yet discovered into what part of it he had come, he sent his soldiers round the country, with orders to cut timber and prepare palisades. Both Macedonians and Greeks had palisades; but the latter had

not adopted the most convenient mode of using them, either with respect to carriage or for the purpose of strengthening their posts. They cut trees, both too large, and too full of branches, for a soldier to carry easily along with his arms: and after they had fenced their camp with a line of these, to demolish them was no difficult matter; for the trunks appearing to view, with great intervals between them, and the numerous and strong shoots affording the hand a good hold, two, or at most three young men, uniting their efforts, used to pull out one tree; which, being removed, left a breach as wide as a gate, and there was nothing at hand with which it could be stopped up. But the Romans cut light stakes, mostly of one fork, with three, or, at the most, four branches; so that a soldier, with his arms slung at his back, can carry several of them together; and then they stick them down so closely, and interweave the branches in such a manner, that it cannot be seen to what extent any branch belongs; besides which, the boughs are so sharp, and wrought so intimately with each other, as to leave no room for a hand to be thrust between; consequently an enemy cannot lay hold of any thing, or, if that could be done, could he draw out the branches thus intertwined, and which mutually bind each other. Nay, even if by accident one should be pulled out, it leaves but a small opening, which is very easily filled up.

6. Next day Quintius, causing his men to carry palisades with them, that they might be ready to encamp on any spot, marched a short way, and took post about six miles from Pheræ; whence he sent scouts to discover in what part of Thessaly the king was, and what appeared to be his intention. Philip was then near Larissa, and as soon as he learned that the Roman general had removed from Thebes, being equally impatient for a decisive engagement, he proceeded towards the enemy, and pitched his camp about four miles from Pheræ. On the day following some light troops went out from both camps, to seize on certain hills which overlooked the city. When, nearly at equal distances from the summit which was intended to be seized, they came within sight of each other, they halted: and sending messengers to their respective camps for directions how they were to proceed on this unexpected meeting, waited their return in quiet. For that day they were recalled to their camps, without having come to action. On the following day there was an engagement between the cavalry, near the same hills, in which the Ætolians bore no small part; and in which the king's troops were defeated, and driven within their trenches. Both parties were greatly impeded in the action by the ground being thickly planted with trees; by the gardens, of which there were many in a place so

near the city; and by the roads being enclosed between walls, and in some places shut up. The commanders, therefore, were equally desirous of removing out of that quarter; and, as if they had preconcerted the matter, they both directed their route to Scotussa—Philip hoping to find there a supply of corn; the Roman intending to get before him, and destroy the crops. The armies marched the whole day without having sight of each other in any place, the view being intercepted by a continued range of hills between them. The Romans encamped at Eretria, in Phthiotis; Philip on the river Onchestus. But though Philip lay at Melambrius, in the territory of Scotussa, and Quintius near Thetidium, in Pharsalia, neither party knew with any certainty where his antagonist was. On the third day there fell a violent rain, which was succeeded by darkness equal to that of night, and this confined the Romans to their camp, through fear of an ambuscade.

7. Philip, intent on hastening his march, suffered not himself to be delayed by the clouds, which, after the rain, covered the face of the country, but ordered his troops to march: and yet so thick a fog had obscured the day, that neither the standard-bearers could see the road, nor the soldiers the standards; so that all, led blindly by the shouts of uncertain guides, fell into disorder, like men wandering by night. When they had passed over the hills called Cynoscephalæ, where they left a strong guard of foot and horse, they pitched their camp. Although the Roman general stayed at Thetidium, yet he detached ten troops of horse, and one thousand foot, to find out where the enemy lay; warning them, however, against ambuscades, which the darkness of the day would cover, even in an open country. When these arrived at the hills where the enemy's guard was posted, struck with mutual fear, both parties stood, as if deprived of the power of motion. They then sent back messengers to their respective commanders; and when the first surprise subsided, they proceeded to action without more delay. The fight was begun by small advanced parties; and afterward the number of the combatants were increased by reinforcements sent to support those who gave way. But the Romans, far inferior to their adversaries, sent message after message to the general, that they were in danger of being overpowered: on which he hastily sent five hundred horse and two thousand foot, mostly Ætolians, under the command of two military tribunes, who relieved them, and restored the fight. The Macedonians, distressed in turn by this change of fortune, sent to beg succour from their king: but as, on account of the general darkness from the fog, he had expected nothing less on that day than a battle,

and had therefore sent a great number of men of every kind to forage, he was for a considerable time in great perplexity, and unable to form a resolution. The messengers still continued to urge him; the covering of clouds was now removed from the tops of the mountains, and the Macedonian party was in view, having been driven up to the highest summit, and trusting for safety rather to the nature of the ground than to their arms. He therefore thought it necessary at all events to hazard the whole, in order to prevent the loss of a part for want of support: and, accordingly, he sent up Athenagoras, general of the mercenaries, with all the auxiliaries, except the Thracians, joined by the Macedonian and Thessalian cavalry. On their arrival the Romans were forced from the top of the hill, and did not face about until they came to the level plain. The principal support which saved them from being driven down in disorderly flight was the Ætolian horsemen. The Ætolians were then by far the best cavalry in Greece; in infantry they were surpassed by some of their neighbours.

8. The accounts of this affair, which were brought to the king, represented it in a more flattering light than the advantages gained could warrant; for people came, one after another, and calling out that the Romans were flying in a panic: so that notwithstanding it was against his judgment, and he demurred, declaring it a rash proceeding, and that he liked not either the place or the time, yet he was prevailed on to draw out his whole force to battle. The Roman general did the same, induced by necessity rather than by the favourableness of the occasion. Leaving the right wing as a reserve, having the elephants posted in front, he, with the left, and all the light infantry, advanced against the enemy; at the same time reminding his men that "they were going to fight the same Macedonians whom they had fought in the passes of Epirus, fenced as they were with mountains and rivers, and whom, after conquering the natural difficulties of the ground, they had dislodged and vanquished; the same, in short, whom they had before defeated under the command of Publius Sulpicius, when they opposed their passage to Eordæa. That the kingdom of Macedonia had been hitherto supported by its reputation, not by real strength. Even that reputation had, at length, vanished." Quintius soon reached his troops, who stood in the bottom of the valley; and they, on the arrival of their general and the army, renewed the fight, and, making a vigorous onset, compelled the enemy again to turn their backs. Philip, with the targeteers, and the right wing of infantry, (the main strength of the Macedonian army, called by them the phalanx,) advanced in a quick pace, having ordered Nicanor, one of his courtiers,

to bring up the rest of his forces with all speed. On reaching the top of the hill, from a few arms and bodies lying there he perceived that there had been an engagement on the spot, and that the Romans had been repulsed from it. When he likewise saw the fight now going on close to the enemy's works, he was elated beyond measure: but presently, observing his men flying back, and the danger of his own, he was much embarrassed, and hesitated for some time whether he should cause his troops to retire into the camp. He was sensible that his party, besides the losses which they suffered as they fled, must be entirely lost, if not speedily succoured; and as, by this time, a retreat would be unsafe, he found himself compelled to put all to hazard before he was joined by the other division of his forces. He placed the cavalry and light infantry that had been engaged on the right wing; and ordered the targeteers, and the phalanx of Macedonians, to lay aside their spears, which their great length rendered unserviceable, and to manage the business with their swords: at the same time, that his line might not be easily broken, he lessened the extent of the front one half, and doubled the files in depth. He ordered them also to close their files, so that men and arms should touch each other.

9. Quintius, having received among the standards and ranks those who had been engaged with the enemy, gave the signal by sound of trumpet. It is said, that such a shout was raised, as was seldom heard at the beginning of any battle; for it happened that both armies shouted at once; not only the troops then engaged, but also the reserves, and those who were just then coming into the field. The king, fighting from the higher ground, had the better on the right wing, by means chiefly of the advantage of situation. On the left all was disorder and confusion; particularly when that division of the phalanx which had marched in the rear was coming up. The centre stood spectators of the fight, as if it no way concerned them. The phalanx, just arrived, (a column rather than a line of battle, and fitter for a march than for a fight,) had scarcely mounted the top of the hill: before these could form, Quintius, though he saw his men in the left wing giving way, charged the enemy furiously, first driving on the elephants against them, for he judged that one part being routed would draw the rest after. There was no dispute. The Macedonians, unable to stand the first shock of the elephants, instantly turned their backs; and the rest, as had been foreseen, followed them in their retreat. Then one of the military tribunes, forming his design in the instant, took with him twenty companies of men; left that part of the army which was evidently victorious; and mak-

ing a small circuit, fell on the rear of the enemy's right wing. Any army whatever must have been disordered by his charge. Such charge and disorder is, indeed, incident to all armies in general, but there was in this case a circumstance particularly aggravating. The phalanx of the Macedonians being heavy, could not readily face about; nor would they have been suffered to do it by their adversaries in front, who, although they gave way to them a little before, on this new occasion pressed them vigorously. Besides, they lay under another inconvenience in respect of the ground; for, by pursuing the retreating enemy down the face of the hill, they had left the top to the party who came round on their rear. Thus attacked on both sides, they were exposed for some time to great slaughter, and then betook themselves to flight, most of them throwing away their arms.

10. Philip, with a small party of horse and foot, ascended a hill somewhat higher than the rest, to take a view of the situation of his troops on the left. Then when he saw them flying in confusion, and all the hills around glittering with Roman standards and arms, he withdrew from the field. Quintius, as he was pressing on the retreating enemy, observed the Macedonians suddenly raising up their spears, and not knowing what they meant thereby, he ordered the troops to halt. Then, on being told that this was the practice of the Macedonians, intimating an intention of surrendering themselves prisoners, he was disposed to spare the vanquished; but the troops not being apprized either of the enemy having ceased fighting, or of the general's intention, made a charge on them, and the foremost being soon cut down, the rest dispersed themselves and fled. Philip hastened with all possible speed to Tempe, and there halted one day at Gonni, to pick up those who might have survived the battle. The victorious Romans rushed into the Macedonian camp with hopes of spoil, but found it, for the most part, plundered already by the Ætolians. Eight thousand of the enemy were killed on that day, five thousand taken. Of the victors, about seven hundred fell. Valerius Antias, who on every occasion exaggerates numbers enormously, says that the killed of the enemy on that day amounted to forty thousand; the prisoners taken, (in which article the deviation from truth is less extravagant,) to five thousand seven hundred, with two hundred and forty-one military standards. Claudius also asserts, that thirty-two thousand of the enemy were slain, and four thousand three hundred taken. We have not given entire credit, even to the smallest of those numbers, but have followed Polybius, a writer whose testimony may be depended on with respect to all the Roman affairs, but especially those which were transacted in Greece.

11. Philip having collected, after the flight, such as, having been scattered by the various chances of the battle, had followed his steps, and having sent people to Larissa to burn the records of the kingdom, lest they should fall into the hands of the enemy, retired into Macedonia. Quintius set up to sale a part of the prisoners and booty, and part he bestowed on the soldiers; and then proceeded to Larissa, without having yet received any certain intelligence to what quarter Philip had betaken himself, or what were his designs. To this place came a herald from the king, apparently to obtain a truce, until those who had fallen in battle should be removed and buried, but in reality to request permission to send ambassadors. Both were obtained from the Roman general; who, besides, desired the messenger to tell the king "not to be too much dejected." This expression gave much offence, particularly to the Ætolians, who were become very assuming, and who complained that "the general was quite altered by success. Before the battle, he was accustomed to transact all business, whether great or small, in concert with the allies; but they had, now, no share in any of his counsels; he conducted all affairs entirely by his own judgment, and was even seeking an occasion of ingratiating himself personally with Philip, in order that, after the Ætolians had laboured through all hardships and difficulties of the war, the Roman might assume to himself all the merit and all the fruits of a peace." Certain it is that he had treated them with less respect than formerly, but they were ignorant of his motives for slighting them. They imagined that he was actuated by an expectation of presents from the king, though he was of a spirit incapable of yielding to a passion of that kind; but he was, with good reason, displeased at the Ætolians, on account of their insatiable greediness for plunder, and of their arrogance in assuming to themselves the honour of the victory—a claim so ill founded, as to offend the ears of all who heard it. Besides, he foresaw that if Philip were removed out of the way, and the strength of the kingdom of Macedonia entirely broken, the Ætolians would hold the place of masters of Greece: for these reasons, on many occasions, he took pains to lessen their importance and reputation in the judgment of the other states.

12. A truce for fifteen days was granted to the Macedonians, and a conference with the king appointed. Before the day arrived on which this was to be held, the Roman general called a council of the allies, and desired their opinions respecting the terms of peace proper to be prescribed. Amynander, king of Athamania, delivered his opinion in a few words; that "the conditions of peace ought to be adjusted in such a manner, as that Greece might have sufficient power

even without the interference of the Romans, to maintain the peace, and also its own liberty." The sentiments delivered by the Ætolians were more harsh; for, after a few introductory observations on the justice and propriety of the Roman general's conduct, in communicating his plans of peace to those who had acted with him as allies in the war, they insisted that "he was utterly mistaken, if he supposed that he could leave the peace with the Romans, or the liberty of Greece, on a permanent footing, unless he deprived Philip, either of his life, or of the throne; both which he could easily accomplish, if he chose to pursue his present success." Quintius, in reply, said, that "the Ætolians, in giving such advice, attended not either to the maxims of the Roman policy, or to the consistency of their own conduct: for, in all the former councils and conferences, wherein the conditions of peace were discussed, they never once urged the pushing of the war to the utter ruin of the Macedonian: and, as to the Romans, besides that they had, from the earliest periods, observed the maxim of sparing the vanquished, they had lately given a signal proof of their clemency in the peace granted to Hannibal and the Carthaginians. But, not to insist on the case of the Carthaginians, how often had the confederates met Philip himself in conference, yet no mention was ever made of his resigning his kingdom: and, because he had been defeated in battle, was that a reason that their animosity should become implacable? Against an armed foe men ought to engage with hostile resentment; towards the vanquished, he that showed most clemency, showed the greatest spirit. The kings of Macedonia were thought to be dangerous to the liberty of Greece. Suppose that kingdom and nation extirpated, the Thracians, Illyrians, and in time, the Gauls, (nations uncivilized and savage,) would pour themselves into Macedonia first, and then into Greece. He therefore warned them, not, by removing inconveniences which lay nearest, to open a passage to others greater and more grievous." Here he was interrupted by Phæneas, pretor of the Ætolians, who called on the assembly to remember the warning he gave them, that "if Philip escaped now, he would soon raise a new and more dangerous war." On which Quintius said—"Cease wrangling, when you ought to deliberate. The peace shall not be encumbered with such conditions as will leave it in his power to raise a war."

13. The convention was then adjourned; and next day the king came to the pass at the entrance of Tempe, the appointed place of meeting; and the third day following was fixed for introducing him to a full assembly of the Romans and allies. On this occasion Philip, with great prudence,

avoided the mention of any of those particulars, without which peace could not be obtained; and he declared that he was ready to comply with all the articles which, in the former conference, were either prescribed by the Romans or demanded by the allies; and to leave all other matters to the determination of the senate. Although he seemed to have hereby precluded every objection, even from the most inveterate of his enemies, yet all the rest remaining silent, Phæneas the Ætolian, said to him,—"What! Philip, do you at last restore to us Pharsalus and Larissa, with Cremaste, Echinus, and Thebes in Phthiotis?" Philip answered, that "he would give no obstruction to their retaking the possession of them." On which a dispute arose between the Roman general and the Ætolians about Thebes; for Quintius affirmed that it became the property of the Roman people by the laws of war; because when, before the commencement of hostilities, he marched his army thither, and invited the inhabitants to friendship, they, although at full liberty to renounce the king's party, yet preferred an alliance with Philip to one with Rome. Phæneas alleged, that, in consideration of their being confederates in the war, it was reasonable that whatever the Ætolians possessed before it began should be restored; and that, besides, there was in the first treaty a provisional clause of that purport, by which the spoils of war, of every kind that could be carried or driven, were to belong to the Romans; the lands and captured cities to the Ætolians. "Yourselves," replied Quintius, "annulled the conditions of that treaty when you deserted us, and made peace with Philip; but supposing it still remained in force, yet that clause could affect only captured cities. Now, the states of Thessaly submitted to us by a voluntary act of their own." —These words were heard by the allies with universal approbation; but to the Ætolians they were highly displeasing at the present, and proved afterward the cause of a war, and of many great disasters attending it. The terms settled with Philip were, that he should give his son Demetrius, and some of his friends, as hostages; should pay two hundred talents;* and send ambassadors to Rome to adjust the other articles: for which purpose there should be a cessation of arms for four months. An engagement was entered into, that, in case the senate should refuse to conclude a treaty, his money and hostages should be returned to him. We are told that one of the principal reasons which made the Roman general wish to expedite the conclusion of a peace was, that he had received certain information of Antiochus intending to commence hostilities, and to pass over into Europe.

* 38,750*l*.

14. About the same time, and, as some writers say, on the same day, the Achæans defeated Androsthenes, the king's commander, in a general engagement near Corinth. Philip, intending to use this city as a citadel to awe the states of Greece, had invited the principal inhabitants to a conference, under pretence of settling with them the number of horsemen which the Corinthians could supply towards the war, and these he detained as hostages. Besides the force already there, consisting of five hundred Macedonians, and eight hundred auxiliaries of various kinds, he had sent thither one thousand two hundred Illyrians, and of Thracians and Cretans (for these served in both the opposite armies) eight hundred. To these were added Bœotians, Thessalians, and Acarnanians, to the amount of one thousand, all carrying bucklers; with as many of the young Corinthians themselves as filled up the number of six thousand effective men,—a force which inspired Androsthenes with such confidence, as to wish for a meeting with the enemy in the field. Nicostratus, pretor of the Achæans, was at Sicyon, with two thousand foot and one hundred horse; but seeing himself so inferior, both in the number and kind of troops, he did not go outside the walls: the king's forces, in various excursions, ravaged the lands of Pellene, Phliasus, and Cleone. At last, reproaching the enemy with cowardice, they passed over into the territory of Sicyon, and sailing round Achaia, wasted the whole coast. As the enemy, while thus employed, spread themselves about too widely, and too carelessly, (the usual consequence of too much confidence,) Nicostratus conceived hopes of attacking them by surprise. He therefore sent secret directions to all the neighbouring states, as to what day, and what number from each state, should assemble in arms at Apelaurus, a place in the territory of Stymphalia. All being in readiness at the time appointed, he marched thence immediately; and, without communicating his intentions to any one, came by night through the territory of the Phliasians to Cleone. He had with him five thousand foot, of whom * * * * * * [1] were light-armed, and three hundred horse: with this force he waited there, having despatched scouts to watch on what quarter the enemy should make their irregular inroads.

15. Androsthenes, utterly ignorant of all these proceedings, left Corinth, and encamped on the Nemea, a river running between the confines of Corinth and Sicyon. Here, dismissing one half of his troops, he divided the remainder into three parts, and ordered all the cavalry of each part to march in separate divisions, and ravage, at the same time,

[1] In the original, the number is omitted, or lost.

the territories of Pellene, Sicyon, and Phliasus. Accordingly, the three divisions set out by different roads. As soon as Nicostratus received intelligence of this at Cleone, he instantly sent forward a numerous detachment of mercenaries, to seize a strong pass at the entrance into the territory of Corinth; and he himself quickly followed, with his troops in two columns, the cavalry proceeding before the head of each, as advanced guards. In one column marched the mercenary soldiers and light infantry; in the other, the shield-bearers of the Achæans and other states, who composed the principal strength of the army. Both infantry and cavalry were now within a small distance of the camp, and some of the Thracians attacked parties of the enemy, who were straggling and scattered over the country, when the sudden alarm reached their tents. The commander there was thrown into the utmost perplexity; for, having never had a sight of the Achæans, except once or twice on the hills before Sicyon, when they did not venture down into the plains, he had never imagined that they would come so far as Cleone. He ordered the stragglers to be recalled by sound of trumpet; commanded the soldiers to take arms with all haste; and, marching out at the head of thin battalions, drew up his line on the bank of the river. His other troops, having scarcely had time to be collected and formed, did not withstand the enemy's first onset; but the Macedonians had attended their standards in greater numbers, and now kept the battle a long time doubtful. At length, being left exposed, by the flight of the rest, and pressed by two bodies of the enemy on different sides, by the light infantry on their flank, and by the shield-bearers and targeteers in front, and seeing victory declare against them, they at first gave ground; soon after, being vigorously pushed, they turned their backs; and most of them throwing away their arms, and having lost all hope of defending their camp, made the best of their way to Corinth. Nicostratus sent the mercenaries in pursuit; and the auxiliary Thracians against the party employed in ravaging the lands of Sicyon: both of which detachments slew great numbers, greater almost than were slain in the battle itself. Of those who had been ravaging Pellene and Phthius, some, returning to their camp, ignorant of all that had happened, and without any regular order, fell in with the advanced guards of the enemy, where they expected their own. Others, from the bustle which they perceived, suspecting the cause, fled and dispersed themselves in such a manner, that, as they wandered up and down, they were cut off by the very peasants. There fell, on that day, one thousand five hundred: three hundred were made prisoners. The great fears under which all Achaia had hitherto laboured, were thus removed.

16. Before the battle at Cynoscephalæ, Lucius Quintius had invited to Corcyra some chiefs of the Acarnanians, the only state in Greece which had continued to maintain its alliance with the Macedonians; and, in concert with them, laid some kind of scheme for a change of measures. Two causes principally had retained them in friendship with the king: one was a principle of honour, natural to that nation; the other, their fear and hatred of the Ætolians. A general assembly was summoned to meet at Leucas; but neither did all the states of Acarnania come thither, nor were those who did attend agreed in opinion. However, the magistrates and leading men prevailed so far, as to get a decree passed, on the authority of a majority of those present, for joining in alliance with the Romans. This gave great offence to those who had not been present; and, in this ferment of the nation, Androcles and Echedemus, two men of distinction among the Acarnanians, being employed by Philip, gained so much influence as to prevail on the assembly, not only to repeal the decree for an alliance with Rome, but also to condemn, as guilty of treason, Archesilaus and Bianor, both men of the first rank in Acarnania, who had been the advisers of that measure; and to deprive Zeuxidas, the pretor, of his office, for having put it to the vote. The persons condemned took a course apparently desperate, but successful in the issue: for, while their friends advised them to yield to the times, and withdraw to Corcyra, to the Romans, they resolved to present themselves to the multitude; and either by that act to mollify their resentment, or endure whatever might befall them. They came, accordingly, into a full assembly; on which, at first, a murmur arose, expressive of surprise; but presently silence took place, partly from respect to their former dignity, partly from commiseration of their present situation. They were even indulged with the liberty of speaking. At first they addressed the assembly in a suppliant manner; but in the progress of their discourse, when they came to refute the charges made against them, they spoke with that degree of confidence which innocence inspires. At last they even ventured to utter some complaints, and to charge the proceedings against them with injustice and cruelty: this had such an effect on the minds of all present, that, with one consent, they annulled all the decrees passed against them. Nevertheless, they came to a resolution to renounce the friendship of the Romans, and return to the alliance with Philip.

17. These decrees were passed at Leucas, the capital of

Acarnania, the place where all the states usually met in council. As soon therefore as the news of this sudden change reached the lieutenant-general, Flamininus, in Corcyra, he instantly set sail with the fleet for Leucas; and coming to an anchor at Heræas, advanced thence towards the walls with every kind of machine used in the attacking of cities; supposing that the first appearance of danger might bend the minds of the inhabitants to submission. But seeing no prospect of effecting any thing, except by force, he began to erect towers, and to bring up the battering-rams and other engines to the walls. The whole of Acarnania, being situated between Ætolia and Epirus, faces towards the west and the Sicilian sea. Leucadia, now an island, separated from Acarnania by a shallow strait, and which is the work of art, was then a peninsula, united on its eastern side to Acarnania by a narrow isthmus: this isthmus was about five hundred paces in length, and in breadth not above one hundred and twenty. At the entrance of this narrow neck stands Leucas, stretching up part of a hill which faces the east and Acarnania: the lower part of the town is level, lying along the sea, which divides Leucadia from Acarnania. Thus it lies open to attacks both from the sea and from the land; for the channel is more like a marsh than a sea, and all the adjacent ground has a depth which renders the construction of works easy. In many places, therefore, at once, the walls were either undermined or demolished by the ram. But all the advantages which the nature of the place afforded to the besiegers were amply counterbalanced by the invincible spirit of the besieged; night and day they employed themselves busily in repairing the shattered parts of the wall; and, stopping up the breaches that were made, fought the enemy with great spirit, and showed a wish to defend the walls by their arms rather than themselves by the walls. And they would certainly have protracted the siege to a length unexpected by the Romans, had not some exiles of Italian birth, who resided in Leucas, admitted a band of soldiers into the citadel: notwithstanding which, when those troops ran down from the higher ground with great tumult and uproar, the Leucadians, drawing up in a body in the forum, withstood them for a considerable time in regular fight. Meanwhile the walls were scaled in many places; and the besiegers, climbing over the rubbish, entered the town through the breaches. And now the lieutenant-general himself surrounded the combatants with a powerful force. Being thus hemmed in, many were slain, the rest laid down their arms, and surrendered to the conqueror. In a few days after, on hearing of the battle at Cynoscephalæ, all the states of Acarnania made their submission to the lieutenant-general.

18. About this time fortune, depressing the same party in every quarter at once, the Rhodians in order to recover from Philip the tract on the continent called Piræa, which had been in possession of their ancestors, sent thither their pretor, Pausistratus, with eight hundred Achæan foot, and about one thousand nine hundred men, made up of auxiliaries of various nations. These were Gauls, Nisuetans, Pisuetans, Tamians, Areans from Africa, and Laodiceniane from Asia. With this force Pausistratus seized by surprise Tendeba, in the territory of Stratonice, a place exceedingly convenient for his purpose. A reinforcement of one thousand Achæan foot, and one hundred horse, called out for the same expedition, came up at the very time, under a commander called Theoxenus. Dinocrates, the king's general, with design to recover the fort, marched his army first to Tendeba, and then to another fort called Astragon, which also stood in the territory of Stratonice. Then, calling in all the garrisons, which were scattered in many different places, and the Thessalian auxiliaries from Stratonice itself, he proceeded to Alabanda, where the enemy lay. The Rhodians were no way averse from a battle, and the camps being pitched near each other, both parties immediately came into the field. Dinocrates placed five hundred Macedonians on his right wing, and the Agrians on his left; the centre he formed of the troops which he had drawn together out of the garrisons of the forts; these were mostly Carians; and he covered the flanks with the cavalry and the Cretan and Thracian auxiliaries. The Rhodians had on the right wing the Achæans; on the left, mercenary soldiers; and in the centre, a chosen band of infantry,—a body of auxiliaries composed of troops of various nations. The cavalry and what light infantry they had were posted on the wings. During that day both armies remained on the banks of a rivulet, which ran between them; and, after discharging a few javelins, they retired into their camps. Next day, being drawn up in the same order, they fought a more obstinate battle than could have been expected, considering the numbers engaged; for there were not more than three thousand infantry on each side, and about one hundred horse: but they were not only on an equality with respect to numbers, and the kind of arms which they used, but they also fought with equal spirit, and equal hopes. First, the Achæans, crossing the rivulet, made an attack on the Agrians; then the whole line passed the river, almost at full speed. The fight continued doubtful for a long time: the Achæans, one thousand in number, drove back the one thousand eight

hundred Agrians. Then the whole centre gave way. On their right wing, composed of Macedonians, no impression could be made, so long as their phalanx preserved its order, each man clinging as it were to another: but when, in consequence of their flank being left exposed, they endeavoured to turn their spears against the enemy, who were advancing on that side, they immediately broke their ranks. This first caused disorder among themselves; they then turned their backs, and at last, throwing away their arms, and flying with precipitation, made the best of their way to Bargylii. To the same place Dinocrates also made his escape. The Rhodians continued the pursuit as long as the day lasted, and then retired to their camp. There is every reason to believe that, if the victors had proceeded with speed to Stratonice, that city would have been gained without a contest; but the opportunity for effecting this was neglected, and the time wasted in taking possession of the forts and villages in Peræa. In the mean time the courage of the troops in garrison at Stratonice revived; and shortly after Dinocrates, with the troops which had escaped from the battle, came into the town, which, after that, was besieged and assaulted without effect; nor could it be reduced until a long time after that, when Antiochus took it. Such were the events that took place in Thessaly, in Achaia, and in Asia, all about the same time.

19. Philip was informed that the Dardanians, expecting to make an easy prey of his kingdom, after the many shocks it had suffered, had passed the frontiers, and were spreading devastation through the upper parts; on which, though he was hard pressed in almost every quarter of the globe, fortune on all occasions defeating his measures, and those of his friends, yet, thinking it more intolerable than death to be expelled from the possession of Macedonia, he made hasty levies through the cities of his dominions; and, with six thousand foot and five hundred horse, surprised and defeated the enemy near Stobi in Pæonia. Great numbers were killed in the fight, and greater numbers of those who were scattered about in quest of plunder. As to such as found a road open for flight, they never thought of trying the chance of an engagement, but hastened back to their own country. After this enterprise, executed with a degree of success beyond what he met in the rest of his attempts, and which raised the drooping courage of his people, he retired to Thessalonica. Seasonable as was the termination of the Punic war, in extricating the Romans from the danger of a quarrel with Philip, the recent triumph over Philip happened still more opportunely, when Antiochus, in Syria, was almost ready to commence hostilities: for besides that it

was easier to wage war against them separately than against their combined strength, a violent insurrection had, a little before this time, broken out in Spain. Antiochus, though he had in the preceding summer reduced under his power all the states in Cœlesyria belonging to Ptolemy, and retired into winter-quarters at Antioch, yet allowed himself no rest: for resolving to exert the whole strength of his kingdom, he collected a most powerful force, both naval and military; and in the beginning of spring, sending forward by land his two sons, Ardues and Mithridates, at the head of the army, with orders to wait for him at Sardis, he himself set out by sea, with a fleet of one hundred decked ships, besides two hundred lighter vessels, barks and fly-boats, designing to attempt the reduction of all the cities under the dominion of Ptolemy along the whole coast of Caria, and Cilicia; and, at the same time, to send troops and ships to the assistance of Philip in the then subsisting war.

20. The Rhodians have signalized their faithful attachment to the Roman people, and their affection for the whole race of the Greeks, by many honourable exertions both on land and sea; but never was their gallantry more eminently conspicuous than on this occasion, when, nowise dismayed at the formidable magnitude of the impending war, they sent ambassadors to tell the king that if he attempted to bring his forces beyond Nephelis, which is a promontory of Cilicia, remarkable for being a boundary mentioned in an old treaty with the Athenians, they would meet him there and oppose him, not out of any ill-will, but because they would not suffer him to join Philip and obstruct the Romans, who were restoring liberty to Greece. At this time Antiochus was pushing on the siege of Coracesium by regular approaches; for, after he had got possession of Zephyrium, Solæ, Aphrodisias, and Corycus; and doubling Anemurium, another promontory of Cilicia, had taken Selinus; when all these, and the other fortresses on that coast, had, either through fear or inclination, submitted without resistance, Coracesium shut its gates, and gave him a delay which he did not expect. Here he gave audience to the Rhodians, and although the purport of their embassy was such as might kindle passion in the breast of a king, yet he stifled his resentment, and answered, that "he would send ambassadors to Rhodes, and would give them instructions to renew the old treaties made by him and his predecessors with that state; and to assure them that they need not be alarmed at his approach; that it would be in no respect detrimental or injurious either to them or their allies; for he was determined not to violate the friendship subsisting between himself and the Romans: and of this, his own late embassy to that people, and the sen-

ate's answers and decrees, so honourable to him, ought to be deemed sufficient proof." Just at that time his ambassadors happened to return from Rome, where they had been heard and dismissed with courtesy, as the juncture required; the event of the war with Philip being yet uncertain. While the king's ambassadors were haranguing to the above purpose, in an assembly of the people at Rhodes, a courier arrived with an account of the battle at Cynoscephalæ having finally decided the fate of the war. In consequence of this intelligence, the Rhodians, now freed from all apprehensions of danger from Philip, resolved to oppose Antiochus with their fleet. Nor did they neglect another object that required their attention; the protection of the freedom of the cities in alliance with Ptolemy, which were threatened with war by Antiochus: for, some they assisted with men, others by forewarning them of the enemy's designs; by which means they enabled the Cauneans, Mindians, Halicarnassians, and Samians, to preserve their liberty. It were needless to attempt enumerating all the transactions as they occurred in that quarter, when I am scarcely equal to the task of recounting those which immediately concern the war in which Rome was engaged.

21. At this time King Attalus, having fallen sick at Thebes, and been carried thence to Pergamus, died at the age of seventy-one, after he had reigned forty-four years. To this man fortune had given nothing which could lead him to form pretensions to a throne except riches. By a prudent, and, at the same time, a splendid use of these, he begat, in himself first, and then in others, an opinion that he was not undeserving of a crown. Afterward, having in one battle utterly defeated the Gauls, which nation was then the more terrible to Asia, as having but lately made its appearance there, he assumed the title of king, and ever after supported a spirit equal to the dignity of the station. He governed his subjects with the most perfect justice, and was singularly faithful to his engagements with his allies, gentle and bountiful to his friends: his wife and four sons survived him; and he left his government established on such solid and firm foundations, that the possession of it descended to the third generation. While this was the posture of affairs in Asia, Greece, and Macedonia, the war with Philip being scarcely ended, and the peace certainly not yet perfected, a desperate insurrection took place in the Farther Spain. Marcus Helvius was governor of that province. He informed the senate by letter that "two chieftains, Colca and Luscinus, were in arms; that Colca was joined by seventeen towns, and Luscinus by the powerful cities of Cardo and Bardo; and that the people of the whole sea-coast, who had

not yet manifested their disposition, were ready to rise on the first motion of their neighbours." On this letter being read by Marcus Sergius, city pretor, the senate decreed that, as soon as the election of pretors should be finished, the one to whose lot the government of Spain fell should without delay consult the senate respecting the commotions in that province.

22. About the same time the consuls came home to Rome, and, on their holding a meeting of the senate in the temple of Bellona, and demanding a triumph, in consideration of their successes against the enemy, Caius Atinius Labeo and Caius Ursanius, plebeian tribunes, insisted that "they should propose their claims of a triumph separately, for they would not suffer the question to be put on both jointly, lest equal honours might be conferred where the merits were unequal." Minucius urged that they had both been appointed to the government of one province, Italy; and that, through the course of their administration, his colleague and himself had been united in sentiments and in counsels; to which Cornelius added, that, when the Boians were passing the Po, to assist the Insubrians and Cænomanians against him, they were forced to return to defend their own country, from Minucius ravaging their towns and lands. In reply, the tribunes acknowledged that the services performed in the war by Cornelius were so great, that "no more doubt could be entertained respecting his triumph than respecting the praise to be given to the immortal gods." Nevertheless they insisted that "neither he nor any other member of the community should possess such power and influence as to be able, after obtaining such honour for himself, to bestow the same on a colleague, who, in claiming it, had betrayed an entire want of modesty. The exploits of Quintus Minucius in Liguria were trifling skirmishes, scarcely deserving mention; and in Gaul he had lost great numbers of soldiers." They mentioned even military tribunes, Titus Juvencius and Cneius Labeo, the plebeian tribune's brother, who had fallen, together with many other brave men, both citizens and allies: and they asserted that "pretended surrenders of a few towns and villages, fabricated for the occasion, had been made, without any pledge of fidelity being taken." These altercations between the consuls and tribunes lasted two days: at last the consuls, overcome by the obstinacy of the tribunes, proposed their claims separately.

23. To Cneius Cornelius a triumph was unanimously decreed: and the inhabitants of Placentia and Cremona added to the applause bestowed on the consul, by returning him thanks, and mentioning to his honour that they had been delivered by him from a siege; and that very many of them,

when in the hands of the enemy, had been rescued from captivity. Quintus Minucius just tried how the proposal of his claim would be received, and finding the whole senate averse from it, declared that by the authority of his office of consul, and pursuant to the example of many illustrious men, he would triumph on the Alban mount. Caius Cornelius, being yet in office, triumphed over the Insubrian and Cænomanian Gauls. He produced a great number of military standards, and carried in the procession abundance of Gallic spoils in captured chariots. Many Gauls of distinction were led before his chariot, and along with them, some writers say, Hamilcar, the Carthaginian general. But what more than all attracted the eyes of the public was, a crowd of Cremonians and Placentians, with caps of liberty on their heads, following his chariot. He carried in his triumph two hundred and thirty-seven thousand five hundred asses,* and of silver denariuses, stamped with a chariot, seventy-nine thousand.† He distributed to each of his soldiers seventy asses,‡ to a horseman double that sum, to a centurion triple. Quintus Minucius, consul, triumphed on the Alban mount, over the Ligurian and Boian Gauls. Although this triumph was less respectable, in regard to the place and the fame of his exploits, and because all knew the expense was not issued from the treasury; yet, in regard of the number of standards, chariots, and spoils, it was nearly equal to the other. The amount of the money also was nearly equal. Two hundred and fifty-four thousand asses§ were conveyed to the treasury, and of silver denariuses, stamped with a chariot, fifty-three thousand two hundred.‖ He likewise gave to the soldiers, horsemen, and centurions, the same sums that his colleague had given.

24. After the triumph, the election of consuls came on. The persons chosen were Lucius Furius Purpureo and Marcus Claudius Marcellus. Next day, the following were elected pretors; Quintus Fabius Buteo, Tiberius Sempronius Longus, Quintus Minucius Thermus, Manius Acilius Glabrio, Lucius Apustius Fullo, and Caius Lælius. Towards the close of this year, a letter came from Titus Quintius, with information that he had fought a pitched battle with Philip in Thessaly, and had totally defeated him. This letter was read by Sergius, the pretor, first in the senate, and then, by their direction, in a general assembly; and supplications of five days' continuance were decreed on account of those successes. Soon after arrived the ambassadors, both from Titus Quintius and from the king. The Macedonians were

* 766*l.* 18*s.* 6 1-2*d.*  † 2,551*l.* 10*d.*  ‡ 4*s.* 6 1-2*d.*
§ 820*l.* 4*s.* 2*d.*  ‖ 1,717*l.* 18*s.* 4*d.*

conducted out of the city to the Villa Publica, where lodgings and every other accommodation were provided for them, and the senate met in the temple of Bellona. Not many words passed; for the Macedonians declared that whatever terms the senate should prescribe, the king was ready to comply with them. It was decreed that, conformably to ancient practice, ten ambassadors should be appointed, and that, in council with them, the general, Titus Quintius, should grant terms of peace to Philip; and a clause was added that, in the number of these ambassadors, should be Publius Sulpicius and Publius Villius, who in their consulships had held the province of Macedonia. On the same day the inhabitants of Cossa presented a petition, praying that the number of their colonists might be enlarged; and an order was accordingly passed that one thousand should be added to the list, with a provision that no person should be admitted into that number who, at any time since the consulate of Publius Cornelius and Tiberius Sempronius, had acted as an enemy to the state.

25. This year the Roman games were exhibited in the circus, and on the stage, by the curule ediles, Publius Cornelius Scipio and Cneius Manlius Vulso, with an unusual degree of splendour, and were beheld with the greater delight in consequence of the late successes in war. They were thrice repeated entire, and the plebeian games seven times. These were exhibited by Acilius Glabrio and Caius Lælius, who also, out of the money arising from fines, erected three brazen statues, to Ceres, Liber, and Libera. Lucius Furius and Marcus Claudius Marcellus, having entered on the consulship [A. U. C. 556. B. C. 196] when the distribution of the provinces came to be agitated, and the senate appeared disposed to vote Italy the province of both, petitioned for liberty to put that of Macedonia to the lot along with Italy. Marcellus, who of the two was the more eager for that province, by assertions that the peace was merely a feigned one, and that if the army were withdrawn thence, the king would renew the war, caused some perplexity in the minds of the senate. The consuls would probably have carried the point, had not Quintus Marcius Rex, and Caius Atinius Labeo, plebeian tribunes, declared that they would enter their protest, unless they were allowed, before any farther proceeding, to take the sense of the people, whether it was their will and order that peace be concluded with Philip. The question was put to the people in the capitol, and every one of the thirty-five tribes voted on the affirmative side. The public found the greater reason to rejoice at the ratification of the peace with Macedonia, as melancholy news was brought from Spain; and a letter was

made public, announcing that "the pretor, Caius Sempronius Tuditanus, had been defeated in battle in the Hither Spain; that his army had been utterly routed and dispersed, and several men of distinction slain in the fight. That Tuditanus, having been grievously wounded, and carried out of the field, expired soon after." Italy was decreed the province of both consuls, in which they were to employ the same legions which the preceding consuls had; and they were to raise four new legions, that two might be in readiness to go wherever the senate should direct. Titus Quintius Flamininus was ordered to continue in the government of his province with the army of two legions, then on the spot. The former prolongation of his command was deemed sufficient.

26. The pretors then cast lots for their provinces. Lucius Apustius Fullo obtained the city jurisdiction; Manlius Acilius Glabrio, that between natives and foreigners; Quintus Fabius Buteo, Farther Spain; Quintus Minucius Thermus, Hither Spain; Caius Lælius, Sicily; Tiberius Sempronius Longus, Sardinia. To Quintus Fabius Buteo and Quintus Minucius, to whom the government of the two Spains had fallen, it was decreed that the consuls, out of the four legions raised by them, should give one each, together with four thousand foot and three hundred horse of the allies and Latine confederates; and those pretors were ordered to repair to their provinces forthwith. This war in Spain broke out in the fifth year after the former had been ended, together with the Punic war. The Spaniards now, for the first time, had taken arms in their own name, unconnected with any Carthaginian commander. Before the consuls stirred from the city, however, they were ordered, as usual, to expiate the reported prodigies. Lucius Julius Sequestrius, on the road to Sabinia, was killed by lightning, together with his horse. The temple of Feronia, in the Capenatian district, was struck by lightning. At the temple of Moneta the shafts of two spears took fire and burned. A wolf, coming in through the Esquiline gate, and running through the most frequented part of the city, down into the forum, passed thence through the Tuscan and Mælian streets; and scarcely receiving a stroke, made its escape out of the Capenian gate. These prodigies were expiated with victims of the larger kinds.

27. About the same time Cneius Cornelius Lentulus, who had held the government of Hither Spain before Sempronius Tuditanus, entered the city in ovation, pursuant to a decree of the senate, and carried in the procession one thousand five hundred and fifteen pounds weight of gold, twenty thousand of silver; and in coin, thirty-four thousand five

hundred and fifty denariuses.* Lucius Stretinius, from the Farther Spain, without making any pretensions to a triumph, carried into the treasury fifty thousand pounds weight of silver; and out of the spoils taken, built two arches in the cattle-market, at the fronts of the temple of Fortune and Mother Matuta, and one of the great Circus; and on these arches placed gilded statues. These were the principal occurrences during the winter. At this time Quintius was in quarters at Elatia. Among many requests, made to him by the allies, was that of the Bœotians, namely, that their countrymen, who had served in the army with Philip, might be restored to them. With this Quintius readily complied; not because he thought them very deserving, but, at a time when there was reason to be apprehensive of the designs of Antiochus, he judged it advisable to conciliate every state in favour of the Roman interest. It quickly appeared how very little gratitude the Bœotians felt on the occasion; for they not only sent persons to give thanks to Philip for the restoration of their fellows, as if that compliment had been paid to him by Quintius and the Romans; but, at the next election, raised to the office of Bœotarch a man named Brachyllas, for no other reason than because he had been commander of the Bœotians serving in the army of Philip; passing by Zeuxippus, Pisistratus, and the others, who had promoted the alliance with Rome. These men were both offended at the present and alarmed about the future consequences; for if such things were done when a Roman army lay almost at their gates, what would become of them when the Romans should have gone away to Italy, and Philip, from a situation so near, should support his own associates, and vent his resentment on those of the opposite party?

28. It was resolved, while they had the Roman army near at hand, to take off Brachyllas, who was the principal leader of the faction which favoured the king; and they chose an opportunity for the deed when, after having been at a public feast, he was returning to his house inebriated, and accompanied by some of his debauched companions, who, for the sake of merriment, had been admitted to the crowded entertainment. He was surrounded and assassinated by six men, of whom three were Italians and three Ætolians. His companions fled, crying out for help; and a great uproar ensued among the people, who ran up and down, through all parts of the city, with lights: but the assassins made their escape through the nearest gate. At the first dawn a full assembly was called together in the theatre, by the voice of a crier, as if some discovery had been made. Many openly

* 1115*l*. 13*s*. 3 1-2*d*.

clamoured that Brachyllas was killed by those detestable wretches who accompanied him; but their private conjectures pointed to Zeuxippus, as author of the murder. It was resolved, however, that those who had been in company with him should be seized and examined. While they were under examination, Zeuxippus, with his usual composure, came into the assembly, for the purpose of averting the charge from himself; yet said that people were mistaken in supposing that so daring a murder was the act of such effeminate wretches as those who were charged with it, urging many plausible arguments to the same purpose. By which behaviour he led several to believe, that if he were conscious of guilt, he would never have presented himself before the multitude, or, uncalled on, have made any mention of the murder. Others were convinced that he intended, by thus pushing impudently forward, to throw off all suspicion from himself. Soon after, those men who were innocent were put to the torture; and, as they knew the universal opinion, they gave information conformable to it, naming Zeuxippus and Pisistratus; but they produced no proof to show that they knew any thing of the matter. Zeuxippus, however, accompanied by a man named Stratonidas, fled by night to Tanagra; alarmed by his own conscience rather than by the assertion of men who were privy to no one circumstance of the affair. Pisistratus, despising the informers, remained at Thebes. A slave of Zeuxippus had carried messages backwards and forwards, and had been intrusted in the management of the whole business. From this man Pisistratus dreaded a discovery; and by that very dread forced him, against his will, to make one. He sent a letter to Zeuxippus, desiring him to "put out of the way the slave who was privy to their crime; for he did not believe him as well qualified for the concealment of the fact as he was for the perpetration of it." He ordered the bearer of this letter to deliver it to Zeuxippus as soon as possible; but he, not finding an opportunity of meeting him, put it into the hands of the very slave in question, whom he believed to be the most faithful to his master of any; and added that it came from Pisistratus about business of the utmost consequence to Zeuxippus. Struck by consciousness of guilt, the slave, after promising to deliver the letter, immediately opened it; and, on reading the contents, fled in a fright to Thebes. Zeuxippus, alarmed by this his flight, withdrew to Athens, where he thought he might live in exile with greater safety. Pisistratus, after being examined several times by torture, was put to death.

29. The murder, and particularly the circumstance of Zeuxippus, one of the first men of the nation, having sub-

orned such a deed, exasperated the Thebans and all the Bœotians to the most rancorous animosity against the Romans. To recommence a war, they had neither strength nor a leader: but they had recourse to private massacres, and cut off many of the soldiers, some as they came to lodge in their houses, others as they travelled from one cantonment to another on various business. Some were killed on the roads by parties lying in wait in lurking places; others were seduced and carried away to inns, which were left uninhabited, and there put to death. At last they committed these crimes, not merely out of hatred, but likewise from a desire of booty; for the soldiers on furlough generally carried money in their purses for the purpose of trading. At first a few at a time, afterward greater numbers used to be missed, until all Bœotia became notorious for those practices, and a soldier was more afraid to go beyond the bounds of the camp than into an enemy's country. Quintius then sent deputies round the states to make inquiry concerning the murders committed. The greatest number of foot soldiers were found about the lake called Copais; there the bodies were dug out of the mud, and drawn up out of the marsh, having had earthen jars or stones tied to them, so as to sink by the weight. Many deeds of this sort were discovered to have been perpetrated at Acrophia and Coronea. Quintius at first insisted that the persons guilty should be given up to him, and that for five hundred soldiers (for so many had been cut off) the Bœotians should pay five hundred talents.* Neither of these requisitions being complied with, and the states only making verbal apologies, declaring that none of those acts had been authorized by the public, Quintius first sent ambassadors to Athens and Achaia to satisfy the allies that the war, which he was about to make on the Bœotians, was conformable to justice and piety; and then, ordering Publius Claudius to march with one half of the troops to Acrophia, he himself, with the remainder, invested Coronea; and these two bodies, marching by different roads from Elatia, laid waste all the country through which they passed. The Bœotians, dismayed by these losses, while every place was filled with fugitives, and while the terror became universal, sent ambassadors to the camp, who were refused admittance; and just at this juncture arrived the Achæans and Athenians. The Achæans had the greater influence as intercessors; and they were resolved, in case they could not procure peace for the Bœotians, to join them in the war. Through the mediation of the Achæans, however, the Bœotians obtained an audience of the Roman gen-

* 96,875l.

eral; who, ordering them to deliver up the guilty, and to pay thirty talents* as a fine, granted them peace, and raised the siege.

30. A few days after this the ten ambassadors arrived from Rome, in pursuance of whose counsel peace was granted to Philip on the following conditions: "That all the Grecian states, as well those in Asia as those in Europe, should enjoy liberty, and their own laws: that from such of them as were in the possession of Philip he should withdraw his garrisons, particularly from the following places in Asia; Euromus, Pedasi, Bargylii, Iassus, Myrina, Abydus; and from Thassus and Perinthus, for it was determined that these likewise should be free: that with respect to the freedom of Cius, Quintius would write to Prusias, king of Bithynia, the resolutions of the senate, and of the ten ambassadors: that Philip should return to the Romans the prisoners and deserters, and deliver up all his decked ships, not excepting even the royal galley,—of a size almost unmanageable, being moved by sixteen banks of oars: that he should not keep more than five hundred soldiers, nor any elephant: that he should not wage war beyond the bounds of Macedonia without permission from the senate: that he should pay to the Roman people one thousand talents:† one half at present, the other by instalments, within ten years." Valerius Antias writes, that there was imposed on him an annual tribute of four thousand pounds weight of silver, for ten years, and an immediate payment of twenty thousand pounds weight. The same author says that an article was expressly inserted, that he should not make war on Eumenes, Attalus's son, who had lately come to the throne. For the performance of these conditions hostages were received, among whom was Demetrius, Philip's son. Valerius Antias adds, that the island of Ægina and the elephants were given as a present to Attalus, who was absent; to the Rhodians, Stratonice in Caria, and other cities which had been in the possession of Philip; and to the Athenians, the islands of Paros, Imbros, Delos, and Scyros.

31. While all the other states of Greece expressed their approbation of these terms of peace, the Ætolians alone, in private murmurs, made severe strictures on the determination of the ten ambassadors. They said, "it consisted merely of an empty piece of writing varnished over with a fallacious appearance of liberty; for why should some cities be put into the hands of the Romans without being named, while others were particularized, and ordered to be enfranchised without such consignment; unless the intent was,

* 5812l. 10s. † 193,750l.

that those in Asia, which, from their distant situation, were more secure from danger, should be free; but those in Greece, not being specified, should be made their property: Corinth, Chalcis, and Oreum; with Eretria and Demetrias." Nor was this charge entirely without foundation; for there was some hesitation with respect to Corinth, Chalcis, and Demetrias; because, in the decree of the senate, in pursuance of which the ten ambassadors had been sent from Rome, all Greece and Asia, except these three, were expressly ordered to be set at liberty; but, with regard to these, ambassadors were instructed, that, whatever other measures the exigences of the state might render expedient, the present they should determine to pursue in conformity to the public good and their own honour. Now they had every reason to believe that Antiochus intended, as soon as he should be able to arrange his affairs at home, to pass into Europe; and they were willing to let these cities, the possession of which would be so advantageous to him, lie open to his attacks. Quintius, with the ten ambassadors, sailed from Elatia to Anticyra, and thence to Corinth. Here the plans they laid down were discussed. Quintius frequently urged, that "every part of Greece ought to be set at liberty, if they wished to refute the cavils of the Ætolians; if they wished that sincere affection and respect for the Roman nation should be universally entertained; or if they wished to convince the world that they had crossed the sea with the design of liberating Greece, not of transferring the sovereignty of it from Philip to themselves." The Macedonians alleged nothing in opposition to the arguments made use of in favour of the freedom of the cities; but "they thought it safer for those cities to remain, for a time, under the protection of Roman garrisons, than to be obliged to receive Antiochus for a master in the room of Philip." Their final determination was, that "Corinth be restored to the Achæans, but that the Roman force should continue in the citadel; and that Chalcis and Demetrias be retained until their apprehensions respecting Antiochus should cease."

32. The stated solemnity of the Isthmian games was at hand. These have ever been attended by very numerous meetings, for two reasons: first, out of the universal fondness entertained by the Corinthians for shows, wherein are seen trials of skill in arts of every kind, besides contests in strength and swiftness of foot: and secondly, because people come thither from every quarter of Greece by means of one or other of the two opposite seas. But on this occasion, all were led, by an eager curiosity, to learn what was thenceforward to be the state of Greece, and what their own condition; while many at the same time not only formed opin-

ions within themselves, but uttered their conjectures in conversation. The Romans took their seats as spectators; and a herald, preceded by a trumpeter, according to custom, advanced into the centre of the theatre, where notice of the commencement of the games is usually made, in a set form of words. Silence being commanded by sound of trumpet, he uttered aloud the following proclamation: "The senate and people of Rome, and Titus Quintius, their general, having subdued Philip and the Macedonians, do hereby order that the following states be free, independent, and ruled by their own laws: the Corinthians, Phocians, and all the Locrians; the island of Eubœa, and the Magnesians; the Thessalians, Perrhæbians, and the Achæans of Phthiotis." He then read a list of all the states which had been under subjection to King Philip. The joy occasioned by hearing these words of the herald was so great, that the people's minds were unable to conceive the matter at once. Scarcely could they believe that they had heard them; and they looked at each other with amazement, as if all were the illusion of a dream. Each inquired of others about what immediately concerned himself. Every one being desirous, not only of hearing, but of seeing the messenger of liberty, the herald was called out again; and he again repeated the proclamation. When they were thus assured of the reality of the joyful tidings, they raised such a shout and clapping of hands, and repeated them so often, as clearly demonstrated, that of all earthly blessings, none is more grateful to the multitude than liberty. The games were then proceeded through with hurry; for neither the thoughts nor eyes of any attended to the exhibitions, so entirely had the single passion of joy preoccupied their minds, as to exclude the sense of all other pleasures.

33. But, when the games were finished, every one eagerly pressed towards the Roman general; so that by the crowd rushing to one spot, all wishing to come near him, and to touch his right hand, and throwing garlands and ribands, he was in some degree of danger. He was then about thirty-three years of age; and besides the vigour of youth, the grateful sensations excited by acknowledgments so eminently glorious to him, increased his strength. Nor did the general exultation last only for that day; but, through the space of many days, was continually revived by sentiments and expressions of gratitude. "There was a nation in the world," they said, "which, at its own expense, with its own labour, and at its own risk, waged wars for the liberty of others. And this it performed, not merely for contiguous states, or, near neighbours, or for countries that made parts of the same continent; but even crossed the seas for the

purpose, that no unlawful power should subsist on the face of the whole earth; but that justice, right, and law, should everywhere have sovereign sway. By one sentence pronounced by a herald, all the cities of Greece and Asia had been set at liberty. To have conceived hopes of this, argued a daring spirit; to have carried it into effect, was a proof of the most consummate bravery and good fortune."

34. Quintius and the ten ambassadors then gave audience to the embassies of the several kings, nations, and states. First of all, the ambassadors of King Antiochus were called. Their proceedings, here, were nearly the same as at Rome; a mere display of words unsupported by facts. But the answer given them was not ambiguous as formerly, during the uncertainty of affairs, and before the conquest of Philip; for the king was required in express terms to evacuate the cities of Asia, which had been in possession either of Philip or Ptolemy; not to meddle with the free cities, or any belonging to the Greeks. Above all, it was insisted on, that he should neither come himself into Europe, nor transport an army thither. The king's ambassadors being dismissed, a general convention of the nations and states was immediately held; and the business was despatched with the greater expedition, because the resolutions of the ten ambassadors mentioned the several states by name. To the people of Orestis, a district of Macedonia, in consideration of their having been the first who came over from the side of the king, their own laws were granted. The Magnesians, Perrhæbians, and Dolopians, were likewise declared free. To the nation of the Thessalians, besides the enjoyment of liberty, the Achæan part of Phthiotis was granted, excepting Phthiotian Thebes and Pharsalus. The Ætolians, demanding that Pharsalus and Leucas should be restored to them in conformity to the treaty, were referred to the senate: but the council united to these, by authority of a decree, Phocis and Locris, places which had formerly been annexed to them. Corinth, Triphylia, and Heræa, another city of Peloponnesus, were restored to the Achæans. The ten ambassadors were inclined to give Oreum and Eretria to King Eumenes, son of Attalus; but Quintius dissenting, the matter came under the determination of the senate, and the senate declared those cities free; adding to them Carystus. Lycus and Parthinia, Illyrian states which had been under subjection to Philip, were given to Pleuratus. Amynander was ordered to retain possession of the forts which he had taken from Philip during the war.

35. When the convention broke up, the ten ambassadors, dividing the business among them, set out by different routes to give liberty to the several cities within their respective

districts. Publius Lentulus went to Bargylii; Lucius Stertinius, to Hephæstia, Thassus, and the cities of Thrace; Publius Villius and Lucius Terentius, to King Antiochus; and Cneius Cornelius to Philip. The last of these, after executing his commission with respect to smaller matters, asked Philip, whether he was disposed to listen to advice not only useful but highly salutary. To which the king answered that he was, and would give him thanks besides, if he mentioned any thing conducive to his advantage. He then earnestly recommended to him, since he had obtained peace with the Romans, to send ambassadors to Rome to solicit their alliance and friendship; lest, in case of Antiochus pursuing any hostile measures, he might be suspected of lying in wait, and watching the opportunity of the times for reviving hostilities. This meeting with Philip was at Tempe in Thessaly; and on his answering that he would send ambassadors without delay, Cornelius proceeded to Thermopylæ, where all the states of Greece are accustomed to meet in general assembly on certain stated days. This is called the Pylaic assembly. Here he admonished the Ætolians, in particular, constantly and firmly to maintain the friendship established between them and the Romans; but some of the principal of these interrupted him with complaints, that the disposition of the Romans towards their nation was not the same since the victory, that it had been during the war; while others censured them with greater boldness, and in a reproachful manner asserted, that "without the aid of the Ætolians, the Romans could neither have conquered Philip, nor even have made good their passage into Greece." To such discourses the Roman forebore giving an answer, lest the matter might end in an altercation, and only said, that if they sent ambassadors to Rome, every thing that was reasonable would be granted to them. Accordingly, they passed a decree for such mission, agreeable to his direction.—In this manner was the war with Philip concluded.

36. While these transactions passed in Greece, Macedonia, and Asia, Etruria was near being converted into a scene of hostilities by a conspiracy among the slaves. To examine into and suppress this, Manius Acilius the pretor, whose province was the administration of justice between natives and foreigners, was sent at the head of one of the two city legions. A number of them, who were by this time formed in a body, he reduced by force of arms, killing and taking many. Some, who had been the ringleaders of the conspiracy, he scourged with rods, and then crucified; some he returned to their masters. The consuls repaired to their provinces. Just as Marcellus entered the frontiers of

the Boians, and while his men were fatigued with marching the whole length of the day, and as he was pitching his camp on a rising ground, Corolam, a chieftain of the Boians, attacked him with a very numerous force, and slew three thousand of his men; several persons of distinction fell in that tumultuary engagement: among others, Tiberius Sempronius Gracchus and Marcus Junius Silanus, prefects of the allies; and Aulus Ogulnius and Publius Claudius, military tribunes in the second legion. The Romans, notwithstanding, had courage enough to finish the fortification of their camp, and to defend it, in spite of an assault made on it by the enemy, after their success in the field. Marcellus remained for some time in the same post, until the wounded were cured, and the spirits of his men revived, after such a disheartening blow. The Boians, a nation remarkably impatient of delay, and quickly disgusted at a state of inaction, separated, and withdrew to their several forts and villages. Marcellus then, suddenly crossing the Po, led his legions into the territory of Comum, where the Insubrians, after rousing the people of the country to arms, lay encamped. They attacked him on his march, and their first onset was so vigorous, as to make a considerable impression on his van. On perceiving which, and fearing lest, if his men should once give ground, they would be obliged to quit the field, he brought up a cohort of Marsians against the enemy, and ordered every troop of the Latine cavalry to charge them. The first and second charges of these having checked the fierceness of the assault, the other troops in the Roman line, resuming courage, advanced briskly on the foe. The Gauls no longer maintained the contest, but turned their backs and fled in confusion. Valerius Antias relates, that in that battle above forty thousand men were killed, five hundred and seven military standards taken, with four hundred and thirty-two chariots, and a great number of gold chains, one of which, of great weight, Claudius says, was deposited as an offering to Jupiter, in his temple in the capitol. The camp of the Gauls was taken and plundered the same day; and the town of Comum was reduced in a few days after. In a little time, twenty-eight forts came over to the consul. There is a doubt among writers whether the consul led his legions, first against the Boians, or against the Insubrians; so as to determine, whether the victory obtained at Comum obliterated the disgrace of the defeat by the Boians, or if that obliterated the honour arising from the present success.

37. Soon after those matters had passed with such variety of fortune, Lucius Furius Purpureo, the other consul, came into the country of the Boians, through the Sappinian tribe. He proceeded almost to the fort of Mutilus, when, beginning

to apprehend that he might be enclosed between the Boians and Ligurians, he marched back by the road he came; and, making a long circuit, through an open and safe country, arrived at the camp of his colleague. After this junction of their forces they overran the territory of the Boians, spreading devastation as far as the city of Felsina. This city, with the other fortresses, and almost all the Boians, excepting only the young men who kept arms in their hands for the sake of plunder, and were at that time skulking in remote woods, made submission. The army was then led away against the Ligurians. The Boians thought that the Romans, as supposing them at a great distance, would be the more careless in guarding their rear, and thereby afford an opportunity of attacking them unawares: with this expectation they followed them by secret paths through the forests. They did not overtake them; and therefore, passing the Po suddenly in ships, they ravaged all the country of the Lævans and Libuans; whence, as they were returning with the spoil of the country, they fell in with the Roman army on the borders of Liguria. A battle was begun with more speed, and with greater fury, than if the parties had met with their minds prepared, and at an appointed time and place. This occurrence showed to what degree of violence anger can stimulate men; for the Romans were so intent on slaughter, that they scarcely left one of the enemy to carry the news of their defeat. On account of these successes, when the letters of the consuls were brought to Rome, a supplication for three days was decreed. Soon after Marcellus came to Rome, and had a triumph decreed him by a unanimous vote of the senate. He triumphed, while in office, over the Insubrians and Comans. The claim of a triumph over the Boians he left to his colleague, because his own arms had been unfortunate in that country; those of his colleague successful. Large quantities of spoils, taken from the enemy, were carried in the procession in captured chariots, and many military standards; also three hundred and twenty thousand asses of brass,* two hundred and thirty-four thousand of silver denariuses,† stamped with a chariot. Eighty asses‡ were bestowed on each foot soldier, and thrice that value on each horseman and centurion.

38. During that year King Antiochus, after having spent the winter at Ephesus, took measures for reducing under his dominion all the cities of Asia which had formerly been members of the empire. As to the rest, being either situated in plains, or having neither walls, arms, nor men, in whom they could confide, he supposed they would without

* 1,033l. 6s. 8d. † 2,331l. 2s. 6d. ‡ 5s. 2 1-4d.

difficulty receive the yoke. But Smyrna and Lampsacus openly asserted their independence; yet, if he complied with the claims of these, whom he feared, there would be reason to apprehend that the rest of the cities in Ætolia and Ionia would follow the example of Smyrna, and those on the Hellespont that of Lampsacus. Wherefore he sent an army from Ephesus to invest Smyrna; and ordered the troops, which were at Abydos, to leave there only a small garrison, and to go and lay siege to Lampsacus. Nor was force the only means that he used to bring them to submission. By sending ambassadors to make gentle remonstrances and reprove the rashness and obstinacy of their conduct, he endeavoured to give them hopes that they might soon obtain the object of their wishes; but not until it should appear clearly, both to themselves and to all the world, that they had gained their liberty through the kindness of the king, and not by any violent efforts of their own. In answer to which they said, that "Antiochus ought neither to be surprised nor displeased if they did not very patiently suffer the establishment of their liberty to be deferred to a distant period." He himself, with his fleet, set sail from Ephesus in the beginning of spring, and steered towards the Hellespont. His army he transported to Madytus, a city in the Chersonese, and there joined his land and sea forces together. The inhabitants having shut their gates, he invested the town; and, when he was just bringing up his machines to the walls, it capitulated. This diffused such fear through the inhabitants of the other cities of the Chersonese, as induced them to submit. He then came, with the whole of his united forces, to Lysimachia; which finding deserted, and almost buried in ruins, (for the Thracians had, a few years before, taken, sacked, and burned it,) he conceived a wish to rebuild a city so celebrated, and so commodiously situated. Accordingly, extending his care to every object at once, he set about repairing the walls and houses, ransomed some of the Lysimachians who were in captivity, sought out and brought home others, who had fled and dispersed themselves through the Chersonese and Hellespontus, enrolled new colonists, whom he invited by prospects of advantages, and used every means to repeople it fully. At the same time, to remove all fear of the Thracians, he went in person, with one half of the land forces, to lay waste the nearest provinces of Thrace; leaving the other half, and all the crews of the ships, employed in the repairs of the place.

39. About this time Lucius Cornelius, who had been commissioned by the senate to accommodate the differences between the kings Antiochus and Ptolemy, stopped at Selymbria; and of the ten ambassadors, Publius Lentulus from

Bargylii, and Publius Villius and Lucius Terentius from Thassus, came to Lysimachia. Hither came, likewise, Lucius Cornelius from Selymbria; and, a few days after, Antiochus, from Thrace. His first meeting with the ambassadors, and an invitation which he afterward gave them, were friendly and hospitable; but when the business of their embassy, and the present state of Asia, came to be treated of, the minds of both parties were exasperated. The Romans did not scruple to declare, that every one of his proceedings, from the time when he set sail from Syria, was displeasing to the senate; and they required restitution to be made to Ptolemy of all the cities which had been under his dominion. "For, as to what related to the cities which had been in the possession of Philip, and which Antiochus, taking advantage of a season when Philip's attention was turned to the war with Rome, had seized into his own hands, it would surely be an intolerable hardship, if the Romans were to have undergone such toils and dangers, on land and sea, for so many years, and Antiochus to appropriate to himself the prizes in dispute. But though his coming into Asia might be passed over unnoticed by the Romans, as a matter not pertaining to them, yet when he proceeded so far as to pass over into Europe with all his land and naval forces, how much was this short of open war with the Romans? Doubtless, had he even passed into Italy, he would deny that intention."

40. To this the king replied, that "for some time past he plainly perceived that the Romans made it their business to inquire into what ought to be done by King Antiochus; but how far they themselves ought to advance on land or sea they never considered. Asia was no concernment of the Romans, in any shape; nor had they any more right to inquire what Antiochus did in Asia, than Antiochus had to inquire what the Roman people did in Italy. With respect to Ptolemy, from whom, they said, cities had been taken, there was a friendly connexion subsisting between him and Ptolemy, and he was taking measures to effect speedily a connexion of affinity also: neither had he sought to acquire any spoils from the misfortunes of Philip, nor had he come into Europe against the Romans, [but to recover the cities and lands of the Chersonese, which having been the property of Lysimachus,*] he considered as part of his own dominions; because, when Lysimachus was subdued, all things belonging to him became, by the right of conquest, the property of Seleucus. That, at times, when his predecessors were occupied by various cares of different kinds, Ptolemy first, and afterward Philip, usurping the rights of others, possessed

* Here is a chasm in the original, which is supplied from Polybius.

themselves of several of these places, as likewise of some of the nearest parts of Thrace, which were indubitably belonging to Lysimachus. To restore these to their ancient state was the intent of his coming, and to build Lysimachia anew, (it having been destroyed by an inroad of the Thracians,) in order that his son Seleucus might have it for the seat of his empire."

41. These disputes had been carried on for several days, when a rumour reached them, but without any authority, that Ptolemy was dead, which prevented the conferences coming to any issue; for both parties made a secret of their having heard it; and Lucius Cornelius, who was charged with the embassy to the two kings, Antiochus and Ptolemy, requested to be allowed a short space of time, in which he could have a meeting with the latter; because he wished to arrive in Egypt before any change of measures should take place in consequence of the new succession to the crown: while Antiochus believed, that if such an event had really happened, Egypt would be his own. Wherefore, having dismissed the Romans, and left his son Seleucus with the land forces, to finish the rebuilding of Lysimachia, he sailed with his whole fleet to Ephesus; sent ambassadors to Quintius to treat with him about an alliance, and then, coasting along the shore of Asia, proceeded to Lycia. Having learned at Pataræ that Ptolemy was living, he dropped the design of sailing to Egypt, but nevertheless steered towards Cyprus; and, when he had passed the promontory of Chelidonium, was detained some little time in Pamphylia, near the river Eurymedon, by a mutiny among his rowers. When he had sailed thence as far as the headlands, as they are called, of Sarus, such a dreadful storm arose as almost buried him and his whole fleet in the deep. Many ships were cast on shore; many swallowed so entirely in the sea that not one man of their crews escaped to land. Great numbers of his men perished on this occasion; not only persons of mean rank, rowers and soldiers; but even of his particular friends in high stations. When he had collected the relics of the general wreck, being in no capacity of making an attempt on Cyprus, he returned to Seleucia, with his force greatly diminished since his departure. Here he ordered the ships to be hauled ashore, for the winter was now at hand, and proceeded to Antioch, where he intended to pass the winter. In this posture stood the affairs of the kings.

42. At Rome, in this year, for the first time, were created offices called triumviri epulones:* these were Caius Lici-

* It was their office to regulate the feasts of the gods.

ains Lucullus, who, as tribune, had proposed the law for their creation, Publius Manlius, and Publius Porcius Læca. These triumvirs, as well as the pontiffs, were allowed by law the privilege of wearing the purple-bordered gown. The body of the pontiffs had this year a warm dispute with the city questors, Quintus Fabius Labeo and Lucius Aurelius. Money was wanted; an order having been passed for making the last payment to private persons of that which had been raised for the support of the war; and the questors demanded it from the augurs and pontiffs, because they had not contributed their share while the war subsisted. The priests in vain appealed to the tribunes, and the contribution was exacted for every year in which they had not paid. During the same year two pontiffs died, and others were substituted in their room: Marcus Marcellus, the consul, in the room of Caius Sempronius Tuditanus, who had been a pretor in Spain; and Lucius Valerius, in the room of Marcus Cornelius Cethegus. An augur also, Quintus Fabius Maximus, died very young, before he had attained to any public office; but no augur was appointed in his place during that year. The consular election was then held by the consul Marcellus. The persons chosen were Lucius Valerius Flaccus and Marcus Porcius Cato. Then were elected pretors, Caius Fabricius Luscinus, Caius Atinius Labeo, Cneius Manlius Vulso, Appius Claudius Nero, Publius Manlius, and Publius Porcius Læca. The curule ediles, Marcus Fulvius Nobilior and Caius Flaminius, made a distribution to the people of one million pecks of wheat, at the price of two asses. This corn the Sicilians had brought to Rome out of respect to Caius Flaminius and his father; and he gave a share of the credit to his colleague. The Roman games were solemnized with magnificence, and exhibited thrice entire. The plebeian ediles, Cneius Domitius Ænobarbus and Caius Scribonius, chief curio, brought many farmers of the public pastures to trial before the people. Three of these were convicted of misbehaviour; and out of the money accruing from fines imposed on them, they built a temple of Faunus in the island. The plebeian games were exhibited for two days, and there was a feast on occasion of the games.

43. Lucius Valerius Flaccus and Marcus Porcius, on the day of their entering into office, consulted the senate respecting the provinces; [A. U. C. 557. B. C. 195;] who resolved, that "whereas the war in Spain was grown so formidable as to require a consular army and commander, it was their opinion, therefore, that the consuls should either settle between themselves, or cast lots, for Hither Spain and Italy, as their provinces. That he to whom Spain fell should

carry with him two legions, five thousand of the Latine confederates, and five hundred horse; together with a fleet of twenty ships of war. That the other consul should raise two legions; for these would be sufficient to maintain tranquillity in the province of Gaul, as the spirits of the Insubrians and Boians had been broken the year before." The lots gave Spain to Cato, and Italy to Valerius. The pretors then cast lots for their provinces: to Caius Fabricius Luscinus fell the city jurisdiction; Caius Atinius Labeo obtained the foreign; Cneius Manlius Vulso, Sicily; Appius Claudius Nero, Farther Spain; Publius Porcius Læca, Pisa, in order that he might be at the back of the Ligurians; and Publius Manlius was sent into Hither Spain, as an assistant to the consul. Quintius was continued in command for the year, as apprehensions were entertained, not only of Antiochus and the Ætolians, but likewise of Nabis, tyrant of Lacedæmon; and it was ordered that he should have two legions, for which, if there was any deficiency in their numbers, the consuls were ordered to raise recruits, and send them into Macedonia. Appius Claudius was permitted to raise, in addition to the legion which Quintus Fabius had commanded, two thousand foot and two hundred horse. The like number of new-raised foot and horse was assigned to Publius Manlius for Hither Spain; and the legion was given to him which had been under the command of Minucius, pretor. To Publius Porcius Læca, for Etruria, near Pisa, were decreed two thousand foot and five hundred horse, out of the army in Gaul. Sempronius Longus was continued in command in Sardinia.

44. The provinces being thus distributed, the consuls, before their departure from the city, proclaimed a sacred spring; which Aulus Cornelius Mammula, pretor, had vowed, in pursuance of a vote of the senate and an order of the people, in the consulate of Cneius Servilius and Caius Flaminius. It was celebrated twenty-one years after the vow had been made. About the same time Caius Claudius Pulcher, son of Appius, was chosen and inaugurated into the office of augur, in the room of Quintus Fabius Maximus, who died the year before. While people in general wondered that so little notice was taken of Spain being in arms, a letter was brought from Quintus Minucius, announcing that "he had fought a pitched battle with the Spanish generals, Budar and Besasis, near the town of Tura, and had gained the victory: that twelve thousand of the enemy were slain; their general Budar taken; and the rest routed and dispersed." The reading of this letter allayed people's fears with respect to Spain, where a very formidable war had been apprehended. The whole anxiety of the public was

directed towards King Antiochus, especially after the arrival of the ten ambassadors. These, after relating the proceedings with Philip, and the conditions on which peace had been granted him, gave information that "there still subsisted a war of no less magnitude to be waged with Antiochus; that he had come over into Europe with a very numerous fleet and a powerful army; that, had not a delusive prospect of an opportunity of invading Egypt, raised by a more delusive rumour, diverted him to another quarter, all Greece would have quickly been involved in the flames of war. Nor would even the Ætolians remain quiet, a race by nature restless, and at that time full of anger against the Romans. That, besides, there was another evil, of a most dangerous nature, lurking in the bowels of Greece,—Nabis, tyrant at present of Lacedæmon, but who would soon, if suffered, become tyrant of all Greece, equalling in avarice and cruelty all the tyrants most remarkable in history: for, if he were allowed to keep possession of Argos, which served as a citadel to awe the Peloponnesus, when the Roman armies should be brought home to Italy, Greece would reap no advantage from being delivered out of bondage to Philip; because, instead of that king, who, supposing no other difference, resided at a distance, she would have for a master a tyrant, close to her side."

45. On this intelligence being received from men of such respectable authority, and who had, besides, examined into all the matters which were reported, the senate, although they deemed the business relating to Antiochus the more important, yet, as the king had for some reason or other gone home into Syria, they thought that the affair respecting the tyrant required more immediate consideration. After debating for a long time whether they should judge the grounds which they had at present sufficient whereon to found a decree for a declaration of war, or whether they should empower Titus Quintius to act in the case respecting Nabis the Lacedæmonian, in such manner as he should judge conducive to the public interest; they at length invested him with full powers: for they thought the business of such a nature, that whether expedited or delayed, it could not very materially affect the general interest of the Roman people. It was deemed more important to endeavour to discover what line of conduct Hannibal and the Carthaginians would pursue in case of a war breaking out with Antiochus. Persons of the faction which opposed Hannibal wrote continually to their several friends, among the principal men in Rome, that "messages and letters were sent by Hannibal to Antiochus, and that envoys came secretly from the king to him. That, as some wild beasts can never be tamed, so the Car-

thaginian's temper was irreclaimable and implacable. That he sometimes complained that the state was debilitated by ease and indolence, and lulled by sloth into a lethargy, from which nothing could rouse it but the sound of arms." These accounts were deemed probable, when people recollected the former war being not only continued, but first set on foot by the efforts of that single man. Besides, he had by a recent act provoked the resentment of many men in power.

46. The order of judges possessed at that time absolute power in Carthage; and this was owing chiefly to their holding the office during life. The property, character, and life of every man was in their disposal. He who incurred the displeasure of one of that order found an enemy in all of them; nor were accusers wanting in a court where the justices were disposed to condemn. While they were in possession of this despotism, (for they did not exercise their exorbitant power with due regard to the rights of others,) Hannibal was elected pretor; and he summoned the questor before him. The questor disregarded the summons, for he was of the opposite faction; and besides, as the practice was, that, after the questorship men were advanced into the order of judges, the most powerful of all, he already assumed a spirit suited to the authority which he was shortly to obtain. Hannibal, highly offended hereat, sent an officer to apprehend the questor; and, bringing him forth into an assembly of the people, he made heavy charges not against him alone, but on the whole order of judges; who, in the fulness of their arrogance and power, set at naught both the magistracy and the laws. Then, perceiving that his discourse was favourably attended to, and that the conduct of those men was offensive to the interest and freedom of the lowest classes, he proposed a law, and procured it to be enacted, that the "judges should be elected annually; and that no person should hold the office two years successively." But, whatever degree of favour he acquired among the commons by this proceeding, he roused in a great part of the nobility an equal degree of resentment. This was followed by another act, by which, while he served the people, he provoked personal enmity against himself. The public revenues were partly wasted through neglect, partly embezzled, and divided among some leading men and magistrates; insomuch, that there was not money sufficient for the regular annual payment of the tribute to the Romans, so that private persons seemed to be threatened with a heavy tax.

47. When Hannibal had informed himself of the amount of the revenues arising from taxes and port duties, for what purposes they were issued from the treasury, how much was

consumed by the ordinary expenses of the state, and how much lost by embezzlement, he asserted in an assembly of the people, that if payment were enforced of the money unapplied to public uses, the taxes might be remitted to the subjects; and that the state would still be rich enough to pay the tribute to the Romans: which assertion he proved to be true. But now those persons who for several years past had maintained themselves by plundering the public were greatly enraged; as if this were ravishing from them their own property, and not as dragging out of their hands their ill-gotten spoil. Accordingly they laboured to draw down on Hannibal the vengeance of the Romans, who were seeking a pretext for indulging their hatred against him. A strenuous opposition was however for a long time made to this by Scipio Africanus, who thought it highly unbecoming the dignity of the Roman people to make themselves a party in the animosities and charges against Hannibal; to interpose the public authority among factions of the Carthaginians, not remaining content with having conquered that commander in the field, but to become as it were his prosecutors in a judicial process, and preferring an action against him. Yet at length the point was carried that an embassy should be sent to Carthage, to represent to the senate there, that Hannibal, in concert with King Antiochus, was forming plans for kindling a war. Three ambassadors were sent, Caius Servilius, Marcus Claudius Marcellus, and Quintus Terentius Culleo. These, on their arrival, by the advice of Hannibal's enemies, ordered that any who inquired the cause of their coming should be told that they came to determine the disputes subsisting between the Carthaginians and Masinissa, king of Numidia; and this was generally believed. But Hannibal was not ignorant that he was the sole object aimed at by the Romans; and that, though they had granted peace to the Carthaginians, their war against him, individually, would ever subsist with unabated rancour. He therefore determined to give way to fortune and the times; and having already made every preparation for flight, he showed himself that day in the forum, in order to guard against suspicion; and, as soon as it grew dark, went in his common dress to one of the gates, with two attendants, who knew nothing of his intention.

48. Finding horses in readiness at a spot where he had ordered, he made a hasty journey by night through a district of the territory of Voca, and arrived in the morning of the following day at a castle of his own between Acholla and Thapsus. There a ship, ready fitted out and furnished with rowers, took him on board. In this manner did Hannibal leave Africa, lamenting the misfortunes of his country oft-

ener than his own. He sailed over the same day to the island of Cercina, where he found in the port a number of merchant ships with their cargoes; and on landing was surrounded by a concourse of people, who came to pay their respects to him; on which he gave orders that, in answer to any inquiries, it should be said that he was going ambassador to Tyre. Fearing, however, lest some of these ships might sail in the night to Thapsus or Acholla, and carry information of his being seen at Cercina, he ordered a sacrifice to be prepared, and the masters of the ships, with the merchants, to be invited to the entertainment, and that the sails and yards should be collected out of the ships to form a shade on shore for the company at supper, as it happened to be the middle of summer. The feast of the day was as sumptuous, and the guests as numerous, as the time and circumstances allowed; and the entertainment was prolonged, with plenty of wine, until late in the night. As soon as Hannibal saw an opportunity of escaping the notice of those who were in the harbour, he set sail. The rest were fast asleep, nor was it early, next day, when they arose, heavily sick from the preceding day's excess; and then, when it was too late, they set about replacing the sails in the ships, and fitting up the rigging, which employed several hours. At Carthage, those who were accustomed to visit Hannibal met in a crowd, at the porch of his house; and when it was publicly known that he was not to be found, the whole multitude assembled in the forum, eager to gain intelligence of the man who was considered as the first in the state. Some surmised that he had fled, as the case was; others, that he had been put to death through the treachery of the Romans; and there was visible in the expression of their countenances that variety which might naturally be expected in a state divided into factions, whereof each supported a different interest. At length an account was brought that he had been seen at Cercina.

49. The Roman ambassadors represented to the council, that "proof had been laid before the senate of Rome, that formerly King Philip had been moved, principally by the instigation of Hannibal, to make war on the Roman people; and that lately Hannibal had, besides, sent letters and messages to King Antiochus. That he was a man who would never be content until he had excited war in every part of the globe. That such conduct ought not to be suffered to pass with impunity, if the Carthaginians wished to convince the Roman people that none of those things were done with their consent, or with the approbation of the state." The Carthaginians answered that they were ready to do whatever the Romans required of them.

Hannibal, after a prosperous voyage, arrived at Tyre; where, in consideration of his illustrious character, he was received by those founders of Carthage with every demonstration of respect, as if he were a native of the country; and here he stayed a few days. He then sailed to Antioch; where, hearing that the king had already left the place, he procured an interview with his son, who was celebrating the anniversary games at Daphne, and who treated him with much kindness; after which he set sail without delay. At Ephesus he overtook the king, whose judgment was still wavering and undetermined respecting a war with Rome: but the arrival of Hannibal proved an incentive of no small efficacy to the prosecution of that design. At the same time, the inclinations of the Ætolians also became unfavourable to the continuance of their alliance with Rome, in consequence of the senate having referred to Quintius their ambassadors, who demanded Pharsalus and Leucas, and some other cities, in conformity to the first treaty.

---

## BOOK XXXIV.

Chap. 1. Amid the serious concerns of so many important wars, some scarcely ended, and others impending, an incident intervened, which may seem too trivial to be mentioned; but which, through the zeal of the parties concerned, occasioned a violent contest. Marcus Fundanius and Lucius Valerius, plebeian tribunes, proposed to the people the repealing of the Oppian law. This law, which had been introduced by Caius Oppius, plebeian tribune, in the consulate of Quintus Fabius and Tiberius Sempronius, during the heat of the Punic war, enacted, that "no woman should possess more than half an ounce of gold, or wear a garment of various colours, or ride in a carriage drawn by horses, in a city, or any town, or any place nearer thereto than one mile; except on occasion of some public religious solemnity." Marcus and Publius Junius Brutus, plebeian tribunes, supported the Oppian law, and declared that they would never suffer it to be repealed; while many of the nobility stood forth to argue for and against the motion proposed. The capitol was filled with crowds who favoured or opposed the law; nor could the matrons be kept at home, either by advice or shame, nor even by the commands of their husbands; but beset every street and pass in the city, beseeching the men, as they went down to the forum, that in the present flourishing state of the commonwealth, when the public prosperity was daily increasing, they would suffer the women so far to partake of it, as to have their former ornaments of dress restored. This throng of women increased daily, for they arrived even from the country towns and villages; and had at length the boldness to come up to the consuls, pretors, and other magistrates, to urge their request. One of the consuls, however, they found inexorable —Marcus Porcius Cato, who, in support of the law proposed to be repealed, spoke to this effect:—

2. "If, Romans, every individual among us had made it a rule to maintain the prerogative and authority of a husband with respect to his own wife, we should have less trouble with the whole sex. But now, our privileges, overpowered at home by female contumacy, are, even here in the forum, spurned and trodden under foot; and because we are unable to withstand each separately, we now dread their collective body. I was accustomed to think it a fabulous and fictitious tale, that, in a certain island, the whole race of males was utterly extirpated by a conspiracy of the women. But the utmost danger may be apprehended equally from either sex, if you suffer cabals and secret consultations to be held: scarcely indeed can I determine, in my own mind, whether the act itself, or the precedent that it affords, is of more pernicious tendency. The latter of these more particularly concerns us consuls, and the other magistrates; the former, you, my fellow-citizens: for, whether the measure proposed to your consideration be profitable to the state or not, is to be determined by you, who are to vote on the occasion. As to the outrageous behaviour of these women, whether it be merely an act of their own, or owing to your instigations, Marcus Fundanius and Lucius Valerius, it unquestionably implies culpable conduct in magistrates. I know not whether it reflects greater disgrace on you, tribunes, or on the consuls: on you certainly, if you have brought these women hither for the purpose of raising tribunitian seditions; on us, if we suffer laws to be imposed on us by a secession of women, as was done formerly by that of the common people. It was not without painful emotions of shame, that I, just now, made my way into the forum through the midst of a band of women. Had I not been restrained by respect for the modesty and dignity of some individuals among them, rather than of the whole number, and been unwilling that they should be seen rebuked by a consul, I should not have refrained from saying to them, 'What sort of practice is this, of running out into public, besetting the streets, and addressing other women's husbands? Could not each have made the same request to her husband at home?

Are your blandishments more seducing in public than in private, and with other women's husbands than with your own? Although if females would let their modesty confine them within the limits of their own rights, it did not become you, even at home, to concern yourselves about any laws that might be passed or repealed here.' Our ancestors thought it not proper that women should perform any, even private business, without a director; but that they should be ever under the control of parents, brothers, or husbands. We, it seems, suffer them, now, to interfere in the management of state affairs, and to thrust themselves into the forum, into general assemblies, and into assemblies of election: for, what are they doing at this moment in your streets and lanes? What, but arguing, some in support of the motion of tribunes; others contending for the repeal of the law? Will you give the reins to their intractable nature, and then expect that themselves should set bounds to their licentiousness, and without your interference? This is the smallest of the injunctions laid on them by usage or the laws, all which women bear with impatience: they long for entire liberty; nay, to speak the truth, not for liberty, but for unbounded freedom in every particular: for what will they not attempt, if they now come off victorious? Recollect all the institutions respecting the sex, by which our forefathers restrained their profligacy, and subjected them to their husbands; and yet, even with the help of all these restrictions, they can scarcely be kept within bounds. If, then, you suffer them to throw these off one by one, to tear them all asunder, and, at last, to be set on an equal footing with yourselves, can you imagine that they will be any longer tolerable? Suffer them once to arrive at an equality with you, and they will from that moment become your superiors.

3. "But, indeed, they only object to any new law being made against them; they mean to deprecate, not justice, but severity. Nay, their wish is, that a law which you have admitted, established by your suffrages, and found in the practice and experience of so many years to be beneficial, should now be repealed; and that by abolishing one law, you should weaken all the rest. No law perfectly suits the convenience of every member of the community; the only consideration is, whether, on the whole, it be profitable to the greater part. If, because a law proves obnoxious to a private individual, it must therefore be cancelled and annulled, to what purpose is it for the community to enact laws, which those, whom they were particularly intended to comprehend, could presently repeal? Let us, however, inquire what this important affair is which has induced the matrons thus to run out into public in this indecorous

manner, scarcely restraining from pushing into the forum and the assembly of the people. Is it to solicit that their parents, their husbands, children, and brothers may be ransomed from captivity under Hannibal? By no means: and far be ever from the commonwealth so unfortunate a situation. Yet, when such was the case, you refused this to the prayers which, on that occasion, their duty dictated. But it is not duty, nor solicitude for their friends; it is religion that has collected them together. They are about to receive the Idæan Mother, coming out of Phrygia from Pessinus. What motive, that even common decency will not allow to be mentioned, is pretended for this female insurrection? Hear the answer: That we may shine in gold and purple; that, both on festival and common days, we may ride through the city in our chariots, triumphing over vanquished and abrogated law, after having captured and wrested from you your suffrages; and that there may be no bounds to our expenses and our luxury. Often have you heard me complain of the profuse expenses of the women—often of those of the men; and that not only of men in private stations, but of the magistrates; and that the state was endangered by two opposite vices, luxury and avarice; those pests which have ever been the ruin of every great state. These I dread the more, as the circumstances of the commonwealth grow daily more prosperous and happy; as the empire increases; as we have passed over into Greece and Asia, places abounding with every kind of temptation that can inflame the passions; and as we have begun to handle even royal treasures: for I greatly fear that these matters will rather bring us into captivity, than we them. Believe me, those statues from Syracuse made their way into this city with hostile effect. I already hear too many commending and admiring the decorations of Athens and Corinth, and ridiculing the earthen images of our Roman gods that stand on the fronts of their temples. For my part, I prefer these gods,—propitious as they are, and I hope will continue, if we allow them to remain in their own mansions. In the memory of our fathers, Pyrrhus, by his ambassador Cineas, made trial of the dispositions, not only of our men, but of our women also, by offers of presents: at that time the Oppian law, for restraining female luxury, had not been made; and yet not one woman accepted a present. What, think you, was the reason? That for which our ancestors made no provision by law on this subject: there was no luxury existing which might be restrained. As diseases must necessarily be known before their remedies, so passions come into being before the laws which prescribe limits to them. What called forth the Licinian law, restricting estates to five hundred acres, but the unbounded desire for enlarging estates? What the Cincian law, concerning gifts and presents, but that the plebeians had become vassals and tributaries to the senate?* It is not, therefore, in any degree surprising that no want of the Oppian law, or of any other, to limit the expenses of the women, was felt at that time, when they refused to receive gold and purple that was thrown in their way, and offered to their acceptance. If Cineas were now to go round the city with his presents, he would find numbers of women standing in the public streets ready to receive them.

4. "There are some passions, the causes or motives of which I can no way account for. To be debarred of a liberty in which another is indulged, may perhaps naturally excite some degree of shame or indignation; yet, when the dress of all is alike, what inferiority in appearance can any one be ashamed of? Of all kinds of shame, the worst, surely, is the being ashamed of frugality or of poverty; but the law relieves you with regard to both; you want only that which it is unlawful for you to have. This equalization, says the rich matron, is the very thing that I cannot endure. Why do not I make a figure, distinguished with gold and purple? Why is the poverty of others concealed under this cover of a law, so that it should be thought that, if the law permitted, they would have such things as they are not now able to procure? Romans, do you wish to excite among your wives an emulation of this sort, that the rich should wish to have what no other can have; and that the poor, lest they should be despised as such, should extend their expenses beyond their abilities? Be assured that when a woman once begins to be ashamed of what she ought not to be ashamed of, she will not be ashamed of what she ought. She who can, will purchase out of her own purse; she who cannot, will ask her husband. Unhappy is the husband, both he who complies with the request, and he who does not; for what he will not give himself, another will. Now, they openly solicit favours from other women's husbands; and, what is more, solicit a law, and votes. From some they obtain them; although, with regard to you, your property, or your children, you would find it hard to obtain any thing from them. If the law ceases to limit the expenses of your wife, you yourself will never be able to limit them. Do not suppose that the matter will hereafter be in the same state in which it was before the law was made on the subject. It is

* Previous to the passing of the Cincian law, about ten years before this time, the advocates who pleaded in the courts received fees and presents; and as all or most of these were senators, the plebeians are here represented as tributary to the senate. By the above law they were forbidden to receive either fees or presents.

safer that a wicked man should never be accused, than that he should be acquitted; and luxury, if it had never been meddled with, would be more tolerable than it will be, now, like a wild beast, irritated by having been chained, and then let loose. My opinion is, that the Oppian law ought on no account to be repealed. Whatever determination you may come to, I pray all the gods to prosper it."

5. After him the plebeian tribunes, who had declared their intention of protesting, added a few words to the same purport. Then Lucius Valerius, who made the motion, spoke thus in support of it: "If private persons only had stood forth to argue for and against the proposition which we have submitted to your consideration, I for my part, thinking enough to have been said on both sides, would have waited in silence for your determination: but since a person of most respectable judgment, the consul, Marcus Porcius, has reprobated our motion, not only by the influence of his opinion, which, had he said nothing, would carry very great weight, but also in a long and laboured discourse, it becomes necessary to say a few words in answer. He has spent more words in rebuking the matrons than in arguing against the measure proposed; and even went so far as to mention a doubt, whether the conduct which he censured in them arose from themselves, or from our instigation. I shall defend the measure, not ourselves: for the consul threw out those insinuations against us, rather for argument's sake, than as a serious charge. He has made use of the terms cabal and sedition; and, sometimes, secession of the women: because the matrons had requested of you, in the public streets, that in this time of peace, when the commonwealth is flourishing and happy, you would repeal a law that was made against them during a war, and in times of distress. I know that to declaim is an easy task; that strong expressions, for the sake of exaggeration, are easily found; and that, mild as Marcus Cato is in his disposition, and gentle in his manners, yet in his speeches he is not only vehement, but sometimes even austere. What new thing, let me ask, have the matrons done in coming out into public in a body? Have they never before appeared in public? I will turn over your own Antiquities,* and quote them against you. Hear now, how often they have done the same, always to the advantage of the public. In the earliest period of our history, even in the reign of Romulus, when the capitol had been taken by the Sabines, and a pitched battle was fought in the forum, was not the fight stopped by the matrons run-

* Alluding to a treatise by Cato, on the antiquities of Italy, entitled Origines, which is the word used here by Valerius.

ning in between the two armies? When, after the expulsion of the kings, the legions of the Volscians, under the command of Marcius Coriolanus, were encamped at the fifth stone, did not the matrons turn away that army, which would have overwhelmed this city? Again, when the city was taken by the Gauls, whence was the gold procured for the ransom of it? Did not the matrons, by unanimous agreement, bring it into the public treasury? In the late war, not to go back to remote antiquity, when there was a want of money, did not the widows supply the treasury? And when new gods were invited hither to the relief of our distressed affairs, did not the matrons go out in a body to the sea-shore to receive the Idæan Mother? 'The cases,' he says, 'are dissimilar.' It is not my purpose to produce similar instances; it is sufficient that I clear these women of having done any thing new. Now, what nobody wondered at their doing, in cases which concerned all in common, both men and women, can we wonder at their doing, in a case peculiarly affecting themselves? But what have they done? We have proud ears, truly, if, though masters disdain not the prayers of slaves, we are offended at being asked a favour by honourable women.

6. "I come now to the question in debate, with respect to which the consul's argument is twofold: for first he is displeased at the thought of any law whatever being repealed; and then, particularly, of that law which was made to restrain female luxury. His mode of arguing, on the former head, in support of the laws in general, appeared highly becoming of a consul; and that, on the latter, against luxury, was quite conformable to the rigid strictness of his morals. Unless, therefore, I shall be able to point out to you which of his arguments, on both heads, are destitute of foundation, you may probably be led away by error. For while I acknowledge, that of those laws which are instituted, not for any particular time, but for eternity, on account of their perpetual utility, not one ought to be repealed; unless either experience evince it to be useless, or some state of the public affairs render it such; I see, at the same time, that those laws which particular seasons have required, are mortal, (if I may use the term,) and changeable with the times. Those made in peace are generally repealed by war; those made in war, by peace; as in the management of a ship, some implements are useful in good weather, others in bad. As these two kinds are thus distinct in their nature, of which kind, do you think, is that law which we now propose to repeal? Is it an ancient law of the kings, coeval with the city itself? Or, what is next to that, was it written in the twelve tables by the decemvirs appointed to form a code of laws?

Is it one, without which our ancestors thought that the honour of the female sex could not be preserved; and, therefore, we also have reason to fear that, together with it, we should repeal the modesty and chastity of our females? Now, is there a man among you who does not know that this is a new law, passed not more than twenty years ago, in the consulate of Quintus Fabius and Tiberius Sempronius? And as, without it, our matrons sustained for such a number of years the most virtuous characters, what danger is there of their abandoning themselves to luxury on its being repealed? For, if the design of passing that law was to check the passions of the sex, there would be reason to fear lest the repeal of it might operate as an incitement to them. But the real reason of its being passed, the time itself will show. Hannibal was then in Italy, victorious at Cannæ, possessed of Tarentum, of Arpi, of Capua, and seemed ready to bring up his army to the city of Rome. Our allies had deserted us. We had neither soldiers to fill up the legions, nor seamen to man the fleet, nor money in the treasury. Slaves, who were to be employed as soldiers, were purchased on condition of their price being paid to the owners at the end of the war. The farmers of the revenues declared that they would contract to supply corn and other matters, which the exigences of the war required, to be paid for at the same time. We gave up our slaves to the oar, in numbers proportioned to our properties, and paid them out of our own pockets. All our gold and silver, in imitation of the example given by the senators, we dedicated to the use of the public. Widows and minors lodged their money in the treasury. We were prohibited from keeping in our houses more than a certain quantity of wrought gold or silver, or more than a certain sum of coined silver or brass. At such a time as this were the matrons so eagerly engaged in luxury and dress, that the Oppian law was requisite to repress such practices? When the senate, because the sacrifice of Ceres had been omitted, in consequence of all the matrons being in mourning, ordered the mourning to end in thirty days. Who does not clearly see that the poverty and distress of the state requiring that every private person's money should be converted to the use of the public, enacted that law, with intent that it should remain in force so long only as the cause of enacting it should remain? For if all the decrees of the senate and orders of the people, which were then made to answer the necessities of the times, are to be of perpetual obligation, why do we refund their money to private persons? Why do we pay ready money to contractors for public services? Why are not slaves brought to serve in the army? Why do we not, private subjects, supply rowers as we did then?

7. "Shall, then, every other class of people, every individual, feel the improvement in the state, and shall our wives alone reap none of the fruits of the public peace and tranquillity? Shall we men have the use of purple, wearing the purple-bordered gown in magistracies and priests' offices? Shall our children wear gowns bordered with purple? Shall we allow the privilege of such a dress to the magistrates of the colonies and borough towns, and to the very lowest of them here at Rome, the superintendents of the streets; and not only of wearing such an ornament of distinction while alive, but of being buried with it when dead; and shall we interdict the use of purple to women alone? And when you, the husband, may wear purple in your great coat, will you not suffer your wife to have a purple cloak? Shall the furniture of your house be finer than your wife's clothes? But with respect to purple, which will be worn out and consumed, I can see an unjust, indeed, but still sort of reason, for parsimony: but with respect to gold, in which, excepting the price of the workmanship, there is no waste, what motive can there be for denying it to them? It rather serves as a useful fund for both public and private exigences, as you have already experienced. He says there will be no emulation between individuals when no one is possessed of it. But, in truth, it will be a source of grief and indignation to all, when they see those ornaments allowed to the wives of the Latine confederates which have been forbidden to themselves; when they see those riding through the city in their carriages, and decorated with gold and purple, while they are obliged to follow on foot, as if empire were seated in the country of the others, not in their own. This would hurt the feelings even of men, and what do you think must be its effect on those of weak women, whom even trifles can disturb? Neither offices of state, nor of the priesthood, nor triumphs, nor badges of distinction, nor military presents, nor spoils, can fall to their share. Elegance of appearance, and ornaments, and dress, these are the women's badges of distinction; in these they delight and glory; these our ancestors called the women's world. What other change in their apparel do they make, when in mourning, except the laying aside their gold and purple? And what, when the mourning is over, except resuming them? How do they distinguish themselves on occasion of public thanksgivings and supplications, but by adding unusual splendour to their dress? But then, if you repeal the Oppian law, should you choose to prohibit any of those particulars which the law at present prohibits, you will not have it in your

power; your daughters, wives, and even the sisters of some, will be less under your control. The bondage of women is never shaken off without the loss of their friends; and they themselves look with horror on that freedom which is purchased with the loss of a husband or parent. Their wish is, that their dress should be under your regulation, not under that of the law; and it ought to be your wish to hold them in control and guardianship, not in bondage; and to prefer the title of father or husband to that of master. The consul just now made use of some invidious terms, calling it a female sedition and secession; because, I suppose, there is danger of their seizing the sacred mount, as formerly the angry plebeians did; or the Aventine. Their feeble nature must submit to whatever you think proper to enjoin; and, the greater power you possess, the more moderate ought you to be in the exercise of your authority."

8. Notwithstanding all these arguments against the motion, the women next day poured out into the public in much greater numbers, and in a body beset the doors of the protesting tribunes; nor did they retire until the tribunes withdrew their protest. There was then no farther demur, but every one of the tribes voted for the repeal. Thus was this law annulled, in the twentieth year after it had been made. The consul Marcus Porcius, as soon as the business of the Oppian law was over, sailed immediately with twenty-five ships of war, of which five belonged to the allies, to the port of Luna, where he ordered the troops to assemble; and having sent an edict along the sea-coast, to collect ships of every description at his departure from Luna, he left orders that they should follow him to the harbour of Pyrenæus, as he intended to proceed thence against the enemy with all the force that he could muster. They accordingly, after sailing by the Ligurian mountains and the Gallic bay, joined him there on the day appointed. From thence they went to Rhoda, and dislodged a garrison of Spaniards that were in that fortress. From Rhoda they proceeded with a favourable wind to Emporiæ, and there landed all the forces, excepting the crews of the ships.

9. At that time, as at present, Emporiæ consisted of two towns, separated by a wall. One was inhabited by Greeks from Phocæa, whence the Massilians also derive their origin; the other by Spaniards. The Greek town being open towards the sea, had but a small extent of wall, not above four hundred paces in circuit; but the Spanish town, being farther back from the sea, had a wall three thousand paces in circumference. A third kind of inhabitants was added by the deified Cæsar settling a Roman colony there, after the final defeat of the sons of Pompey. At present they are

all incorporated in one mass; the Spaniards first, and at length the Greeks, having been admitted to the privilege of Roman citizens. Whoever had, at that period, observed the Greeks exposed on one side to the open sea, and on the other to the Spaniards, a fierce and warlike race, would have wondered by what cause they were preserved. Deficient in strength, they guarded against danger by regular discipline; of which, among even more powerful people, the best preservative is fear. That part of the wall which faced the country they kept strongly fortified, having but one gate, at which some of the magistrates were continually on guard. During the night a third part of the citizens kept watch on the walls, posting their watches, and going their rounds, not merely from the force of custom, or in compliance with the law, but with as much vigilance as if an enemy were at their gates. They never admitted any Spaniard into the city, nor did they go outside the walls without precaution. The passage to the sea was open to every one; but, through the gate next to the Spanish town none ever passed, but in a large body; these were generally the third division, which had watched on the walls the preceding night. The cause of their going out was this: the Spaniards, ignorant of maritime affairs, were fond of trafficking with them, and glad of an opportunity of purchasing for their own use the foreign goods which the others imported in their ships; and, at the same time, of finding a market for the produce of their lands. Sensible of the advantages resulting from a mutual intercourse, the Spaniards gave the Greeks free admittance into their city. Another thing which contributed to their safety was being sheltered under the friendship of the Romans, which they cultivated with as much cordial zeal, though not possessed of equal abilities, as the Massilians. On this account they received the consul and his army with every demonstration of courtesy and kindness. Cato stayed there a few days, until he could learn what force the enemy had, and where they lay; and, not to be idle during even that short delay, he spent the whole time in exercising his men. It happened to be the season of the year when people have the corn in their barns. He therefore ordered the purveyors not to purchase any corn, and sent them home to Rome, saying, that the war would maintain itself. Then, setting out from Emporiæ, he laid waste the lands of the enemy with fire and sword, spreading terror and desolation over the whole country.

10. At the same time, as Marcus Helvius was going home from Farther Spain, with an escort of six thousand men, given him by the pretor, Appius Claudius, the Celtiberians, with a numerous army, met him near the city of

Illiturgi. Valerius says that they had twenty thousand effective men; that twelve thousand of them were killed, the town of Illiturgi taken, and all the adult males put to the sword. Helvius soon after arrived at the camp of Cato; and as he had now no danger to apprehend from the enemy, in the country through which he was to pass, he sent back the escort to Farther Spain, and proceeded to Rome, where, on account of his successful services, he received the honour of an ovation. He carried into the treasury, of silver bullion, fourteen thousand pounds weight; of coined, seventeen thousand and twenty-three denariuses;* and Oscan† denariuses, twenty thousand four hundred and thirty-eight.‡ The reason for which the senate refused him a triumph was, because he fought under the auspices and in the province of another. As he had not come home until the second year after the expiration of his office, because after he had resigned the government of the province to Quintius Minucius he was detained there during the succeeding year by a severe and tedious sickness, he entered the city in ovation, only two months before the triumph of his successor. The latter brought into the treasury thirty-four thousand eight hundred pounds weight of silver, seventy-eight thousand denariuses,§ and of Oscan denariuses two hundred and seventy-eight thousand.‖

11. Meanwhile, in Spain, the consul lay encamped at a small distance from Emporiæ. Thither came three ambassadors from Bilistages, chieftain of the Ilergetians, one of whom was his son, representing that "their fortresses were besieged, and that they had no hopes of being able to hold out unless the Romans sent them succour. Five thousand men," they said, "would be sufficient;" and they added that, "if such a force came to their aid, the enemy would evacuate the country." To this the consul answered that "he was truly concerned for their danger and their fears; but that his army was far from being so numerous, as that, while there lay in his neighbourhood such a powerful force of the enemy with whom he daily expected a general engagement, he could safely diminish his strength by dividing his forces." The ambassadors, on hearing this, threw themselves at the consul's feet, and with tears conjured him "not to forsake them at such a perilous juncture; for, if rejected by the Romans, to whom could they apply? They had no other allies, no other hope on earth. They might have escaped the present hazard, if they had consented to forfeit

* 519*l.* 14*s.*

† Osca, now Huesca, was a city in Spain, remarkable for silver mines near it.

‡ 659*l.* 11*s.* 9 1-2*d.* § 2,430*l.* 11*s.* 3*d.* ‖ 8,880*l.* 6*s.* 9*d.*

their faith, and to conspire with the rest; but no menaces, no appearances of danger had been able to shake their constancy; because they hoped to find in the Romans abundant succour and support. If there was no farther prospect of this; if it was refused them by the consul, they called gods and men to witness that it was contrary to their inclination, and in compliance with necessity, that they should change sides, to avoid such sufferings as the Saguntines had undergone; and that they would perish together with the other states of Spain, rather than alone."

12. They were that day dismissed without any positive answer. During the following night the consul's thoughts were greatly perplexed and divided. He was unwilling to abandon these allies, yet equally so to diminish his army, which might either oblige him to decline a battle, or render an engagement too hazardous. At length he determined not to lessen his forces, lest he should suffer some disgrace from the enemy; and therefore he judged it expedient, instead of real succour, to hold out hopes to the allies: for he considered that in many cases, but especially in war, mere appearances have had all the effect of realities; and that a person, under a firm persuasion that he can command resources, virtually has them; that very prospect inspiring him with hope and boldness in his exertions. Next day he told the ambassadors that "although he had many objections to lending a part of his forces to others, yet he considered their circumstances and danger more than his own." He then gave orders to the third part of the soldiers of every cohort to make haste and prepare victuals, which they were to carry with them on board ships, which he ordered to be got in readiness against the third day. He desired two of the ambassadors to carry an account of these proceedings to Bilistages and the Ilergetians; but, by kind treatment and presents, he prevailed on the chieftain's son to remain with him. The ambassadors did not leave the place until they saw the troops embarked on board the ships; then reporting this at home, they spread, not only among their own people, but likewise among the enemy, a confident assurance of the approach of Roman succours.

13. The consul, when he had carried appearances as far as he thought sufficient, to create a belief of his intending to send aid, ordered the soldiers to be landed again from the ships; and as the season of the year now approached when it would be proper to enter on action, he pitched a winter-camp at the distance of a mile from Emporiæ. From this post he frequently led out his troops to ravage the enemy's country; sometimes to one quarter, sometimes to another, as opportunity offered, leaving only a small guard in the

camp. They generally began their march in the night, that they might proceed as far as possible, and surprise the enemy unawares; by which practice the new-raised soldiers gained a knowledge of discipline, and great numbers of the enemy were cut off; so that they no longer dared to venture beyond the walls of their forts. When he had made himself thoroughly acquainted with the temper of the enemy, and of his own men, he ordered the tribunes and the prefects, with all the horsemen and centurions, to be called together, and addressed them thus: "The time is arrived which you have often wished for, when you might have an opportunity of displaying your valour. Hitherto you have waged war, rather as marauders than as regular troops; you shall now meet your enemies face to face, in regular fight. Henceforward you will have it in your power, instead of pillaging country places, to rifle the treasures of cities. Our fathers, at a time when the Carthaginians had in Spain both commanders and armies, and they themselves had neither commander nor soldiers there, nevertheless insisted on its being an article of treaty that the river Iberus should be the boundary of their empire. Now, when two pretors of the Romans, one of their consuls, and three armies are employed in Spain, and, for near ten years past, no Carthaginian has been in either of its provinces, yet we have lost that empire on the hither side of the Iberus. This it is your duty to recover by your valour and arms; and to compel this nation, which is in a state rather of giddy insurrection than of steady warfare, to receive again the yoke which it has shaken off." After thus exhorting them, he gave notice that he intended to march by night to the enemy's camp; and then dismissed them to take refreshment.

14. At midnight, after having duly performed what related to the auspices, he began his march, that he might take possession of such ground as he chose before the enemy should observe him. Having led his troops beyond their camp, he formed them in order of battle, and at the first light sent three cohorts close to their very ramparts. The barbarians, surprised at the Romans appearing on their rear, ran hastily to arms. In the mean time the consul observed to his men, "Soldiers, you have no room for hope, but in your own courage; and I have purposely taken care that it should be so. The enemy are between us and our tent; behind us is an enemy's country. What is most honourable is likewise safest: to place all our hopes in our own valour." He then ordered the cohorts to retreat, in order to draw out the barbarians by the appearance of flight. Every thing happened as he had expected. The enemy, thinking that the Romans retired through fear, rushed out of the gate, and filled the

whole space between their own camp and the line of their adversaries. While they were hastily marshalling their troops, the consul, who had all his in readiness, and in regular array, attacked them before they could be properly formed. He caused the cavalry from both wings to advance first to the charge: but those on the right were immediately repulsed, and, retiring in disorder, spread confusion among the infantry also. On seeing this, the consul ordered two chosen cohorts to march round the right flank of the enemy, and show themselves on their rear, before the two lines of infantry should close. The alarm which this gave the enemy remedied the disadvantage occasioned by the cowardice of the cavalry, and restored the fight to an equality. But such a panic had taken possession of both the cavalry and infantry of the right wing, that the consul was obliged to lay hold of several with his own hand, and turn them about with their faces to the enemy. As long as the fight was carried on with missile weapons, success was doubtful: and, on the right wing, where the disorder and flight had first begun, the Romans with difficulty kept their ground. On their left wing the barbarians were hard pressed in front; and looked back with dread at the cohorts that threatened their rear. But when, after discharging their iron darts and large javelins, they drew their swords, the battle, in a manner, began anew. They were no longer wounded by random blows from a distance, but closing foot to foot, placed all their hope in courage and strength.

15. When the consul's men were now spent with fatigue, he reanimated their courage by bringing up into the fight some subsidiary cohorts from the second line. These formed a new front, and being fresh themselves, and with fresh weapons attacking the wearied enemy in the form of a wedge, by a furious onset they first made them give ground; and then, when they were once broken, put them completely to flight, and compelled them to seek their camp with all the speed they could make. When Cato saw the rout become general, he rode back to the second legion, which had been posted in reserve, and ordered it to advance in quick motion, and attack the camp of the enemy. If any of them, through too much eagerness, pushed forward beyond his rank, he himself rode up and struck them with his javelin, and also ordered the tribunes and centurions to chastise them. By this time the camp was attacked, though the Romans were kept off from the works by stones, poles, and weapons of every sort. But, on the arrival of the fresh legion, the assailants assumed new courage, and the enemy fought with redoubled fury in defence of their rampart. The consul attentively examined every place himself, that he might make

his push where he saw the weakest resistance. At a gate on the left he observed that the guard was thin, and thither he led the first-rank men and spearmen of the second legion. The party posted at the gate were not able to withstand their assault; while the rest, seeing the enemy within the rampart, abandoned the defence of the camp, and threw away their standards and arms. Great numbers were killed at the gates, being stopped in the narrow passages by the throng; and the soldiers of the second legion cut off the hindmost, while the rest were in search of plunder. According to the account of Valerius Antias, there were above forty thousand of the enemy killed on that day. Cato himself, who was not apt to be too sparing in his own praise, says that a great many were killed, but he specifies no number.

16. The conduct of Cato on that day is judged deserving of commendation in three particulars. First, in leading round his army so far from his camp and fleet, as to put the enemy between it and them when he engaged, that his men might look for no safety but in their courage. Secondly, in throwing the cohorts on the enemy's rear. Thirdly, in ordering the second legion, when all the rest were disordered by the eagerness of their pursuit, to advance at a full pace to the gate of the camp, in compact and regular order under their standards. He delayed not to improve his victory; but having sounded a retreat, and brought back his men laden with spoil, he allowed them a few hours of the night for rest; and then led them out to ravage the country. They spread their depredations the wider, as the enemy were dispersed in their flight; and this disaster, operating not less forcibly than the defeat of the preceding day, obliged the Spaniards of Emporiæ, and those of their neighbourhood, to make a submission. Many also, belonging to other states, who had made their escape to Emporiæ, surrendered; all of whom the consul received with kindness, and after refreshing them with victuals and wine, dismissed to their several homes. He quickly decamped thence, and wherever the army proceeded on its march he was met by ambassadors, surrendering their respective states; so that by the time when he arrived at Tarraco, all Spain on this side of Iberus was in a state of perfect subjection; and the Roman prisoners, and those of their allies and the Latine confederates, who, by various chances, had fallen into the hands of the enemies in Spain, were brought back by the barbarians and presented to the consul. A rumour afterward spread abroad that Cato intended to lead his army into Turdetania; and it was given out, with equal falsehood, that he meant to proceed to the remote inhabitants of the mountains. On this groundless, unauthenticated report, [illegible]

en forts of the Bergistans revolted; but the Roman, marching thither, reduced them to subjection without much fighting. In a short time after, when the consul returned to Tarraco, and before he removed to any other place, the same persons revolted again. They were again subdued; but, on this second reduction, met not the same mild treatment; they were all sold by auction, to put an end to their continual rebellions.

17. In the mean time the pretor Publius Manlius, having received the army from Quintius Minucius, whom he had succeeded, and joined to it the old army of Appius Claudius Nero, from Farther Spain, marched into Turdetania. Of all the Spaniards, the Turdetanians are reckoned the least warlike; nevertheless, relying on their great numbers, they went to oppose the march of the Romans. One charge of the cavalry immediately broke their line; and, with the infantry, there was hardly any dispute. The veteran soldiers, well acquainted with the enemy and their manner of fighting, effectually decided the battle. This engagement however did not terminate the war. The Turdulans hired ten thousand Celtiberians, and prepared to carry on the war with foreign troops. The consul, meanwhile, alarmed at the rebellion of the Bergistans, and suspecting that the other states would act in like manner, when occasion offered, took away their arms from all the Spaniards on this side of the Iberus; which proceeding affected them so deeply, that many laid violent hands on themselves, thinking, according to the notions of that fierce race, that without arms life was nothing. When this was reported to the consul, he summoned before him the senators of every one of the states, to whom he spoke thus: "It is not more our interest, than it is your own, that you should not rebel; since your insurrections have, hitherto, always drawn more misfortune on the Spaniards, than labour on the Roman armies. To prevent such things happening in future, I know but one method, which is, to put it out of your power to rebel. I wish to effect this in the gentlest way, and that you would assist me therein with your advice. I will follow none with greater pleasure than what yourselves shall offer." They all remained silent; and then he told them that he would give them a few days' time to consider the matter. They were again called together; but, even in the second meeting, they uttered not a word. On which, in one day, he razed the walls of all their fortresses, and, marching against those who had not yet submitted, he received, in every country as he passed through, the submission of all the neighbouring states. Segestica alone, a strong and opulent city, he reduced by a regular siege.

18. Cato had greater difficulties to surmount in subduing the enemy than had those commanders who came first into Spain; for this reason, that the Spaniards, through disgust at the Carthaginian government, came over to their side; whereas, he had the task of enforcing their submission to slavery, in a manner, after they had been in full enjoyment of liberty. Besides, he found the whole province in a state of commotion; insomuch that some were in arms, and others, because they refused to join in the revolt, were held besieged, and would not have been able to hold out if they had not received timely succour. But so vigorous was the spirit and capacity of the consul, that there was no kind of business, whether great or small, which he did not himself attend to and perform: and he not only planned and ordered, but generally executed in person such measures as were expedient; nor did he practise greater strictness and severity over any one than over himself. In spare diet, watching, and labour, he vied with the meanest of his soldiers; nor, excepting the honour of his post and the command, had he any peculiar distinction above the rest of the army.

19. The Celtiberians, hired by the enemy as above mentioned, rendered the war in Turdetania difficult to the pretor, Publius Manlius. The consul, therefore, in compliance with a letter from the pretor, led his legions thither. The Celtiberians and Turdetanians were lying in separate camps at the approach of the Romans, who began immediately to skirmish with the Turdetanians, making attacks on their advanced guards; and they constantly came off victorious, though sometimes they engaged too rashly. The consul ordered some military tribunes to enter into a conference with the Celtiberians, and to offer them their choice of three proposals: first, to come over to the Romans, and receive double the pay for which they had agreed with the Turdetanians; the second, to depart to their own homes, on receiving assurance, under the sanction of the public faith, that no resentment should be shown of their behaviour in joining the enemies of the Romans; the third was, that if they were absolutely determined on war, they should appoint a day and place to decide the matter with him by arms. The Celtiberians desired a day's time for consideration; but numbers of the Turdetanians mixing in their assembly, caused so great a confusion, as to prevent them from forming any resolution. Although it was uncertain whether there was to be war or peace with the Celtiberians, the Romans nevertheless, just as though the latter were determined on, brought provisions from the lands and forts of the enemy, and soon ventured to go within their fortifications, relying on private truces as they would on a common inter-

course established by authority. When the consul found that he could not entice the enemy to a battle, he first led out a number of cohorts, lightly accoutred, in regular order, to ravage a part of the country which was yet unhurt; then, hearing that all the baggage of the Celtiberians was deposited at Saguntia, he proceeded thither to attack that town, but was unable, notwithstanding, to provoke them to stir. Paying, therefore, his own troops and those of Minucius, he left the bulk of his army in the pretor's camp, and, with seven cohorts, returned to the Iberus.

20. With that small force he took several towns. The Sidetonians, Ausetanians, and Suessetanians, came over to his side. The Lacetanians, a remote and wild nation, still remained in arms; partly through their natural ferocity, and partly through consciousness of guilt, in having laid waste, by sudden incursions, the country of the allies, while the consul and his army were employed in the war with the Turdetanians. He therefore marched to attack their capital, not only with the Roman cohorts, but also with the troops of the allies, who were justly incensed against them. The town was stretched out into considerable length, but had not proportionable breadth. At the distance of about four hundred paces from it he halted, and leaving there a party composed of chosen cohorts, he charged them not to stir from that spot until he himself should come to them; and then he led round the rest of the men to the farther side of the town. The greater part of his auxiliary troops were Suessetanians, and these he ordered to advance and assault the wall. The Lacetanians, knowing their arms and standards, and remembering how often they had themselves, with impunity, committed every kind of outrage and insult in their territory,—how often defeated and routed them in pitched battles,—hastily threw open a gate, and all, in one body, rushed out against them. The Suessetanians scarcely stood their shout, much less their onset; and the consul on seeing this happen, just as he had foreseen, galloped back under the enemy's wall to his cohorts, brought them up quickly to that side where all was silence and solitude, in consequence of the Lacetanians having sallied out on the Suessetanians, led them into the town, and took possession of every part of it before the return of its people; who, having nothing now left but their arms, soon surrendered themselves also.

21. The conqueror marched thence, without delay, to the fort of Vergium; which being now converted almost entirely into a receptacle of robbers and plunderers, incursions were made on the peaceable parts of the province. One of the principal inhabitants deserted out of the place to

the consul, and endeavoured to excuse himself and his countrymen; alleging that "the management of affairs was not in their hands; for the robbers, having gained admittance, had reduced the fort entirely under their own power." The consul ordered him to return home, and pretend some plausible reason for having been absent; and then, "when he should see him advancing to the walls, and the robbers intent on making a defence, to seize the citadel with such men as favoured his party." This was executed according to his directions. The double alarm, from the Romans scaling the walls in front, and the citadel being seized on their rear, at once entirely confounded the barbarians. The consul having taken possession of the place, ordered that those who had secured the citadel should, with their relations, be set at liberty, and enjoy their property; the rest of the natives he commanded the questor to sell, and he put the robbers to death. Having restored quiet, he settled the iron and silver mines on such a footing, that they produced a large revenue; and, in consequence of the regulations then made, the province daily increased in riches. On account of these services performed in Spain, the senate decreed a supplication for three days. During this summer, the other consul, Lucius Valerius Flaccus, fought a pitched battle with a body of the Boians in Gaul, near the forest of Litinæ, and gained a complete victory. We are told that eight thousand of the Gauls were killed; the rest, desisting from farther opposition, retired to their several villages and lands. During the remainder of the season the consul kept his army near the Po, at Placentia and Cremona, and repaired the buildings in these cities which had been ruined in the war.

22. While the affairs of Italy and Spain were in this posture, Titus Quintius had spent the winter in Greece, in such a manner that, excepting the Ætolians, who neither had gained rewards of victory adequate to their hopes, nor were capable of being long contented with a state of quiet, all Greece, being in full enjoyment of the blessings of peace and liberty, were highly pleased with their present state; and they admired not more the Roman general's bravery in arms than his temperance, justice, and moderation in success. And now a decree of the senate was brought to him, containing a denunciation of war against Nabis the Lacedæmonian. On reading it, Quintius summoned a convention of deputies from all the allied states, to be held on a certain day at Corinth. Accordingly, many persons of the first rank came together from all quarters, forming a very full assembly, from which even the Ætolians were not absent. He then addressed them in this manner:—"Although

the Romans and Greeks, in the war which they waged against Philip, were united in affections and councils, yet they had each their separate reasons for entering into it. He had violated friendship with the Romans; first by aiding our enemies, the Carthaginians; and then, by attacking our allies here; and, towards you, his conduct was such, that even if we were willing to forget our own injuries, those offered by him to you would be reason sufficient to make us declare war against him. But the business to be considered this day rests wholly on yourselves: for the subject which I propose to your consideration is, whether you choose to suffer Argos, which, as you know, has been seized by Nabis, to remain under his dominion; or whether you judge it reasonable that a city of such high reputation and antiquity, seated in the centre of Greece, should be restored to liberty, and placed in the same state with the rest of the cities of Peloponnesus and of Greece. This question, as you see, merely respects yourselves; it concerns not the Romans in any degree, excepting so far as the one city being left in subjection to tyranny hinders their glory, in having liberated Greece, from being full and complete. If, however, you are not moved by regard for that city, nor by the example, nor by the danger of the contagion of that evil spreading wider, we, for our parts, shall rest content. On this subject I desire your opinions, resolved to abide by whatever the majority of you shall determine."

23. When the Roman general had ended his discourse, the several deputies proceeded to give their opinions. The ambassador of the Athenians extolled, to the utmost of his power, and expressed the greatest gratitnde for the kindness of the Romans towards Greece, "in having, when applied to for assistance, brought them succours against Philip; and now, without being applied to, voluntarily offering assistance against the tyrant Nabis." He, at the same time, severely censured the conduct of some, who, in their discourses, "depreciated those kindnesses, and propagated evil surmises of the future, when it would better become them rather to return thanks for the past." It was evident that this was pointed at the Ætolians; wherefore Alexander, deputy of that nation, began with inveighing against the Athenians, who, having formerly been the most strenuous supporters of liberty, now betrayed the general cause, for the sake of recommending themselves by flattery. He then complained that "the Achæans, formerly soldiers of Philip, and lately, on the decline of his fortune, deserters from him, had regained possession of Corinth, and were aiming at the possession of Argos; while the Ætolians, who had first opposed their arms to Philip, who had always been allies of

the Romans, and who had stipulated by treaty, that on the Macedonians being conquered, the lands and cities should be theirs, were defrauded by Echinus and Pharsalus." He charged the Romans with insincerity, because, "while they made empty professions of establishing universal liberty, they held forcible possession of Demetrias and Chalcis; though, when Philip hesitated to withdraw his garrisons from those places, they always urged against him, that the Grecians would never be free while Demetrias, Chalcis, and Corinth, were in the hands of others. And lastly, that they named Argos and Nabis merely as a pretext for remaining in Greece, and keeping their armies there. Let them carry home their legions, and the Ætolians were ready to undertake, either that Nabis should voluntarily evacuate Argos on terms, or they would compel him by force of arms to comply with the unanimous judgment of Greece."

24. This arrogant speech called up, first, Aristænus, pretor of the Achæans, who said:—"Forbid it, Jupiter, supremely good and great, and imperial Juno, the tutelar deity of Argos, that that city should lie as a prize between the Lacedæmonian tyrant and the Ætolian plunderers, under such unhappy circumstances, that its being retaken by us should be productive of more calamitous consequences than its capture by him. Titus Quintius, the sea lying between us does not secure us from those robbers; what then will become of us, should they procure themselves a stronghold in the centre of Peloponnesus? They have nothing Grecian but the language, as they have nothing human but the shape. They live like beasts of prey, and are, in their manners and rites, more brutally savage than any barbarians. Wherefore, Romans, we beseech you, not only to recover Argos from Nabis, but also to establish the affairs of Greece on such a footing, as to leave these countries in a state of security from the robberies of the Ætolians." The rest concurring in these censures on the Ætolians, the Roman general said, that "he had himself intended to have answered them, but that he perceived all so highly incensed against those people, that the general resentment required rather to be appeased than irritated. Satisfied therefore with the sentiments entertained of the Romans, and of the Ætolians, he would simply put this question:—what was the general opinion concerning war with Nabis, in case of his refusing to restore Argos to the Achæans?" Every one voted for war; whereon he recommended to them to send in their shares of auxiliary troops, each state in proportion to its ability. He even sent an ambassador to the Ætolians, rather to make them disclose their sentiments, in which he succeeded, than with any hope of obtaining their concurrence. He gave or-

ders to the military tribunes to bring up the army from Elatia. To the ambassadors of Antiochus, who at this time proposed to treat of an alliance, he answered, that "he could say nothing on the subject in the absence of the ten ambassadors: they must go to Rome, and apply to the senate."

25. As soon as the troops arrived from Elatia, Quintius put himself at their head, and began his march towards Argos. Near Cleone he was met by the pretor Aristænus, with ten thousand Achæan foot and one thousand horse; and having joined forces, they pitched their camp at a small distance from thence. Next day they marched down into the plains of Argos, and fixed their post about four miles from that city. The commander of the Lacedæmonian garrison was Pythagoras, the tyrant's son-in-law, and his wife's brother: who, on the approach of the Romans, posted strong guards on both the citadels, for Argos has two, and in every other place that was commodious for defence or exposed to danger. But, while thus employed, he could by no means dissemble the dread inspired by the approach of the Romans; and, to the alarm from abroad, was added an insurrection within. There was an Argive, named Damocles, a youth of more spirit than prudence, who held conversations with proper persons on a design of expelling the garrison; at first, with the precaution of imposing an oath, but afterward, through his eager desire to add strength to the conspiracy, he trusted to people's sincerity with too little reserve. While he was in conference with his accomplices, an officer, sent by the commander of the garrison, summoned him to appear before him, and this convinced him that his plot was betrayed; on which, exhorting the conspirators, who were present, to take arms with him, rather than be tortured to death, he went on with a few companions towards the forum, crying out to all who wished the preservation of the state to follow him: he would lead them to liberty, and assert its cause. He could prevail on none to join him; for they saw no prospect of any attainable advantage, and much less any support on which they could rely. While he exclaimed in this manner, the Lacedæmonians surrounded him and his party, and put them to death. Many others were afterward seized, the greater part of whom were executed, and the remaining few thrown into prison. During the following night great numbers, letting themselves down from the walls by ropes, came over to the Romans.

26. These men affirmed, that if the Roman army had been at the gates, the commotion would not have ended without effect: and that, if the camp was brought nearer, the townsmen would not remain inactive. Quintius therefore sent some horsemen and infantry, lightly accoutred, who, meet-

ing at the Cylarabis, a place of exercise, less than three hundred paces from the city, a party of Lacedæmonians, who sallied out of a gate, engaged them, and, without much difficulty, drove them back into the town; and the Roman general encamped on the very spot where the battle was fought. There he passed one day, watching if any new commotion might arise; but perceiving that the inhabitants were quite disheartened, he called a council to determine whether he should lay siege to Argos. All the deputies of Greece, except Aristænus, were of one opinion, that, as that city was the sole object of the war, with it the war should commence. This was by no means agreeable to Quintius; but he listened, with evident marks of approbation, to Aristænus, arguing in opposition to the joint opinion of all the rest; while he himself added, that "as the war was undertaken in favour of the Argives, against the tyrant, what could be less proper than to leave the enemy in quiet, and lay siege to Argos? For his part, he was resolved to point his arms against the main object of the war, Lacedæmon and Nabis." He then dismissed the meeting, and sent out light-armed cohorts to collect forage. Whatever was ripe in the adjacent country they reaped, and brought together; and what was green they trod down and destroyed, to prevent its being of use to the enemy. He then proceeded over Mount Parthenius, and, passing by Tygæa, encamped on the third day at Caryæ; where he waited for the auxiliary troops of the allies before he entered the enemy's territory. Fifteen hundred Macedonians came from Philip, and four hundred horsemen from Thessaly; and now the Roman general had no occasion to wait for more auxiliaries, having abundance; but he was obliged to stop for supplies of provisions, which he had ordered the neighbouring cities to furnish. He was joined also by a powerful naval force: Lucius Quintius came from Leucas with forty ships, as did eighteen ships of war from the Rhodians; and King Eumenes was cruising among the Cyclades, with ten decked ships, thirty barks, and smaller vessels of various sorts. Of the Lacedæmonians themselves, also, a great many, who had been driven from home by the cruelty of the tyrants, came into the Roman camp, in hopes of being reinstated in their country; for the number was very great of those who had been banished by the several despots, during many generations, since they first got Lacedæmon into their power. The principal person among the exiles was Agesipolis, to whom the crown of Lacedæmon belonged in right of his birth; but who had been driven out when an infant by Lycurgus, after the death of Cleomenes, the first tyrant of Lacedæmon.

27. Although Nabis was enclosed between such powerful

armaments on land and sea, and who, on a comparative view of his own and his enemy's strength, could scarcely conceive any degree of hope, yet neglected not preparing for a defence, but brought from Crete a thousand chosen young men of that country, in addition to a thousand whom he had before; he had, besides, under arms, three thousand mercenary soldiers, and ten thousand of his countrymen, with the peasants, who were vassals to the proprietors of land.* He fortified the city with a ditch and rampart; and, to prevent any intestine commotion, curbed the people's spirits by fear, punishing them with extreme severity. As he could not hope for good wishes towards a tyrant, and had reason to suspect some designs against his person, he drew out all his forces to a field called Dromos, (the course,) and ordered the Lacedæmonians to be called to an assembly without their arms. He then formed a line of armed men round the place where they were assembled, observing briefly, "that he ought to be excused if, at such a juncture, he feared and guarded against every thing that might happen; and that, if the present state of affairs subjected any to suspicion, it was their advantage to be prevented from attempting any design, rather than to be punished for the attempt: he therefore intended," he said, "to keep certain persons in custody, until the storm which then threatened should blow over; and would discharge them as soon as the country should be clear of the enemy, from whom the danger would be less when proper precaution was taken against internal treachery." He then ordered the names of about eighty of the principal young men to be called over, and, as each answered to his name, he put them in custody. On the night following they were all put to death. Some of the Ilotans, or helotes, a race of rustics, who have been vassals even from the earliest times, being charged with an intention to desert, they were driven with stripes through all the streets, and put to death. The terror which this excited so enervated the multitude, that they gave up all thoughts of any attempt to effect a revolution. He kept his forces within the fortifications, knowing that he was not a match for the enemy in the field; and, besides, he was afraid to leave the city, while all men's minds were in a state of such suspense and uncertainty.

28. Quintius, having finished every necessary preparation, decamped; and, on the second day, came to Sellasia, on the river Œnus, on the spot where it is said Antigonus, king of Macedonia, fought a pitched battle with Cleomenes, tyrant of Lacedæmon. Being told that the ascent from

* These were the helotes, kept in a state of slavery.

thence was through a difficult and narrow pass, he made a short circuit by the mountains, sending forward a party to make a road, and came, by a broad and open passage, to the river Eurotas, where it flows almost immediately under the walls of the city. Here the tyrant's auxiliary troops attacked the Romans, while they were forming their camp; together with Quintius himself, (who, with a division of cavalry and light troops, had advanced beyond the rest,) and threw all into fright and confusion; for they had not expected any impediment on their whole march: they had met no kind of molestation, passing, as it were, through the territory of friends. The disorder lasted a considerable time, the infantry calling for aid on the cavalry, and the cavalry on the infantry, each relying on the others more than on themselves. At length the foremost ranks of the legions came up; and no sooner had the cohorts of the vanguard taken part in the fight, than those who had lately spread terror round them were driven back into the city. The Romans, retiring so far from the wall as to be out of the reach of weapons, stood there for some time in battle array; and then, none of the enemy coming out against them, retired to their camp. Next day Quintius led on his army in regular order along the bank of the river, passed the city, to the foot of the mountain of Menelaus, the legionary cohorts marching in front, and the cavalry and light infantry bringing up the rear. Nabis kept his mercenary troops, on whom he placed his whole reliance, in readiness, and drawn up in a body, within the walls, intending to attack the rear of the enemy; and, as soon as the last of their troops passed by, these rushed out of the town, from several places at once, with as great fury as the day before. The rear was commanded by Appius Claudius, who, having beforehand prepared his men to expect such an event, that they might not be disconcerted when it happened, instantly made his troops face about, and presented an entire front to the enemy. A regular engagement therefore took place, as if two complete lines had encountered, and it lasted a considerabie time; but, at length, Nabis's troops betook themselves to flight, which would have been attended with less dismay and danger, if they had not been closely pressed by the Achæans, who were well acquainted with the ground. These made dreadful havoc, and, dispersing them entirely, obliged the greater part to throw away their arms. Quintius encamped near Amyclæ; and, afterward, when he had utterly laid waste all the pleasant and thickly inhabited country round the city, the enemy not venturing out of the gates, he removed his camp to the river Eurotas. From thence he sent out parties that ravaged the valley lying under Taygetus, and the country reaching as far as the sea.

29. About the same time Lucius Quintius got possession of the towns on the sea-coast; of some, by their voluntary surrender, of others, by fear or force. Then, learning that the Lacedæmonians made Gythium the repository of all their naval stores, and that the Roman camp was at no great distance from the sea, he resolved to attack that town with his whole force. It was, at that time, a place of considerable strength; well furnished with great numbers of native inhabitants and settlers from other parts, and with every kind of warlike stores. Very seasonably for Quintius, at the commencement of an enterprise of no easy nature, King Eumenes and the Rhodian fleet joined him. The vast multitude of seamen, collected out of the three fleets, finished in a few days all the works requisite for the siege of a city so strongly fortified, both on the land side and on that next the sea. Covered galleries were soon brought up; the wall was undermined, and, at the same time, shaken with battering-rams. By the frequent shocks given with these, one of the towers was thrown down, and, by its fall, the adjoining wall on each side was laid flat. The Romans on this attempted to force in, both on the side next the port, to which the approach was more level than to the rest, hoping to divert the enemy's attention from the more open passage, and, at the same time, to enter the breach caused by the falling of the wall. They were near effecting their design of penetrating into the town, when the assault was suspended by a proposal of a capitulation; which, however, came to nothing. Dexagoridas and Gorgopas commanded there with equal authority. Dexagoridas had sent to the Roman general the proposal of surrendering; and, after the time and the mode of proceeding had been agreed on, he was slain as a traitor by Gorgopas, and the defence of the city was maintained with redoubled vigour by this single commander. The farther prosecution of the siege would have been much more difficult, had not Titus Quintius arrived with a body of four thousand chosen men. He showed his army in order of battle, on the brow of a hill at a small distance from the city; and, on the other side, Lucius Quintius plied the enemy hard with his engines, both on the quarter of the sea, and of the land; on which Gorgopas was compelled to follow the plan which, in the case of another, he had punished with death. After stipulating for liberty to carry away the soldiers whom he had there as a garrison, he surrendered the city to Quintius. Previous to the surrender of Gythium, Pythagoras, who commanded at Argos, left that place, intrusting the defence of the city to Timocrates of

Pellene; and with a thousand mercenary soldiers, and two thousand Argives, came to Lacedæmon and joined Nabis.

30. Although Nabis had been greatly alarmed at the first arrival of the Roman fleet, and the loss of the towns on the sea-coast, yet as long as Gythium was held by his troops, the small degree of hope which that afforded had helped to quiet his apprehensions; but when he heard that Gythium too was given up to the Romans, and saw that he had no room for any kind of hope on the land, where every place round was in the hands of the enemy, and that he was totally excluded from the sea, he found himself under the necessity of yielding to fortune. He first sent an officer, with a wand of parley, into the Roman camp, to learn whether permission would be given to send ambassadors. This being consented to, Pythagoras came to the general, with no other commission than to propose a conference between that commander and the tyrant. A council was summoned on the proposal, and every one present agreeing in opinion that a conference should be granted, a time and place were appointed. They came with moderate escorts to some hills in the interjacent ground; and leaving their cohorts there, in posts open to the view of both parties, they went down to the place of meeting; Nabis attended by a select party of his life-guards; Quintius by his brother, King Eumenes, Sosilaus the Rhodian, Aristænus, pretor of the Achæans, and a few military tribunes.

31. Then the tyrant, having the choice given him to speak either before or after the Roman, began thus: "Titus Quintius, and you who are present, if I could collect from my own reflections the reason of your having either declared or actually made war against me, I should have waited in silence the issue of my destiny. But in the present state of things, I could not repress my desire of knowing, before I am ruined, the cause for which my ruin is resolved on. And, in truth, if you were such men as the Carthaginians are represented,—men who considered the obligation of faith, pledged in alliances, as in no degree sacred, I should not wonder if you were the less scrupulous with respect to your conduct towards me. But, instead of that, when I look at you, I perceive that you are Romans; men who allow treaties to be the most solemn of religious acts, and faith, pledged therein, the strongest of human ties. Then, when I look back at myself, I am confident I am one who, as a member of the community, am, in common with the rest of the Lacedæmonians, included in a treaty subsisting with you of very ancient date; and likewise have, lately, during the war with Philip, concluded anew, in my own name, a personal friendship and alliance with you. But I

have violated and cancelled that treaty, by holding possession of the city of Argos. In what manner shall I defend this? By the consideration of the fact, or of the time? The consideration of the fact furnishes me with a twofold defence: for, in the first place, in consequence of an invitation from the inhabitants themselves, and of their voluntary act of surrender, I accepted the possession of that city, and did not seize it by force. In the next place, I accepted it when the city was in league with Philip, not in alliance with you. Then the consideration of the time acquits me, for this reason; that when I was in actual possession of Argos, you entered into an alliance with me, and stipulated that I should send you aid against Philip, not that I should withdraw my garrison from that city. In this dispute, therefore, so far as it relates to Argos, I have unquestionably the advantage, both from the equity of the proceeding, as I gained possession of a city which belonged not to you, but to your enemy; and as I gained it by its own voluntary act, and not by forcible compulsion; and also from your own acknowledgment; since, in the articles of our alliance, you left Argos to me. But then the name of tyrant and my conduct are strong objections against me: that I call forth slaves to a state of freedom; that I carry out the indigent part of the populace, and give them settlements in lands. With respect to the title by which I am styled, I can answer thus: that, let me be what I may, I am the same now that I was at the time when you yourself, Titus Quintius, concluded an alliance with me. I remember that I was then styled king by you; now, I see, I am called tyrant. If, therefore, I had since altered the style of my office, I might be chargeable with fickleness: as you chose to alter it, the charge falls on you. As to what relates to the augmenting the number of the populace, by giving liberty to slaves, and the distribution of lands to the needy; on this head, too, I might defend myself on the ground of a reference to the time of the facts charged. These measures, of what complexion soever they are, I had practised before you formed friendship with me, and received my aid in the war against Philip. But, if I did the same things at this moment, I would not say to you, how did I thereby injure you, or violate the friendship subsisting between us? but, I would insist, that in so doing, I acted agreeably to the practice and institutions of my ancestors. Do not estimate what is done at Lacedæmon by the standard of your own laws and constitution. I need not compare every particular: you are guided in your choice of a horseman by the quantity of his property; in your choice of a foot soldier, by the quantity of his property; and your plan is, that a few should abound in wealth, and that the body of the people should be in subjection to them. Our lawgiver did not choose that the administration of government should be in the hands of a few, such as you call a senate; or that this or that order of citizens should have a superiority over the rest: but he proposed, by equalizing the property and dignity of all, to multiply the number of those who were to bear arms for their country. I acknowledge that I have enlarged on these matters beyond what consists with the conciseness customary with my countrymen, and that the sum of the whole might be comprised in few words: that, since I first commenced a friendship with you, I have given you no just cause of displeasure."

32. The Roman general answered: "We never contracted any friendship or alliance with you, but with Pelops, the right and lawful king of Lacedæmon; whose authority, while the Carthaginian, Gallic, and other wars, succeeding one another, kept us constantly employed, the tyrants, who after him held Lacedæmon under forced subjection, usurped into their own hands, as did you also during the late war with Macedonia. For what could be less consistent with propriety than that we, who were waging war against Philip, in favour of the liberty of Greece, should contract friendship with a tyrant, and a tyrant who carried his violence and cruelty towards his subjects to as great an excess as any that ever existed? But, even supposing that you had not either seized or held Argos by iniquitous means, it would be incumbent on us, when we are giving liberty to all Greece, to reinstate Lacedæmon also in its ancient freedom, and the enjoyment of its own laws, which you just now spoke of, as if you were another Lycurgus. Shall we take pains to make Philip's garrisons evacuate Tassus and Bargylii; and shall we leave Lacedæmon and Argos, those two most illustrious cities, formerly the lights of Greece, under your feet, that their continuance in bondage may tarnish our title of deliverers of Greece? But the Argives took part with Philip: we excuse you from taking any concern in that cause, so that you need not be angry with them on our behalf. We have received sufficient proof that the guilt of that proceeding is chargeable on two only, or at most three persons, and not on the state; just, indeed, as in the case of the invitation given to you and to your army, and your reception in the town, not one step was taken by public authority. We know that the Thessalians, Phocians, and Locrians, to a man, unanimously joined in espousing the cause of Philip; and when, notwithstanding this, we have given liberty to all the rest of Greece, how, I ask you, can you suppose we shall conduct ourselves towards the Argives, who are acquitted of having publicly authorized misconduct? You

said that your inviting slaves to liberty, and the distribution of lands among the indigent, were objected to you as crimes; and crimes surely they are of no small magnitude. But what are they in comparison with those atrocious deeds that are daily perpetrated by you and your adherents in continual succession? Show us a free assembly of the people, either at Argos or Lacedæmon, if you wish to hear a true recital of the crimes of the most abandoned tyranny. To omit all other instances of older date, what a massacre did your son-in-law, Pythagoras, make at Argos, almost before my eyes? What another did you yourself perpetrate when I was on the borders of Laconia? Now, give orders that the persons whom you took out of the midst of an assembly and committed to prison, after declaring, in the hearing of all your countrymen, that you would keep them in custody, be produced in their chains, that their wretched parents may know that they are alive, and have no cause for their mourning. Well, but you say, though all these things were so, Romans, how do they concern you? Can you say this to the deliverers of Greece; to people who crossed the sea in order to deliver it, and have maintained a war, on sea and land, to effect its deliverance? Still you tell us you have not directly violated the alliance, or the friendship established between us. How many instances must I produce of your having done so? But I will not go into a long detail; I will bring the matter to a short issue. By what acts is friendship violated? Most effectually by these two: by treating our friends as foes; and by uniting yourself with our enemies. Now, which of these has not been done by you? For Messene, which had been united to us in friendship, by one and the same bond of alliance with Lacedæmon, you, while professing yourself our ally, reduced to subjection by force of arms, though you knew it was in alliance with us; and you contracted with Philip, our professed enemy, not only an alliance, but even an affinity, through the intervention of his general, Philocles; and waging actual war against us, with your piratical ships, you made the sea round Malea unsafe, and you captured and slew more Roman citizens almost than Philip himself; and it was less dangerous for our ships to bring supplies for our armies by the coast of Macedonia, than by the promontory of Malea. Cease therefore to vaunt your good faith, and the obligations of treaties; and, dropping your affectation of popular sentiments, speak as a tyrant, and as an enemy."

33. Aristænus then began, at first to advise, and afterward even to beseech Nabis, while it was yet in his power, and while the state of affairs permitted, to consider what was best for himself and his interests. He then mentioned the

names of several tyrants in the neighbouring states who had resigned their authority, and restored liberty to their people, and afterward lived to old age, not only in safety, but with the respect of their countrymen. After this conversation had passed, the approach of night broke up the conference. Next day Nabis said that he was willing to cede Argos, and withdraw his garrison, since such was the desire of the Romans, and to deliver up the prisoners and deserters; and if they demanded any thing farther, he requested that they would set it down in writing, that he might deliberate on it with his friends. Thus the tyrant gained time for consultation, and Quintius also, on his part, called a council, to which he summoned the chiefs of the allies. The greatest part were of opinion, that "they ought to persevere in the war until the tyrant should be stripped of all power; otherwise the liberty of Greece would never be secure. That it would have been much better never to have entered on the war than to drop it after it was begun: for this would be a kind of approbation of his tyrannical usurpation, and which would establish him more firmly, as giving the countenance of the Roman people to his ill-acquired authority, while the example would quickly spirit up many in other states to plot against the liberty of their countrymen. The wishes of the general himself tended rather to peace; for he saw that, as the enemy were shut up in the town, nothing remained but a siege, and that must be very tedious: for it was not Gythium that they must besiege, though even that place had been gained by capitulation, not by assault; but Lacedæmon, a city most powerful in men and arms. The only hope which they could have formed was that, on the first approach of their army, dissensions and insurrections might have been raised within: but, though the standards had been seen to advance almost to the gates, not one person had stirred. To this he added, that Villius the ambassador, returning from Antiochus, brought intelligence that nothing but war was to be expected from that quarter; and that the king had come over into Europe with a much more powerful armament by sea and land than before. Now, if the army should be engaged in the siege of Lacedæmon, with what other forces could the war be maintained against a king of his great power and strength?" These arguments he urged openly; but he was influenced by another motive which he did not avow, his anxiety lest one of the new consuls should be appointed to the province of Greece; and then the honour of terminating the war, in which he had proceeded so far, must be yielded to a successor.

34. Finding that he could not by opposition make any alteration in the sentiments of the allies, by pretending to go

over to their opinion, he led them all into a concurrence in his scheme. "Be it so," said he, "and may success attend us: let us lay siege to Lacedæmon, since that is your choice. However, as a business so slow in its progress, as you know the besieging of cities to be, very often wears out the patience of the besiegers sooner than that of the besieged, you ought, before you proceed a step farther, to consider that we must pass the winter under the walls of Lacedæmon. If this tedious enterprise brought only toil and danger, I would recommend to you to prepare your minds and bodies to support these. But, in the present case, vast expenses also will be requisite for the construction of works, for machines and engines, sufficient for the siege of so great a city, and for procuring stores of provisions for the winter to serve you and us: therefore, to prevent your being suddenly disconcerted, or shamefully deserting an enterprise which you had engaged in, I think it will be necessary for you to write home to your respective states, and learn what degree of spirit and of strength each possesses. Of auxiliary troops I have a sufficient number, and to spare; but the more numerous we are, the more numerous will be our wants. The country of the enemy has nothing left but the naked soil. Besides, the winter is at hand, which will render it difficult to convey what we may stand in need of from distant places." This speech first turned their thoughts to the domestic evils prevailing in their several states; the indolence of those who remained at home; the envy and misrepresentations to which those who served abroad were liable; the difficulty of procuring unanimity among men in a state of freedom; the emptiness of the public treasury, and people's backwardness to contribute out of their private property. These considerations wrought such a sudden change in their inclinations, that they gave full power to the general to do whatever he judged conducive to the general interest of the Roman people and their allies.

35. Then Quintius, consulting only his lieutenants-general and military tribunes, drew up the following conditions on which peace should be made with Nabis: "That there should be a suspension of arms for six months, between Nabis on the one part, and the Romans, King Eumenes, and the Rhodians on the other. That Titus Quintius and Nabis should immediately send ambassadors to Rome, in order that the peace might be ratified by authority of the senate. That, whatever day a written copy of these conditions should be delivered to Nabis, on that day should the armistice commence; and within ten days after, his garrisons should be withdrawn from Argos, and all other towns in the territory of the Argives; all which towns should be entirely evac-

uated, restored to freedom, and in that state delivered to the Romans. That no slave, whether belonging to the king, the public, or a private person, be removed out of any of them; and if any had been removed before, that they be faithfully restored to their owners. That he should give up the ships, which he had taken from the maritime states; and should not have any other than two barks; and these to be navigated with no more than sixteen oars. That he should restore to all the states, in alliance with the Roman people, the prisoners and deserters in his hands; and to the Messenians, all the effects that could be discovered, and which the owners could prove to be their property. That he should, likewise, restore to the exiled Lacedæmonians their children, and their wives, who chose to follow their husbands; provided that no woman should be obliged, against her will, to go with her husband into exile. That such of the mercenary soldiers of Nabis as had deserted him, and gone either to their own countries or to the Romans, should have all their effects faithfully returned to them. That he should hold possession of no city in the island of Crete; and that such as were then in his possession, should be given up to the Romans. That he should not form any alliance or wage war with any of the Cretan states, or with any other. That he should withdraw all his garrisons from those cities which he should give up, and which had put themselves and their country under the dominion and protection of the Roman people; and should take care that, in future, neither he, nor any of his subjects, should give them any disturbance. That he should not build any town or fort in his own or any other territory. That, to secure the performance of these conditions, he should give five hostages, such as the Roman general should choose, and among them his own son; and should pay at present one hundred talents of silver; and fifty talents annually for eight years."

36. These articles were put into writing and sent into Lacedæmon, the camp having been removed, and brought nearer to the town. The tyrant saw nothing in them that gave him much satisfaction, excepting that, beyond his hopes, no mention had been made of reinstating the exiles. But what mortified him most of all, was, the depriving him of his shipping, and of the maritime towns: for the sea had been a source of great profit to him; his piratical vessels having continually infested the whole coast from the promontory of Malea. Besides, he found in the young men of those towns recruits for his army, who made by far the best of his soldiers. Though he discussed those conditions in private with his confidential friends, yet, as the ministers in the courts of kings, faithless in other respects, are particularly

so with respect to the concealing of secrets, they soon became the subject of common conversation. The public, in general, expressed not so great a disapprobation of the whole of the terms, as did individuals of the articles particularly affecting themselves. Those who had the wives of the exiles in marriage, or had possessed themselves of any of their property, were provoked, as if they were to lose what was their own, and not to make restitution of what belonged to others. The slaves who had been set at liberty by the tyrant, perceived plainly, not only that their enfranchisement would be annulled, but that their servitude would be much more severe than it had been before, when they should be again put under the power of their incensed masters. The mercenary soldiers saw, with uneasiness, that, in consequence of a peace, their pay would cease; and they knew also, that they could not return among their own countrymen, who detested not tyrants more than they did their abettors.

37. They at first spoke of these matters, in their circles, with murmurs of discontent; and afterward, suddenly ran to arms. From which tumultuous proceeding the tyrant perceived that the passions of the multitude were of themselves inflamed as highly as he could wish; he therefore immediately ordered a general assembly to be summoned. Here he explained to them the terms which the Romans strove to impose, to which he falsely added others more severe and humiliating. While, on the mention of each particular, sometimes the whole assembly, sometimes different parties, raised a shout of disapprobation, he asked them "What answer they wished him to give; or what they would have him do?" On which all, as it were with one voice, cried out, "To give no answer, to continue the war;" and they began, as is common with a multitude, every one to encourage the rest, to keep up their spirits, and cherish good hopes, observing, that "fortune favours the brave." Animated by these expressions, the tyrant assured them that Antiochus and the Ætolians would come to their assistance; and that he had, in the mean time, a force abundantly sufficient for the maintenance of a siege. Every thought of peace vanished from their minds, and unable to contain themselves longer in quiet, they ran out in parties against the advanced guards of the enemy. The sally of these few skirmishers, and the weapons which they threw, immediately demonstrated to the Romans, beyond a doubt, that the war was to continue. During the four following days several slight encounters took place, without any certain advantage; but, on the fifth day after, in a kind of regular engagement, the Lacedæmonians were beaten back into the town in such a panic, that several Roman soldiers, pressing

close on their rear, entered the city through open spaces, not secured with a wall, of which, at that time, there were several.

38. Then Quintius, having by this repulse, effectually checked the sallies of the enemy, and being fully convinced that he had now no alternative, but must besiege the city, sent persons to bring up all the marine forces from Gythium; and in the mean time rode himself, with some military tribunes, round the walls, to take a view of the situation of the place. In former times Sparta had no wall; of late, the tyrants had built walls, in the places where the ground was open and level; but the higher places and those more difficult of access they secured by placing guards of soldiers instead of fortifications. When he had sufficiently examined every circumstance, he resolved on making a general assault; and, for that purpose, surrounded the city with all his forces, the number of which, Romans and allies, horse and foot, naval and land forces, all together, amounted to fifty thousand men. Some brought scaling ladders, some firebrands, some other matters, wherewith they might either assail the enemy, or strike terror. The orders were, that on raising the shout, all should advance at once, in order that the Lacedæmonians, being alarmed at the same time in every quarter, might be at a loss where, first, to make head, or whither to bring aid. The main force of his army he formed in three divisions, and ordered one to attack on the side of the Phœbeum, another on that of the Dictynneum, and the third near a place called Heptagoniæ, all which are open places without walls. Though surrounded on all sides by such a violent alarm, the tyrant, at first, attentive to every sudden shout and hasty message, either ran up himself, or sent others, wherever the greatest danger pressed; but afterward, he was so stunned by the horror and confusion that prevailed all around, as to become incapable either of giving proper directions, or of hearing what was said, and to lose, not only his judgment, but almost his reason.

39. For some time the Lacedæmonians maintained their ground against the Romans in the narrow passes; and three armies on each side fought at one time, in different places. Afterward, when the heat of the contest increased, the combatants were by no means on an equal footing; for the Lacedæmonians fought with missile arms, against which, the Roman soldiers, by means of their large shields, easily defended themselves, and many of their blows either missed, or were very weak; for, the narrowness of the place causing them to be closely crowded together, they neither had room to discharge their weapons with a previous run, which gives great force to them, nor clear and steady footing while

they made their throw. Of those, therefore, discharged against the front of the Romans, none pierced their bodies, few even their shields: but several were wounded by those who stood on higher places on each side of them; and presently, when they advanced a little, they were hurt unawares, both with javelins, and tiles also thrown from the tops of the houses. On this they raised their shields over their heads, and joining them so close together as to leave no room for injury from such random casts, or even for the insertion of a javelin, by a hand within reach, they pressed forward under cover of this tortoise fence. For some time the narrow streets, being thronged with the soldiers of both parties, considerably retarded the progress of the Romans; but when once, by gradually pushing back the enemy, they gained the wider passes, the impetuosity of their attack could no longer be withstood. While the Lacedæmonians, having turned their backs, fled precipitately to the higher places, Nabis, being utterly confounded, as if the town were already taken, began to look about for a way to make his escape. Pythagoras, through the whole affair, displayed the spirit and conduct of a general, and was now the sole means of saving the city from being taken: for he ordered the buildings nearest to the wall to be set on fire, and these being instantly in a blaze, those who on another occasion would have brought help to extinguish the fire, now helping to increase it, the roofs tumbled on the Romans; and not only fragments of the tiles, but also the half-burned timber reached the soldiers: the flames spread wide, and the smoke caused a degree of terror even greater than the danger. In consequence, the Romans who were without the city, and were just then advancing to the assault, retired from the wall; and those who were within, fearing lest the fire, rising behind them, should put it out of their power to rejoin the rest of the army, began to retreat. Whereon Quintius, seeing how matters stood, ordered a general retreat to be sounded.—Thus, after they had almost mastered the city, they were obliged to quit it, and return to their camp.

40. Quintius conceiving greater hopes from the fears of the enemy, than from the immediate effect of his operations, kept them in a continual alarm during the three succeeding days; sometimes harassing them with assaults, sometimes enclosing several places with works, so as to leave no passage open for flight. These menaces had such an effect on the tyrant, that he again sent Pythagoras to solicit peace. Quintius at first rejected him with disdain, ordering him to quit the camp; but afterward, on his suppliant entreaties, and throwing himself at his feet, he admitted him to an audience in form. The purport of his discourse,

at first, was an offer of implicit submission to the will of the Romans; but this availed nothing, being considered as nugatory and indecisive. The business was, at length, brought to this issue, that a truce should be made on the conditions delivered in writing a few days before, and the money and hostages were accordingly received. While the tyrant was kept shut up by the siege, the Argives, receiving frequent accounts one after another, that Lacedæmon was on the point of being taken, and having themselves resumed courage on the departure of Pythagoras, with the strongest part of his garrison, looked now with contempt on the small number remaining in the citadel; and, being headed by a person named Archippus, drove the garrison out. They gave Timocrates of Pellene leave to retire, with solemn assurance of sparing his life, in consideration of the mildness which he had shown in his government. In the midst of their rejoicing for this event, Quintius arrived, after having granted peace to the tyrant, dismissed Eumenes and the Rhodians from Lacedæmon, and sent back his brother Lucius Quintius to the fleet.

41. The Nemæan games, the most celebrated of all the Roman festivals, and their most splendid public spectacle, had been omitted at the regular time, on account of the disasters of the war: the state, now in the fulness of their joy, ordered them to be celebrated on the arrival of the Roman general and his army; and appointed the general himself president of the games. Many circumstances concurred to render their happiness complete: their countrymen, whom Pythagoras, lately, and, before that, Nabis, had carried away, were brought home from Lacedæmon: those who on the discovery of the conspiracy by Pythagoras, and when the massacre was already begun, had fled from home, now returned: they saw their liberty restored after a long interval, and beheld in their city the Romans, the authors of its restoration, whose only view in making war on the tyrant was the support of their interest. The freedom of the Argives was also solemnly announced, by the voice of a herald, on the very day of the Nemæan games. Whatever pleasure the Achæans felt on Argos being reinstated in the general council of Achaia, it was, in a great measure, allayed by Lacedæmon being left in slavery, and the tyrant close at their side. As to the Ætolians, they loudly railed at that measure in every meeting. They remarked, that "the war with Philip was not ended until he evacuated all the cities of Greece. But Lacedæmon was left to the tyrant, while the lawful king, who had been at the time in the Roman camp, and others, the noblest of the citizens, must live in exile: so that the Roman nation was become a partisan of

Nabis's tyranny." Quintius led back his army to Elatia, whence he had set out to the Spartan war. Some writers say that the tyrant's method of carrying on hostilities was not by sallies from the city, but that he encamped in the face of the Romans; and that after he had declined fighting a long time, waiting for succours from the Ætolians, he was forced to come to an engagement, by an attack which the Romans made on his foragers, when, being defeated in that battle, and beaten out of his camp, he sued for peace, after fifteen thousand of his men had been killed, and more than four thousand made prisoners.

42. Nearly at the same time arrived at Rome a letter from Titus Quintius, with an account of his proceedings at Lacedæmon; and another out of Spain from Marcus Porcius the consul: whereon the senate decreed a supplication for three days in the name of each. The other consul, Lucius Valerius, as his province had remained quiet since the defeat of the Boians at the wood of Litana, came home to Rome to hold the elections. Publius Cornelius Scipio Africanus, a second time, and Tiberius Sempronius Longus, were elected consuls. The fathers of these two had been consuls in the first year of the second Punic war. The election of pretors was then held, and the choice fell on Publius Cornelius Scipio, two Cneius Corneliuses Merenda, and Blasio, Cneius Domitius Ænobarbus, Sextus Digitius, and Titus Juvencius Thalna. As soon as the elections were finished, the consul returned to his province. The inhabitants of Ferentinum, this year, laid claim to a privilege unheard of before; that Latines, giving in their names for a Roman colony, should be deemed citizens of Rome. Some colonists, who had given in their names for Puteoli, Salernum, and Buxentum, assumed, on that ground, the character of Roman citizens; but the senate determined that they were not.

43. In the beginning of the year, [A. U. C. 558. B. C. 194,] wherein Publius Scipio Africanus, a second time, and Tiberius Sempronius Longus, were consuls, two ambassadors from the tyrant Nabis came to Rome. The senate gave them audience in the temple of Apollo, outside the city. They entreated that a peace might be concluded on the terms settled with Quintius, which was granted. When the question was put concerning the provinces, the majority of the senate were of opinion, that, as the wars in Spain and Macedonia were at an end, Italy should be the province of both the consuls; but Scipio contended that one consul was sufficient for Italy, and that Macedonia ought to be decreed to the other: that "there was every reason to apprehend a dangerous war with Antiochus, for he had already, of his

own accord, come into Europe; and how did they suppose he would act in future, when he should be encouraged to a war, on one hand by the Ætolians, avowed enemies of their state, and stimulated on the other by Hannibal, a general famous for his victories over the Romans?" While the consular provinces were in dispute, the pretors cast lots for theirs. The city jurisdiction fell to Cneius Domitius; the foreign to Titus Juvencius; Farther Spain to Publius Cornelius; Hither Spain to Sextus Digitius; Sicily to Cneius Cornelius Blasio; Sardinia to Cneius Cornelius Merenda. It was resolved that no new army should be sent into Macedonia, but that the one which was there should be brought home to Italy by Quintius, and disbanded: that the army which was in Spain. under Marcus Porcius Cato, should likewise be disbanded: that Italy should be the province of both the consuls, for the defence of which they should raise two city legions: so that, after the disbanding of the armies, mentioned in the resolution of the senate, the whole military establishment should consist of eight Roman legions.

44. A sacred spring had been celebrated, in the preceding year, during the consulate of Marcus Porcius and Lucius Valerius; but Publius Licinius, one of the pontiffs, having made a report, first, to the college of pontiffs, and afterward, by their direction, to the senate, that it had not been duly performed, a vote was passed that it should be celebrated anew, under the direction of the pontiffs; and that the great games, vowed together with it, should be exhibited at the usual expense; that the sacred spring should be deemed to comprehend all the cattle born between the calends of March and the day preceding the calends of May, in the year of the consulate of Publius Cornelius Scipio and Tiberius Sempronius Longus. Then followed the election of censors. Sextus Ælius Pætus and Caius Cornelius Cethegus being created censors, named as prince of the senate the consul Publius Scipio, whom the former censors likewise had appointed. They passed by only three senators in the whole, none of whom had enjoyed the honour of a curule office. They obtained, on another account, the highest degree of credit with that body; for, at the celebration of the Roman games, they ordered the curule ediles to set apart places for the senators, distinct from those of the people; whereas, hitherto, all the spectators used to sit promiscuously. Of the knights, also, very few were deprived of their horses; nor was severity shown towards any rank of men. The gallery of the temple of Liberty, and the Villa Publica, were repaired and enlarged by the same censors. The sacred spring, and the votive games, were celebrated, pursuant to the vow of Servius Sulpicius Galba, when consul. While

every one's thoughts were engaged by the shows then exhibited, Quintius Pleminius, who, for the many crimes against gods and men committed by him at Locri, had been thrown into prison, procured men who were to set fire by night to several parts of the city at once, in order that, during the general consternation which such a disturbance would occasion, the prison might be broken open. But some of the accomplices discovered the design, and the affair was laid before the senate. Pleminius was thrown into the dungeon, and there put to death.

45. In this year colonies of Roman citizens were settled at Puteoli, Vulturnum, and Liternum; three hundred men in each place. The lands allotted to them had formerly belonged to the Campanians. Colonies of Roman citizens were likewise established at Salernum and Buxentum. The commissioners for conducting these settlements were, Tiberius Sempronius Longus, then consul, Marcus Servilius, and Quintus Minucius Thermus. Other commissioners also, Decius Junius Brutus, Marcus Bæbius Tamphilus, and Marcus Helvius, led a colony of Roman citizens to Sipontum, into a district which had belonged to the Arpinians. To Tempsa, likewise, and to Croto, colonies of Roman citizens were led out. The lands of Tempsa had been taken from the Bruttians, who had formerly expelled the Greeks from them. Croto was possessed by Greeks. In ordering these establishments, there were named, for Croto, Cneius Octavius, Lucius Æmilius Paulus, and Caius Pletorius; for Tempsa, Lucius Cornelius Merula, and Caius Salonius. Several prodigies were observed at Rome that year, and others reported from other places. In the forum, comitium, and capitol, drops of blood were seen, and several showers of earth fell, and the head of Vulcan was surrounded with a blaze of fire. It was reported that a stream of milk ran in the river at Interamna; that, in some reputable families at Ariminum, children were born without eyes and nose; and one, in the territory of Picenum, that had neither hands nor feet. These prodigies were expiated according to an order of the pontiffs, and the nine days' festival was celebrated, in consequence of a report from Adria that a shower of stones had fallen in that neighbourhood.

46. In Gaul, Lucius Valerius Flaccus, proconsul, in a pitched battle, near Mediolanum, completely overthrew the Insubrian Gauls and the Boians; who, under the command of Dorulacus, had crossed the Po, to rouse the Insubrians to arms. Ten thousand of the enemy were slain. About this time his colleague, Marcus Porcius Cato, triumphed over Spain. He carried in the procession twenty-five thousand pounds weight of unwrought silver, one hundred and

three thousand silver denariuses,* five hundred and forty of Oscan silver,† and one thousand four hundred pounds weight of gold. Out of the booty he distributed to each of his soldiers two hundred and seventy asses;‡ double that sum to each centurion, and triple to each horseman. Tiberius Sempronius, consul, proceeding to his province, led his legions, first, into the territory of the Boians. At this time Boiorix, their chieftain, with his two brothers, after having drawn out the whole nation into the field to renew the war, pitched his camp on level ground, with an evident intention to fight the enemy, in case they should pass the frontiers. When the consul understood what a numerous force, and what a degree of resolution the enemy had, he sent an express to his colleague, requesting him, "if he thought proper, to hasten to join him;" adding, that "he would act on the defensive, and defer engaging in battle until his arrival." The same reason which made the consul wish to decline an action, induced the Gauls, whose spirits were raised by the backwardness of their antagonists, to bring it on as soon as possible, that they might finish the affair before the two consuls should unite their forces. However, during two days, they did nothing more than stand in readiness for battle, if any should come out against them. On the third, they advanced furiously to the rampart, and assaulted the camp on every side at once. The consul immediately ordered his men to take arms, and kept them quiet under arms for some time; both to add to the foolish confidence of the enemy, and to arrange his troops at the gates, through which each party was to sally out. The two legions were ordered to march by the two principal gates; but, in the very pass of the gates, the Gauls opposed them in such close bodies as to stop up the way. The fight was maintained a long time in these narrow passes; nor were their hands or swords much employed in the business, but pushing with their shields and bodies, they pressed against each other, the Romans struggling to force their way out, the Gauls to break into the camp, or at least to hinder the Romans from issuing forth. However, neither party could make the least impression on the other, until Quintus Victorius, a first centurion, and Caius Atinius, a military tribune, the former of the second, the latter of the fourth legion, had recourse to an expedient often tried in desperate cases; snatching the standards from the officers who carried them, and throwing them among the enemy. In the struggle to recover the standards, the men of the second legion first made their way out of the gate.

47. These were now fighting on the outside of the ram-

* 96l. 17s. 6d. † 17l. 8s. 9d. ‡ 17s. 5 1-2d.

part, the fourth legion still entangled in the gate, when a new alarm arose on the opposite side of the camp. The Gauls had broke in by the Questorian gate, and had slain the questor, Lucius Postumius, surnamed Tympanus, with Marcus Atinius and Publius Sempronius, prefects of the allies, who made an obstinate resistance; and also, near two hundred soldiers. The enemy were masters of that part of the camp, until a cohort of those which are called extraordinaries, sent by the consul to defend the Questorian gate, killed some who had got within the rampart, drove out the rest, and opposed others who were attempting to break in. About the same time the fourth legion, and two cohorts of extraordinaries, burst out of the gate: and thus there were three battles, in different places, round the camp; while the various kinds of shouts raised by them called off the attention of the combatants from the fight in which they themselves were immediately engaged, to the dangers which threatened their friends. The battle was maintained until midday with equal strength, and with nearly equal hopes. At length the fatigue and heat so far got the better of the soft relaxed bodies of the Gauls, who are incapable of enduring thirst, as to make most of them give up the fight; and the few who stood their ground were attacked by the Romans, routed, and driven to their camp. The consul then gave the signal for retreat, which the greater part obeyed; but some, eager to continue the fight, and hoping to get possession of the camp, pressed forward to the rampart, on which the Gauls, despising their small number, rushed out in a body. The Romans were then routed in turn, and compelled, by their own fear and dismay, to retreat to their camp, which they had refused to do at the command of their general. Thus both parties experienced in turn the vicissitudes of flight and victory. The Gauls, however, had eleven thousand killed, the Romans but five thousand. The Gauls retreated into the heart of their country, and the consul led his legions to Placentia. Some writers say that Scipio, after joining his forces to those of his colleague, overran and plundered the country of the Boians and Ligurians, as far as the woods and marshes suffered him to proceed; others, that, without having effected any thing material, he returned to Rome to hold the elections.

48. Titus Quintius passed the entire winter season of this year at Elatia, where he had established the winter-quarters of his army, in adjusting political arrangements, and reversing the measures which had been introduced in the several states under the arbitrary domination of Philip and his deputies, while they crushed the rights and liberties of others, in order to augment the power of those who formed

a faction in their favour. Early in the spring he came to Corinth, where he had summoned a general convention. Ambassadors having attended from every one of the states, so as to form a numerous assembly, he addressed them in a long speech, in which, beginning from the first commencement of friendship between the Romans and the nation of the Greeks, he enumerated the proceedings of the commanders who had been in Macedonia before him, and likewise his own. His whole narration was heard with the warmest approbation, until he came to make mention of Nabis; and then they expressed their opinion, that it was utterly inconsistent with the character of the deliverer of Greece to have left seated, in the centre of one of its most respectable states, a tyrant, who was not only insupportable to his own country, but a terror to all the states in his neighbourhood. Whereon Quintius, who well knew their sentiments on the occasion, freely acknowleged, that "if the business could have been accomplished without the entire destruction of Lacedæmon, no mention of peace with the tyrant ought ever to have been listened to; but that, as the case stood, when it was not possible to crush him without involving the city in utter ruin, it was judged more eligible to leave Nabis in a state of debility, stripped of almost every kind of power to do injury, than to suffer the city, which must have perished in the very process of its delivery being effectuated, to sink under remedies too violent for it to support."

49. To the recital of matters past he subjoined, that "his intention was to depart shortly for Italy, and to carry with him all his troops; that they should hear, within ten days, of the garrisons having evacuated Demetrias; and that Chalcis, the citadel of Corinth, should instantly be delivered up to the Achæans; that all the world might know which deserved better the character of deceivers, the Romans or the Ætolians, who had spread insinuations, that when the cause of liberty was intrusted to the Romans, it was put into dangerous hands, and that they had only changed masters, being subjugated now to the Romans, as formerly to the Macedonians. But they were men who never scrupled what they either said or did. The rest of the nations he advised to form their estimate of friends from deeds, not from words; and to satisfy themselves whom they ought to trust, and against whom they ought to be on their guard; to use liberty with moderation; for, when regulated by prudence, it was productive of happiness both to individuals and to states; but when pushed to excess, it became not only obnoxious to others, but precipitated the possessors of it themselves into dangerous rashness and extravagance. He recommended that those at the head of affairs, and all the several ranks

of men in each particular state, should cultivate harmony between themselves; and that all should direct their views to the general interest of the whole: for, while they acted in concert, no king or tyrant would ever be able to overpower them; but discord and dissention gave every advantage to the arts of an adversary, as the party worsted in a domestic dispute generally chose to unite with foreigners rather than submit to a countryman of their own. He then exhorted them, as the arms of others had procured their liberty, and the good faith of foreigners had returned it safe into their hands, to apply now their own diligent care to the watching and guarding of it, that the Roman people might perceive that those on whom they had bestowed liberty were deserving of it, and that their kindness was not ill placed."

50. On hearing these admonitions, such as parental tenderness might dictate, every one present shed tears of joy; and so great were their transports, that they affected his feelings to such a degree as to interrupt his discourse. For some time a confused noise prevailed, all together expressing their approbation, and charging each other to treasure up those expressions in their minds and hearts, as if they had been uttered by an oracle. Then silence ensuing, he requested of them to make diligent search for such Roman citizens as were in servitude among them, and to send them into Thessaly to him within two months; observing, that "it would not redound to their honour if, in a land restored to liberty, its deliverers should remain in servitude." This was answered with a shout of applause; and they acknowleged, as an obligation added to the rest, his reminding them of the discharge of a duty so indispensably incumbent on their gratitude. There was a vast number of these who had been made prisoners in the Punic war, and sold by Hannibal when their countrymen refused to ransom them. That they were very numerous is proved by what Polybius says, that this business cost the Achæans one hundred talents,* though they had fixed the price to be paid for each captive to the owner so low as five hundred denariuses:† for, at that rate, there were one thousand two hundred in Achaia. Calculate now, in proportion to this, how many were probably in all Greece.

51. Before the convention broke up, they saw the garrison march down from the citadel of Corinth, proceed forward to the gate, and depart. The general followed them, accompanied by the whole assembly, who, with loud acclamations, blessed him as their preserver and deliverer. At

* 19,375*l.*  † 16*l.* 2*s.* 11*d.*

length, taking leave of these, and dismissing them, he returned to Elatia by the same road through which he came. He thence sent Appius Claudius, lieutenant-general, with all his troops, ordering him to march through Thessaly and Epirus, and to wait for him at Oricum, where he intended to embark the army for Italy. He also wrote to his brother, Lucius Quintius, lieutenant-general and commander of the fleet, to collect thither transport ships from all the coasts of Greece. He himself proceeded to Chalcis; and, after sending away the garrisons, not only from that city, but likewise from Oreum and Eretria, he held there a congress of the Eubœan states, whom he reminded of the condition in which he had found their affairs, and of that in which he was leaving them; and then dismissed the assembly. He then proceeded to Demetrias, and removed the garrison. Accompanied by all the citizens, as at Corinth and Chalcis, he pursued his route into Thessaly, where the states were not only to be set at liberty, but also to be reduced from a state of utter anarchy and confusion into some tolerable form; for they had been thrown into disorder, not only through the faults of the times, and the arbitrary acts of the king and his adherents, but also through the restless disposition of the nation, who, from the earliest times, even to our days, have never conducted any election, or assembly, or council, without dissensions and tumult. He chose both senators and judges, with regard principally to their property, and vested the chief share of power in that part of the state which was more particularly interested in its safety and tranquillity.

52. When he had completed these regulations in Thessaly, he went on, through Epirus, to Oricum, whence he intended to take his passage, all the troops being transported thence to Brundusium. From this place to the city, they passed the whole length of Italy, in a manner, like a triumph; the captured effects which they brought with them forming a train as large as that of the troops themselves. When they arrived at Rome, the senate assembled outside the city, to receive from Quintius a recital of his services; and, with high satisfaction, voted him a triumph, which he had so justly merited. His triumph lasted three days. On the first day were carried in procession armour, weapons, brazen and marble statues, of which he had taken greater numbers from Philip than from the states of Greece. On the second, gold and silver wrought, unwrought, and coined. Of unwrought silver there were eighteen thousand pounds weight; and of wrought, two hundred and seventy thousand; consisting of many vessels of various sorts, most of them engraved, and several of excellent workmanship; also a great

many others made of brass; and, besides these, ten shields of silver. The coined silver amounted to eighty-four thousand of the Attic coin called tetradrachmus, containing each of silver about the weight of four denariuses.* Of gold there were three thousand seven hundred and fourteen pounds, and one shield of massy gold; and of the gold coin called philippics, fourteen thousand five hundred and fourteen.† On the third day were carried golden crowns, presented by the several states, in number one hundred and fourteen; then the victims. Before his chariot went many illustrious captives with the hostages, among whom were Demetrius, son of King Philip, and Armenes, a Lacedæmonian, son of the tyrant Nabis. Then Quintius himself rode into the city, followed by a numerous body of soldiers, as the whole army had been brought home from the province. Among these he distributed two hundred and fifty asses‡ to each footman, double to a centurion, triple to a horseman. Those who had been redeemed from captivity added to the grandeur of the procession, walking after him with their heads shaven.

53. In the latter part of this year Quintus Ælius Tubero, plebeian tribune, in pursuance of a decree of the senate, proposed to the people, and the people ordered, that "two Latine colonies should be settled, one in Bruttium, the other in the territory of Thurium." For making these settlements commissioners were appointed, who were to hold the office for three years; for Bruttium, Quintus Nævius, Marcus Minucius Rufus, and Marcus Furius Crassipes; and for the district of Thurium, Cneius Manlius, Quintus Ælius, and Lucius Apustius. The assemblies of election to these two appointments were held in the capitol by Cneius Domitius, city pretor. Several temples were dedicated this year; one of Juno Sospita, in the herb market, vowed and contracted for four years before, in the time of the Gallic war, by Cneius Cornelius, consul; and the same person, now censor, performed the dedication. Another of Faunus, the building of which had been agreed for two years before, and a fund formed for it out of fines estreated by the ediles, Caius Scribonius and Cneius Domitius; the latter of whom, now city pretor, dedicated it. Quintus Marcius Ralla, constituted commissioner for the purpose, dedicated the temple of Fortuna Primigenia, on the Quirinal Hill. Publius Sempronius Sophus had vowed this temple ten years before, in the Punic war; and being afterward censor, had employed persons to build it. Caius Servilius, duumvir, also dedicated a temple of Jupiter, in the island. This had been vowed in the Gallic war, six years before, by Lucius Furius Purpureo,

* 10,849*l.* 18*s.*　　† 936*l.* 10*s.*　　‡ 16*s.* 1 1-4*d.*

who afterward, when consul, contracted for the building. Such were the transactions of that year.

54. Publius Scipio came home from his province of Gaul to choose new consuls; and the people, in assembly, elected Lucius Cornelius Merula aud Quintus Minucius Thermus. Next day were chosen pretors, Lucius Cornelius Scipio, Marcus Fulvius Nobilior, Caius Scribonius, Marcus Valerius Messala, Lucius Porcius Licinus, and Caius Flaminius. The curule ediles of this year, Caius Atilius Serranus and Lucius Scribonius, first exhibited the Megalesian games, in which were introduced performances on the stage. At the Roman games, celebrated by these ediles, the senators, for the first time, sat separate from the people, which, as every innovation usually does, gave occasion to various observations. Some considered this as "an honour, shown at length to that most respectable body, and which ought to have been done long before;" while others contended that "every addition made to the grandeur of the senate, was a diminution of the dignity of the people; and that all such distinctions as tended to set the orders of the state at a distance from each other, were equally subversive of liberty and concord. During five hundred and fifty-eight years," they asserted, "all the spectators had sat promiscuously; what reason then had now occurred, on a sudden, that should make the senators disdain to have the commons intermixed with them, or make the rich scorn to sit in company with the poor? It was an unprecedented gratification of pride and overbearing vanity, never even desired, or certainly not assumed, by the senate of any other nation." It is said that even Africanus himself at last became sorry for having proposed that matter in his consulship: so difficult is it to bring people to approve of any alteration of ancient customs; they are always naturally disposed to adhere to old practices, unless experience evidently proves their inexpediency.

55. In the beginning of the year, which was the consulate of Lucius Cornelius and Quintus Minucius, such frequent reports of earthquakes were brought, that people grew weary, not only of the matter itself, but of the religious rites enjoined in consequence; for neither could the senate be convened, nor the business of the public be transacted, the consuls were so constantly employed in sacrifices and expiations. At last, the decemvirs were ordered to consult the books; and in pursuance of their answer, a supplication was performed during three days. People offered prayers at all the shrines, with garlands on their heads. An order was published, that all the persons belonging to one family should pay their worship together; and the consuls, by direction of the senate, published an edict, that, on any day

whereon religious rites should be ordered, in consequence of the report of an earthquake, no person should report another earthquake on that day. Then the consuls first, afterward the pretors, cast lots for their provinces. Cornelius obtained Gaul; Minucius, Liguria; Caius Scribonius, the city jurisdiction; Marcus Valerius, the foreign; Lucius Cornelius, Sicily; Lucius Portius, Sardinia; Caius Flaminius, Hither Spain; and Marcus Fulvius, Farther Spain.

56. While the consuls supposed that, for that year, they should have no employment in the military line, a letter was brought from Marcus Cincius, who was commander at Pisæ, announcing that "twenty thousand armed Ligurians, in consequence of a conspiracy of that whole nation, formed in the meetings of their several districts, had first wasted the lands of Luna, and then passing through the territory of Pisæ, had overrun the whole sea-coast." In consequence of this intelligence, the consul Minucius, whose province Liguria was, by direction of the senate, mounted the rostrum, and published orders, that "the two legions, enlisted the year before, should, on the tenth day from that, attend him at Arretium;" and mentioned his intention of levying two legions for the city in their stead. [A. U. C. 559. B. C. 193.] He likewise gave notice to the magistrates and ambassadors of such of the allies,* and of the Latine confederates, as were bound to furnish soldiers, to attend him in the capitol. Of these he wrote out a list, amounting to fifteen thousand foot and five hundred horse, proportioning the contingent of each state to the number of its young men, and ordered those present to go directly from the spot to the gate of the city; and, in order to expedite the business, to proceed to their homes to raise the men. To Fulvius and Flaminius were assigned equal numbers of men, to each three thousand Roman foot, and a reinforcement of one hundred horse, with five thousand foot of the Latine allies, and two hundred horse; and orders were given to those pretors to disband the old troops immediately on their arrival in their provinces. Although great numbers of the soldiers belonging to the city legions had made application to the plebeian tribunes to take cognizance of the cases of such men as claimed exemption from the service, on account either of having served out their time, or of bad health; yet a letter from Tiberius Sempronius banished all thoughts of such proceeding; for he sent an account that "fifteen thousand of the Ligurians had come into the lands of Placentia, and

* It was not customary to levy recruits from all the states of the allies at once, but from a certain number of them at a time; so that they all furnished supplies in their turn, except when a pressing exigency demanded an extraordinary force.

wasted them with fire and sword, to the very walls of that city and the bank of the Po; and that the Boian nation also appeared disposed to renew hostilities." In consequence of this information, the senate passed a vote that "there was a Gallic tumult subsisting, and that it would be improper for the plebeian tribunes to take cognizance of the claims of the soldiers, so as to prevent their attending pursuant to the proclamation;" and they added an order, that the Latine confederates, who had served in the army of Publius Cornelius and Tiberius Sempronius, and had been discharged by those consuls, should reassemble, on whatever day and in whatever place of Etruria the consul Lucius Cornelius should appoint; and that the consul Lucius Cornelius, on his way to his province, should enlist, arm, and carry with him, all such persons as he should think fit, in the several towns and countries through which he was to pass, and should have authority to discharge such of them, and at such times, as he might judge proper.

57. After the consuls had finished the levies, and were gone to their provinces, Titus Quintius demanded that "the senate should receive an account of the regulations which he, in concert with the ten ambassadors, had settled; and, if they thought proper, ratify them by their authority." He told them that "it would facilitate this business if they were first to give audience to the ambassadors, who had come from all parts of Greece, and a great part of Asia, and to those from the two kings." These embassies were introduced to the senate by the city pretor Caius Scribonius, and all received kind answers. As the discussion of the affair with Antiochus required too much time, it was referred to the ten ambassadors, some of whom had conferred with the king in Asia, or at Lysimachia. Directions were given to Titus Quintius that, in conjunction with these, he should hear what the king's ambassadors had to say, and should give them such answer as comported with the dignity and interest of the Roman people. At the head of the embassy were Menippus and Hegesianax; the former of whom said that "he could not conceive what intricacy there was in the business of their embassy, as they came simply to ask friendship, and conclude an alliance. Now, there were three kinds of treaties, by which kings and states formed friendships with each other: one, when terms were dictated to a people vanquished in war; for after every thing has been surrendered to him who has proved superior in war, he has the sole power of judging and determining what share shall remain to the vanquished, and what they shall forfeit. The second, when parties, equally matched in war, conclude a treaty of peace and friendship on terms of equality; for then demands

are proposed and restitution made, reciprocally, in a convention; and if, in consequence of the war, confusion has arisen with respect to any parts of their properties, the matter is adjusted on the footing either of ancient right or of the mutual convenience of the parties. The third kind was, when parties who had never been foes, met to form a friendly union by a social treaty; these neither dictate nor receive terms, for that is the case between a victor and a party vanquished. As Antiochus came under this last description, he wondered, he said, at the Romans taking upon them to dictate terms to him; and to prescribe, which of the cities of Asia they chose should be free and independent, which tributary, and which of them the king's troops and the king himself should be prohibited to enter. This might be a proper method of concluding a peace with Philip, who was their enemy, but not of making a treaty of alliance with Antiochus, their friend."

58. To this Quintius answered: "Since you choose to deal methodically, and enumerate the several modes of contracting amity, I also will lay down two conditions, without which, you may tell your king, that he must not expect to contract any friendship with the Romans. One, that if he does not choose that we should concern ourselves in the affairs of the cities in Asia, he must refrain from interfering, in any particular, with the affairs of Europe. The other, that if he does not confine himself within the limits of Asia, but passes over into Europe, the Romans will think themselves at full liberty to maintain the friendships which they have already formed with the states of Asia, and also to contract new ones." On this Hegesianax exclaimed, that "such propositions were highly improper to be listened to, as their tendency was to exclude Antiochus from the cities of Thrace and the Chersonese,—places which his great-grandfather, Seleucus, had acquired with great honour, after vanquishing Lysimachus in war, and killing him in battle, and had left to his successors; and part of which, after they had been seized by the Thracians, Antiochus had, with equal honour, recovered by force of arms: as well as others which had been deserted,—as Lysimachia, for instance, he had repeopled, by calling home the inhabitants;—and several, which had been destroyed by fire, and buried in ruins, he had rebuilt at a vast expense. What kind of resemblance was there, then, in the cases of Antiochus being ejected from possessions so acquired, so recovered; and of the Romans refraining from intermeddling with Asia, to which they never had any claim? Antiochus wished to obtain the friendship of the Romans; but he wished it on terms that would redound to his honour, not to his shame.

In reply to this, Quintius said,—"Since honour is the point on which our disquisitions turn, and which, indeed, with a people who held the first rank among the nations of the world, and with so great a king, ought to be the sole, or at least the primary object of regard; tell me, I pray you, which do you think more honourable, to wish to give liberty to all the Grecian cities in every part of the world, or to make them slaves and vassals? Since Antiochus thinks it conducive to his glory, to reduce to slavery those cities which his great-grandfather held by the right of arms, but which his grandfather or father never occupied as their property; while the Roman people, having undertaken the patronage of the liberty of the Greeks, deem it incumbent on their faith and constancy not to abandon it. As they have delivered Greece from Philip, so they intend to deliver, from Antiochus, all the states of Asia which are of the Grecian race: for colonies were not sent into Ætolia and Ionia to be enslaved to kings; but with design to increase the population, and to propagate that ancient race in every part of the globe."

59. Hegesianax hesitating, as he could not deny that the cause which professed the bestowing of liberty carried a more honourable semblance than one that pointed to slavery, Publius Sulpicius, who was the eldest of the ten ambassadors, said,—"Let us cut the matter short. Choose one of the two conditions clearly propounded just now by Quintius, or cease to speak of friendship." But Menippus replied: "We neither will, nor can, accede to any proposition which tends to lessen the dominions of Antiochus." Next day Quintius brought into the senate house all the ambassadors of Greece and Asia, in order that they might learn the dispositions entertained by the Roman people, and by Antiochus, towards the Grecian states. He then acquainted them with his own demands and those of the king; and desired them to "assure their respective states that the same disinterested zeal and courage which the Roman people had displayed in defence of their liberty against the encroachments of Philip, they would likewise exert against those of Antiochus, if he should refuse to retire out of Europe." On this, Menippus earnestly besought Quintius and the senate, "not to be hasty in forming their determination, which, in its effects, might disturb the peace of the whole world; to take time to themselves, and allow the king time for consideration; that, when informed of the conditions proposed, he would consider them, and either obtain some relaxation in the terms or accede to them." Accordingly, the business was deferred entire; and a resolution passed, that the same ambassadors should be sent to

the king, who had attended him at Lysimachia,—Publius Sulpicius, Publius Villius, and Publius Ælius.

60. Scarcely had these begun their journey, when ambassadors from Carthage brought information that Antiochus was evidently preparing for war, and that Hannibal was employed in his service; which gave reason to fear that the Carthaginians might take arms at the same time. Hannibal, on leaving his own country, had gone to Antiochus, as was mentioned before, and was held by the king in high estimation, not so much for his other qualifications, as because, to a person who had long been revolving schemes for a war with Rome, there could not be any fitter counsellor to confer with on such a subject. His opinion was always one and the same: that Italy should be made the seat of the war: because "Italy would supply a foreign enemy both with men and provisions; but, if it were left in quiet, and the Roman people were allowed to employ the strength and forces of Italy, in making war in any other country, no king or nation would be able to cope with them." He demanded for himself, one hundred decked ships, ten thousand foot, and one thousand horse. "With this force," he said, "he would first repair to Africa; and he had confident hopes that he should be able to prevail on the Carthaginians to revive hostilities. If they should hesitate, he would raise a war against the Romans in some part of Italy. That the king ought to cross over into Europe with all the rest of his force, and keep his army in some part of Greece; not to pass over immediately into Italy, but to be in readiness to do so; which would be sufficient to give the war a formidable appearance, and impress a terrifying notion of its magnitude."

61. When he had brought the king to agree in his opinion, he judged it necessary to predispose the minds of his countrymen in favour of the design; but he durst not send a letter, lest it might, by some accident, be intercepted, and his plans by that means be discovered. He had found at Ephesus a Tyrian called Aristo, and in several less important commissions, had discovered him to possess a good degree of ingenuity. This man he now loaded with presents and promises of rewards, which were confirmed by the king himself, and sent him to Carthage with messages to his friends. He told him the names of the persons to whom they were to be delivered, and furnished him with secret tokens, by which they would know, with certainty, that the messages came from him. On this Aristo's appearing at Carthage, the reason of his coming was not discovered by Hannibal's friends sooner than by his enemies. At first they spoke of the matter publicly, in their circles and

their tables; and at last some persons declared in the senate that "the banishment of Hannibal answered no purpose, if, while resident in another country, he was still able to propagate designs for changing the administration, and disturbing the quiet of the state, by his intrigues. That a Tyrian stranger named Aristo had come with a commission from Hannibal and King Antiochus; that certain men daily held secret conferences with him, and caballed in private, the consequences of which would soon break out, to the ruin of the public." This produced a general outcry, that Aristo ought to be summoned, and examined respecting the reason of his coming; and if he did not disclose it, to be sent to Rome with ambassadors accompanying him; that they had already suffered enough of punishment in atonement of the headstrong rashness of one individual; that the faults of private citizens should be at their own risk, and the state should be preserved free, not only from guilt, but even from the suspicion of it." Aristo, being summoned, contended for his innocence; and urged as his strongest defence, that he had brought no letter to any person whatever; but he gave no satisfactory reason for his coming, and was chiefly embarrassed to obviate the charge of conversing solely with men of the Barcine faction. A warm debate ensued: some earnestly pressing that he should be immediately seized as a spy, and kept in custody; while others insisted, that there were not sufficient grounds for such violent measures; that "putting strangers into confinement without reason was a step that afforded a bad precedent; for doubtless the same treatment would be retaliated on the Carthaginians at Tyre, and other marts, where they frequently traded." They came to no determination that day. Aristo practised on the Carthaginians an artifice suited to their own genius; for having early in the evening hung up a written tablet, in the most frequented place in the city, over the tribunal where the magistrates daily sat, he went on board his ship at the third watch, and fled. Next day, when the suffetes had taken their seats to administer justice, the tablet was observed, taken down, and read. Its contents were, that "Aristo came not with a private commission to any person, but with a public one to the elders:" by this name they called the senate. The imputation being thus thrown on the state, less pains were taken in searching into the suspicions harboured of a few individuals: however, it was determined that ambassadors should be sent to Rome, to represent the affair to the consuls and the senate, and at the same time to complain of injuries received from Masinissa.

62. When Masinissa observed that the Carthaginians were looked on with jealousy by others, and were full of dissen-

sions among themselves, the nobles being suspected by the senate, on account of their conferences with Aristo, and the senate by the people, in consequence of the information given by the same Aristo, he thought that at such a conjuncture he might successfully encroach on their rights; and accordingly he laid waste their country along the sea-coast, and compelled several cities, which were tributary to the Carthaginians, to pay their taxes to him. This tract they call Emporia; it forms the shore of the lesser Syrtis, and has a fertile soil; one of its cities is Leptis, which paid a tribute to the Carthaginians of a talent a day. At this time Masinissa not only ravaged that whole tract, but, with respect to a considerable part of it, disputed the right of possession with the Carthaginians; and when he learned that they were sending to Rome, both to justify their conduct, and, at the same time, to make complaints of him, he likewise sent ambassadors to Rome, to aggravate the suspicions entertained of them, and to manage the dispute about the right to the taxes. The Carthaginians were heard first, and their account of the Tyrian stranger gave the senate no small uneasiness, as they dreaded being involved in war with Antiochus and the Carthaginians at the same time. What contributed chiefly to strengthen a suspicion of evil designs was, that though they had resolved to seize Aristo, and send him to Rome, they had not placed a guard either on himself or his ship. Then began the controversy with the king's ambassadors on the claims of the territory in dispute. The Carthaginians supported their cause, by insisting, that "it must belong to them, as being within the limits which Scipio, after conquering the country, had fixed as the boundaries of the Carthaginian territory; and also by the acknowledgment of the king, who, when he was going in pursuit of Aphir, a fugitive from his kingdom, then hovering about Cyrene, with a party of Numidians, had solicited as a favour a passage through that very district, as being confessedly a part of the Carthaginian dominions." The Numidians insisted "that they were guilty of misrepresentation with respect to the limits fixed by Scipio; and if a person chose to recur to the real origin of their property, what title had the Carthaginians to call any land in Africa their own; foreigners and strangers, to whom had been granted as a gift, for the purpose of building a city, as much ground as they could encompass with the cuttings of a bull's hide? Whatever acquisitions they had made beyond Byrsa, their original settlement, they held by fraud and violence; for, in relation to the land in question, so far were they from being able to prove uninterrupted possession from the time when it was first acquired, that they cannot even prove that they ever possessed it for any considerable time. As occasion offered, sometimes they, sometimes the kings of Numidia, had held the dominion of it; and the possession of it always fell to the party which had the stronger army. They requested the senate to suffer the matter to remain on the same footing on which it stood before the Carthaginians became enemies to the Romans, or the king of Numidia their friend and ally; and to interfere, so as to hinder whichever party was able, from keeping possession."—The senate resolved to tell the ambassadors of both parties that they would send persons into Africa to determine, on the spot, the controversy between the people of Carthage and the king. They accordingly sent Publius Scipio Africanus, Caius Cornelius Cethegus, and Marcus Minucius Rufus; who, after viewing the ground, and hearing what could be said on both sides, left every thing as they found it, without giving any opinion. Whether they acted in this manner from their own judgment, or in pursuance of directions received at home, is by no means certain; but thus much is most certain, that as affairs were circumstanced, it was highly expedient to leave the dispute undecided; for, had the case been otherwise, Scipio alone, either from his own knowledge of the business, or the influence which he possessed, and to which he had a just claim on both parties, could, with a nod, have ended the controversy.

---

## BOOK XXXV.

Chap. 1. In the beginning of the same year Sextus Digitius, pretor in the Hither Spain, fought with those states, which after the departure of Marcus Cato had recommenced hostilities, a great number of battles, but none deserving of particular mention; and all so unfavourable to him, that he scarcely delivered to his successor half the number of men that he had received. In consequence of this, every state in Spain would certainly have resumed new courage, and have taken up arms, had not the other pretor, Publius Cornelius Scipio, son of Cneius, been successful in several engagements on the other side of the Iberus; and, by these means, diffused such a general terror, that no less than fifty towns came over to his side. These exploits Scipio performed in his pretorship. Afterward, when propretor, as the Lusitanians, after ravaging the farther province, were returning home, with an immense booty, he attacked them on their march, and continued the engagement from the third hour of the day to the eighth, before any advantage was gained on either side. He was inferior to the enemy in number of men, but he had the advantage of them in other respects: with his troops formed in a compact body, he attacked a long train, encumbered with multitudes of cattle, and with his soldiers fresh, engaged men fatigued by a long march; for the enemy had set out at the third watch, and besides travelling the remainder of the night, had continued their route to the third hour of the day; nor had they been allowed any rest, as the battle immediately succeeded the march. Wherefore, though at the beginning they retained some vigour of body and mind, and at first threw the Romans into disorder, yet after some time the fight became equal. In this critical situation the propretor made a vow to celebrate games in honour of Jupiter, in case he should defeat and cut off the enemy. The Romans then made a more vigorous push, which the Lusitanians could not withstand, but in a little time turned their backs. The victors pursued them briskly, killed no less than twelve thousand of them, and took five hundred and forty prisoners, most of whom were horsemen. There were taken, besides, a hundred and thirty-four military standards. Of the Roman army, but seventy-three men were lost. The battle was fought at a small distance from the city of Ilipa. Thither Publius Cornelius led back his victorious army, amply enriched with spoil; all which was exposed to view under the walls of the town, and permission given to the owners to claim their effects. The remainder was put into the hands of the questor to be sold, and the money produced by the sale was distributed among the soldiers.

2. At the time when these occurrences happened in Spain, Caius Flaminius, the pretor, had not yet set out from Rome: therefore he and his friends took pains to represent, in the strongest colours, both the successes and the misfortunes experienced there; and he laboured to persuade the senate that, as a very formidable war had blazed out in his province, and he was likely to receive from Sextus Digitius a very small remnant of an army, and that too terrified and disheartened, they ought to decree one of the city legions to him, in order that, when he should have united to it the soldiers levied by himself, pursuant to decree, he might select from the whole number three thousand five hundred foot, and three hundred horse. He said that "with such a legion as that (for very little confidence could be placed on the troops of Sextus Digitius) he should be able to manage the war." But the elder part of the senate insisted that "decrees of the senate ought not to be passed on every groundless rumour,

fabricated by private persons for the purpose of humouring magistrates; and that no intelligence should be deemed authentic except it were either written by the pretors from their provinces, or brought by their deputies. If there was a tumultuous commotion in Spain, they advised a vote that tumultuary soldiers should be levied by the pretor in some other country than Italy." The senate's intention was that such description of men should be raised in Spain. Valerius Antias says that Caius Flaminius sailed to Sicily for the purpose of levying troops, and that, on his voyage thence to Spain, being driven by a storm to Africa, he enlisted there many stragglers who had belonged to the army of Publius Africanus; and that, to the levies made in those two provinces, he added a third in Spain.

3. In Italy, the war commenced by the Ligurians grew daily more formidable. They now invested Pisæ with an army of forty thousand men; for multitudes flocked to them continually, led by the favourable reports of their proceedings, and the expectation of booty. The consul, Minucius, came to Aretium, on the day which he had fixed for the assembling of the troops. Thence he led them, in order of battle, towards Pisæ; and though the enemy had removed their camp to the other side of the river, at the distance of no more than three miles from the place, the consul marched into the city, which evidently owed its preservation to his coming. Next day, he also encamped on the opposite shore, about a mile from the enemy; and by sending out parties from that post, to attack those of the enemy, protected the lands of the allies from their depredations. He did not think it prudent to hazard a general engagement, because his troops were raw, composed of many different kinds of men, and not yet sufficiently acquainted with each other, to act together with confidence. The Ligurians depended so much on their numbers, that they not only came out and offered battle, willing to risk every thing on the issue of it; but from their superfluity of men they sent out many parties along the frontiers to plunder; and whenever a large quantity of cattle and other prey was collected, there was an escort always in readiness to convey it into their forts and towns.

4. While the operations remained at a stand at Pisæ, the other consul, Lucius Cornelius Merula, led his army through the extreme borders of the Ligurians into the territory of the Boians, where the mode of proceeding was quite the reverse of that which took place in the war of Liguria. The consul offered battle; the enemy refused to fight; and the Romans, when they could not urge them to it, went out in parties to plunder, while the Boians chose to let their

country be utterly wasted with fire and sword without opposition, rather than venture an engagement in defence of it. When the ravage was completed, the consul quitted the enemy's lands, and marched towards Mutina in a careless manner, as through a tract where no hostility was to be apprehended. The Boians, when they learned that the Roman had withdrawn beyond their frontiers, followed him as secretly as possible, watching an opportunity for an ambuscade; and, having gone by his camp in the night, took possession of a defile through which the Romans were to pass. But they were not able to effect this without being discovered; and the consul, who usually began his march late in the night, now waited until day, lest in the disorderly fight likely to ensue, darkness might increase the confusion; and though he did not stir before it was light, yet he sent forward a troop of horse to explore the country. On receiving intelligence from them of the number and situation of the enemy, he ordered the baggage to be heaped together in the centre, and the veterans to throw up a rampart round it; and then, with the rest of the army in order of battle, he advanced towards the enemy. The Gauls did the same, when they found that their stratagem was detected, and that they were to engage in a fair and regular battle, where success must depend on valour alone.

5. The battle began about the second hour. The left brigade of the allies and the extraordinaries formed the first line, and were commanded by two lieutenants-general of consular dignity, Marcus Marcellus and Tiberius Sempronius, who had been consul the year before. The present consul was sometimes employed in the front of the line, sometimes in keeping back the legions in reserve, that they might not, through eagerness for fighting, come up to the attack until they received the signal. He ordered the two Minuciuses, Quintus and Publius, military tribunes, to lead off the cavalry of the legions into open ground, at some distance from the line; and "when he should give them the signal, to charge the enemy through the clear space." While he was thus employed, a message came from Tiberius Sempronius Longus, that the extraordinaries could not support the onset of the Gauls; that great numbers had already fallen; and that partly through weariness, partly through fear, the ardour of the survivors was much abated. He recommended it therefore to the consul, if he thought proper, to send up one or other of the two legions, before the army suffered disgrace. The second legion was accordingly sent, and the extraordinaries were ordered to retire. By the legion coming up, with its men fresh, and the ranks complete in their numbers, the fight was renewed with vigour. The left

wing was withdrawn out of the action, and the right took its place in the van. The intense heat of the sun discomposed the Gauls, whose bodies were very ill qualified to endure it; nevertheless, keeping their ranks close, and leaning sometimes on each other, sometimes on their bucklers, they withstood the attack of the Romans; which, when the consul observed, in order to break their ranks, he ordered Caius Livius Salinator, commander of the allied cavalry, to charge them at full speed, and the legionary cavalry to remain in reserve. This shock of the cavalry first confused and disordered, and at length entirely broke the line of the Gauls; yet it did not make them fly. That was prevented by their officers, who, when they quitted their posts, struck them on the back with their spears, and compelled them to return to their ranks; but the allied cavalry, riding in among them, did not suffer them to recover their order. The consul exhorted his soldiers to "continue their efforts a little longer, for victory was within their reach; to press the enemy while they saw them disordered and dismayed; for if they were suffered to recover their ranks, they would enter on a fresh battle, the success of which must be uncertain." He ordered the standard-bearers to advance with the standards, and then, all exerting themselves at once, they at length forced the enemy to give way. As soon as they turned their backs, and fled precipitately on every side, the legionary cavalry was sent in pursuit of them. On that day fourteen thousand of the Boians were slain; one thousand and ninety-two taken—as were seven hundred and twenty-one horsemen, and three of their commanders, with two hundred and twelve military standards, and sixty-three chariots. Nor did the Romans gain the victory without loss of blood; of themselves, or their allies, were lost above five thousand men, twenty-three centurions, four prefects of the allies, and two military tribunes of the second legion, Marcus Genucius and Marcus Marcius.

6. Letters from both the consuls arrived at Rome nearly at the same time. That of Lucius Cornelius gave an account of the battle fought with the Boians at Mutina; that of Quintus Minucius, from Pisæ, mentioned, that "the holding of the elections had fallen to his lot, but that affairs in Liguria were in such a critical posture, that he could not leave that country without bringing ruin on the allies, and material injury on the commonwealth. He therefore advised that, if the senate thought proper, they should direct his colleague (as in his province the fate of the war was determined) to repair to Rome to hold the elections. He said, if Cornelius should object to this, because that employment had not fallen to his lot, he would certainly do whatever the senate should

order; but he begged them to consider carefully, whether it would not be less injurious to the public that an interregnum should take place, than that the province should be left by him in such a state." The senate gave directions to Caius Scribonius to send two deputies of senatorian rank to the consul, Lucius Cornelius, to communicate to him the letter sent by his colleague to the senate, and to acquaint him that if he did not come to Rome to elect new magistrates, the senate were resolved, rather than Quintus Minucius should be called away from a war, in which no progress had been made, to suffer an interregnum to take place. The deputies sent brought back his answer, that he would come to Rome to elect new magistrates. The letter of Lucius Cornelius, which contained an account of the battle with the Boians, occasioned a debate in the senate; for Marcus Claudius, lieutenant-general, in private letters to many of the members, had written, "that they might thank the fortune of the Roman people, and the bravery of the soldiers, for the success of their arms. That the conduct of the consul had been the cause of a great many men being lost, and of the enemy's army, which might have been entirely cut off, making its escape. That what made the loss of men the greater was the reinforcements, necessary to support them when distressed, coming up too late from the reserve; and that what enabled the enemy to slip out of their hands, was the signal being given too tardily to the legionary cavalry, and their not being allowed to pursue the fugitives." It was agreed that no resolution should be hastily passed on the subject; and the business was accordingly adjourned until there should be a fuller meeting.

7. Another concern demanded their attention. The public was heavily distressed by usurious practices; and although avarice had been restricted by many laws respecting usury, yet these had been evaded by a fraudulent artifice of transferring the securities to subjects of some of the allied states, who were not bound by those laws, by which means usurers, freed from all restraint, overwhelmed their debtors under accumulated loads. On considering of the best method for putting a stop to this evil, the senate decreed that a certain day should be fixed on for it; the next approaching festival of the infernal deities; and that any of the allies who should from that day lend money to the Roman citizens should register the transaction; and that all proceedings respecting such money, lent after that day, should be regulated by the laws of whichever of the two states the debtor should choose. In some time after, when the great amount of debt, contracted through this kind of fraud, was discovered by means of the registries, Marcus Sempronius,

plebeian tribune, by direction of the senate, proposed to the people, and the people ordered, that all proceedings relative to money lent, between Roman citizens and subjects of any of the allied states, or Latine confederacy, should be regulated by the same laws as those wherein both parties were Roman citizens. Such were the transactions in Italy, civil and military. In Spain the war was far from being so formidable as the exaggerations of report had represented it. In Hither Spain, Caius Flaminius took the town of Ilucia, in the country of the Oretanians, and then marched his army into winter-quarters. Several engagements took place during the winter, but none deserving of particular mention, the adversaries being rather bands of robbers, than regular soldiers; and yet the success was various, and some men were lost. More important services were performed by Marcus Fulvius. He fought a pitched battle near the town of Toletum, against the Vaccæans, Vectonians, and Celtiberians; routed and dispersed their combined forces, and took prisoner their king, Hilermus.

8. While this passed in Spain, the day of election drawing near, Lucius Cornelius, consul, left Marcus Claudius, lieutenant-general, in command of the army, and came to Rome. After representing in the senate the services which he had performed, and the present state of the province, he expostulated with the conscript fathers on their not having ordered a thanksgiving to the immortal gods, when so great a war was so happily terminated by one successful battle; and then demanded that the same might be decreed, and also a triumph to himself. But before the question was put, Quintus Metellus, who had been consul and dictator, said, that "letters had been brought at the same time from the consul, Lucius Cornelius, to the senate, and from Marcus Marcellus to a great part of the senators, which letters contradicted each other; and for that reason the consideration of the business had been adjourned, in order that it might be debated when the writers of those letters should be present. He had expected therefore that the consul, who knew that the lieutenant-general had written something to his disadvantage, would, when he was coming home, have brought him to Rome; especially as the command of the army would, with more propriety, have been committed to Tiberius Sempronius, who was already invested with authority, than to the lieutenant-general. As the case stood at present it appeared as if the latter was kept out of the way designedly, lest he might assert in person the same things which he had written in his letters; and, face to face, either substantiate his charges, or, if his allegations were ill founded, be convicted of misrepresentation, so that the truth would

be clearly discovered. For this reason he was of opinion that the senate should not, at present, assent to either of the decrees demanded by the consul." The latter, nevertheless, persisted in putting the question, on a thanksgiving being ordered, and himself allowed to ride into the city in triumph: but two plebeian tribunes, Marcus and Caius Titinius, declared that they would enter their protest if the senate passed any decree on the subject.

9. In the preceding year Sextus Ælius Pætus and Caius Cornelius Cethegus were created censors. Cornelius now closed the lustrum. The number of citizens rated was a hundred and forty-three thousand seven hundred and four. Extraordinary quantities of rain fell in this year, and the Tiber overflowed the lower parts of the city; by which inundation some buildings near the Flumentan gate were laid in ruins. The Cœlimontan gate was struck by lightning, as was the wall on each side of it, in several places. At Aricia, Lanuvium, and on the Aventine, showers of stones fell. From Capua a report was brought that a very large swarm of wasps flew into the forum, and pitched on the temple of Mars; that they had been carefully collected, and burnt. On account of these prodigies, the decemvirs were ordered to consult the books; the nine days' festival was celebrated, a supplication proclaimed, and the city purified. At the same time Marcus Porcius Cato dedicated a chapel to Maiden Victory, near the temple of Victory, two years after he had vowed it. During this year a Latine colony was established in the Thurian territory by commissioners appointed for the purpose, Cneius Manlius Vulso, Lucius Apustius Fullo, and Quintus Ælius Tubero, who had proposed the order for its settlement. There went out thither, three thousand foot and three hundred horsemen; a very small number in proportion to the quantity of land lying waste. Thirty acres might have been given to each footman, and sixty to a horseman; but, by the advice of Apustius, a third part was reserved, that they might afterward, when they should judge proper, send out thither a new colony. The footmen received twenty acres each, the horsemen forty.

10. The year was now near a close: and with regard to the election of consuls, the heat of competition was kindled to a degree beyond what was ever known before. The candidates, both patrician and plebeian, were many and powerful: Publius Cornelius Scipio, son to Cneius, and who had lately come home from Spain, where he had gained great honour by his exploits; Lucius Quintius Flamininus, who had commanded the fleet in Greece; and Cneius Manlius Vulso: these were the patricians. Then there were, of ple-

beian rank, Caius Lælius, Cneius Domitius, Caius Livius Salinator, and Manius Acilius. The eyes of all men were turned on Quintius and Cornelius; for, being both patricians, they sued for one place, and they were both of them recommended by high and recent renown in war. Above every thing else, the brothers of the candidates, the two most illustrious generals of the age, increased the violence of the struggle. Scipio's fame was the more splendid; and, in proportion to its greater splendour, the more obnoxious to envy. Quintius's was the more recent, as he had triumphed in the course of that very same year. Besides, the former had now for almost ten years been continually in people's sight; which circumstance, by the mere satiety which it creates, diminishes the reverence felt for great characters. He had been a second time consul, after the final defeat of Hannibal, and also censor. All Quintius's claims to the favour of the public were fresh and new; since his triumph he had neither asked nor received any thing from the people; "he solicited," he said, "in favour of his own brother, not of a half-brother; in favour of his lieutenant-general, and partner in the administration of the war, his brother having conducted the operations by sea while he did the same on land." Such were the arguments by which he carried his point. His brother was preferred to the brother of Africanus, though supported by the whole Cornelian family, and while one of the same family presided at the election; and notwithstanding the very honourable testimony given by the senate in his favour, when he judged him to be the best man in the state; and as such, appointed him to receive the Idæan Mother into the city, when she was brought from Pessinus. Lucius Quintius and Cneius Domitius Ahenobarbus were elected consuls; so that, not even with respect to the plebeian consul, could Africanus prevail; for he employed his interest in favour of Caius Lælius. Next day were elected pretors, Lucius Scribonius Libo, Marcus Fulvius Centumalus, Aulus Atilius Serranus, Marcus Bæbius Tamphilus, Lucius Valerius Tappus, and Quintus Salonius Sarra. The ediles of this year, Marcus Æmilius Lepidus and Lucius Æmilius Paulus, distinguished themselves highly: they prosecuted to conviction many of the farmers of the public pastures, and, with the money accruing from the fines, placed gilded shields in the upper part of the temple of Jupiter. They built one colonnade on the outside of the gate Tergemina, to which they added a wharf on the Tiber; and another, reaching from the Frontinal gate to the altar of Mars, to serve as a passage into the field of Mars.

11. For a long time nothing worth recording had occur-

red in Liguria, but towards the end of this year the Roman affairs there were twice brought into great peril; for the consul's camp, being assaulted, was with difficulty saved from falling into the enemy's hands; and a short time after, as the Roman army was marching through a defile, the Ligurians seized on the opening through which they were to pass. The consul, when he found that passa
faced about, resolved to return by the way he
entrance behind, also, was occupied by a party
and the disaster of Caudium not only occurred to the memory of the Romans, but was in a manner represented to their eyes. The consul had, among his auxiliary troops, about eight hundred Numidian horsemen, whose commanding officer undertook to force a passage with his troops on whichever side the consul should choose. He only desired
villages lay;
for on them he meant to make an attack: and the first thing
to the houses, in order that

it, running
out. The
contempt, conceived from their appearance, they took pains to increase; sometimes falling from their horses, and making themselves objects of derision and ridicule. The consequence was, that the enemy, who at first had been alert, and ready on their posts, in case of an attack, now, for the most part, laid aside their arms, and, sitting down, amused themselves with looking at them. The Numidians often rode up, then galloped back, but still contrived to get nearer the pass, as if they were unable to manage their horses, and were carried away against their will. At last, setting spurs to them, they broke out through the midst of the enemy's posts, and getting into the open country, set fire to all the houses near the road. The nearest village was soon in flames, while they ravaged all around with fire and sword. At first the sight of the smoke, then the shouts of the affrighted inhabitants, at last the old people and children, who fled for shelter, created great disorder in the camp. In consequence of which the whole of their army, without plan,

and without command, ran off, each to take care of his own: the camp was in a moment deserted; and the consul, delivered from the blockade, made good his march to the place whither he intended to go.

12. But neither the Boians nor the Spaniards, though professed enemies at that time, were such bitter and inveterate foes to the Romans as the nation of the Ætolians. These, after the departure of the Roman armies from Greece, had for some time entertained hopes that Antiochus would come and take possession of Europe without opposition; and that neither Philip nor Nabis would continue quiet. But seeing no active measures begun in any quarter, they resolved, lest their designs might be damped by delay, to set on foot some plan of disturbance; and with this view they summoned a general assembly at Naupactum. Here Thoas, their pretor, after complaining of the injurious behaviour of the Romans, and the present state of Ætolia, and asserting that "of all the nations and states of Greece, they were treated with the greatest indifference, after the victory which they themselves had been the means of obtaining," moved, that ambassadors should be sent to each of the kings; not only to sound their dispositions, but, by such incentives as suited the temper of each, to urge them to a war with Rome. Damocritus was sent to Nabis, Nicander to Philip, and Dicæarchus, the pretor's brother, to Antiochus. To the Lacedæmonian tyrant, Damocritus represented, that, "by the maritime cities being taken from him, his government was left quite destitute of strength; for from them he used to draw supplies of soldiers, as well as of ships and seamen. He was now pent up, almost within the walls of his capital, while he saw the Achæans domineering over the whole Peloponnesus. Never would he have another opportunity of recovering his rights, if he neglected to improve the one that now offered. There was no Roman army in Greece, nor would the Romans deem Gythium, or the other towns on the coast of Laconia, sufficient cause for transporting their legions a second time into that country." These arguments were used for the purpose of provoking the passions of Nabis; in order that when Antiochus should come into Greece, the other, conscious of having infringed the treaty of amity with Rome by injuries offered to its allies, might unite himself with him. Nicander endeavoured to rouse Philip by arguments somewhat similar; and he had more copious matter for discourse, as the king had been degraded from a more elevated state than the tyrant, and had sustained greater losses. Besides these topics, he introduced the ancient renown of the Macedonian kings, and the victorious arms of that nation, displayed through every quarter of the

globe. "The plan which he proposed," he said, "was free from any danger, either in the commencement, or in the issue: for he did not advise that Philip should stir until Antiochus should have come into Greece with an army; and, considering that, without the aid of Antiochus, he had maintained a war so long against the combined forces of the Romans and Ætolians, with what possible force could the Romans withstand him, when joined by Antiochus, and supported by the aid of the Ætolians, who, on the former occasion, were more dangerous enemies than the Romans?" He added the circumstance of Hannibal being general; "a man born a foe to the Romans, who had slain greater numbers, both of their commanders and soldiers, than were left surviving." Such were the incitements held out to Philip by Nicander. Dicæarchus addressed other arguments to Antiochus. In the first place, he told him, that "although the Romans reaped the spoils of Philip, the honour of the victory over him was due to the Ætolians; that, to the Ætolians alone, the Romans were obliged for having gained admittance into Greece, and that the same people supplied them with the strength which enabled them to conquer." He next set forth the numerous forces, both horse and foot, which they were willing to furnish to Antiochus for the purpose of the war; what quarters they would assign to his land forces, what harbours for his ships. He than asserted whatever falsehoods he pleased, respecting Philip and Nabis; that "both were ready to recommence hostilities, and would greedily lay hold on the first opportunity of recovering what they had lost in war." Thus did the Ætolians labour in every part of the world to stir up war against the Romans. Of the kings, however, one refused to engage in the business, and the other engaged in it too late.

13. Nabis immediately despatched emissaries through all the towns on the coast to sow dissensions among the inhabitants: some of the men in power he brought over to his party by presents; others, who more firmly adhered to the alliance with Rome, he put to death. The charge of protecting all the Lacedæmonians on the coast had been committed by Titus Quintius to the Achæans; they therefore instantly sent ambassadors to the tyrant, to remind him of his treaty with the Romans, and to warn him against violating a peace which he had so earnestly sued for. They also sent succours to Gythium which he had already besieged, and ambassadors to Rome to make known these transactions. King Antiochus having this winter solemnized the nuptials of his daughter with Ptolemy, king of Egypt, at Raphia, in Phœnicia, returned thence to Antioch, and came, towards the end of the season, through Cilicia, after passing mount

Taurus, to the city of Ephesus. Early in the spring, he sent his son Antiochus thence into Syria, to guard the remote frontiers of his dominions, lest, during his absence, any commotion might arise behind him; and then he marched himself, with all his land forces, to attack the Pisidians, inhabiting the country near Sida. At this time, Publius Sulpicius and Publius Villius, the Roman ambassadors, who were sent to Antiochus, as above mentioned, having received orders to wait on Eumenes, first came to Elæa, and thence went up to Pergamus, where that monarch kept his court. Eumenes was very desirous of war being undertaken against Antiochus, for he thought that if peace continued, a king, so much superior in power, would be a troublesome neighbour; but that in case of hostilities, he would prove no more a match for the Romans, than Philip had been; and that either he would be entirely removed out of the way, or, should peace be granted to him, after a defeat, he (Eumenes) might reasonably expect that a great deal of what should be taken from Antiochus would fall to his own share; so that in future, he might be very well able to defend himself against him, without any aid from his ally; and even if any misfortune were to happen, it would be better for him, in conjunction with the Romans, to undergo any turn of fortune, than, standing alone, either suffer himself to be ruled by Antiochus, or, on refusal, be compelled to submission by force of arms. Therefore, with all his influence, and every argument which he could devise, he urged the Romans to a war.

14. Sulpicius, falling sick, stayed at Pergamus. Villius, on hearing that the king was carrying on war in Pisidia, went on to Ephesus, and, during a few days that he halted in that city, took pains to procure frequent interviews with Hannibal, who happened to be there at the time. His design was merely to discover his intentions, if possible, and to remove his apprehensions of danger threatening him from the Romans. No other business of any kind was mentioned at these meetings; yet they accidentally produced an important consequence, as effectually as if it had been intentionally sought; the lowering Hannibal in the esteem of the king, and rendering him more obnoxious to suspicion in every matter. Claudius, following the history written in Greek by Acilius, says, that Publius Africanus was employed in this embassy, and that it was he who conversed with Hannibal at Ephesus. He even relates one of their conversations, in which Scipio asked Hannibal, "What man it was whom he thought the greatest captain?" who answered, "Alexander, king of Macedonia; because, with a small band, he defeated armies whose numbers were beyond reckoning; and because he carried his victorious arms through

the remotest boundaries of the world, the merely visiting of which would be a task which no other man could hope to accomplish." Scipio then asked, "to whom he gave the second place?" and he replied, "to Pyrrhus; for he first taught the method of encamping; and besides, no one ever showed more exquisite judgment, in choosing his ground, and disposing his posts; while he also possessed the art of conciliating esteem to such a degree, that the nations of Italy wished him, though a foreign prince, to hold the sovereignty among them, rather than the Romans, who had so long possessed the dominion of that part of the world." On his proceeding to ask "the name of him whom he esteemed the third?" Hannibal replied, "myself beyond doubt." On this Scipio, smiling, said, "What would you have said if you had conquered me?" "Then," replied the other, "I would have placed Hannibal, not only before Alexander and Pyrrhus, but before every other commander that ever lived." This answer, conveying, with a turn of Punic artifice, an indirect compliment, and an unexpected kind of flattery, was highly grateful to Scipio, as it set him apart from the crowd of commanders, beyond competition, as if his abilities were not to be estimated.

15. From Ephesus Villius proceeded to Apamea, whither Antiochus, on hearing of the coming of the Roman delegates, came to meet him. In this congress, at Apamea, the debates were similar to those which passed at Rome between Quintius and the king's ambassadors; and the conferences were broken off by news arriving of the death of Antiochus, the king's son, who, as just now mentioned, had been sent into Syria. This youth was greatly lamented and regretted at court; for he had given such specimens of his character, as afforded evident proof, that had a longer life been allotted him, he would have displayed the talents of a great and just prince. The more he was beloved and esteemed by all, the stronger were the suspicions excited by his death; that his father, thinking that his heir shared too largely of the public favour, while he himself was declining in old age, had him taken off by poison by some eunuchs, a kind of people who recommend themselves to kings by the perpetration of such foul deeds. People mentioned also, as another motive of that clandestine act of villany, that as he had given Lysimachia to his son Seleucus, he had no establishment of the like kind which he could give to Antiochus, for the purpose of banishing him also to a distance, under pretext of doing him honour. Nevertheless an appearance of deep mourning was maintained in the court for several days; and the Roman ambassador, lest his presence at that time might be troublesome, retired to Pergamus.

The king, dropping the prosecution of the war which he had begun, went back to Ephesus; and there, keeping himself shut up in the palace, under colour of grief, held secret consultations with a person called Minio, who was his principal favourite. Minio was utterly ignorant of the state of all foreign nations; and, accordingly, estimating the strength of the king from his successes in Syria or Asia, he was confident that Antiochus had superiority from the merits of his cause, and that the demands of the Romans were highly unreasonable; imagining also, that he would prove the more powerful in war. As the king wished to avoid farther debate with the envoys, either because he had found no advantage to result from the former conference, or because he was too much discomposed by recent grief, Minio undertook to say whatever was requisite for his interest, and persuaded him to invite for that purpose the ambassadors from Pergamus.

16. By this time Sulpicius had recovered his health; both himself and Villius, therefore, came to Ephesus. Minio apologized for the king not being present, and the business was entered on. Then Minio, in a studied speech, said, "I find, Romans, that you profess very specious intentions, (the liberating of the Grecian states,) but your actions do not accord with your words. You lay down one rule for Antiochus, and follow another yourselves. For, how are the inhabitants of Smyrna and Lampsacus better entitled to the character of Greeks, than the Neapolitans, Rhegians, and Tarentines, from whom you exact tribute, and ships, in pursuance of a treaty? Why do you send yearly to Syracuse, and other Grecian cities of Sicily, a pretor, vested with sovereign power, and attended by his rods and axes? You can, certainly, allege no other reason than this, that, having conquered them in war, you imposed these terms on them. Admit, then, on the part of Antiochus, the same reason with respect to Smyrna and Lampsacus, and the cities belonging to Ionia and Æolia. Conquered by his ancestors, they were subjected to tribute and taxes, and he only reclaims an ancient right. Answer him on these heads, if you mean a fair discussion, and do not merely seek a pretence for war." Sulpicius answered, "Antiochus has shown some modesty in choosing, that since no other arguments could be produced in his favour, any other person should utter these rather than himself: for what similarity is there in the cases of those states which you have brought into comparison? From the Rhegians, Neapolitans, and Tarentines, we require what they owe us by treaty, in virtue of a right invariably exercised, in one uniform course, since they first came under our power; a right always as-

serted, and never intermitted. Now, can you assert, that as these states have, neither of themselves, or through any other, ever refused conforming to the treaty, so the Asiatic states, since they once came under the power of Antiochus's ancestors, have been held in uninterrupted possession by your reigning kings; and that some of them have not been subject to the dominion of Philip, some to that of Ptolemy; and that others have not, for many years, maintained themselves in a state of independence, their title to which was not called in question? For, if the circumstance of their having been once subject to a foreigner, when crushed under the severity of the times, conveys a right to enforce that subjection again after a lapse of so many generations, what can be said of our having delivered Greece from Philip, but that we have laboured in vain; and that his successors may reclaim Corinth, Chalcis, Demetrias, and the whole nation of Thessaly? But why do I plead the cause of those states, which it would be fitter that both we and the king should hear pleaded by themselves?"

17. He then desired that the deputies of those states should be called, for they had been prepared beforehand, and kept in readiness by Eumenes, who reckoned that every share of strength that should be taken away from Antiochus, would become an accession to his own kingdom. Many of them were introduced; and, while each enforced his own complaints, and sometimes demands, some reasonable, many unreasonable, they changed the debate into a mere altercation. The ambassadors therefore without conceding or carrying any one point, returned to Rome, and left every thing in the same unsettled state in which they found it. On their departure the king held a council, on the subject of a war with Rome, in which all the members vied with each other in the violence of their harangues; for every one thought, that the greater acrimony he showed towards the Romans, the greater share of favour he might expect to obtain. One inveighed against the insolence of their demands, in which they presume to impose terms on Antiochus, the greatest king in Asia, as they would on the vanquished Nabis. "Although to Nabis they left absolute power over his own country, and its capital, Lacedæmon, yet they insist on the impropriety of Smyrna and Lampsacus yielding obedience to Antiochus."—Others said, that "to so great a monarch, those cities were but a trivial ground of war, scarcely worth mention; but unjust pretensions to authority were always urged, at first, in matters of little consequence; unless indeed it could be supposed that the Persians, when they demanded earth and water from the Lacedæmonians, stood in need of a morsel of the one, or a

draught of the other. The proceedings of the Romans, respecting the two cities, were meant as a trial of the same sort. The rest of the states, when they saw that two had shaken off the yoke, would go over to the party of that nation which professed the patronage of liberty. If freedom was not actually preferable to servitude, yet the hope of bettering their circumstances by a change was more flattering to every one than any present situation."

18. There was in the council an Acarnanian named Alexander, who had formerly been a friend of Philip, but had lately left him, to follow the more opulent court of Antiochus. This man, being well skilled in the affairs of Greece, and not unacquainted with the Romans, was admitted by the king into such a degree of intimacy, that he shared even in his secret counsels. As if the question to be considered were not, whether there should be war or not, but where and in what manner it should be carried on, he affirmed that "he saw an assured prospect of victory, provided the king would pass into Europe, and choose some part of Greece for the seat of war. In the first place, the Ætolians, who lived in the centre of Greece, would be found in arms, ready to take the lead in the most perilous operations. Then, in the two extremities of Greece, Nabis, on the side of Peloponnesus, would put every thing in motion, to recover the city of Argos, and the maritime cities, from which he had been expelled by the Romans, and pent up within the walls of Lacedæmon; while, on the side of Macedonia, Philip would be ready for the field the moment he heard the alarm sounded. He knew," he said, "his spirit, he knew his temper; he knew that, (as is the case with wild beasts, confined by bars or chains,) for a long time past, the most violent rage had been boiling in his breast. He remembered also how often during the war that prince had prayed to all the gods to grant him Antiochus as an assistant; and, if that prayer were now heard with favour, he would not hesitate an instant to resume his arms. It was only requisite that there should be no delay, no procrastination; for success depended chiefly on securing beforehand commodious posts and proper allies: besides, Hannibal ought to be sent immediately into Africa, in order to distract the attention of the Romans."

19. Hannibal was not called to this consultation, because the king had harboured suspicions of him on account of his conferences with Villius, and had not since shown him any mark of regard. This affront, at first, he bore in silence; but afterward thought it better to take some proper opportunity to inquire the reason of the king's suddenly withdrawing his favour, and to clear himself of blame. Without any

preface, he asked the cause of the king's displeasure; and on being told it, said, "Antiochus, when I was yet an infant, my father Hamilcar, at a time when he was offering sacrifice, brought me up to the altars, and made me take an oath that I never would be a friend to the Roman people. Under the obligation of this oath, I carried arms against them for thirty-six years: this oath, on peace being made, drove me out of my country, and brought me an exile to your court; and this oath shall guide me, should you disappoint my hopes, until I traverse every quarter of the globe, where I can understand that there is either strength or arms, to find out enemies to the Romans. If therefore your courtiers have conceived the idea of ingratiating themselves with you, by insinuating suspicions of me, let them seek some other means of advancing their own reputation, rather than the depressing of mine. I hate, and am hated by the Romans. That I speak the truth in this, my father Hamilcar and the gods are witnesses. Whenever therefore you shall employ your thoughts on a plan of waging war with Rome, consider Hannibal as one of your firmest friends. If circumstances force you to adopt peaceful measures, on such a subject employ some other counsellor." This discourse affected the king much, and even reconciled him to Hannibal. The resolution of the council, at their breaking up, was, that the war should be undertaken.

20. At Rome, [A. U. C. 560. B. C. 192,] people talked, indeed, of a breach with Antiochus as an event very likely to happen, but, except talking of it, they had hitherto made no preparation. Italy was decreed the province of both the consuls, who received directions to settle between themselves, or draw lots, which of them should preside at the elections of the year; and it was ordered that he who should be disengaged from that business should hold himself in readiness, in case there should be occasion, to lead the legions anywhere out of that country. The consul, so commissioned, had leave given him to levy two new legions, and twenty thousand foot, and nine hundred horse, among the allies and Latine confederates. To the other consul were decreed the two legions which had been commanded by Lucius Cornelius, consul of the preceding year; and from the same army a body of allies and Latines, amounting to fifteen thousand foot, and five hundred horse. Quintus Minucius was continued in command, and had assigned to him the forces which he then had in Liguria; as a supplement to which, four thousand Roman foot, and five hundred horse, were ordered to be enlisted, and five thousand foot, and two hundred and fifty horse, to be demanded from the allies. The province of going out of Italy, wherever the senate should or-

der, fell to Cneius Domitius; Gaul, and the holding the elections, to Lucius Quintius. The pretors then cast lots for their provinces: to Marcus Fulvius Centumalus fell the city jurisdiction; to Lucius Scribonius Libo, the foreign; Lucius Valerius Tappus obtained Sicily; Quintus Salonius Sarra, Sardinia; Marcus Bæbius Tamphilus, Hither Spain, and Marcus Atilius Serranus, Farther Spain. But the provinces of the two last were changed, first by a decree of the senate, which was afterward confirmed by an order of the people. The fleet and Macedonia were assigned to Atilius; Bruttium to Bæbius. Flaminius and Fulvius were continued in command in both the Hither and Farther Spain. To Bæbius Tamphilus, for the business of Bruttium, were decreed the two legions which had served in the city the year before; and he was ordered to demand from the allies, for the same service, fifteen thousand foot and five hundred horse. Atilius was ordered to build thirty ships of five banks of oars; to bring out from the docks any old ones that were fit for service, and to raise seamen. An order was also given to the consul to supply him with two thousand of the allied and Latine footmen, and a thousand Roman. The destination of these two pretors, and their two armaments, one on land, and the other on sea, was declared to be intended against Nabis, who was now carrying on open hostilities against the allies of the Roman people. But it was thought proper to wait the return of the ambassadors sent to Antiochus, and the senate ordered the consul Cneius Domitius not to leave the city until they arrived.

21. The pretors, Fulvius and Scribonius, whose province was the administration of justice at Rome, were charged to provide a hundred quinqueremes, besides the fleet which Atilius was to command. Before the consul and pretors set out for their provinces, a supplication was performed on account of some prodigies. A report was brought from Picenum that a goat had produced six kids at a birth. It was said that a boy was born at Arretium who had but one hand; that, at Amiternum, a shower of earth fell; a gate and wall at Formiæ were struck by lightning; and, what was more alarming than all, an ox, belonging to the consul Cneius Domitius, spoke these words,—"Rome, take care of thyself." To expiate the other prodigies, a supplication was performed; the ox was ordered by the aruspices to be carefully preserved and fed. The Tiber, pouring into the city with more destructive violence than last year, swept away two bridges, and many buildings, particularly about the Flumentan gate. A huge rock, loosened from its seat, either by the rains, or by an earthquake, so slight that no other effect of it was perceived, tumbled down from the capitol into the

Jugarian street, and buried many people under it. In the country, many parts of which were overflowed, much cattle was carried away, and many houses thrown down. Previous to the arrival of the consul, Lucius Quintius, in his province, Quintus Minucius fought a pitched battle with the Ligurians, in the territory of Pisæ, slew nine thousand of the enemy, and putting the rest to flight, drove them within their works, which were assaulted and defended with obstinate valour until night came on. During the night the Ligurians stole away unobserved; and, at the first dawn, the Romans took possession of their deserted camp, where the quantity of booty was the less, because it was a frequent practice with the enemy to send home the spoil taken in the country. Minucius, after this, allowed them no respite. From the territory of Pisæ, he marched into that of the Ligurians, and, with fire and sword, utterly destroyed their forts and towns, where the Roman soldiers were abundantly enriched with the spoils which the enemy had collected in Etruria and sent home.

22. About this time the ambassadors who had been sent to the kings returned to Rome. As they brought no information of such a nature as called for any immediate declaration of war, (except against the Lacedæmonian tyrant, whom the Achæan ambassadors also represented as ravaging the sea-coast of Laconia, in breach of treaty,) Atilius, the pretor, was sent with the fleet to Greece, for the protection of the allies. It was resolved that, as there was nothing to be apprehended from Antiochus at present, both the consuls should go to their provinces; and, accordingly, Domitius marched into the country of the Boians, by the shorter road, through Ariminum, and Quintius through Liguria. The two armies of the consuls, proceeding by these different routes, spread devastation wide over the enemy's country. In consequence of which, first, a few of their horsemen, with their commanders, then their whole senate, and, at last, all who possessed either property or dignity, to the number of one thousand five hundred, came over and joined the consuls. In both Spains, likewise, success attended the Roman arms during this year; for, in one, Caius Flaminius, after a siege, took Litabrum, a strong and opulent city, and made prisoner Corribilo, a powerful chieftain; and, in the other, Marcus Fulvius, proconsul, fought two battles, with two armies of the enemy, and was victorious in both. He captured Vescelia and Holo, towns belonging to the Spaniards, with many of their forts, and others voluntarily submitted to him. Then, advancing into the territory of Oretum, and having, there also, taken two cities, Noliba and Cusibis, he proceeded to the river Tagus. Here stood Toletum, a small

city, but strong from its situation. While he was besieging this place, a numerous army of Vectonians came to relieve their friends in the town, but he overthrew them in a general engagement, and, after their defeat, took Toletum by means of his works.

23. At this juncture, the wars, in which they were actually engaged, caused not so great anxiety in the minds of the senate, as the expectation of one with Antiochus; for although, through their ambassadors, they had, from time to time, made careful inquiries into every particular, yet rumours, rashly propagated, without authentic foundation, intermixed many falsehoods with the truth. Among the rest, a report was spread that Antiochus intended, as soon as he should come into Ætolia, to send a fleet immediately to Sicily. The senate, therefore, though they had already despatched the pretor, Atilius, with a squadron to the Ionian sea, yet, considering that not only a military force, but also the influence of characters entitled to respect, would be necessary towards securing the attachment of the allies, they sent into Greece, in quality of ambassadors, Titus Quintius, Caius Octavius, Cneius Servilius, and Publius Villius; at the same time ordering, in their decree, that Marcus Bæbius should lead forward his legions from Bruttium to Tarentum and Brundusium, so that, if occasion required, he might transport them thence into Macedonia. They also ordered that Marcus Fulvius, pretor, should send a fleet of thirty ships to protect the coast of Sicily; and that, whoever had the direction of that fleet, should be invested with the authority of a commander-in-chief. To this commission was appointed Lucius Oppius Salinator, who had been plebeian edile the year before. They likewise determined that the same pretor should write to his colleague, Lucius Valerius, that "there was reason to apprehend that the ships of King Antiochus would pass over from Ætolia to Sicily; for which reason the senate judged it proper that, in addition to the army, which he then had, he should enlist tumultuary soldiers to the number of twelve thousand foot, and four hundred horse, which might enable him to defend that coast of his province which lay next to Greece." These troops the pretor collected, not only out of Sicily, but from the circumjacent islands; placing strong garrisons in all the towns on the coast opposite to Greece. The rumours already current were, in some degree, confirmed by the arrival of Attalus, the brother of Eumenes; for he brought intelligence that King Antiochus had crossed the Hellespont with his army, and that the Ætolians were putting themselves into such a posture that, when he arrived, he expected to find them in arms. Thanks were given to Eumenes in his absence, and to At-

talus, who was present; and an order was passed that the latter should be furnished with a house, and every accommodation; that he should be presented with two horses, two suits of horseman's armour, vases of silver to a hundred pounds weight, and of gold to twenty pounds.

24. As accounts were continually arriving that the war was on the point of breaking out, it was judged expedient that consuls should be elected as soon as possible. Wherefore the senate passed a decree, that the pretor, Marcus Fulvius, should instantly despatch a letter to the consul, informing him that it was the will of the senate that he should leave the command of the province and army to his lieutenants-general, and return to Rome; and that, when on the road, he should send on before him an edict appointing the day for the election of consuls. The consul complied with the letter; and having sent forward the edict, arrived at Rome. There was this year also a warm competition, three patricians suing for one place: Publius Cornelius Scipio, son to Cneius, who had suffered a disappointment the year before; Lucius Cornelius Scipio, and Cneius Manlius Vulso. The consulship was conferred on Publius Scipio, that it might appear that the honour had only been delayed, and not refused to a person of such character. The plebeian colleague joined with him was Manius Acilius Glabrio. Next day were created pretors, Lucins Æmilius Paulus, Marcus Æmilius Lepidus, Marcus Junius Brutus, Aulus Cornelius Mammula, Caius Livius, and Lucius Oppius; the two last, both of them, surnamed Salinator. This was the same Oppius who had conducted the fleet of thirty ships to Sicily. While the new magistrates were settling the distribution of their provinces, orders were despatched to Marcus Bæbius to pass over with all his forces, from Brundusium to Epirus, and to keep the army stationed near Apollonia; and Marcus Fulvius, city pretor, was commissioned to build fifty new quinqueremes.

25. Such were the precautions taken by the Roman people to guard against every attempt of Antiochus. At this time Nabis did not disavow his hostile intentions, but, with his utmost force, carried on the siege of Gythium; and, being incensed against the Achæans, for having sent succours to the besieged, he ravaged their lands. The Achæans would not presume to engage in war until their ambassadors should come back from Rome, and acqnaint them with the sentiments of the senate; but as soon as these returned, they summoned a council at Sicyon, and also sent deputies to Titus Quintius to ask his advice. In the council, all the members were inclined to vote for an immediate declaration of war; but a letter from Titus Quintius, in which he re-

commended waiting for the Roman pretor and fleet, caused some hesitation. While many of the members persisted in their first opinion, and others arguing that they ought to follow the counsel of the person to whom they of themselves had applied for advice, the generality waited to hear the sentiments of Philopœmen. He was pretor of Achæa at the time, and surpassed all his contemporaries both in wisdom and influence. He first observed, that "it was a wise rule, established among the Achæans, that their pretor, when he proposed a question concerning war, should not have a vote:" and then he desired them to "fix their determination among themselves as soon as possible;" assuring them that "their pretor would faithfully and carefully carry their decrees into execution; and would use his best endeavours that, as far as depended on human prudence, they should not repent of them, whether they were for peace or war." These words conveyed a more efficacious incitement to war than if, by openly arguing in favour of it, he had betrayed an ambition to distinguish himself in command. War was therefore unanimously resolved on: the time and mode of conducting it were left entirely to the pretor. Philopœmen's own judgment, indeed, besides it being the opinion of Quintius, pointed it out as best to wait for the Roman fleet, which might succour Gythium by sea; but he feared that the business would not endure delay, and that not only Gythium, but the party which had been sent to its aid, would fall into the hands of the enemy, and therefore he drew out what ships the Achæans had.

26. The tyrant also, with the view of cutting off any supplies that might be brought to the besieged by sea, had fitted out a small squadron, consisting of only three ships of war, with some barks and cutters, as his former fleet had been given up to the Romans, according to the treaty. In order to try the activity of these vessels, as they were then new, and to have every thing in a fit condition for a battle, he put out to sea every day, and exercised both the rowers and marines in mock fights; for he thought that all his hopes of succeeding in the siege depended on his preventing any succours being brought to them by ships. The pretor of the Achæans, in respect of skill for conducting operations on land, was equal to any of the most celebrated commanders both in capacity and experience, yet with naval affairs he was quite unacquainted. Being an inhabitant of Arcadia, an inland country, he was even ignorant in foreign affairs, excepting that he had once served in Crete as commander of a body of auxiliaries. There was an old ship of four banks of oars, which had been taken eighty years before, as it was conveying Nicæa, the wife of Craterus, from Nau-

pactum to Corinth. Led by the reputation of this ship, for it had been reckoned a remarkably fine vessel when in the king's fleet, he ordered it, though now quite rotten, and falling asunder through age, to be brought out from Ægium. The fleet sailed with this ship at its head, Tiso of Patræ, the commander, being on board it, when the ships of the Lacedæmonians from Gythium came within view. At the first shock, against a new and firm vessel, that old one, which before admitted the water through every joint, was shattered to pieces, and the whole crew were made prisoners. On the loss of the commander's ship, the rest of the fleet fled as fast as their oars could carry them. Philopœmen himself made his escape in a light advice boat, nor did he stop his flight until he arrived at Patræ. This untoward event did not in the least damp the spirit of a man so well versed in military affairs, and who had experienced so many vicissitudes of fortune. On the contrary, as he had failed of success in the naval line, in which he had no experience, he even conceived, thence, the greater hopes of succeeding in another, wherein he had acquired knowledge; and he affirmed that he would quickly put an end to the tyrant's rejoicing.

27. Nabis, elated by this adventure, and confident that he had not now any danger to apprehend from the sea, resolved to shut up the passages on the land also, by parties stationed in proper posts. With this view he drew off a third part of his forces from the siege of Gythium, and encamped them at Bææ, a place which commands both Leucæ and Acriæ, on the road by which he supposed the enemy's army would advance. While he lay on this station, where very few of his men had tents, (the generality of them having formed huts of reeds interwoven, and which they covered with leaves of trees, to serve as a defence from the weather,) Philopœmen, before he came within sight, resolved to surprise him by an attack of such a kind as he did not expect. He drew together a number of small ships in a remote creek, on the coast of the territory of Argos, and embarked on board them a body of soldiers, mostly targeteers, furnished with slings, javelins, and other light kinds of weapons. He then coasted along the shore until he came to a promontory near Nabis's post. Here he landed, and made his way by night, through paths with which he was well acquainted, to Bææ. He found the sentinels fast asleep; for they had not conceived the least apprehension of an enemy being near; and he immediately set fire to the huts in every part of the camp. Great numbers perished in the flames before they could discover the enemy's arrival, and those who did discover it could give no assistance; so that nearly the whole was destroyed by fire and sword. From

both these means of destruction, however, a very small number made their escape, and fled to the principal camp before Gythium. Philopœmen having by this blow given a severe check to the presumption of the enemy, led on his forces to ravage the district of Tripolis, a part of the Lacedæmonian territory lying next to the frontiers of Megalopolis; and, carrying off thence a vast number of men and cattle, withdrew before the tyrant could send a force from Gythium to protect the country. He then collected his whole force at Tegea, to which place he summoned a council of the Achæans and their allies; at which were present, also, deputies from the Epirots and Acarnanians. Here it was resolved that, as the minds of his men were now sufficiently recovered from the shame of the disgrace suffered at sea, and those of the enemy dispirited, he should march directly to Lacedæmon; for that was judged to be the only effectual means to draw off the enemy from the siege of Gythium. On entering their country, he encamped the first day at Caryæ; and, on that very day, Gythium was taken. Ignorant of that event, Philopœmen advanced to the Barbosthenes, a mountain ten miles from Lacedæmon. On the other side, Nabis, after taking possession of Gythium, set out, at the head of a body of light troops, marched hastily by Lacedæmon, and seized on a place called the Camp of Pyrrhus, which post he believed the Achæans intended to occupy. From thence he proceeded to meet the enemy. The latter, being obliged by the narrowness of the road to extend their train to a great length, occupied a space of almost five miles. The cavalry, and the greatest part of the auxiliaries, covered the rear, Philopœmen expecting that the tyrant would attack him on that quarter with his mercenary troops, in whom he placed his principal confidence. Two unforseen circumstances at once filled him with uneasiness; one, the post at which he aimed being pre-occupied; the other, the enemy having met him in front, where, as the road lay through very uneven ground, he did not see how the battalions could advance without the support of the light troops.

28. Philopœmen was possessed of an admirable degree of skill and experience in conducting a march and choosing his station; having made these points his principal study, not only in times of war, but likewise during peace. Whenever, in travelling, he came to a defile where the passage was difficult, it was his practice, first, to examine the nature of the ground on every side. When journeying alone, he meditated within himself: if he had company, he asked them, "If an enemy should appear in that place, what would be the proper method of proceeding; what, if they should

attack him in front; what, if on this flank, or on that; what, if on the rear? for he might happen to meet them while his men were formed with a regular front; or when they were in the loose order of march, fit only for the road." He would proceed to examine, either in his own mind, or by asking questions, "What ground he ought to choose; what number of soldiers, or what kind of arms, (which was a very material point,) he ought to employ; where he should deposite the baggage, where the soldiers' necessaries, where the unarmed multitude; what number and what kind of troops he should appoint to guard them; and whether it would be better to prosecute his march as intended, or to return back by the way he came; what spot, also, he should choose for his camp; what space he should enclose within the lines; where he could be conveniently supplied with water; where a sufficiency of forage and wood could be had; which would be his safest road on decamping next day, and in what form the army should march?" In such studies and inquiries he had, from his early years, so frequently exercised his thoughts, that on any emergency of the kind occurring, no expedient that could be devised was new to him. On this occasion he first ordered the army to halt; then sent forward to the van the auxiliary Cretans, and the horsemen called Tarentines, each leading two spare horses; and, ordering the rest of the cavalry to follow, he seized on a rock which stood over a rivulet, from which he might be supplied with water. Here he collected together all the baggage, with all the sutlers and followers of the army, placing a guard of soldiers around them; and then he fortified his camp as the nature of the place required. The pitching of tents in such rugged and uneven ground was a difficult task. The enemy were distant not more than five hundred paces. Both drew water from the same rivulet, under escorts of light troops; but, before any skirmish took place, as usual, between men encamped so near to each other, night came on. It was evident, however, that they must unavoidably fight next day at the rivulet, in support of the watering parties. Wherefore, during the night, Philopœmen concealed, in a valley remote from the view of the enemy, as great a number of targeteers as could conveniently lie in the place.

29. At break of day the Cretan light infantry, and the Tarentine horse, began an engagement on the bank of the rivulet. Lafemnastus, a Cretan, commanded his countrymen; Lycortas of Megalopolis the cavalry. The enemy's watering-party also was guarded by Cretan auxiliaries and Tarentine horsemen. The fight was for a considerable time doubtful, as the troops on both sides were of the same kind, and armed alike; but, as the contest advanced, the tyrant's

auxiliaries gained an advantage, both by their superiority of numbers, and because Philopœmen had given directions to his officers that, after maintaining the contest for a short time, they should betake themselves to flight, and draw the enemy on to the place of the ambuscade. The latter, pursuing the runaways in disorderly haste through the valley, were most of them wounded and slain before they discovered their concealed foe. The targeteers had posted themselves in such order, as far as the breadth of the valley allowed, that they easily gave a passage to their flying friends through openings in their ranks; then starting up themselves, hale, fresh, and in regular order, they briskly attacked the enemy, whose ranks were broken, who were scattered in confusion, and were, besides, exhausted with fatigue and wounds. This decided the victory: the tyrant's troops instantly turned their backs, and, flying with much more precipitation than they had pursued, were driven into their camp. Great numbers were killed and taken in the pursuit; and the consternation would have spread through the camp also, had not Philopœmen ordered a retreat to be sounded: for he dreaded the ground (which was rough, and dangerous to advance on without caution) more than he did the enemy. Judging, both from the issue of the battle and from the disposition of the enemy's leader, that he was not a little dismayed, he sent to him one of the auxiliary soldiers in the character of a deserter, to assure him positively that the Achæans had resolved to advance next day to the river Eurotas, which runs almost close to the walls, in order to cut off the tyrant's retreat to the city, and to prevent any provisions being brought thence to the camp; and that they intended, at the same time, to try whether any could be prevailed on to desert his cause. Although the deserter did not gain implicit credit, yet he afforded Nabis's captain, who was full of apprehensions, a plausible pretext for leaving his camp. On the day following he ordered Pythagoras, with the auxiliaries and cavalry, to mount guard before the rampart; and then, marching out himself with the main body of the army, as if intending to offer battle, he ordered them to return with all haste to the city.

30. When Philopœmen saw their army marching precipitately through a narrow and steep road, he sent all his cavalry, together with the Cretan auxiliaries, against the guard of the enemy stationed in the front of their camp. These, seeing their adversaries approach, and perceiving that their friends had abandoned them, at first attempted to retreat within their works; but then, observing the whole force of the Achæans advancing in order of battle, they were seized with fear, lest, together with the camp itself,

they might be taken: they resolved therefore to follow the body of their army, which by this time had proceeded to a considerable distance. Immediately, the targeteers of the Achæans assailed the camp, and the rest set out in pursuit of the enemy. The road was such that a body of men, even when undisturbed by any fear of a foe, could not, without difficulty, make its way through it. But when an attack was made on their rear, and the shouts of terror raised by the affrighted troops behind reached to the van, they threw down their arms, and fled different ways into the adjacent woods. In an instant of time the way was stopped up with heaps of weapons, particularly spears, which, falling mostly with their points towards the pursuers, formed a kind of palisade across the road. Philopœmen ordered the auxiliaries to push forward in pursuit of the enemy, who would find it a difficult matter, the horsemen particularly, to continue their flight; while he himself led away the heavy troops, through more open ground, to the river Eurotas. There he pitched his camp a little before sunset, and waited for the light troops which he had sent in chase of the enemy. These arrived at the first watch, and brought intelligence that Nabis, with a few attendants, had made his way into the city; and that the rest of his army, unarmed and dispersed, were straggling through all parts of the woods: whereon he ordered them to refresh themselves, while he himself chose out a party of men who, having come earlier into camp, were by this time both recruited by food and rest; and, ordering them to carry nothing with them but their swords, he marched them out directly, and posted them in the roads which led from two of the gates, one towards Pheræ, the other towards the Barbosthenes: for he supposed that through these the flying enemy would endeavour to make their retreat. Nor was he disappointed therein; for the Lacedæmonians, as long as any light remained, retreated through the centre of the woods in the most retired paths. As soon as it grew dusk, and they saw lights in the enemy's camp, they kept themselves concealed from view; but, having passed it by, they then thought that all was safe, and came down into the open roads, where they were intercepted by the parties lying in wait; and such numbers of them were killed and taken, that, of the whole army, scarcely a fourth part effected their escape. As Nabis was now pent up within the city, Philopœmen employed the greatest part of thirty succeeding days in ravaging the lands of the Lacedæmonians; and then, after greatly reducing and almost annihilating the strength of the tyrant, he returned home, while the Achæans extolled him as equal, on the merit of

The Athenians seemed to be the best qualified for this purpose, by reason of the high reputation of their state, and also from an amity long subsisting between them and the Ætolians. Quintius therefore requested of them to send ambassadors to the Panætolic council. At the first meeting Thoas made a report of the business of his embassy. After him Menippus was introduced, who said, that "it would have been happy for all the Greeks residing both in Greece and Asia, if Antiochus could have taken a part in their affairs, while the power of Philip was yet unbroken; for then every one would have had what of right belonged to him, and the whole would not have come under the dominion and absolute disposal of the Romans. But even as matters stand at present," said he, "provided you have constancy enough to carry into effect the measures which you have adopted, Antiochus will be able, with the assistance of the gods, and the alliance of the Ætolians, to reinstate the affairs of Greece in their former rank of dignity, notwithstanding the low condition to which they have been reduced. But this dignity consists in a state of freedom supported by its own strength, and not dependant on the will of another." The Athenians, who were permitted to deliver their sentiments next after the king's ambassadors, avoiding all mention of Antiochus, reminded the Ætolians of their alliance with Rome, and the benefits conferred by Titus Quintius on the whole body of Greece; and recommended to them, "not inconsiderately to break off that connexion by too hasty councils; observing, that passionate and adventurous schemes, however flattering at first view, prove difficult in the execution, and disastrous in the issue: that as the Roman ambassadors, and among them Titus Quintius, were within a small distance, it would be better, before any violent step was taken, to discuss in amicable conference any matters in dispute, than to rouse Europe and Asia to a dreadful war."

33. The multitude, ever fond of novelty, warmly espoused the cause of Antiochus, and gave their opinion, that the Romans should not even be admitted into the council; but by the influence chiefly of the elder members a vote was passed that the council should give audience to the Romans. On being acquainted by the Athenians with this determination, Quintius resolved on going into Ætolia; for he thought that "either he should be able to effect some change in their designs, or that it would be manifest to all mankind that the blame of the war would lie on the Ætolians, and that the Romans would be warranted to take arms by justice, and in a manner by necessity." On arriving there, Quintius, in his discourse to the council, began with the first formation of the alliance between the Romans and the Ætolians, and enu-

merated the many trangressions of the terms of the treaty, of which the latter had been guilty. He then enlarged a little on the rights of the states concerned in the dispute, and added, that "notwithstanding, if they thought that they had any reasonable demand to make, it would surely be infinitely better to send ambassadors to Rome, whether they choose to argue the case or to make a request to the senate, than that the Roman people should enter the lists with Antiochus, while the Ætolians acted as marshals of the field; an event which would cause a great convulsion in the affairs of the world, and the utter ruin of Greece." He concluded with asserting, that "no people would feel the fatal consequences of such a war sooner than the first promoters of it." This prediction of the Roman was disregarded. Thoas and others of the same faction were then heard with general approbation; and they prevailed so far, that, without adjourning the meeting, or waiting for the absence of the Romans, the assembly passed a decree that Antiochus should be invited to vindicate the liberty of Greece, and decide the dispute between the Ætolians and the Romans. To the insolence of this decree their pretor, Damocritus, added a personal affront; for on Quintius asking him for a copy of the decree, without any respect to the dignity of the person to whom he spoke, he told him that "he had, at present, more pressing business to despatch; but he would shortly give him the decree, and an answer, in Italy, from his camp on the banks of the Tiber." Such was the degree of madness which possessed, at that time, both the nation of the Ætolians and their magistrates.

34. Quintius and the ambassadors returned to Corinth. The Ætolians, that they might not appear to depend merely on Antiochus, and to sit inactive, waiting for his arrival, though they did not, after the departure of the Romans, hold a general diet of the nation, yet endeavoured by their Apocleti (a more confidential council, composed of persons selected from the rest) to devise schemes for setting Greece in commotion. They were sensible that in the several states the principal people, particularly those of the best characters, were disposed to maintain the Roman alliance, and well pleased with the present state of affairs; but that the populace, and especially such as were in needy circumstances, wished for a general revolution. The Ætolians, at one day's sitting, formed a scheme, the very conception of which argued not only boldness, but impudence,—being no less than the making themselves masters of Demetrias, Chalcis, and Lacedæmon. One of their principal men was sent to each of these places; Thoas to Chalcis, Alexamenus to Lacedæmon, Diocles to Demetrias. This last was assisted by the exile

Eurylochus, whose flight and the cause of it have been mentioned above, and who had no other prospect of being restored to his country. Eurylochus, by letter, instructed his friends and relations, and those of his own faction, to order his wife and children to assume a mourning dress; and, holding the badges of supplicants, to go into a full assembly, and to beseech each individual, and the whole body, not to suffer a man, who was innocent and uncondemned, to grow old in exile. The simple and unsuspecting were moved by compassion; the ill-disposed and seditious, by the hope of seeing all things thrown into confusion, in consequence of the tumults which the Ætolians would excite; and every one voted for his being recalled. These preparatory measures being effected, Diocles, at that time general of the horse, with all the cavalry, set out under pretext of escorting to his home the exile, who was his guest. Having, during that day and the following night, marched an extraordinary length of way, and arrived within six miles of the city at the first dawn, he chose out three troops, at the head of which he went on, before the rest of the cavalry, whom he ordered to follow. When he came near the gate he made all his men dismount and lead their horses by the reins, without keeping their ranks, but like travellers on a journey, in order that they might appear to be the retinue of the general, rather than a military force. Here he left one troop at the gate, lest the cavalry, who were coming up, might be shut out; and then holding Eurylochus by the hand, conducted him to his house through the middle of the city and the forum, and through crowds who met and congratulated him. In a little time the city was filled with horsemen, and convenient posts were seized; and then parties were sent to the houses of persons of the opposite faction to put them to death. In this manner Demetrias fell into the hands of the Ætolians.

35. The plan to be executed at Lacedæmon was, not to attempt the city by force, but to entrap the tyrant by stratagem: for though he had been stripped of the maritime towns by the Romans, and afterward shut up within the walls of his city by the Achæans, they supposed that whoever took the first opportunity of killing him would engross the whole thanks of the Lacedæmonians. The pretence which they had for sending to him was, that he had long solicited assistance from them, since by their advice he had renewed the war. A thousand foot were put under the command of Alexamenus, with thirty horsemen, chosen from among the youth. These received a charge from Damocritus, the pretor, in the select council of the nation, mentioned above, "not to suppose that they were sent to act against

the Achæans; or even on other business, which any might think he had discovered from his own conjectures. Whatever sudden enterprise circumstances might direct Alexamenus to undertake, that (however unexpected, rash, or daring) they were to hold themselves in readiness to execute with implicit obedience; and should understand that to be the matter, for the sole purpose of effecting which they had been sent abroad." With these men, thus pre-instructed, Alexamenus came to the tyrant, and at his first arrival filled him with very flattering hopes; telling him that "Antiochus had already come over into Europe; that he would shortly be in Greece, and would cover the lands and seas with men and arms; that the Romans would find that they had not Philip to deal with; that the numbers of the horsemen, footmen, and ships, could not be reckoned; and that the train of elephants, by their mere appearance, would effectually daunt the enemy; that the Ætolians were resolved to come to Lacedæmon with their entire force whenever occasion required; but that they wished to show the king, on his arrival, a numerous body of troops; that Nabis himself, likewise, ought to take care not to suffer his soldiers to be enervated by inaction, and by spending their time in houses; but to lead them out, and make them perform their evolutions under arms, which, while it exercised their bodies, would also rouse their courage; that the labour would become lighter by practice, and might even be rendered not unpleasing by the affability and kindness of their commander." Thenceforward, the troops used frequently to be drawn out under the walls of the city, in a plain near the river Eurotas. The tyrant's life-guards were generally posted in the centre. He himself, attended by three horsemen at the most, of whom Alexamenus was commonly one, rode about in front, and went to view both wings to their extremities. On the right wing were the Ætolians; both those who had been before in his army as auxiliaries, and the thousand who came with Alexamenus. Alexamenus made it his custom to ride about with Nabis through a few of the ranks, making such remarks as he thought proper; then to join his own troops in the right wing; and presently after, as if having given the necessary orders, to return to the tyrant. But, on the day which he had fixed for the perpetration of the deed of death, after accompanying the tyrant for a little time, he withdrew to his own soldiers, and addressed the horsemen, sent from home with him, in these words: "Young men, you are now to perform, and that with boldness and resolution, the business which you were ordered to execute at my command. Have your courage and your hands ready, that none may fail to second me in whatever he sees me attempt. If any one shall hesitate, and let any scheme of his own interfere with mine, that man most certainly shall never return to his home." Horror seized them all, and they well remembered the charge which they had received at setting out. Nabis was now coming from the left wing. Alexamenus ordered his horsemen to rest their lances, and keep their eyes fixed on him; and in the mean time he himself re-collected his spirits from the hurry into which they had been thrown by the thoughts of such a desperate attempt. As soon as the tyrant came near, he charged him; and driving his spear through his horse, brought the rider to the ground. All the horsemen aimed their lances at him as he lay, and after many ineffectual strokes against his coat of mail, their points at length penetrated his body, so that, before relief could be sent from the centre, he expired.

36. Alexamenus, with all the Ætolians, hastened away to sieze on the palace. Nabis's life-guards were at first struck with horror and dismay, the act being perpetrated before their eyes; then, when they observed the Ætolian troops leaving the place, they gathered round the tyrant's body, where it was left, forming, instead of avengers of his death, a mere group of spectators. Nor would any one have stirred, if Alexamenus had immediately called the people to an assembly, there made a speech suitable to the occasion, and afterward kept a good number of Ætolians in arms, without offering to commit any act of violence. Instead of which, by a fatality which ought to attend all designs founded in treachery, every step was taken that could tend to hasten the destruction of the actors in this villanous enterprise. The commander, shut up in the palace, wasted a day and a night in searching out the tyrant's treasures; and the Ætolians, as if they had stormed the city, of which they wished to be thought the deliverers, betook themselves to plunder. The insolence of their behaviour, and, at the same time, contempt of their numbers, gave the Lacedæmonians courage to assemble in a body, when some said that they ought to drive out the Ætolians and resume their liberty, which had been ravished from them at the very time when it seemed to be restored; others, that for the sake of appearance, they ought to associate with them some one of the royal family, to give authority to their proceedings. There was a very young boy of that family, named Laconicus, who had been educated with the tyrant's children; him they mounted on a horse, and taking arms, slew all the Ætolians whom they met straggling through the city. They then assaulted the palace, where they killed Alexamenus, who, with a small party, attempted resistance. Others of the Ætolians,

who had collected together round the Chalciæcon, that is, the brazen temple of Minerva, were cut to pieces. A few, throwing away their arms, fled, some to Tegea, others to Megalopolis, where they were seized by the magistrates, and sold as slaves. Philopœmen, as soon as he heard of the murder of the tyrant, went to Lacedæmon, where, finding all in confusion and consternation, he called together the principal inhabitants, to whom he addressed a discourse, (such as ought to have been made by Alexamenus,) which had so great an effect, that the Lacedæmonians joined the confederacy of the Achæans. To this they were the more easily persuaded, because, at that very juncture, Aulus Atilius happened to arrive at Gythium with twenty-four quinqueremes.

37. Meanwhile Thoas, in his attempt on Chalcis, was not near so fortunate as Eurylochus had been in getting possession of Demetrias; although (by the intervention of Euthymidas, a man of considerable consequence, who, after the arrival of Titus Quintius and the ambassadors, had been banished by those who adhered to the Roman alliance; and also of Herodorus, who was a merchant of Cios, and who, by means of his wealth, possessed a powerful influence at Chalcis) he had engaged a party, composed of Euthymidas's faction, to betray the city into his hands. Euthymidas went from Athens, where he had fixed his residence, first to Thebes, and thence to Salganea; Herodorus to Thronium. At a small distance, on the Malian bay, Thoas had two thousand foot and two hundred horse, with thirty light transport ships. With these vessels, carrying six hundred footmen, Herodorus was ordered to sail to the island of Atalanta, that, as soon as he should perceive the land forces approaching Aulus and the Euripus, he might pass over to Chalcis; to which place Thoas himself led the rest of his forces, marching mostly by night, and with all possible expedition.

38. Mictio and Xenoclides, who were now, since the banishment of Euthymidas, at the head of affairs in that city, either of themselves suspected the matter, or received some information of it, and were at first so greatly terrified, that they saw no prospect of safety but in flight; but afterward, when their fright subsided, and they considered that by such a step they would betray and desert not only their country, but the Roman alliance, they struck out the following plan. It happened that, at that very time, there was a solemn anniversary festival celebrated at Eretria, in honour of Diana Amarynthis, which was always attended by great numbers, not only of the natives, but also of the Carystians; thither they sent envoys to beseech the Eretrians and Carystians, "as having been born in the same isle, to compassionate their sit-

uation; and, at the same time, to show their regard to the friendship of Rome; not to suffer Chalcis to become the property of the Ætolians, who, if they once got that city into their power, would soon possess themselves of all Eubœa; and to remind them that they had found the Macedonians grievous masters, but that the Ætolians would be much more intolerable." Those states were influenced chiefly by motives respecting the Romans, as they had lately experienced both the bravery in war, and the justice and liberality in success, which characterized that people. Both states therefore armed, and sent the main strength of their young men. To these the people of Chalcis intrusted the defence of the walls; and they themselves, with their whole force, crossed the Euripus, and encamped at Salganea. From that place they despatched, first a herald, and afterward ambassadors, to ask the Ætolians for what word or act of theirs, friends and allies came thus to attack them. Thoas, commander of the Ætolians, answered, that "he came not to attack them, but to deliver them from the Romans: that they were fettered at present with a brighter chain indeed, but a much heavier one, than when they had a Macedonian garrison in their citadel." The men of Chalcis replied, that "they were neither under bondage nor in need of protection." The ambassadors then withdrew from the meeting, and returned to their countrymen. Thoas and the Ætolians (who had no other hopes than in a sudden surprise, and were by no means in a capacity to undertake a regular war, and the siege of a city so well secured against any attack from the land or the sea) returned home. Euthymidas, on hearing that his countrymen were encamped at Salganea, and that the Ætolians had retired, went back from Thebes to Athens. Herodorus, after waiting several days at Atalanta, attentively watching for the concerted signal in vain, sent an advice-boat to learn the cause of the delay; and, understanding that the enterprise was abandoned by his associates, returned to Thronium.

39. Quintius, being informed of these proceedings, came with the fleet from Corinth, and met Eumenes in the Euripus of Chalcis. It was agreed between them that King Eumenes should leave there five hundred of his soldiers, as a garrison to the city, and should go himself to Athens. Quintius proceeded to Demetrias, as he had purposed from the first, hoping that the relief of Chalcis would prove a strong inducement to the Magnetians to renew the alliance with Rome: and, in order that such of them as favoured his views might have some support at hand, he wrote to Eunomus, pretor of the Thessalians, to arm the youth of his nation; sending Villius forward to Demetrias, to sound the

inclinations of the people: for he was determined not to take any step in the business, unless a considerable number of them were disposed to revive the former treaty of amity. Villius, in a ship of five banks of oars, came to the mouth of the harbour, and the whole multitude of the Magnetians hastened out thither. Villius then asked, whether they chose that he should consider himself as having come to friends or to enemies? Eurylochus the Magnetarch answered, that "he had come to friends; but desired him not to enter the harbour, but to suffer the Magnetians to live in freedom and harmony; and not to attempt, under the show of friendly converse, to seduce the minds of the populace." Then followed an altercation, not a conference, the Roman upbraiding the Magnetians with ingratitude, and forewarning them of the calamities impending over them; the multitude, on the other side, clamorously reproaching him, and reviling, sometimes the senate, sometimes Quintius. Villius, therefore, unable to effect any part of his business, went back to Quintius, who despatched orders to the Thessalian pretor to lead his troops home, while himself returned by sea to Corinth.

40. I have let the affairs of Greece, blended with those of Rome, carry me away, as it were, out of the course; not that they were in themselves deserving of a recital, but because they gave rise to a war with Antiochus. After the consular election, for thence I digressed, the consuls, Lucius Quintius and Cneius Domitius, repaired to their provinces; Quintius to Liguria, Domitius against the Boians. These latter kept themselves quiet: nay, the senators, with their children, and the commanding officers of the cavalry, with their troops, amounting in all to one thousand five hundred, surrendered to the consul. The other consul laid waste the country of the Ligurians to a wide extent, and took some forts: in which expeditions he not only acquired booty of all sorts, together with many prisoners, but he also recovered several of his countrymen, and of the allies, who had been in the hands of the enemy. In this year a colony was settled at Vibo, in pursuance of a decree of the senate and an order of the people; three thousand seven hundred footmen, and three hundred horsemen, went out thither, conducted by the commissioners, Quintus Nævius, Marcus Minucius, and Marcus Furius Crassipes. Fifteen acres of ground were assigned to each footman, double that quantity to a horseman. This land had been last in possession of the Bruttians, who had taken it from the Greeks. About this time two dreadful alarms happened at Rome, one of which continued long, but produced less mischief than the other. An earthquake lasted through thirty-eight days; during all

which time there was a total cessation of business, so strong were people's anxiety and fears. On account of this event a supplication was performed of three days' continuance. The other was not a mere fright, but attended with the loss of many lives. In consequence of a fire breaking out in the cattle-market, the conflagration, among the houses near to the Tiber, continued through all that day and the following night; and all the shops, with wares of very great value, were reduced to ashes.

41. The year was now almost at an end, while the rumors of impending hostility, and consequently the anxiety of the senate, daily increased. They therefore set about adjusting the provinces of the magistrates elect, in order that they might be all the more attentive in their several departments. They decreed that those of the consuls should be Italy, and whatever other place the senate should vote, for every one knew that a war against Antiochus was now a settled point. That he to whose lot the latter province fell should have under his command,—of Roman citizens, four thousand foot and three hundred horse; and of the Latine confederates, six thousand foot and four hundred horse. The consul, Lucius Quintius, was ordered to levy these troops, that the new consul might have nothing to prevent his proceeding immediately to any place which the senate should appoint. Concerning the provinces of the pretors, also, it was decreed, that the first lot should comprehend the two jurisdictions, both that between natives and that between them and foreigners; the second should be Bruttium; the third, the fleet, to sail wherever the senate should direct; the fourth, Sicily; the fifth, Sardinia; the sixth, Farther Spain. An order was also given to the consul Lucius Quintius to levy two new legions of Roman citizens, and of the allies and Latines twenty thousand foot and eight hundred horse. This army they assigned to the pretor to whom should fall the province of Bruttium. Two temples were dedicated this year to Jupiter in the capitol; one of which had been vowed by Lucius Furius Purpureo, when pretor during the Gallic war; the other by the same, when consul. Quintus Marcius Ralla, duumvir, dedicated both. Many severe sentences were passed this year on usurers, who were prosecuted by the curule ediles, Marcus Tuccius and Publius Junius Brutus. Out of the fines imposed on those who were convicted, gilded chariots, with four horses, were placed in the recess of Jupiter's temple in the capitol, over the canopy of the shrine, and also twelve gilded bucklers. The same ediles built a portico on the outside of the Triple Gate, in the Carpenters'-square.

42. While the Romans were busily employed in prepar-

ing for a new war, Antiochus, on his part, was not idle. He was detained some time by three cities, Smyrna, Alexandria in Troas, and Lampsacus, which hitherto he had not been able either to reduce by force, or to persuade into a treaty of amity; and he was unwilling, on going into Europe, to leave these as enemies. The difficulty of forming a fixed determination respecting Hannibal occasioned him farther delay. First, the open ships, which the king was to have sent with him to Africa, were not readily fitted out; and, afterward, doubts were raised, whether he ought to be sent at all. This was owing chiefly to Thoas, the Ætolian; who, after setting all Greece in commotion, came with the account of Demetrias being in the hands of his countrymen; and as he had, by false representations concerning the king, and multiplying, in his assertions, the number of his forces, exalted the expectations of many in Greece; so now, by the same artifices, he puffed up the hopes of the king; telling him, that "every one, with earnest wishes, longed for his coming; and that, wherever they got a view of the royal fleet, they would all run down to the shore to welcome him." He even had the audacity to attempt altering the king's judgment respecting Hannibal, when it was nearly settled: for he alleged, that "the fleet ought not to be weakened by sending away any part of it; but that, if ships must be sent, no person was less fit for the command than Hannibal; for he was an exile, and a Carthaginian; to whom his own circumstances, or his disposition, might daily suggest a thousand new schemes. Then, as to his military fame, which, like a large dowry, recommended him to notice, it was too splendid for an officer acting under Antiochus. The king ought to be the grand object of view; the king ought to appear the sole leader, the sole commander. If Hannibal should lose a fleet or an army, the amount of the damage would be the same as if the loss were incurred by any other general; but should success be obtained, all the honour would be ascribed to Hannibal. Besides, if the war should prove so fortunate as to terminate finally in the defeat of the Romans, could it be expected that Hannibal would live under a king; subject, in short, to an individual; he who could not brook subjection to the government of his own country? His conduct, from early youth, had been of a very different cast; for he was a man who grasped at nothing less than the dominion of the world. It was therefore not likely that in his maturer age he would be able to endure a master. The king wanted not Hannibal as a general: as an attendant and a counsellor in the business of the war, he might properly employ him. A moderate use of such abilities would be neither unprofitable nor dangerous; but, if advantages of the highest nature were sought through him, the probable consequences would be the destruction both of the agent and the employer."

43. There are no dispositions more prone to envy than those of persons whose mental qualifications are inferior to their birth and rank in life: such always harbour an antipathy to merit, as a treasure in which they cannot share. The design of the expedition to be commanded by Hannibal, the only one thought of that could be of use in the beginning of the war, was immediately laid aside. The king, highly flattered by the defection of Demetrias from the Romans to the Ætolians, resolved to pass into Greece without farther delay. Before the fleet weighed anchor he went up from the shore to Ilium, to offer sacrifice to Minerva. Immediately on his return, he set sail with forty decked ships and sixty open ones, followed by two hundred transports, laden with provisions and warlike stores. He first touched at the island of Imbrus; thence he passed over to Sciathus; whence, after collecting the ships which had been separated during the voyage, he proceeded to Pteleum, the nearest part of the continent. Here, Eurylochus the Magnetarch, and other principal Magnetians from Demetrias, met him. Being greatly gratified by their numerous appearance, he carried his fleet the next day into the harbour of their city. At a small distance from the town he landed his forces, which consisted of ten thousand foot, five hundred horse, and six elephants; a force scarcely sufficient to take possession of Greece, if there were to be no foreign opposition, much less to withstand the armies of Rome. The Ætolians, as soon as they were informed of Antiochus's arrival at Demetrias, convened a general council, and passed a decree, inviting him into their country. The king had already left Demetrias, (for he knew that such a decree was to be passed,) and had advanced as far as Phalera on the Malian bay. Here the decree was presented to him, and then he proceeded to Lamia, where he was received by the populace with marks of the warmest attachment, with clapping of hands and shouting, and other signs by which the vulgar express extravagant joy.

44. When he came to the place where the council sat, he was introduced by Phæneas, the pretor, and other persons of eminence, who, with difficulty, made way for him through the crowd. Then, silence being ordered, the king addressed himself to the assembly. He began with accounting for his having come with a force so much smaller than every one had hoped and expected. "That," he said, "ought to be deemed the strongest proof of the warmth of his good will towards them; because, though he was not sufficiently pre-

pared in any particular, and though the season was yet too early for sailing, he had, without hesitation, complied with the call of their ambassadors, and had believed that, when the Ætolians should see him among them, they would be satisfied, that in him, even if he were unattended, they might be sure of every kind of support. But he would also abundantly fulfil the hopes of those whose expectations seemed at present to be disappointed: for, as soon as the season of the year rendered navigation safe, he would cover all Greece with arms, men, and horses, and all its coasts with fleets. He would spare neither expense, nor labour, nor danger, until he should remove the Roman yoke from their necks, and render Greece really free, and the Ætolians the first among its states. That, together with the armies, stores of all kinds were to come from Asia. For the present, the Ætolians ought to take care that his men might be properly supplied with corn, and other accommodations, at reasonable rates."

45. Such was the purport of the king's discourse, which was received with universal approbation, and he then withdrew. After his departure, a warm debate ensued between two of the Ætolian chiefs, Phæneas and Thoas. Phæneas declared his opinion, that it would be better to employ Antiochus as a mediator of peace, and an umpire respecting the matters in dispute with the Roman people, than as leader in a war. That "his presence, and his dignified station, would impress the Romans with awe, more powerfully than his arms. That in many cases men, for the sake of avoiding war, remit pretensions, which force and arms would never compel them to forego." Thoas, on the other hand, insisted that "Phæneas's motive was not a love of peace, but a wish to embarrass them in their preparations for war, with the view that, through the tediousness of the proceedings, the king's vigour might be relaxed, and the Romans gain time to put themselves in readiness. That they had abundant proof from experience, after so many embassies sent to Rome, and so many conferences with Quintius in person, that nothing reasonable could ever be obtained from the Romans in the way of negotiation; and that they would not, until every hope of that sort was out of sight, have implored the aid of Antiochus. That, as he had appeared among them sooner than any had expected, they ought not to sink into indolence, but rather to petition the king, that, since he had come in person, which was the great point of all, to support the rights of Greece, he would also send for his fleets and armies: for the king, at the head of an army, might obtain something; but, without that, could have very little influence with the Romans, either in the cause of the Ætolians, or even in his own." This opinion was adopted, and the

council voted that the title of general should be conferred on the king. They also nominated thirty of their number, as a council with whom he might deliberate on business, when he should think proper. The council was then broken up, and all went home to their respective states.

46. Next day the king held a consultation with their select council, respecting the most eligible place for beginning his operations. They judged it best to make the first trial on Chalcis, which had lately been attempted in vain by the Ætolians; and they thought that the business required rather expedition than any great exertion or preparation. Accordingly the king, with a thousand foot, who had followed him from Demetrias, took his route through Phocis; and the Ætolian chiefs, going by another road, met at Cheronæa a small number of their young men, whom they had called to arms, and thence, in ten decked ships, proceeded after him. Antiochus pitched his camp at Salganea, while himself, with the Ætolian chiefs, crossed the Euripus in the ships. When he had advanced a little way from the harbour, the magistrates, and other chief men of Chalcis, came out before their gate. A small number, from each side, met to confer together. The Ætolians warmly recommended to the others, "without violating the friendship subsisting between them and the Romans, to receive the king also, as a friend and ally: for his coming into Europe was not for the purpose of making war, but of vindicating the liberty of Greece; and of vindicating it in reality, not in words and pretence merely, as the Romans had done. Nothing could be more advantageous to the states of Greece than to possess the friendship of both those powers; as they would then be always secure against ill treatment from either, under the guarantee and protection of the other. If they refused to receive the king, they ought to consider the immediate difficulties which they must encounter; the aid of the Romans being far distant, and Antiochus, whom with their own strength they could not possibly resist, in character of an enemy at their gates." To this Mictio, one of the Chalcian deputies, answered, that "he wondered who those people were, for the vindicating of whose liberty Antiochus had left his own kingdom, and come over into Europe: for his part, he knew not any state in Greece which either was awed by a garrison, or paid tribute to the Romans, or was bound by a disadvantageous treaty, and obliged to submit to terms which it did not like. The people of Chalcis, therefore, stood not in need, either of any assertor of their liberty, which they already enjoyed, or of any armed protector; since, through the kindness of the Roman people, they were in possession of both liberty and peace. They did not slight

the friendship of the king, nor that of the Ætolians themselves. The first instance of friendship, therefore, that they could give, would be to quit the island and go home: for, as to themselves, they were fully determined, not only not to admit them within their walls, but not even to agree to any alliance, but with the approbation of the Romans."

47. When an account of this conference was brought to the king, at the ships, where he had stayed, he resolved for the present to return to Demetrias; for he had not with him a sufficient number of men to attempt any thing by force. At Demetrias he held another consultation with the Ætolians, to determine what was next to be done, as their first effort had proved fruitless. It was agreed that they should make trial of the Bœotians, Achæans, and Amynander, king of Athamania. The Bœotian nation they believed to be disaffected to the Romans, ever since the death of Brachyllas, and the consequences which attended it. Philopœmen, chief of the Achæans, they supposed to hate, and be hated by, Quintius, in consequence of a rivalship for fame in the war of Laconia. Amynander had married Apamia, daughter of a Megalopolitan, called Alexander, who, pretending to be descended from Alexander the Great, had given the names of Philip and Alexander to his two sons, and that of Apamia to his daughter; and when she was raised to distinction, by her marriage to the king, Philip, the elder of her brothers, followed her into Athamania. This man, who was naturally vain, the Ætolians and Antiochus persuaded to hope that, as he was really of the royal family, he should be put in possession of the kingdom of Macedonia, on condition of his prevailing on Amynander and the Athamanians to join Antiochus; and these empty promises produced the intended effect, not only on Philip, but likewise on Amynander.

48. In Achaia, the ambassadors of Antiochus, and the Ætolians, were admitted to an audience of the council at Ægium, in the presence of Titus Quintius. The ambassador of Antiochus was heard prior to the Ætolians. He, with all that pomp and parade which is common among those who are maintained in the courts of kings, covered, as far as the empty sound of words could go, both lands and seas with forces. He said that "an innumerable body of cavalry was coming over the Hellespont into Europe; some of them cased in coats of mail, whom they call Cataphracti; others discharging arrows on horseback; and, what rendered it impossible to guard against them, shooting with the surest aim even when their backs were turned, and their horses in full gallop." To this army of cavalry, sufficient to crush the forces of all Europe, collected into one body, he

added another of infantry of many times its number; and to terrify them, repeated the names of nations scarcely ever heard of before; talking of Dahans, Medes, Elymæans, and Cadusians. "As to the naval forces, no harbours in Greece were capable of containing them; the right squadron was composed of Sidonians and Tyrians; the left of Aradians and Sidetians, from Pamphylia—nations which none other had ever equalled either in courage, or skill in sea affairs. Then, as to money, and other requisites for the support of war, it was needless for him to speak. They themselves knew that the kingdoms of Asia had always abounded in gold. The Romans, therefore, had not now to deal with Philip, or with Hannibal; the one a principal member of a commonwealth, the other confined merely to the limits of the kingdom of Macedonia; but with the great monarch of all Asia, and part of Europe. Nevertheless, though he had come to the remotest bounds of the East to give freedom to Greece, he did not demand any thing from the Achæans that could injure the fidelity of their engagements with the Romans, their former friends and allies; for he did not require them to take arms on his side against them; but only, that they should not join themselves to either party. That, as became common friends, they should wish for peace to both parties, and not intermeddle in the war." Archidamus, ambassador of the Ætolians, made nearly the same request: that, as was their easiest and safest way, they should stand neuter; and, as mere spectators of the war, wait for the issue, which would affect only the interests of others, while their own affairs were exposed to no manner of hazard. He afterward allowed himself to be transported into such intemperance of language, as to utter invectives, sometimes against the Romans in general, sometimes against Quintius himself in particular; charging them with ingratitude, and upbraiding them, as being indebted to the valour of the Ætolians, not only for the victory over Philip, but even for their preservation; for, "by their exertions, both Quintius himself and his army had been saved. What duty of a commander had he ever discharged? He used to see him, indeed, in the field, taking auspices; sacrificing, and offering vows, like an insignificant soothsaying priest: while he himself was, in his defence, exposing his person to the weapons of the enemy."

49. To this Quintius replied, that "Archidamus had calculated his discourse for the numerous auditors, rather than for the persons to whom it was particularly addressed: for the Achæans very well knew that the bold spirit of the Ætolians consisted entirely in words, not in deeds, and was more displayed in their councils and assemblies than in the field.

He had therefore been indifferent concerning the sentiments of the Achæans, to whom he and his countrymen were conscious that they were thoroughly known, and studied to recommend himself to the king's ambassadors, and, through them, to their absent master. But, if any person had been hitherto ignorant of the cause which had effected a junction between Antiochus and the Ætolians, it was easy to discover it from the language of their ambassadors. By the false representations made by both parties, and boasts of strength which neither possessed, they mutually puffed up each other, and were themselves puffed up with vain expectations; one party talking of Philip being vanquished by them, the Romans being protected by their valour, and the rest of what you have just heard; and that you, and the other states and nations, would follow their lead; the king, on the other side, boasting of clouds of horsemen and footmen, and covering the seas with his fleets. Their representations," he added, "are exceedingly like a supper that I remember at the house of my host at Chalcis, who is both a man of worth and an excellent conductor of a feast. He gave a cheerful entertainment to a party of us at midsummer; and on our wondering how he could, at that time of the year, procure such plenty and variety of game, he, not being so vain-glorious as these men, told us, with a pleasant smile, that the variety was owing to the dressing, and that what appeared to be the flesh of many different wild animals, was entirely of tame swine. This may be aptly applied to the forces of the king, so ostentatiously displayed a while ago; that those men, in various kinds of armour, and nations whose names were never mentioned before, Dahans, and Medes, and Cadusians, and Elymæans, are nothing more than Syrians, a race possessed of such grovelling souls, as to be much fitter for slaves than for soldiers. I wish, Achæans, that I could exhibit to your view the rapid excursions of this mighty monarch from Demetrias; first, to Lamia, to the council of the Ætolians; then to Chalcis. I would show you, in the royal camp, about the number of two small legions, and these incomplete. You should see the king, now, in a manner begging corn from the Ætolians, to be measured out to his soldiers; then, striving to borrow money at interest to pay them; again, standing at the gates of Chalcis; and presently, on being refused admittance, returning thence into Ætolia, without having effected any thing, except indeed the taking a peep at Aulis and the Euripus. Both have been duped: Antiochus by the Ætolians, and the Ætolians by the king's vain and empty boastings: for which reason, you ought to be the more on your guard against their deceptions, and rather to confide in the tried and approved fidelity of the Romans: for, with respect to a neutrality, which they recommend as your wisest plan, nothing, in fact, can be more contrary to your interest; for the inevitable consequence must be, that, without gaining thanks or esteem from either, you will become a prey to the conqueror."

50. His arguments, in opposition to both, were deemed conclusive, and there was no difficulty in bringing an audience, prepossessed in his favour, to give their approbation to his discourse. In fact there was no debate or doubt started, but all concurred in voting that the nation of the Achæans would treat, as their friends or foes, those who were judged to be such by the Roman people, and in ordering war to be declared against both Antiochus and the Ætolians. They also, by the direction of Quintius, sent immediate succours of five hundred men to Chalcis, and five hundred to the Piræus; for affairs at Athens were in a state not far from a civil war, in consequence of the endeavours used by some to seduce the venal populace, by hopes of largesses, to take part with Antiochus. But at length Quintius was called thither by those who were of the Roman party; and Apollodorus, the principal adviser of a revolt, being publicly charged therewith by one Leon, was condemned and driven into exile. Thus, from the Achæans also, the king's embassy returned with a discouraging answer. The Bœotians made no explicit declaration; they only said, that when Antiochus should come into Bœotia, they would then deliberate on the measures proper to be pursued. When Antiochus heard that both the Achæans and King Eumenes had sent reinforcements to Chalcis, he resolved to act with the utmost expedition, that his troops might get the start of them, and, if possible, intercept the others as they came; and he sent thither Menippus, with about three thousand soldiers, and Polyxenidas with the whole fleet. In a few days after he marched himself, at the head of six thousand of his own soldiers, and a smaller number of Ætolians, as many as could be collected in haste, out of those who were at Lamia. The five hundred Achæans, and a small party sent by King Eumenes, being guided by Xenoclides, of Chalcis, (the roads being yet open,) crossed the Euripus, and arrived at Chalcis in safety. The Roman soldiers, who were likewise about five hundred, came, after Menippus had fixed his camp under Salganea, at Hermæus, the place of passage from Bœotia to the island of Eubœa. They had with them Mictio, who had been sent express from Chalcis to Quintius, to solicit the reinforcement; and when he perceived that the passes were blocked up by the enemy, he quitted the road to Aulis, and turned away to Delium, with intent to pass over thence to Eubœa.

51. Delium is a temple of Apollo, standing over the sea, five miles distant from Tanagra; and the passage thence, to the nearest part of Eubœa, is less than four miles. As they were in this sacred building and grove, sanctified with all that religious awe and those privileges which belong to temples, called by the Greeks asylums, (war not being yet either proclaimed, or so far commenced as that they had heard of swords being drawn, or blood shed anywhere,) the soldiers, in perfect tranquillity, amused themselves, some with viewing the temple and groves; others with walking about unarmed, on the strand; and a great part had gone different ways in quest of wood and forage; when on a sudden Menippus attacked them in that scattered condition, slew many, and took fifty of them prisoners. Very few made their escape, among whom was Mictio, who was received on board a small trading vessel. Though this event caused much grief to Quintius and the Romans, on account of the loss of their men, yet it tended greatly to the justification of their cause in making war on Antiochus. Antiochus, when arrived with his army so near as Aulis, sent again to Chalcis a deputation, composed partly of his own people, and partly of Ætolians, to treat on the same grounds as before, but with heavier denunciations of vengeance; and, notwithstanding all the efforts of Mictio and Xenoclides to the contrary, he carried his point, and the gates were opened to him. Those who adhered to the Roman interest, on the approach of the king, withdrew from the city. The soldiers of the Achæans, and Eumenes, held Salganea; and the few Romans who had escaped raised for the security of the place a little fort on the Euripus. Menippus laid siege to Salganea, and the king himself to the fort. The Achæans and Eumenes' soldiers first surrendered, on the terms of being allowed to retire in safety. The Romans defended their fortress with more obstinacy. But even these, when they found themselves completely invested both by land and sea, and saw the machines and engines prepared for an assault, could hold out no longer. The king, having thus got possession of the capital of Eubœa, the other cities of the island did not even attempt resistance; and he seemed to himself to have signalized the commencement of the war by an important acquisition, in having brought under his power so great an island, and so many cities so conveniently situated.

# BOOK XXXVI.

CHAP. 1. PUBLIUS CORNELIUS SCIPIO, son of Cneius, and Manius Acilius Glabrio, consuls, [A. U. C. 561. B. C. 191,] on their assuming the administration, were ordered by the senate, before they settled any thing respecting their provinces, to perform sacrifices, with victims of the greater kinds, at all the shrines, where the Lectisternium was usually celebrated for the greater part of the year; and to offer prayers, that the business which the state had in contemplation concerning a new war might terminate prosperously and happily for the senate and people of Rome. At every one of those sacrifices appearances were favourable, and the propitious omens were found in the first victims. Accordingly the aruspices gave this answer:—That by this war the boundaries of the Roman empire would be enlarged, and that victory and triumph were portended. When this answer was reported, the senate, having their minds now freed from every religious scruple, ordered this question to be proposed to the people; "was it their will, and did they order that war should be undertaken against King Antiochus, and all who should join his party?" And that if that order passed, then the consuls were, if they thought proper, to lay the business entire before the senate. Publius Cornelius got the order passed; and then the senate decreed that the consuls should cast lots for the provinces of Italy and Greece; that he to whose lot Greece fell, should, in addition to the number of soldiers enlisted and raised from the allies by Quintius for that province, pursuant to a decree of the senate, take under his command that army, which, int he preceding year, Marcus Bæbius, pretor, had, by order of the senate, carried over to Macedonia. Permission was also granted him to receive succours from the allies out of Italy, if circumstances should so require, provided their number did not exceed five thousand. It was resolved that Lucius Quintius, consul of the former year, should be commissioned as a lieutenant-general in that war. The other consul, to whom Italy fell, was ordered to carry on the war with the Boians, with whichever he should choose of the two armies commanded by the consuls of the last year; and to send the other to Rome; and these were ordered to be the city legions, and ready to march to whatever place the senate should direct.

2. Things being thus adjusted in the senate, excepting the assignment of his particular province to each of the magistrates, the consuls were ordered to cast lots. Greece fell to Acilius, Italy to Cornelius. The lot of each being now determined, the senate passed a decree, that "inasmuch as the

Roman people had ordered war to be declared against King Antiochus, and those who were under his government, the consuls should command a supplication to be performed on account of that business; and that Manius Acilius, consul, should vow the great games to Jupiter, and offerings at all the shrines." This vow was made by the consul in these words, which were dictated by Publius Lcinius, chief pontiff: "If the war which the people has ordered to be undertaken against King Antiochus, shall be concluded agreeably to the wishes of the senate and people of Rome, then, O Jupiter, the Roman people will, through ten successive days, exhibit the great games in honour of thee, and offerings shall be presented at all the shrines, of such value as the senate shall direct. Whatever magistrate shall celebrate those games, and at whatever time and place, let the celebration be deemed proper, and the offerings rightly and duly made." The two consuls then proclaimed a supplication for two days. When the consuls had determined their provinces by lots, the pretors, likewise, immediately cast lots for theirs. The two civil jurisdictions fell to Marcus Junius Brutus; Bruttium, to Aulus Cornelius Mammula; Sicily, to Marcus Æmilius Lepidus; Sardinia, to Lucius Oppius Salinator; the fleet, to Caius Livius Salinator; and Farther Spain, to Lucius Æmilius Paulus. The troops for these were settled thus:—to Aulus Cornelius were assigned the new soldiers, raised last year by Lucius Quintius, consul, pursuant to the senate's decree; and he was ordered to defend the whole coast near Tarentum and Brundusium. Lucius Æmilius Paulus was directed to take with him into Farther Spain (to fill up the numbers of the army, which he was to receive from Marcus Fulvius, propretor,) three thousand new-raised foot, and three hundred horse, of whom two thirds should be Latine allies, and the other third Roman citizens. An equal reinforcement was sent to Hither Spain to Caius Flaminius, who was continued in command. Marcus Æmilius Lepidus was ordered to receive both the province and army from Lucius Valerius, whom he was to succeed; and, if he thought proper, to retain Lucius Valerius as propretor in the province, which he was to divide with him in such a manner, that one division should reach from Agrigentum to Pachynum, and the other from Pachynum to Tyndarium, the sea-coast whereof Lucius Valerius was to protect with a fleet of twenty ships of war. The same pretor received a charge to levy two tenths of corn, and to take care that it should be carried to the coast, and thence conveyed into Greece. Lucius Oppius was likewise commanded to levy a second tenth in Sardinia; but with directions that it should be transported, not into Greece, but to Rome. Caius Livius, the pretor, whose lot was the command of the fleet, was ordered to sail directly to Greece, with thirty ships, which were ready, and to receive the other fleet from Atilius. The pretor Marcus Junius was commissioned to refit and arm the old ships which were in the dock-yards; and, for the manning of these, to enlist the sons of freemen as seamen.

3. Commissaries were sent into Africa, three to Carthage, and a like number to Numidia, to procure corn to be carried into Greece; for which the Roman people were to pay the value. And so particularly attentive was the state to the making of every preparation and provision necessary for the carrying on of this war, that the consul, Publius Cornelius, published an edict, that "no senator, nor any who had the privilege of giving an opinion in the senate, nor any of the inferior magistrates, should go so far from the city of Rome as that they could not return the same day; and that not more than five of the senators should be absent at the same time." The exertions of the pretor, Caius Livius, in fitting out the fleet, were for some time retarded by a dispute which arose with the maritime colonies: for when he insisted on their manning the ships, they appealed to the tribunes of the people, by whom the cause was referred to the senate. The senate, without one dissenting voice, resolved, that those colonies were not entitled to exemption from the sea-service. The colonies which disputed this point with the pretor were, Ostia, Fregenæ, Castrumnovum, Pyrgi, Antium, Tarracina, Minturnæ, and Sinuessa. The consul, Manius Acilius, then, by direction of the senate, consulted the college of heralds, "whether a declaration of war should be made to Antiochus in person, or whether it would be sufficient to declare it at some of his garrison towns; whether they directed a separate declaration against the Ætolians, and whether their alliance and friendship ought not to be renounced before war was declared." The heralds answered, that "they had given their judgment before, when they were consulted respecting Philip, that it was of no consequence whether the declaration were made to himself in person, or at one of his garrisons. That in their opinion, friendship had been already renounced; because, after their ambassadors had so often demanded restitution, the Ætolians had not thought proper to make either restitution or apology. That these, by their own act, had made a declaration of war against themselves, when they seized by force Demetrias, a city in alliance with Rome; when they laid siege to Chalcis by land and sea; and brought King Antiochus into Europe, to make war on the Romans." Every preparatory measure being now completed, the consul, Manius Acilius, issued an edict, that "the soldiers enlisted or raised from

among the allies by Titus Quintius, and who were under orders to go with him to his province; as, likewise, the military tribunes of the first and third legions, should assemble at Brundusium on the ides of May."* He himself, on the fifth before the nones of May,† set out from the city in his military robe of command. The pretors likewise departed for their respective provinces.

4. A little before this time, ambassadors came to Rome from the two kings, Philip of Macedonia and Ptolemy of Egypt, offering aid of men, money, and corn, towards the support of the war. From Ptolemy was brought a thousand pounds weight of gold, and twenty thousand pounds weight of silver. None of this was accepted. Thanks were returned to the kings. Both of them offered to come, with their whole force, into Ætolia. Ptolemy was excused from that trouble; and Philip's ambassadors were answered, that the senate and people of Rome would consider it as a kindness if he lent his assistance to the consul Manius Acilius. Ambassadors came, likewise, from the Carthaginians, and from King Masinissa. The Carthaginians made an offer of sending a thousand pecks‡ of wheat and five hundred thousand of barley to the army, and half that quantity to Rome; which they requested the Romans to accept from them as a present. They also offered to fit out a fleet at their own expense, and to give in, immediately, the whole amount of the annual tribute money which they were bound to pay for many years to come. The ambassadors of Masinissa promised that their king should send five hundred thousand pecks of wheat, and three hundred thousand of barley, to the army in Greece, and three hundred thousand of wheat, and two hundred and fifty thousand of barley, to Rome; also five hundred horse, and twenty elephants, to the consul Acilius. The answer given to both, with regard to the corn, was, that the Roman people would make use of it, provided they would receive payment for the same. With regard to the fleet offered by the Carthaginians, no more was accepted than such ships as they owed by treaty; and as to the money, they were told that none would be taken before the regular days of payment.

5. While affairs at Rome proceeded in this manner, Antiochus, during the winter season at Chalcis, endeavoured to bring over several of the states by ambassadors sent among them; while many of their own accord sent deputies to him;

* 15th May. † 3d May.

‡ Here is, doubtless, some word dropped in the original; so small a quantity could never have been deemed an object for one powerful state to offer to another. Commentators suppose it to have been one hundred thousand.

as the Epirots, by the general voice of the nation, and the Eleans from Peleponnesus. The Eleans requested aid against the Achæans; for they supposed that, since the war had been declared against Antiochus contrary to their judgment, the Achæans would first turn their arms against them. One thousand foot were sent to them, under the command of Euphanes, a Cretan. The embassy of the Epirots showed no mark whatever of a liberal or candid disposition. They wished to ingratiate themselves with the king; but, at the same time, to avoid giving cause of displeasure to the Romans. They requested him "not hastily to make them a party in the dispute; exposed as they were, opposite to Italy, and in the front of Greece, where they must necessarily undergo the first assault of the Romans. If he himself, with his land and sea forces, could take charge of Epirus, the inhabitants would joyfully receive him in all their ports and cities. But if circumstances allowed him not to do that, then they earnestly entreated him not to subject them, naked and defenceless, to the arms of the Romans." Their intention in sending him this message evidently was, that if he declined going into Epirus, which they rather supposed would be the case, they stood clear of all blame with regard to the Romans, while they sufficiently recommended themselves to the king by their willingness to receive him on his coming; and that, on the other hand, if he should come, even then they were not without hopes of being pardoned by the Romans, for having yielded to the strength of a prince who was in the heart of their country, without waiting for succour from them, who were so far distant. To this evasive embassy, as he did not readily think of a proper answer, he replied, that he would send ambassadors to confer on such matters as were of common concernment both to him and them.

6. Antiochus went himself into Bœotia, where the ostensible causes held out for the public resentment to the Romans were those already mentioned; the death of Brachyllas, and the attack made by Quintius on Coronea, on account of the massacre of the Roman soldiers; while the real ones were, that the former excellent policy of that nation, with respect both to public and private concerns, had, for several generations, been on the decline; and that great numbers were in such circumstances, that they could not long subsist without some change in affairs. Through multitudes of the principal Bœotians, who everywhere were flocked out to meet him, he arrived at Thebes. There, notwithstanding that he had (both at Delium, by the attack made on the Roman troops, and also at Chalcis) already commenced hostilities, by enterprises of neither a trifling nor of a dubious nature,

yet, in a general council of the nation, he delivered a speech of the same import with that which he delivered in the first conference at Chalcis, and that used by his ambassadors in the council of the Achæans; that "what he required of them was, to form a league of friendship with him, not to declare war against the Romans." But not a man among them was ignorant of his meaning. However, a decree, disguised under a slight covering of words, was passed in his favour against the Romans. After securing this nation also on his side, he returned to Chalcis; and having despatched letters, summoning the chief Ætolians to meet him at Demetrias, that he might deliberate with them on the general plan of operations, he went thither by sea. Amynander, likewise, was called from Athamania to the consultation; and Hannibal, who, for a long time before, had not been asked to attend, was present at this assembly. The subject of their deliberation was, the mode of conduct proper to be pursued towards the Thessalian nation; and every one present was of opinion, that it was necessary to obtain their concurrence. The only points on which opinions differed were, that some thought the attempt ought to be made immediately, while others judged it better to defer it for the winter season, which was then about half spent, until the beginning of spring. Some advised to send ambassadors; others, that the king should go at the head of all his forces, and, if they hesitated, terrify them into compliance.

7. Although the present debate turned chiefly on these points, Hannibal being called on by name to give his opinion, led the king, and those who were present, into the consideration of the general conduct of the war, by a speech to this effect:—"If I had been employed in your councils since we came first into Greece, when you were consulting about Eubœa, the Achæans, and Bœotia, I would have offered the same advice which I shall offer you this day, when your thoughts are employed about the Thessalians. My opinion is, that, above all things, Philip and the Macedonians should by some means or other be engaged to act as confederates in this war; for as to Eubœa, as well as the Bœotians and Thessalians, is it not perfectly clear that, having no strength of their own, they will ever court the power that is present, and will make use of the same fear which governs their counsels as an argument for obtaining pardon? That, as soon as they shall see a Roman army in Greece, they will change sides, and attach themselves to that government to which they have been accustomed? Nor are they to blame [illegible] when the Romans were at so great a distance, they did [illegible]hoose to try your force, and that of your army, who [illegible] on the spot. How much more advisable, therefore,

and more advantageous would it be, to unite Philip to us, than these; as, if he once embarks in the cause, he will have no room for retreat, and as he will bring with him such a force as will not only be an accession to a power at war with Rome, but was able, lately, of itself, to withstand the Romans? With such an ally, (I wish to speak without offence,) how could I harbour a doubt about the issue? When I should see the very persons who enabled the Romans to overcome Philip, now ready to act against them? The Ætolians, who, as all agree, conquered Philip, will fight in conjunction with Philip against the Romans. Amynander and the Athamanian nation, who, next to the Ætolians, performed the greatest services in that war, will stand on our side. The Macedonian, at the time when you remained inactive, sustained the whole burden of the war. Now, you and he, two of the greatest kings, will, with the force of Asia and Europe, wage war against one state; which, to say nothing of my own contests with them, either prosperous or adverse, was certainly, in the memory of our fathers, unequal to a dispute with a single king of Epirus; what then, I say, must it be in competition with you two? But it may be asked, what circumstances induce me to believe that Philip may be brought to a union with us? First, common utility, which is the strongest cement of union; and next, my reliance, Ætolians, on your veracity; for Thoas, your ambassador, among the other arguments which he used to urge for the purpose of drawing Antiochus into Greece, always laid particular stress on this assertion, that Philip expressed extreme indignation at being reduced to the condition of a slave under the appearance of conditions of peace; comparing the king's anger to that of a wild beast chained, or shut up, and wishing to break the bars that confined it. Now, if his temper of mind is such, let us loose his chains; let us break these bars, that he may vent, on the common foe, this anger so long pent up. But should our embassy fail of producing any effect on him, let us then take care that, if we cannot unite him to ourselves, he may not be united to our enemies. Your son, Seleucus, is at Lysimachia; and if, with the army which he has there, he shall pass through Thrace, and once begin to make depredations on the nearest parts of Macedonia, he will effectually divert Philip from carrying aid to the Romans, and will oblige him to endeavour, in the first place, to protect his own dominions. Thus much respecting Philip. With regard to the general plan of the war, you have, from the beginning, been acquainted with my sentiments; and if my advice had been listened to, the Romans would not now hear that Chalcis in Eubœa was taken, and a fort on the Euripus reduced, but that Etruria, and the whole coast of Liguria and Cisalpine Gaul, were in a blaze of war; and, what would strike more terror into them all, that Hannibal was in Italy. Even as matters stand at present, I recommend it to you to call home all your land and sea forces; let store-ships with provisions follow the fleet; for, as we are here too few for the exigences of the war, so are we too many for the scanty supplies of necessaries. When you shall have collected together the whole of your force, you will divide the fleet, and keep one division stationed at Corcyra, that the Romans may not have a clear and safe passage; and the other you will send to the coast of Italy, opposite Sardinia and Africa; while you yourselves, with all the land forces, will proceed to the territory of Byllium. In this position you will hold the command of all Greece; you will give the Romans reason to think that you intend to sail over to Italy; and you will be in readiness to do so, if occasion require. This is my advice; and though I may not be the most skilful in every kind of warfare, yet surely I must be allowed to have learned, in a long series of both good and bad fortune, how to wage war against the Romans. For the execution of the measures which I have advised, I offer you my most faithful and zealous endeavours. Whatever plan you shall prefer, may the gods grant it their approbation!"

8. Such, nearly, was the counsel given by Hannibal, which the hearers commended indeed at the time, but never carried into effect: for not one article of it was executed, except the sending Polyxenidas to bring over the fleet and army from Asia. Ambassadors were sent to Larissa, to the diet of the Thessalians. The Ætolians and Amynander appointed a day for the assembling of their troops at Pheræ; and the king, with his forces, came thither immediately. While he waited there for Amynander and the Ætolians, he sent Philip, the Megalopolitan, with two thousand men, to collect the bones of the Macedonians round Cynoscephalæ, where had been fought the battle which decided the war with King Philip; being advised to this, either in order to gain favour with the Macedonians, and draw their displeasure on the king for having left his soldiers unburied, or having of himself, through the spirit of vain-glory incident to kings, conceived such a design,—splendid, indeed, in appearance, but really insignificant. There is a mount there formed of the bones which had been scattered about, and were then collected into one heap. Although this step procured him no thanks from the Macedonians, yet it excited the heaviest displeasure of Philip; in consequence of which, he who had hitherto intended to regulate his counsels by the fortune of events, now sent instantly a messenger to the

propretor, Marcus Bæbius, to inform him that "Antiochus had made an irruption into Thessaly; and to request of Bæbius, if he thought proper, to move out of his winter-quarters; which, if he did, he himself would advance to meet him, that they might consider together what was proper to be done."

9. While Antiochus lay encamped near Pheræ, where the Ætolians and Amynander had joined him, ambassadors came to him from Larissa, desiring to know on account of what act or words of theirs he had made war on the Thessalians; at the same time requesting him to withdraw his army; and if he had conceived any reason of disagreement, to discuss it amicably by commissioners. In the mean time they sent five hundred soldiers, under the command of Hippolochus, to reinforce Pheræ; but these, being debarred of access by the king's troops, who blocked up all the roads, retired to Scotussa. The king answered the Larissan ambassadors in mild terms, that "he came into their country, not with a design of making war, but of protecting and establishing the liberty of the Thessalians." He sent a person to make a similar declaration to the people of Pheræ; who, without giving him any answer, sent to the king, in quality of an ambassador, Pausanias, the first magistrate of their state. He offered remonstrances of a similar kind with those which had been urged in behalf of the people of Chalcis, at the first conference, on the strait of the Euripus, as the cases were similar, and he even proceeded to a greater degree of boldness; on which the king desired that they would consider seriously before they adopted a resolution which, while they were over-cautious and provident of futurity, would give them immediate cause of repentance; and then dismissed him. When the Pheræans were acquainted with the result of this embassy, without the smallest hesitation, they determined to endure whatever the fortune of war might bring on them, rather than violate their engagements with the Romans. They accordingly exerted their utmost efforts to provide for the defence of the place; while the king, on his part, resolved to assail the walls on every side at once; and considering, what was evidently the case, that it depended on the fate of this city, the first which he had besieged, whether he should for the future be despised or dreaded by the whole nation of the Thessalians, he put in practice, everywhere, all possible means of striking them with terror. The first fury of the assault they supported with great firmness; but in some time, great numbers of their men being either slain or wounded, their resolution began to fail. However, they were soon so far reanimated by the rebukes of their leaders, as to resolve on persevering in their

resistance; and having abandoned the exterior circle of the wall, for the defence of which their numbers were now insufficient, they withdrew to the interior part of the city, round which had been raised a fortification of less extent. At last, being overcome by distresses of every kind, and fearing that, if they were taken by storm, they might meet no mercy from the conqueror, they capitulated. The king then lost no time; but, while the alarm was fresh, sent four thousand men against Scotussa, which surrendered without delay, the garrison taking warning from the recent example of those in Pheræ; who, notwithstanding their obstinate refusal at first, were at length compelled by sufferings to submit. Together with the town, Hippolochus and the Larissan garrison were yielded to him, all of whom he dismissed unhurt; hoping that such behaviour would operate powerfully towards conciliating the esteem of the Larissans.

10. Having accomplished all this within the space of ten days after his arrival at Pheræ, he marched, with his whole force, to Cranon, which submitted on his first approach. He then took Cypæra and Metropolis, and the forts in their neighbourhood; and now every town, in all that tract, was in his power, except Atrax and Gyrton. He next resolved to lay siege to Larissa, for he hoped that (either through dread inspired by the storming of the other towns, or in consideration of his kindness in dismissing the troops of their garrison, or being led by the example of so many cities surrendering themselves) they would now lay aside their obstinacy. Having ordered the elephants to advance in front of the battalions, for the purpose of striking terror, he approached the city with his army in order of battle; which had such an effect on a great number of the Larissans, that they became irresolute and perplexed, between their fears of the enemy at their gates, and their respect for their distant allies. Meantime, Amynander, with the Athamanian troops, seized on Pellinæus; while Menippus, with three thousand Ætolian foot and two hundred horse, marched into Perrhæbia, where he took Mallæa and Cyretia by assault, and ravaged the lands of Tripolis. After executing these enterprises with despatch, they marched back to Larissa, where they joined the king, just when he was holding a council on the method of proceeding with regard to that place. On this occasion there were opposite opinions; for some thought that force should be applied; that there was no time to be lost, but that the walls should be immediately attacked with works and machines on all sides at once; especially as the city stood in a plain, the entrances open, and the approaches everywhere level. While others represented at one time the strength of the city, greater beyond

comparison than that of Pheræ; at another, the approach of the winter season, unfit for any operation of war, much more so for besieging and assaulting cities. While the king's judgment hung in suspense between hope and fear, his courage was raised by ambassadors happening to arrive just at the time from Pharsalus, to make surrender of the same. In the mean time, Marcus Bæbius had a meeting with Philip in Dassaretia; and, in conformity to their joint opinion, sent Appius Claudius to reinforce Larissa, who, making long marches through Macedonia, arrived at that summit of the mountains which overhang Gonni. The town of Gonni is twenty miles distant from Larissa, standing at the opening of the valley called Tempe. Here, by enlarging the extent of his camp beyond what his numbers required, and kindling more fires than were necessary, he imposed on the enemy the opinion which he wished, that the whole Roman army was there, and King Philip along with them. Antiochus therefore, pretending the near approach of winter as his motive, stayed but one day longer, then withdrew from Larissa, and returned to Demetrias. The Ætolians and Athamanians retired to their respective countries. Appius, although he saw that, by the siege being raised, the purpose of his commission was fulfilled, yet resolved to go down to Larissa to strengthen the resolution of the allies against future contingences. Thus the Larissans enjoyed a twofold happiness, from the departure of the enemy out of their country, and from seeing a Roman garrison in their city.

11. Antiochus went from Demetrias to Chalcis, where he became captivated with a young woman, daughter of Cleoptolemus. Her father was unwilling to enter into a connexion which might probably involve him in difficulties, until at length, by messages, and afterward by personal importunities, he gained his consent; and then he celebrated his nuptials in the same manner as if it were a time of profound peace. Forgetting the two important undertakings in which he was engaged,—the war with Rome, and the liberating of Greece,—he banished every thought of business from his mind, and spent the remainder of winter in feasting and carousals; and when fatigued, rather than cloyed, with these, in sleep. The same spirit of dissipation seized all his officers, who commanded in the several winter quarters, particularly those stationed in Bœotia; and even the common men abandoned themselves to the same indulgences; not one of whom ever put on his armour, or kept watch or guard, or did any part of the duty or business of a soldier. This was carried to such a length, that when in the beginning of spring the king came through Phocis to Chæronea,

where he had appointed the general assembly of all the troops, he perceived at once that the discipline of the army during the winter had not been more rigid than that of their commander. He ordered Alexander, an Acarnanian, and Menippus, a Macedonian, to lead his forces thence to Stratum, in Ætolia; and he himself, after offering sacrifice to Apollo at Delphi, proceeded to Naupactum. After holding a council of the chiefs of Ætolia, he went by the road which leads by Chalcis and Lysimachia to Stratum, to meet his army, which was coming along the Malian bay. Mnesilochus, a man of distinction among the Acarnanians, being bribed by many presents, not only laboured himself to dispose that nation in favour of the king, but had brought to a concurrence in the design their pretor, Clitus, who was at that time invested with the highest authority. This latter, finding that the people of Leucas, the capital of Acarnania, could not be easily prevailed on to violate their former engagements, because they were afraid of the Roman fleets, one under Atilius, and another at Cephalenia, practised an artifice against them. He observed in the council that the inland parts of Acarnania should be guarded from danger, and that all who were able to bear arms ought to march out to Medio and Thurium, to prevent those places from being seized by Antiochus, or the Ætolians; on which some said that there was no occasion to call out all the people in that hasty manner, for a body of five hundred men would be sufficient for the purpose. Having got this number of soldiers at his disposal, he placed three hundred in garrison at Medio, and two hundred at Thurium, with the design that they should fall into the hands of the king, and serve hereafter as hostages.

12. At this time ambassadors from the king came to Medio, whose proposal being heard, the assembly began to consider what answer to give; when some advised to adhere to the alliance with Rome, and others, not to reject the friendship of the king; but Clitus offered an opinion, which seemed to take a middle course between the other two, and which was therefore adopted. It was, that ambassadors would be sent to the king, to request of him to allow the people of Medio to deliberate on a subject of such great importance in a general assembly of the Acarnanians. Care was taken that this embassy should be composed of Mnesilochus, and some others of his faction; who, sending a private message to the king to bring up his army, wasted time on purpose; so that they had scarcely set out when Antiochus appeared in the territory, and presently at the gates of the city; and, while those who were not concerned in the plot were all in hurry and confusion, and hastily called the young men to arms, he

was conducted into the place by Clitus and Mnesilochus. One party of the citizens now joined him through inclination, and those who were of different sentiments were compelled by fear to attend him. He then calmed their apprehensions by a discourse full of mildness: and his clemency being reported abroad, several of the states of Acarnania, in hopes of meeting the same treatment, went over to his side. From Medio he went to Thurium, whither he had sent on before him the same Mnesilochus, and his colleagues in the embassy. But the detection of the treachery practised at Medio rendered the Thurians more cautious, not more timid. They answered him explicitly, that they would form no new alliance without the approbation of the Romans: they then shut their gates, and posted soldiers on the walls. Most seasonably for confirming the resolution of the Acarnanians, Cneius Octavius, being sent by Quintus, and having received a party of men and a few ships from Aulus Postumius, whom Atilius had appointed his lieutenant to command at Cephalenia, arrived at Leucas, and filled the allies with the strongest hopes; assuring them, that the consul Manius Acilius had already crossed the sea with his legions, and that the Roman forces were encamped in Thessaly. As the season of the year, which was by this time favourable for sailing, strengthened the credibility of this report, the king, after placing a garrison in Medio, and some other towns of Acarnania, retired from Thurium, and, taking his route through the cities of Ætolia and Phocis, returned to Chalcis.

13. Marcus Bæbius and King Philip, after the meeting which they had in the winter in Dassaretia, when they sent Appius Claudius into Thessaly to raise the siege of Larissa, had returned to winter-quarters, the season not being sufficiently advanced for entering on action; but now in the beginning of spring, they united their forces, and marched into Thessaly. Antiochus was then in Acarnania. As soon as they entered that country, Philip laid siege to Mallæa, in the territory of Perrhæbia, and Bæbius to Phacium. This town of Phacium he took almost at the first attempt, and then reduced Phæstus with as little delay. After this he retired to Atrax; and having seized on Cyretia and Phricium, and placed garrisons in the places which he had reduced, he again joined Philip, who was carrying on the siege of Mallæa. On the arrival of the Roman army, the garrison, either awed by its strength, or hoping for pardon, surrendered themselves, and the combined forces marched, in one body, to recover the towns which had been seized by the Athamanians. These were Æginium, Ericinum, Gomphi, Silana, Tricca, Meliboea, and Phaloria. Then they invested Pellinæum, where Philip of Megalopolis was in garrison, with five hun-

dred foot and forty horse; but before they made an assault, they sent a person to warn Philip, not to expose himself to the last extremities; to which he answered, with much confidence, that he could intrust himself either to the Romans or the Thessalians, but never would put himself in the power of the Macedonian. The confederate commanders now saw that they must have recourse to force, and thought that Limnæa might be attacked at the same time; it was therefore agreed that the king should go against Limnæa, while Bæbius stayed to carry on the siege of Pellinæum.

14. It happened that, just at this time, the consul, Manius Aeilius, having crossed the sea with twenty thousand foot, two thousand horse, and fifteen elephants, ordered some military tribunes, chosen for the purpose, to lead the infantry to Larissa, and he himself with the cavalry came to Limnæa, to Philip. Immediately on the consul's arrival, the town capitulated; and the king's garrison, together with the Athamanians, were delivered up. From Limnæa the consul went to Pellinæum. Here the Athamanians surrendered first, and afterward Philip of Megalopolis. King Philip, happening to meet the latter as he was coming out from the town, ordered his attendants, in derision, to salute him with the title of king; and he himself, coming up to him, with a sneer, highly unbecoming his own exalted station, accosted him by the name of brother. He was brought before the consul, who ordered him to be kept in confinement, and soon after sent him to Rome in chains. All the rest of the Athamanians, together with the soldiers of King Antiochus, who had been in garrison in the towns which surrendered about that time, were delivered over to Philip. They amounted to three thousand men. The consul went thence to Larissa, in order to hold a consultation on the general plan of operations; and on his way was met by ambassadors from Pieria and Metropolis, with the surrender of those cities. Philip treated the captured, particularly the Athamanians, with great kindness, in expectation of gaining, through them, the favour of their countrymen; and having hence conceived hopes of getting Athamania into his possession, he first sent forward the prisoners to their respective states, and then marched his army thither. The representations given by these of the king's clemency and generosity towards them, operated strongly on the minds of the people; and Amynander, who, by his presence, had retained many in obedience, through the respect paid to his dignity, began now to dread that he might be delivered up to Philip, who had been long his professed enemy, or to the Romans, who were justly incensed against him for his late defection. He, therefore, with his wife and children,

quitted the kingdom, and retired to Ambracia. Thus all Athamania came under the authority and dominion of Philip. The consul delayed a few days at Larissa, for the purpose chiefly of refreshing the horses, which, by the voyage first, and marching afterward, had been much harassed and fatigued; and when he had renewed the vigour of his army by a moderate share of rest, he marched to Cranon. On his way, Pharsalus, Scotussa, and Pheræ, were surrendered to him, together with the garrisons placed in them by Antiochus. He asked these men whether any of them chose to remain with him; and one thousand having declared themselves willing, he gave them to Philip; the rest he sent back, unarmed, to Demetrias. After this he took Proerna, and the forts adjacent; and then marched forward towards the Malian bay. When he drew near to the pass on which Thaumaci is situated, all the young men of that place took arms; and, quitting the town, placed themselves in ambush in the woods adjoining the roads, and thence, with the advantage of higher ground, made attacks on the Roman troops as they marched. The consul first sent people to talk with them, and warn them to desist from such a mad proceeding; but, finding that they persisted in their undertaking, he sent round a tribune, with two companies of soldiers, to cut off the retreat of the men in arms, and took possession of the defenceless city. On this, the parties in ambush, hearing from behind the shouts occasioned by that event, fled homeward from all parts of the woods, but were intercepted and cut to pieces. From Thaumaci the consul came, on the second day, to the river Sperchius; and, sending out parties, laid waste the country of the Hypatæans.

15. During these transactions, Antiochus was at Chalcis; and now, perceiving that he had gained nothing from Greece to recompense his trouble, except pleasing winter-quarters and a disgraceful marriage, he warmly blamed Thoas, and the fallacious promises of the Ætolians; while he admired Hannibal, as a man endowed not only with wisdom, but with a kind of prophetic skill, which had enabled him to foretel all that had come to pass. However, that he might not contribute to the failure of his inconsiderate enterprise by his own inactivity, he sent requisitions to the Ætolians, to arm all their young men, and assemble in a body He went himself immediately into their country, at the head of about ten thousand foot, (the number having been filled up out of the troops which had come after him from Asia,) and five hundred horse. Their assembly on this occasion was far less numerous than ever before, none attending but the chiefs with a few of their vassals. These affirmed that they had, with the utmost diligence, tried every

method to bring into the field as great a number as possible out of their respective states, but had not been able, either by argument, persuasion, or authority, to overcome the general aversion to the service. Being disappointed thus on all sides, both by his own people, who delayed in Asia, and by his allies, who did not fulfil those engagements by which they had prevailed on him to comply with their invitation, the king retired beyond the pass of Thermopylæ. A range of mountains here divides Greece in the same manner as Italy is divided by the ridge of the Apennines. Outside the strait of Thermopylæ, towards the north, lie Epirus, Perrhæbia, Magnesia, Thessaly, the Achæan Phthiotis, and the Malian bay; on the inside, towards the south, the greater part of Ætolia, Acarnania, Phocis, Locris, Bœotia, and the adjacent island of Eubœa, the territory of Attica, which stretches out like a promontory into the sea, and, behind that, the Peloponnesus. This range of mountains, which extends from Leucas and the sea on the west, through Ætolia to the opposite sea on the east, is so closely covered with thickets and craggy rocks, that, not to speak of an army, even persons lightly equipped for travelling can with difficulty find paths through which they can pass. The hills at the eastern extremity are called Œta, and the highest of them Callidromus; in a valley, at the foot of which, reaching to the Malian bay, is a passage not broader than sixty paces. This is the only military road by which an army can be led, even supposing no opposition. The place is therefore called Pylæ, the gate; and by some, on account of a warm spring, rising just at the entrance of it, Thermopylæ. It is rendered famous by the glorious stand made there by a party of Lacedæmonians against the Persians, and by their still more glorious death.

16. With a very inferior portion of spirit, Antiochus now pitched his camp within the enclosures of this pass, the difficulties of which he increased by raising fortifications; and when he had completely strengthened every part with a double rampart and trench, and, wherever it seemed requisite, with a wall formed of the stones which lay scattered about in abundance, being very confident that the Roman army would never attempt to force a passage there, he sent away one half of the four thousand Ætolians, the number that had joined him, to garrison Heraclea, which stood opposite the entrance of the defile, and the other half to Hypata; for he concluded that the consul would undoubtedly attack Heraclea, and he received accounts from many hands of depredations committed on the country round Hypata. The consul, after ravaging the lands of Hypata first, and then those of Heraclea, in both which places the Ætolian detach-

ments proved useless, encamped opposite to the king, in the very entrance of the pass, near the warm springs; both parties of the Ætolians shutting themselves up in Heraclea. Antiochus, who, before he saw the enemy, thought every spot perfectly well fortified, and secured by guards, now began to apprehend that the Romans might discover some paths among the hills above through which they could make their way; for he had heard that the Lacedæmonians formerly had been surrounded in that manner by the Persians, and Philip, lately by the Romans themselves. He therefore despatched a messenger to the Ætolians at Heraclea, desiring them to afford him so much assistance, at least in the war, as to seize and secure the tops of the hills, so as to put it out of the power of the Romans to pass them. The delivery of this message raised a dissension among the Ætolians: some insisted that they ought to obey the king's orders, and go where he desired; others, that they ought to lie still at Heraclea, and wait the issue, be it what it might; for if the king should be defeated by the consul, their forces would be fresh, and in readiness to carry succour to their own states in the neighbourhood; and if he were victorious, they could pursue the Romans while scattered in their flight. Each party not only adhered positively to its own plan, but even carried it into execution; two thousand lay still at Heraclea; and two thousand, divided into three parties, took possession of the summits called Callidromus, Rhoduntia, and Tichiuns.

17. When the consul saw that the heights were possessed by the Ætolians, he sent against those posts two men of consular rank, who acted as lieutenants-general, with two thousand chosen troops;—Lucius Valerius Flaccus against Rhoduntia and Tichiuns, and Marcus Porcius Cato against Callidromus. Then, before he led on his forces against the enemy, he called them to an assembly, employing a short exhortation to this effect: "Soldiers, I see that the greater part of you who are present, of all ranks, are men who served in this same province, under the conduct and auspices of Titus Quintius. I therefore wish to remind you, that in the Macedonian war, the pass at the river Aous was much more difficult than this before us: for this is only a gate, a single passage, formed as it were by nature; every other in the whole tract between the two seas being utterly impracticable. In the former case, there were stronger fortifications, and more advantageously situated. The enemy's army was both more numerous, and composed of very superior men; for they were Macedonians, Thracians, and Illyrians,—people remarkable for the ferocity of their courage: your present opponents are Syrians, and Asiatic Greeks,

the most unsteady of men, and born slaves. The commander, there, was a king of extraordinary warlike abilities, improved by practice from his early youth in wars against his neighbours, the Thracians and Illyrians, and all the adjoining nations. The king with whom we have now to deal is one who (to say nothing of his former life, after coming over from Asia into Europe to make war on the Roman people) has, during the whole length of the winter, accomplished no more memorable exploit, than the taking a wife to gratify his amorous inclinations out of a private house, and a family obscure even among its neighbours; and now, this newly married man, after indulging in the luxury of nuptial feasts, comes out to fight. His chief reliance was on the strength of the Ætolians,—a nation of all others the most faithless and ungrateful, as you have formerly experienced, and as Antiochus now experiences; for they neither joined him with the great numbers that were promised, nor could they be kept in the field; and, besides, they are now in a state of dissension among themselves. Although they demanded to be intrusted with the defence of Hypata and Heraclea, yet they defended neither; but one half of them fled to the tops of the mountains, while the others shut themselves up in Heraclea. The king himself plainly confessing, that so far from daring to meet us in battle on the level plain, he durst not even encamp in open ground, has abandoned all that tract in front, which he boasted of having taken from us and Philip, and has hid himself behind the rocks; not even appearing in the opening of the pass, as it is said the Lacedæmonians did formerly, but drawing back his camp within the strait. Does not this demonstrate just the same degree of fear, as if he had shut himself up within the walls of a city to stand a siege? But neither shall the straits protect Antiochus, nor the hills which they have seized, the Ætolians. Sufficient care and precaution have been used on every quarter, that you shall have nothing to contend with in the fight but the enemy himself. On your parts, you have to consider, that you are not fighting merely for the liberty of Greece; although, were that all, it would be an achievement highly meritorious to deliver that country now from Antiochus and the Ætolians, which you formerly delivered from Philip; and that the wealth in the king's camp will not be the whole prize of your labour; but that the great collection of stores, daily expected from Ephesus, will likewise become your prey; and also, that you will open a way for the Roman power into Asia and Syria, and all the most opulent realms to the extremity of the East. What then must be the consequence, but that, from Gades to the Red Sea,* we shall have no limit but the ocean, which encircles the whole orb of the earth; and that all mankind shall regard the Roman name with a degree of veneration next to that which they pay to the divinities? for the attainment of prizes of such magnitude, be ready to exert a spirit adequate to the occasion, that, to-morrow, with the aid of the gods, we may decide the matter in the field."

18. After this discourse, he dismissed the soldiers, who, before they went to their repast, got ready their armour and weapons. At the first dawn, the signal of battle being displayed, the consul formed his troops with a narrow front, adapted to the nature and the straitness of the ground. When the king saw the enemy's standards in motion, he likewise drew out his forces. He placed in the van, before the rampart, a part of his light infantry; and behind them, as a support, close to the fortifications, the main strength of his Macedonians, whom they call Sarissophori, spearmen. On the left wing of these, at the foot of the mountain, he posted a body of javelin-bearers, archers, and slingers; that from the higher ground they might annoy the naked flank of the enemy; and on the right of the Macedonians, to the extremity of the works, where the deep morasses and quicksands, stretching thence to the sea, render the place impassable, the elephants with their usual guard; in the rear of them, the calvalry; and then, with a moderate interval between, the rest of his forces as a second line. The Macedonians, posted before the rampart, for some time easily withstood the efforts which the Romans made everywhere to force a passage; for they received great assistance from those who poured down from the higher ground a shower of leaden balls from their slings, and of arrows, and javelins, all together. But afterward, the enemy pressing on with greater and now irresistible force, they were obliged to give ground, and, filing off from the rear, retire within the fortification. Here, by extending their spears before them, they formed as it were a second rampart, for the rampart itself was of such a moderate height, that while its defenders enjoyed the advantage of the higher ground, they, at the same time, by the length of their spears, had the enemy within reach underneath. Many of the assailants, inconsiderately approaching the work, were run through the body; and they must either have abandoned the attempt and retreated, or have lost very great numbers, had not Marcus Porcius come from the summit of Callidromus, whence he had dislodged

* The ancients supposed the earth to have a flat circular surface, round the extremity of which flowed a body of water, called by them the ocean. The eastern quarter of the ocean they called the Red Sea, from the ruddy colour of the rising sun.

the Ætolians, after killing the greater part of them. These he had surprised, quite unprepared, and mostly asleep, and now he appeared on the hill which overlooked the camp. Flaccus had not met the same good fortune at Tichiuns and Rhoduntia; having failed in his attempts to approach those fastnesses.

19. The Macedonians and others in the king's camp, as long as, on account of the distance they could distinguish nothing more than a body of men in motion, thought they were the Ætolians, who, on seeing the fight, were coming to their aid. But when, on a nearer view, they knew the standards and arms, and thence discovered their mistake, they were all instantly seized with such a panic, that they threw down their arms and fled. The pursuit was somewhat retarded by the fortifications, and by the narrowness of the valley through which the troops had to pass: and, above all, by the elephants being on the rear of the flying enemy, so that it was with difficulty that the infantry could make their way. This, indeed, the cavalry could by no means do, their horses being so frightened, that they threw one another into greater confusion than would be occasioned by a battle. The plundering of the camp, also, caused a considerable delay. But, notwithstanding all this, the Romans pursued the enemy that day as far as Scarphia, killing and taking on the way great numbers both of men and horses, and also killing such of the elephants as they could not secure; and then they returned to their post. This had been attacked, during the time of the action, by the Ætolians quartered at Heraclea; but the enterprise, which certainly showed no want of boldness, was not attended with any success. The consul, at the third watch of the following night, sent forward his cavalry in pursuit of the enemy; and, as soon as day appeared, set out at the head of the legions. The king had got far before him, for he fled with the utmost speed, and never halted until he came to Elatia. There he first endeavoured to collect the scattered remains of his army; and then, with a very small body of half-armed men, he continued his retreat to Chalcis. The Roman cavalry did not overtake the king himself at Elatia; but they cut off a great part of his soldiers, who either halted through weariness, or wandered out of the way through mistake, as they fled without guides through unknown roads; so that out of the whole army, not one escaped, except five hundred, who kept close about the king; and even of the ten thousand men, whom, on the authority of Polybius, we have mentioned as brought over by the king from Asia, a very trifling number got off. But what shall we say to the account given by Valerius Antias, that there were in the king's

army sixty thousand men, of whom forty thousand fell, and above five thousand were taken, with two hundred and thirty military standards? Of the Romans were slain in the action itself a hundred and fifty; and of the party that defended the camp against the assault of the Ætolians, not more than fifty.

20. As the consul marched through Phocis and Bœotia, the revolted states, conscious of their demerits, and dreading lest they should be exposed as enemies to the ravages of the soldiers, presented themselves at the gates of their cities, with the badges of suppliants; but the army proceeded, during the whole time, just as if they were in the country of friends, without offering violence of any sort, until they reached the territory of Coronea. Here a statue of King Antiochus, standing in the temple of Minerva Itonia, kindled such violent resentment, that permission was given to the soldiers to plunder the surrounding lands. But the reflection quickly occurred, that, as the statue had been erected by a general vote of all the Bœotian states, it was unreasonable to resent it on the single district of Coronea. The soldiers were therefore immediately recalled, and the depredations stopped. The Bœotians were only reprimanded for their ungrateful behaviour to the Romans in return for great obligations so recently conferred. At the very time when the battle was fought, ten ships belonging to the king, with their commander Isidorus, lay at anchor near Thronium, in the Malian bay. To them Alexander of Acarnania, being grievously wounded, made his escape, and gave an account of the unfortunate issue of the battle; on which the fleet, alarmed at the immediate danger, sailed away in haste to Cenæus in Eubœa. There Alexander died, and was buried. Three other ships, which came from Asia to the same port, on hearing the disaster which had befallen the army, returned to Ephesus. Isidorus sailed over from Cenæus to Demetrias, supposing that the king might perhaps have directed his flight thither. About this time, Aulus Atilius, commander of the Roman fleet, intercepted a large convoy of provisions going to the king, just as they had passed the strait at the island of Andros: some of the ships he sunk, and took many others. Those who were in the rear tacked about, and steered back to Asia. Atilius, with the captured vessels in train, sailed back to Piræus, his former station, and distributed a vast quantity of corn among the Athenians, and the other allies in that quarter.

21. Antiochus, quitting Chalcis before the consul arrived there, sailed first to Tenus, and thence passed over to Ephesus. When the consul came to Chalcis, the gates were open to receive him; for Aristoteles, who commanded for

the king, on hearing of his approach, had withdrawn from the city. The rest of the cities of Eubœa also submitted without opposition; and peace being restored all over the island within the space of a few days, without inflicting punishment on any, the army, which had acquired much higher praise for moderation after victory, than even for the attainment of it, marched back to Thermopylæ. From this place the consul despatched Marcus Cato to Rome, that the senate and people might learn what had passed from unquestionable authority. He set sail from Creusa, a sea-port belonging to the Thespians, seated at the bottom of the Corinthian gulf, and steered to Petræ, in Achaia. From Petræ he coasted along the shores of Ætolia and Acarnania, as far as Corcyra, and thence he passed over to Hydruntum in Italy. Proceeding hence with rapid expedition by land, he arrived on the fifth day at Rome. Having come into the city before day, he went on directly from the gate to Marcus Junius, the pretor, who, at the first dawn, assembled the senate. Here, Lucius Cornelius Scipio, who had been despatched by the consul several days before Cato, and on his arrival had heard that the latter had outstripped him, and was then in the senate, came in, just as he was giving a recital of the transactions. The two lieutenants-general were then, by order of the senate, conducted to the assembly of the people, where they gave the same account, as in the senate, of the services performed in Ætolia. Hereon a decree was passed, that a supplication of three days' continuance should be performed; and that the pretor should offer sacrifice to such of the gods as his judgment should direct, with forty victims of the larger kinds. About the same time Marcus Fulvius Nobilior, who, two years before, had gone into Farther Spain, in the office of pretor, went through the city in ovation. He carried in the procession a hundred and thirty thousand silver denariuses,* and, besides the coin, twelve thousand pounds' weight of silver, and a hundred and twenty-seven pounds' weight of gold.

22. The consul Acilius sent on from Thermopylæ a message to the Ætolians in Heraclea, warning them, "then at least, after the experience which they had of the emptiness of the king's professions, to return to a proper way of thinking; and, by surrendering Heraclea, to endeavour to procure from the senate a pardon for their past madness, or error, if they rather chose so to call it;" and he observed that "other Grecian states also had, during the present war, revolted from the Romans, to whom they were under the highest

* 4097*l.* 16*s.* 4*d.*

obligations: but that inasmuch as, after the flight of the king, whose presence had inspired that confidence which led them astray from their duty, they had not added obstinacy to their other crimes, they were readmitted into friendship. In like manner, although the Ætolians had not followed the king's lead, but had invited him, and had been principals in the war, not auxiliaries; nevertheless, if they could prevail on themselves to show a proper sense of their misconduct, they might still ensure their safety." Their answer showed nothing like a pacific disposition; wherefore, seeing that the business must be determined by force of arms, and that, notwithstanding the defeat of the king, the war of Ætolia was as far from a conclusion as ever, Acilius led up his army from Thermopylæ to Heraclea; and, on the same day, rode on horseback entirely round the walls, in order to discover the strength of the city. Heraclea is situated at the foot of Mount Œta; the town itself is in the plain, but has a citadel overlooking it, which stands on an eminence of considerable height, terminated on all sides by precipices. Having examined every part which he wished to see, the consul determined to make the assault in four places at once. On the side next the river Asopus, where is also the Gymnasium, he gave the direction of the works to Lucius Valerius. He assigned to Tiberius Sempronius Longus the attack of a part of the suburbs, which was as thickly inhabited as the city itself. He appointed Marcus Bæbius to act on the side opposite the Malian bay, where the access was far more easy; and Appius Claudius, on the side next to another rivulet, called Melas the black, opposite to the temple of Diana. These exerted themselves with such vigorous emulation, that within a few days the towers, rams, and other machines used in the besieging of towns, were all completed. The lands round Heraclea, naturally marshy, and abounding with tall trees, furnished timber in abundance for every kind of work; and then, as the Ætolians had fled into the city, the deserted suburbs supplied not only beams and boards, but also bricks and mortar, and stones of every size for all their various occasions.

23. The Romans carried on their approaches by means of works more than of personal exertions; the Ætolians maintained their defence by dint of arms: for when the walls were shaken by the ram, they did not, as is usual, intercept and turn aside the strokes by the help of nooses formed on ropes, but sallied out in large armed bodies, with parties carrying fire in order to burn the machines. They had likewise arched passages through the parapet, for the purpose of making sallies; and when they built up the wall anew, in the room of any part that was demolished, they

left a great number of these sallyports, that they might rush out in many places at once. In several days, at the beginning, while their strength was unimpaired, they carried on this practice in numerous parties, and with much spirit; but then, both their numbers and spirit daily decreased: for though they had a multiplicity of difficulties to struggle with, what above all things utterly consumed their vigour, was the want of sleep, as the Romans, having plenty of men, relieved each other regularly in their posts; while among the Ætolians, their numbers being small, the same persons were obliged to toil on without intermission. During a space of twenty-four days they were kept day and night in one continued course of unremitting exertion against the attacks carried on by the enemy in four different quarters at once; so that they never had an hour's respite from action. When the consul, from computing the time, and from the reports of deserters, judged that the Ætolians were thoroughly fatigued, he adopted the following plan:—At midnight he gave the signal of retreat, and drawing off all his men at once from the assault, kept them quiet in the camp until the third hour of the next day. The attacks were then renewed, and continued until midnight, when they ceased, until the third hour of the day following. The Ætolians imagined that the Romans suspended the attack from the same cause by which they felt themselves distressed,—excessive fatigue. As soon therefore as the signal of retreat was given to the Romans, as if themselves were thereby recalled from duty, every one gladly retired from his post, nor did they again appear in arms on the walls before the third hour of the day.

24. The consul having put a stop to the assault at midnight, renewed it on three of the sides, at the fourth watch, with the utmost vigour; ordering Tiberius Sempronius, on the fourth, to keep his party alert, and ready to obey his signal; for he concluded assuredly, that, in the tumult by night, the enemy would all run to those quarters where they heard the shouts. Of the Ætolians, such as had gone to rest with difficulty roused their bodies from sleep, exhausted as they were with fatigue and watching; and such as were still awake ran in the dark to the places where they heard the noise of fighting. Meanwhile the Romans endeavoured to climb over the ruins of the walls, through the breaches; in others, strove to scale the walls with ladders; while the Ætolians hastened to defend the parts attacked. In one quarter, where the buildings stood outside the city, there was neither attack nor defence; but a party stood ready, waiting for the signal to make an attack, but there was none within to oppose them. The day now began to

dawn, and the consul gave the signal; on which the party, without any opposition, made their way into the town; some through breaches, others scaling the walls where they were entire. As soon as the Ætolians heard them raise the shout, which denoted the place being taken, they everywhere forsook their posts, and fled into the citadel. The victors sacked the city; the consul having given permission, not for the sake of gratifying resentment or animosity, but that the soldiers, after having been restrained from plunder in so many captured cities, might at last, in some one place, enjoy the fruits of victory. About midday he recalled the troops; and, dividing them into two parts, ordered one to be led round by the foot of the mountain to a rock, which was of equal height with the citadel, and seemed as if it had been broken off from it, leaving a hollow between; but the summits of these eminences are so nearly contiguous, that weapons may be thrown into the citadel from their tops. With the other half of the troops the consul intended to march up from the city to the citadel, as soon as he should receive a signal from those who were to mount the rock on the farther side. The Ætolians in the citadel could not support the shout of the party which had seized the rock, and the consequent attack of the Romans from the city; for their courage was now broken, and the place was by no means in a condition to hold out a siege of any continuance; the women, children, and great numbers of other helpless people, being crowded together in a fort, which was scarce capable of containing, much less of affording protection to such a multitude. On the first assault, therefore, they laid down their arms and submitted. Among the rest was delivered up Damocritus, chief magistrate of the Ætolians, who at the beginning of the war, when Titus Quintius asked for a copy of the decree passed by the Ætolians for inviting Antiochus, told him, that, "in Italy, when the Ætolians were encamped there, it should be delivered to him." This presumptuous insolence of his, enhanced the satisfaction which the victors felt at his being put into their hands.

25. At the same time, while the Romans were employed in the reduction of Heraclea, Philip by concert besieged Lamia. He had an interview with the consul as he was returning from Bœotia, at Thermopylæ, whither he came to congratulate him and the Roman people on their successes, and to apologize for his not having taken an active part in the war, being prevented by sickness; and then they went from thence by different routes to lay siege to the two cities at once. The distance between these places is about seven miles; and as Lamia stands on high ground, and has an open prospect on that side particularly, the distance seems

very short, and every thing that passes can be seen from thence. The Romans and Macedonians, with all the emulation of competitors for a prize, employed the utmost exertions, both night and day, either in the works or in fighting; but the Macedonians encountered greater difficulty on this account, that the Romans made their approaches by mounds, covered galleries, and other works, which were all above ground; whereas the Macedonians worked under ground by mines, and, in that stony soil, often met a flinty rock, which iron could not penetrate. The king seeing that little progress could be made in that way, endeavoured, by reasoning with the principal inhabitants, to prevail on them to surrender the place; for he was fully persuaded that if Heraclea should be taken first, the Lamians would then choose to surrender to the Romans rather than to him; and that the consul would take to himself the merit of relieving them from a siege. Nor was he mistaken in that opinion; for no sooner was Heraclea reduced, than a message came to him to raise the siege; because "it was more reasonable that the Roman soldiers, who had fought the Ætolians in the field, should reap the fruits of the victory." Thus was Lamia relieved, and the misfortune of a neighbouring city proved the means of its escaping a like disaster.

26. A few days before the capture of Heraclea, the Ætolians, having assembled a council at Hypata, sent ambassadors to Antiochus, among whom was Thoas, who had visited him before in the same capacity. Their instructions were, in the first place, to request the king again to assemble his land and marine forces, and come into Greece; and, in the next place, if it should be inconvenient to him to leave home, then to send them supplies of men and money. They were to remind him that "it concerned his dignity and his honour not to abandon his allies; and it likewise concerned the safety of his kingdom not to leave the Romans at full leisure, after ruining the nation of the Ætolians, to carry their whole force into Asia." Their remonstrances were well founded, and therefore made the deeper impression on the king; in consequence of which, he immediately supplied the ambassadors with the money requisite for the exigences of the war, and assured them that he would send them succours both of troops and ships. He kept with him Thoas, who was not unwilling to stay, as he hoped that his presence might accelerate the performance of the king's promises.

27. But the loss of Heraclea entirely broke the spirits of the Ætolians; insomuch that, within a few days after they had sent ambassadors into Asia for the purpose of renewing the war, and inviting the king, they threw aside all thoughts of fighting, and despatched deputies to the consul to sue for

peace. When these began to speak, the consul interrupting them, said that he had other business to attend to at present; and, ordering them to return to Hypata, granted them a truce for ten days, sending with them Lucius Valerius Flaccus, to whom he desired whatever business they intended to have proposed to himself might be communicated, with any other that they thought proper. On their arrival at Hypata, the chiefs of the Ætolians held a consultation, at which Flaccus was present, on the method to be used in treating with the consul. They showed an inclination to begin with setting forth the ancient treaties, and the services which they had performed to the Roman people; on which Flaccus desired them to "speak no more of treaties, which they themselves had violated and annulled." He told them that "they might expect more advantage from an acknowledgment of their fault, and submissive entreaty; for their hopes of safety rested not on the merits of their cause, but on the clemency of the Roman people. That if they acted in a suppliant manner, he would himself be a solicitor in their favour, both with the consul and with the senate at Rome; for thither also they must send ambassadors." This appeared to all the only way to safety: "to submit themselves entirely to the faith of the Romans: for, in that case, the latter would be ashamed to do injury to suppliants; while themselves would, nevertheless, retain the power of consulting their own interest, should fortune offer any thing more advantageous."

28. When they came into the consul's presence, Phæneas, who was at the head of the embassy, made a long speech, in which he endeavoured, by a variety of pathetic representations, to mitigate the wrath of the conqueror; and he concluded with saying, that "the Ætolians surrendered themselves and all belonging to them to the faith of the Roman people." The consul, on hearing this, said, "Ætolians, consider well whether you will yield on these terms:" and then Phæneas produced the decree, in which the conditions were expressly mentioned. "Since, then," said the consul, "you submit in this manner, I demand that, without delay, you deliver up to me Dicæarchus, your countryman, Menetas the Epirot," who had, with an armed force entered Naupactum, and compelled the inhabitants to abandon the cause of Rome, "and also Amynander, with the Athamanian chiefs, by whose advice you revolted from us." Phæneas, scarcely waiting until the Roman had done speaking, answered,—"We surrendered ourselves, not into slavery, but to your faith; and I take it for granted that, from not being sufficiently acquainted with us, you fall into the mistake of commanding what is inconsistent with the practice of the

Greeks."—"Nor in truth," replied the consul, "do I much concern myself, at present, what the Ætolians may think conformable to the practice of the Greeks; while I, conformably to the practice of the Romans, exercise authority over men, who just now surrendered themselves by a decree of their own, and were before that conquered by my arms. Wherefore, unless my commands are quickly complied with, I order that you be put in chains." At the same time he ordered chains to be brought forth, and the lictors to surround the ambassadors. This effectually subdued the arrogance of Phæneas and the other Ætolians; and, at length, they became sensible of their situation. Phæneas then said, that "as to himself and his countrymen there present, they knew that his commands must be obeyed; but it was necessary that a council of the Ætolians should meet, to pass decrees accordingly; and that, for that purpose, he requested a suspension of arms for ten days." At the intercession of Flaccus this was granted, and the Ætolians returned to Hypata. When Phæneas related here, in the select council, called Apocleti, the orders which they had received, and the treatment which they had narrowly escaped, although the melancholy condition to which they were reduced drew forth the deepest lamentations from the members present, nevertheless they were of opinion that the conqueror must be obeyed, and that the Ætolians should be summoned from all their towns to a general assembly.

29. But when the assembled multitude heard the same account, they were so highly exasperated both by the harshness of the order, and the indignity offered, that, even if they had been in a pacific temper before, the violent impulse of anger which they then felt would have been sufficient to rouse them to war. There occurred besides the difficulty of executing the orders; for, "how was it possible for them, for instance, to deliver up King Amynander?" It happened also that a favourable prospect seemed to open to them; for Nicander, returning from King Antiochus at that juncture, filled the minds of the people with unfounded assurances that immense preparations for war were going on both by land and sea. This man, after finishing the business of his embassy, set out on his return to Ætolia, and the twelfth day after he embarked reached Phalara, on the Malian bay. Having conveyed thence to Lamia the money that he had brought, he, with a few light troops, directed, in the evening, his course towards Hypata, by known paths, through the country which lay between the Roman and Macedonian camps. Here he fell in with an advanced guard of the Macedonians, and was conducted to the king, who had not yet risen from dinner. Philip, being told of his coming, re-

ceived him as a guest, not an enemy; desired him to take a seat, and a share of the entertainment; and afterward, when he dismissed the rest, detained him alone, and told him that he had nothing to fear for himself. He censured severely the conduct of the Ætolians, in bringing, first the Romans, and afterward Antiochus, into Greece; designs which originated in a want of judgment, and always fell heavy on their own heads. But "he would forget," he said, "all past transactions, which it was easier to blame than to amend; nor would he act in such a manner as to appear to insult their misfortunes. On the other hand, it would become the Ætolians to lay aside, at length, their animosity towards him; and it would become Nicander himself, in his private capacity, to remember that day on which he was to be indebted to him for his preservation." He then gave him an escort to a place of safety; and Nicander arrived at Hypata, while his countrymen were consulting about the peace with Rome.

30. Manius Acilius having sold, or given to the soldiers, the booty found near Heraclea, and having learned that the counsels adopted at Hypata were not of a pacific nature, but that the Ætolians had hastily assembled at Naupactum, with intention to make a stand there against all their adversaries, sent forward Appius Claudius, with four thousand men, to seize the tops of the hills, where the passes were difficult; and he himself, ascending Mount Œta, offered sacrifice to Hercules in the spot called Pyra,* because there the mortal part of that demigod was burned. He then set out with the main body of the army, and marched all the rest of the way with tolerable ease and expedition. But when they came to Corax, a very high mountain between Callipolis and Naupactum, great numbers of the beasts of burden, together with their loads, tumbled down the precipices, by which many of the men were hurt. This clearly showed an extraordinary degree of negligence in the enemy, who had not secured the pass by a guard, and which must have greatly incommoded the Romans; for, even as the case was, the army suffered considerably. Hence he marched down to Naupactum; and having erected a fort against the citadel, he invested the other parts of the city, dividing his forces according to the situation of the walls. Nor was this siege likely to prove less difficult and laborious than that of Heraclea.

31. At the same time, the Achæans laid siege to Messene in Peloponnesus, because it refused to become a member of their body; for the two states of Messene and Elis were unconnected with the Achæan confederacy, and favoured the

* The funeral pile.

designs of the Ætolians. However, the Eleans, after Antiochus had been driven out of Greece, answered the deputies sent by the Achæans with more moderation; that "when the king's troops were removed, they would consider what part they should take." But the Messenians had dismissed the deputies without an answer, and prepared for war. Alarmed afterward at the danger of their situation, when they saw the enemy ravaging their country without control, and pitching their camp almost at their gates, they sent deputies to Chalcis, to Titus Quintius, the author of their liberty, to acquaint him that "the Messenians were willing, both to open their gates and surrender their city to the Romans, but not to the Achæans." On hearing this, Quintius immediately set out, and despatched from Megalopolis a messenger to Diophanes, pretor of the Achæans, requiring him to draw off his army instantly from Messene, and to come to him. Diophanes obeyed the order; raising the siege, he hastened forward himself before the army, and met Quintius near Andania, a small town between Megalopolis and Messene. When he began to explain the reasons for commencing the siege, Quintius gently reproving him for undertaking a business of that importance without consulting him, ordered him to disband his forces, and not to disturb a peace which had been established on terms highly beneficial to all. He commanded the Messenians to recall the exiles, and to unite themselves to the confederacy of the Achæans; and if there were any particulars to which they chose to object, or any precautions judged requisite against future contingencies, they might apply to him at Corinth. He then gave directions to Diophanes to convene immediately a general council of the Achæans, that he might settle some business with them.

32. In this assembly he complained of their having acquired possession of the island of Zacynthus by unfair means, and demanded that it should be restored to the Romans. Zacynthus had formerly belonged to Philip, king of Macedonia, and he had made it over to Amynander, in requital of his having given him leave to march an army through Athamania, into the upper part of Ætolia, on that expedition wherein he reduced the Ætolians to despair, and compelled them to sue for peace. Amynander gave the government of the island to Philip, the Megalopolitan; and afterward, during the war in which he acted in conjunction with Antiochus against the Romans, having called out Philip to a command in the field, he sent as his successor, Hierocles of Agrigentum. This man, after the defeat of Antiochus at Thermopylæ, and the expulsion of Amynander from Athamania by Philip, sent emissaries of his own accord to

Diophanes, pretor of the Achæans; and having bargained for a sum of money, put the Achæans in possession of the island. This acquisition, made during the war, the Romans claimed as their own; for they said that "it was not for Diophanes and the Achæans that the consul Manius Acilius, and the Roman legions, fought at Thermopylæ." Diophanes, in answer, sometimes apologized for himself and his nation; sometimes insisted on the justice of the proceeding. But several of the Achæans testified that they had, from the beginning, disapproved of that business, and they now blamed the obstinacy of the pretor. Pursuant to their advice, a decree was made, that the affair should be left entirely to the disposal of Titus Quintius. As Quintius was severe to such as made opposition, so, when complied with, he was easily appeased. Laying aside therefore every thing stern in his voice and looks, he said, "If, Achæans, I thought the possession of that island advantageous to you, I would be the first to advise the senate and people of Rome to leave it in your hands. But as I see that a tortoise, when collected within its natural covering, is safe against blows of any kind, and whenever it thrusts out any of its members, it feels whatever it has thus uncovered weak and liable to every injury; so you, Achæans, being enclosed on all sides by the sea, can easily unite among yourselves, and maintain by that union all that is comprehended within the limits of Peloponnesus; but whenever, through ambition of enlarging your possessions, you overstep these limits, then all that you hold beyond them is naked and exposed to every attack." The whole assembly declaring their assent, and Diophanes not daring to give farther opposition, Zacynthus was ceded to the Romans.

33. When the consul was on his march to Naupactum, King Philip proposed that, if it was agreeable to him, he would in the mean time retake those cities that had revolted from their alliance with Rome. Having obtained permission so to do, he about this time marched his army to Demetrias, where he knew that great distraction prevailed; for the garrison, being destitute of all hope of succour since they were abandoned by Antiochus, and having no reliance on the Ætolians, daily and nightly expected the arrival of Philip or the Romans, whom they had most reason to dread, as these were more justly incensed against them. There was in the place an irregular multitude of the king's soldiers, a few of whom had been at first stationed there as a garrison, but the greater part had fled thither after the defeat of his army, most of them without arms, and without either strength or courage sufficient to sustain a siege. Wherefore, Philip's sending on messengers to offer them hopes of

favourable terms, they answered that their gates were open for the king. On his first entrance, several of the chiefs left the city; Eurylochus killed himself. The soldiers of Antiochus, in conformity to a stipulation, were escorted through Macedonia and Thrace by a body of Macedonians, and conducted to Lysimachia. There were also a few ships at Demetrias, under the command of Isidorus, which, together with their commander, were dismissed. Philip then reduced Dolopia, Aperantia, and several cities of Perrhæbia.

34. While Philip was thus employed, Titus Quintius, after receiving from the Achæan council the cession of Zacynthus, crossed over to Naupactum, which had stood a siege of near two months, but was now reduced to a desperate condition; and it was supposed that, if it should be taken by storm, the whole nation of the Ætolians would be sunk thereby in utter destruction. But although he had good reason to be angry with the Ætolians, from the recollection that they alone had attempted to depreciate his merits when he was giving liberty to Greece, and had refused to pay any regard to his advice when he endeavoured, by forewarning them of the events which had since occurred, to deter them from their mad undertaking,—nevertheless, thinking it particularly incumbent on him, who had asserted the freedom of the country, to prevent any of its states from being entirely subverted, he first walked about near the walls, that he might be easily known by the Ætolians. He was quickly distinguished by the first advanced guards, and the news spread from rank to rank that Quintius was there. On this the people from all sides ran to the walls, and eagerly stretching out their hands, all in one joint cry besought Quintius by name to assist and save them. Although he was much affected by these entreaties, yet for that time he made signs with his hand that they were to expect no assistance from him. However, when he met the consul he accosted him thus:—"Manius Acilius, are you unapprized of what is passing; or do you know it, and think it immaterial to the interest of the commonwealth?" These words raising the consul's curiosity, he requested him to explain what he meant. Quintius then said, "Do you not see that, since the defeat of Antiochus, you have been wasting time in besieging two cities, though the year of your command is near expiring; but that Philip, who never faced the enemy, or even saw their standards, has annexed to his dominions such a number, not only of cities, but of nations,—Athamania, Perrhæbia, Aperantia, Dolopia? But, surely, we are not so deeply interested in diminishing the strength and resources of the Ætolians as in hindering those of Philip from being augmented beyond measure; and in you and your soldiers

not having yet gained, to reward your victory, as many towns as Philip has gained Grecian states."

35. The consul assented to the justness of his remarks, but was ashamed to let himself be foiled in his attempt, and to raise the siege. At length the matter was left entirely to the management of Quintius. He went again to that part of the wall whence the Ætolians had called to him a little before; and on their entreating him now, with still greater earnestness, to take compassion on the nation of the Ætolians, he desired that some of them might come out to him. Accordingly Phæneas himself, with some others of the principal men, instantly came, and threw themselves at his feet. He then said, "Your condition causes me to restrain my resentment and my reproofs. The events which I foretold have come to pass, and you have not even so much consolation left as the reflection that you have not deserved what has fallen on you. Nevertheless, since fate has in some manner destined me to the office of cherishing the interests of Greece, I will not cease to show kindness even to the unthankful. Send a suppliant embassy to the consul, and let them petition him for a suspension of hostilities, for so long a time as will allow you to send ambassadors to Rome to surrender yourselves to the will of the senate. I will intercede, and plead in your favour with the consul." They did as Quintius directed; nor did the consul reject their application. He granted them a truce for a certain time, until an account might be brought from Rome of the result of their embassy; and then, raising the siege, he sent his army into Phocis. The consul, with Titus Quintius, crossed over thence to Ægium, to confer with the council of the Achæans, where the business of the Eleans was introduced, and also a proposal of restoring the Lacedæmonian exiles. But neither was carried into execution, because the Achæans chose to reserve to themselves the merit of effecting the latter; and the Eleans preferred being united to the Achæan confederacy by a voluntary act of their own rather than through the mediation of the Romans. Ambassadors came hither to the consul from the Epirots, who, it was well known, had not fulfilled with sincerity the engagements to which they were bound by the treaty of alliance. Although they had not furnished Antiochus with any soldiers, yet they were charged with having assisted him with money; and they did not disavow the having sent ambassadors to him. They requested that they might be permitted to continue on the former footing of friendship. To which the consul answered, that "he did not yet know whether he was to consider them as friends or foes. The senate must be the judge of that matter. He would therefore take no

step in the business, but leave it to be determined at Rome; and for that purpose he granted them a truce of ninety days." When the Epirots who were sent to Rome addressed the senate, they rather enumerated hostile acts which they had not committed, than cleared themselves of those laid to their charge; and they received an answer of such a kind as showed that they had rather obtained pardon than proved their innocence. About the same time ambassadors from King Philip were introduced to the senate, and presented his congratulations on their late successes. They asked leave to sacrifice in the capitol, and to deposite an offering of gold in the temple of Jupiter supremely good and great. This was granted by the senate, and they presented a golden crown of a hundred pounds weight. The senate not only answered the ambassadors with kindness, but gave them Demetrius, Philip's son, who was at Rome as a hostage, to be conducted home to his father. Such was the conclusion of the war waged in Greece by the consul Manius Acilius, against Antiochus.

36. The other consul, Publius Cornelius Scipio, to whose lot the province of Gaul had fallen, before he set out to take the field against the Boians, demanded of the senate by a decree, to order him money for the exhibition of games, which, when acting as propretor in Spain, he had vowed at a critical time of a battle. His demand was deemed unprecedented and unreasonable, and they therefore voted that "whatever games he had vowed on his own single judgment, without consulting the senate, he should celebrate out of the spoils, if he had reserved any for the purpose; otherwise at his own expense." Accordingly, Publius Cornelius exhibited those games through the space of ten days. About this time the temple of the great Idæan Mother was dedicated; which deity, on her being brought from Asia in the consulate of Publius Cornelius Scipio, afterward surnamed Africanus, and Publius Licinius, the above mentioned Publius Cornelius had conducted from the sea side to the Palatine. In pursuance of a decree of the senate, Marcus Livius and Caius Claudius, censors, in the consulate of Marcus Cornelius and Publius Sempronius, had contracted with builders to erect the goddess's temple; and, thirteen years after that, it was dedicated by Marcus Junius Brutus, and games were celebrated on occasion of its dedication; in which, according to the account of Valerius Antias, dramatic entertainments were, for the first time, introduced into the Megalesian games. Likewise Caius Licinius Lucullus, being appointed duumvir, dedicated the temple of Youth in the great circus. This temple had been vowed sixteen years before, by Marcus Livius, consul, on the day whereon he

cut off Hasdrubal and his army; and the same person, when censor, in the consulate of Marcus Cornelius and Publius Sempronius, had contracted for the building of it. Games were also exhibited on occasion of this consecration, and every thing was performed with the greater degree of religious zeal, on account of the impending war with Antiochus.

37. At the beginning of the year in which those transactions passed, after Manius Acilius had gone to open the campaign, and while the other consul, Publius Cornelius, yet remained in Rome, two tame oxen, it is said, climbed up by ladders on the tiles of a house in the Carinæ. The aruspices ordered them to be burned alive, and their ashes to be thrown into the Tiber. It was reported that several showers of stones had fallen at Tarracina and Amiternum; that at Minturnæ the temple of Jupiter, and the shops round the forum, were struck by lightning; that, at Vulturnum, in the mouth of the river, two ships were struck by lightning and burnt to ashes. On occasion of these prodigies, the decemvirs, being ordered by a decree of the senate to consult the Sibylline books, declared that "a fast ought to be instituted in honour of Ceres, and the same observed every fifth year; that the nine days' worship ought to be solemnized, and a supplication for one day; and that, when employed in the supplication, the people should wear garlands on their heads; also, that the consul Publius Cornelius should sacrifice to such deities, and with such victims as the decemvirs should direct." When he had used every means to avert the wrath of the gods, by duly fulfilling vows, and expiating prodigies, the consul went to his province; and ordering the proconsul Cneius Domitius to disband his army, and go home to Rome, he marched his own legions into the territory of the Boians.

38. Nearly at the same time, the Ligurians, having collected an army under the sanction of their devoting law, made an unexpected attack, in the night, on the camp of the proconsul Quintus Minucius. Minucius kept his troops until daylight drawn up within the rampart, and watchful to prevent the enemy from scaling any part of the fortifications. At the first light he made a sally by two gates at once; but the Ligurians did not, as he had expected, give way to his first onset; on the contrary, they maintained a dubious contest for more than two hours. At last, as supplies of troops continually came out from the camp, and fresh men took the places of those who were wearied in the fight, the Ligurians, who, besides other hardships, felt a great loss of strength from the loss of sleep, after a severe struggle betook themselves to flight. Above four thousand of the enemy were killed; the Romans and allies lost not quite three hundred. About two months after this, the consul Publius Cornelius fought a

pitched battle with the army of the Boians with extraordinary success. Valerius Antias affirms, that twenty-eight thousand of the enemy were slain, and three thousand four hundred taken, with a hundred and twenty-four military standards, one thousand two hundred and thirty horses, and two hundred and forty-seven wagons; and that of the conquerors there fell one thousand four hundred and eighty-four. Though we may not entirely credit this writer with respect to the numbers, as he always exaggerates most extravagantly, yet it is certain that the victory on this occasion was very complete; because the enemy's camp was taken, while, immediately after the battle, the Boians surrendered themselves; and because a supplication was decreed by the senate on account of it, and victims of the greater kinds were sacrificed.

39. The consul Publius Cornelius having received hostages from the Boians, punished them so far as to appropriate almost one half of their lands for the use of the Roman people, and into which they might afterward, if they chose, send colonies. Then returning home in full confidence of a triumph, he dismissed his troops, and ordered them to attend on the day of his rejoicing at Rome. The next day after his arrival, he held a meeting of the senate in the temple of Bellona; and, after recounting his services, demanded permission to ride through the city in triumph. Publius Sempronius Blæsus, tribune of the people, advised that "the honour of a triumph should not be refused to Scipio, but postponed. Wars of the Ligurians," he said, "were always united with wars of the Gauls; for these nations lying so near, sent mutual assistance to each other. If Publius Scipio, after subduing the Boians in battle, had either gone himself, with his victorious army, into the country of the Ligurians, or sent a part of his forces to Quintus Minucius, who was detained there, now the third year, by a war of which the issue was still uncertain, that with the Ligurians might have been brought to an end; instead of which, he had, in order to procure a full attendance on his triumph, brought home the troops, who might have performed most material services to the state; and might do so still, if the senate thought proper, by deferring this token of victory, to redeem the omission occasioned by haste to obtain distinction. If they would order the consul to return with his legions into his province, and to give his assistance towards subduing the Ligurians, (for unless these were reduced under the dominion and jurisdiction of the Roman people, neither would the Boians ever remain quiet,) there must be either peace or war with both. When the Ligurians should be subdued, Publius Cornelius, in quality of proconsul, might triumph a few months later,

as had been the case of many, who did not attain that honour until the expiration of their office."

40. To this the consul answered, that "neither had the province of Liguria fallen to his lot, nor had he waged war with the Ligurians, nor did he demand a triumph over them. He confidently hoped that in a short time Quintus Minucius, after completing their reduction, would demand and obtain a well-deserved triumph; for his part, he demanded that note of celebrity from having vanquished the Boian Gauls, whom he had driven out of their camp; of whose whole nation he had received an absolute submission within two days after the fight; and from whom he had brought home hostages to secure peace in future. But there was another circumstance of much greater magnitude; he had slain in battle so great a number of Gauls, that no commander before him could say that he ever met in the field so many thousands, at least of the Boians. Out of fifty thousand men, more than one half were killed; and many thousands made prisoners; so that the Boians had now remaining only old men and boys. Could it, then, be a matter of surprise to any one, that a victorious army, which had not left one enemy in the province, should come to Rome to attend the triumph of their consul? And if the senate should choose to employ the services of these troops in another province also,—of the two kinds of treatment, which could be supposed would make them enter on a new course of danger and fatigue with the greater alacrity, the paying them the reward of their former toils and dangers without defalcation; or the sending them away with the shadow instead of the substance, after their first hopes had terminated in disappointment? As to what concerned himself personally, he had acquired a stock of glory sufficient for his whole life on that day when the senate adjudged him to be the best man in the state, and commissioned him to give a reception to the Idæan Mother. With this inscription (though neither consulship nor triumph were added) the statue of Publius Scipio Nasica would be sufficiently honoured and dignified." The senate not only gave their unanimous vote for the solicited honour, but by their influence prevailed on the tribune to desist from his intention of protesting against it. Publius Cornelius, consul, triumphed over the Boians. In this procession he carried, on Gallic wagons, arms, standards, and spoils of all sorts; the brazen utensils of the Gauls; and, together with the prisoners of distinction, he led a train of captured horses. He deposited in the treasury a thousand four hundred and seventy golden chains; and besides these, two hundred and forty-five pounds weight of gold; two thousand three hundred and forty pounds weight of silver, some unwrought,

and some formed in vessels of the Gallic fashion, not without beauty; and two hundred and thirty-three thousand denariuses.* To the soldiers who followed his chariot, he distributed three hundred and twenty-five asses† each, double to a centurion, triple to a horseman. Next day he summoned an assembly, and after expatiating on his own services, and the ill treatment shown him by the tribune, who wanted to entangle him in a war which did not belong to him, in order to defraud him of the fruits of his success, he absolved the soldiers of their oath, and discharged them.

41. While this passed in Italy, Antiochus was at Ephesus, divested of all concern respecting the war with Rome, as supposing that the Romans had no intention of coming into Asia; into which state of security he was lulled by the erroneous opinions or the flattering representations of the greater part of his friends. Hannibal alone, whose judgment was at that time the most highly respected by the king, declared, that "he rather wondered the Romans were not already in Asia, than entertained a doubt of their coming. The passage was easier from Greece to Asia, than from Italy to Greece, and Antiochus was a much more inviting object than the Ætolians: for the Roman wars were not less powerful on sea than on land. Their fleet had long been at Malea, and he had heard that a reinforcement of ships and a new commander had lately come from Italy, with intent to enter on action. He therefore advised Antiochus not to form to himself vain hopes of peace. He must necessarily in a short time maintain a contest with the Romans, both by sea and land; in Asia, and for Asia itself; and must either wrest the power out of hands that grasped at the empire of the world, or lose his own dominions." Hannibal seemed to be the only person who had judgment to foresee, and sincerity to foretel what was to happen. The king therefore, with the ships which were in readiness, sailed to the Chersonesus, in order to secure the places there with garrisons, lest the Romans should happen to come by land. He left orders with Polyxenidas to fit out the rest of the fleet, and put to sea; and sent out advice-boats among the islands to procure intelligence of every thing that was passing.

42. When Caius Livius, commander of the Roman fleet, sailed with fifty decked ships from Rome, he went to Neapolis, where he had appointed the rendezvous of the undecked ships, which were due by treaty from the allies on that coast; and thence he proceeded to Sicily, where, as he sailed through the strait beyond Messana, he was joined by six Carthaginian ships, sent to his assistance; and then, having

---

* 7623*l.* 16*s.* 2*d.* † 1*l.* 4*s.* 2 1-2*d.*

collected the vessels due from the Rhegians, Locrians, and other allies, who were bound by the same conditions, he purified the fleet at Lacinium, and put forth into the open sea. On his arrival at Corcyra, which was the first Grecian country where he touched, inquiring about the state of the war, (for the commotions in Greece were not yet entirely composed,) and about the Roman fleet, he was told that the consul and the king were posted at the pass of Thermopylæ, and that the fleet lay at Piræus: on which, judging expedition necessary on every account, he sailed directly forward to Peloponnesus. Having on his passage ravaged Samos and Zacynthus, because they favoured the party of the Ætolians, he bent his course to Malea; and, meeting very favourable weather, arrived in a few days at Piræus, where he joined the old fleet. At Scyllæum he was met by King Eumenes, with three ships, who had long hesitated at Ægina whether he should go home to defend his own kingdom, on hearing that Antiochus was preparing both marine and land forces at Ephesus; or whether he should unite himself inseparably to the Romans, on whose destiny his own depended. Aulus Atilius, having delivered to his successor twenty-five decked ships, left Piræus, and sailed for Rome. Livius, with eighty-one beaked ships, besides many others of inferior rates, some of which were open and furnished with beaks, others without beaks, fit for advice-boats, crossed over to Delos.

43. At this time the consul Acilius was engaged in the siege of Naupactum. Livius was detained several days at Delos by contrary winds, for that tract among the Cyclades, which are separated in some places by larger straits, in others by smaller, is remarkably subject to storms. Polyxenidas, receiving intelligence from his scout-ships, which he had stationed in various places, that the Roman fleet lay at Delos, sent off an express to the king, who, quitting the business in which he was employed in Hellespontus, and taking with him all the ships of war, returned to Ephesus with all possible speed, and instantly called a council to determine whether he should risk an engagement at sea. Polyxenidas affirmed, that "it was particularly requisite so to do, before the fleet of Eumenes and the Rhodian ships should join the Romans; in which case, even, they would scarcely be inferior in number, and in every other particular would have a great superiority, by reason of the agility of their vessels, and a variety of favourable circumstances; for the Roman ships being unskilfully constructed, were slow in their motions; and, besides that, as they were coming to an enemy's coast, they would be heavily laden with provisions; whereas their own, leaving none but friends in all the countries round, would have nothing on board but men and arms.

They would, also, have a great advantage in their knowledge of the sea, of the adjacent lands, and of the winds; of all which the Romans being ignorant, would find themselves much distressed." Every one was convinced by his arguments, especially as the same person who gave the advice was also to carry it into execution. Two days only were passed in making preparations; and on the third, setting sail with a hundred ships, of which seventy had decks, and the rest were open, but all of the smaller rates, they steered their course to Phocæa. The king, as he did not intend to be present in the naval combat, on hearing that the Roman fleet was approaching, withdrew to Magnesia, near Sipylus, to collect his land forces, while his ships proceeded to Cyssus, a port of Erythræa, where it was supposed they might with more convenience wait for the enemy. The Romans, as soon as the north wind, which had held foi several days, ceased, sailed from Delos to Phanæ, a port in Chios, opposite the Ægæan sea. They afterward brought round the fleet to the city of Chios, and having taken in provisions there, sailed over to Phocæa. Eumenes, who had gone to join his fleet at Elæa, returned a few days after with twenty-four decked ships, and a greater number of open ones, to Phocæa, where he found the Romans, who were fitting and preparing themselves for a sea-fight. The fleet, which now consisted of a hundred and five decked ships, and about fifty open ones, on setting sail, was for some time driven forcibly towards the land, by a north wind blowing across its course. The ships were thereby obliged to go, for the most part singly, one after another, in a thin line; afterward, when the violence of the wind abated, they endeavoured to stretch over to the harbour of Corycus, beyond Cyssus.

44. When Polyxenidas heard that the enemy were approaching, rejoiced at an opportunity of engaging them, he drew out the left squadron towards the open sea, at the same time ordering the commanders of the ships to extend the right division towards the land; and then advanced to the fight, with his fleet in a regular line of battle a-head. The Roman commander, on seeing this, furled his sails, lowered his masts, and, at the same time adjusting his rigging, waited for the ships which were coming up. There were now about thirty in the line; and in order that his left squadron might form a front in like direction, he hoisted his top-sail, and stretched out into the deep, ordering the others to push forward, between him and the land, against the right squadron of the enemy. Eumenes brought up the rear; who, as soon as he saw the bustle of taking down the rigging begin, likewise led on his division with all possible speed. All their ships were by this time in sight; two Carthaginians, how

ever, which advanced before the Romans, were attacked by three belonging to the king. As the numbers were unequal, two of the king's ships fell on one, and, in the first place, swept away the oars from both its sides; the armed mariners then boarded, and killing some of the crew, and driving others into the sea, took the ship. The one which had engaged in an equal contest, on seeing her companion taken, lest she should be surrounded by the three, fled back to the fleet. Livius, fired with indignation, bore down against the enemy. The two which had overpowered the Carthaginian ship, in hopes of the same success against this one, advanced to the attack, on which he ordered the rowers on both sides to plunge their oars into the water in order to hold the ship steady, and to throw grappling-irons into the enemy's vessels as they came up. Having by these means rendered the business something like a fight on land, he desired his men to act with the courage of Romans, and to consider that their adversaries were the slaves of a king. Accordingly, this single ship now defeated and captured the two, with more ease than the two had before taken one. By this time the entire fleets were engaged and intermixed with each other. Eumenes, who had come up last, and after the battle was begun, when he saw the left squadron of the enemy thrown into disorder by Livius, directed his own attack against their right, where the contest was yet equal.

45. In a short time the left squadron began to fly: for Polyxenidas, perceiving that he was evidently overmatched with respect to the bravery of the men, hoisted his top-sails, and got away; and, quickly after, those who were engaged with Eumenes near the land did the same. The Romans and Eumenes pursued with much perseverance as long as the rowers were able to hold out, and they had any prospect of annoying the rear of the enemy: but, finding that the latter, by reason of the lightness and fleetness of their ships, baffled every effort that could be made by theirs, loaded as they were with provisions, they at length desisted, having taken thirteen ships, together with the soldiers and rowers, and sunk ten. Of the Roman fleet, only the one Carthaginian ship, which, at the beginning of the action, had been attacked by two, was lost. Polyxenidas continued his flight until he got into the harbour of Ephesus. The Romans stayed, during the remainder of that day, in the port from which the king's fleet had sailed out, and, on the day following, proceeded in the pursuit. About midway, they were met by twenty-five Rhodian decked ships, commanded by Pausistratus; and, in conjunction with these, followed the runaways to Ephesus, where they stood for some time, in order of battle, before the mouth of the harbour. Hav-

ing thus extorted from the enemy a full confession of their being defeated, the Romans sent home the Rhodians and Eumenes, and steered their course to Chios. When they had passed Phænicus, a port of Erythræa, they cast anchor for the night; and proceeding next day to the island, came up to the city itself. After halting here a few days, for the purpose chiefly of refreshing the rowers, they sailed over to Phocæa. Here they left four quinqueremes for the defence of the city, while the rest of the fleet proceeded to Canæ, where, as the winter now approached, the ships were hauled on shore, and surrounded with a trench and rampart. At the close of the year the elections were held at Rome, in which were chosen consuls, Lucius Cornelius Scipio and Caius Lælius, from whom all men expected the conclusion of the war with Antiochus. Next day were elected pretors, Marcus Tuccius Lucius Aurunculeius, Cneius Fulvius, Lucius Æmilius, Publius Junius, and Caius Atinius Labeo.

---

## BOOK XXXVII.

CHAP. 1. ON the commencement of the consulship of Lucius Cornelius Scipio and Caius Lælius, [A. U. C. 562. B. C. 190,] the first business introduced in the senate, after the concerns of religion, was that of the Ætolians, whose ambassadors were importunate to have it brought on, because the period of the truce granted them was short; and they were seconded by Titus Quintius, who had by this time come home from Greece to Rome. The Ætolians, as they rested their hopes on the compassion of the senate, more than on the merits of their cause, acted the parts of suppliants, humbly representing their former services, as a counterbalance to their late misbehaviour. While present, they were teased by all the senators with questions tending to draw from them a confession of guilt rather than information; and, after they were ordered to withdraw, they became the subject of a warm dispute. Resentment had more power in their case than compassion; for the senate were incensed against them not merely as enemies, but as an uncivilized and unsocial race. After a debate, which lasted several days, it was at last resolved that peace should neither be granted nor refused. The option was given them of two conditions; either to submit themselves absolutely to the disposal of the senate, or to pay one thousand talents,* and

* 193,750l.

have no other allies or enemies than those who were such to Rome. They wished to have the extent of that power defined, which the senate was to exercise over them, but received no positive answer. They were therefore dismissed, without having concluded any treaty of peace, and were ordered to quit the city that very day, and Italy within fifteen days. The next business proceeded on was the appointing the provinces of the consuls. Both of these wished for Greece. Lælius had a powerful interest in the senate; and when an order was passed there that the consuls should either cast lots for the provinces, or settle them between themselves, he observed, that they would act more judiciously in leaving that matter to the wisdom of the senators, than to the decision of lot. To this Scipio answered, that he would take advice how he ought to act. He consulted his brother only, who desired him to leave it with confidence to the senate; and then he answered his colleague, that he would do as he was recommended. This mode of proceeding was either perfectly new, or, if there had been any precedent, it was of so old a date, that all memory of it was lost; a warm debate was therefore expected on its being proposed to the senate. But Publius Scipio Africanus offering, that "if they decreed that province to his brother, Lucius Scipio, he would go along with him, as his lieutenant-general;" his proposal was received with universal approbation, and put an end to all dispute. The senate were well pleased to make the trial, whether King Antiochus should receive more effectual aid from the vanquished Hannibal, or the Roman consul and legions from his conqueror Africanus; and they almost unanimously voted Greece to Scipio, and Italy to Lælius. The pretors then cast lots for their provinces: Lucius Aurunculeius obtained the city jurisdiction, Cneius Fulvius the foreign; Lucius Æmilius Regillus, the fleet; Publius Junius Brutus, Tuscany; Marcus Tuccius, Apulia and Bruttium; and Caius Atinius, Sicily.

2. Orders were then issued that the consul to whom the province of Greece had been decreed should, in addition to the army which he was to receive from Manius Acilius, and which consisted of two legions, have a reinforcement of three thousand Roman foot, and one hundred horse; and of the Latine confederates, five thousand foot, and two hundred horse: and it was farther ordered, that if, when he arrived in his province, he should judge it conducive to the public interest, he should be at liberty to carry over the army into Asia. To the other consul was decreed an army entirely new; two Roman legions, and of the Latine confederates fifteen thousand foot, and six hundred horse. Quin-

tus Minucius was ordered to remove his forces out of Liguria (which province, according to his letters, was entirely reduced, the whole nation having submitted,) into the country of the Boians, and to give up the command to Publius Cornelius, proconsul. The two city legions, enlisted the year before, were brought home from the country taken from the Boians, and assigned to Marcus Tuccius, pretor, together with fifteen thousand foot and six hundred horse of the Latine confederates, for the defence of Apulia and Bruttium. Aulus Cornelius, a pretor of the preceding year, who had the command of an army in Bruttium, received an order that, if the consul judged it proper, he should transport his legions into Ætolia, and give them to Manius Acilius, provided the latter was inclined to remain there; but if Acilius wished to come to Rome, that then Aulus Cornelius should stay in Ætolia with that army. It was resolved that Caius Atinius Labeo should receive from Marcus Æmilius the province of Sicily and the army there; and should, if he deemed it proper, enlist in the province itself two thousand foot and one hundred horse to fill up deficiencies. Publius Junius Brutus was ordered to raise a new army for Tuscany, consisting of one Roman legion, and ten thousand Latine foot, and four hundred horse. Lucius Æmilius was ordered to receive from Marcus Junius, pretor of the former year, twenty ships of war, with their crews, and himself to enlist one thousand marines and two thousand foot-soldiers, with which ships and soldiers he was to sail to Asia, and receive the command of the fleet from Caius Livius. The present governors of the two Spains and of Sardinia were continued in command, and ordered to keep the same armies. Sicily and Sardinia were this year assessed in two tenths of their corn. All the corn from Sicily was ordered to be carried into Ætolia, to the army there; of that to be collected from Sardinia, one half to Rome, and the other half into Ætolia, for the same use as the corn from Sicily.

3. It was judged proper that, previous to the departure of the consuls for their provinces, the prodigies which had occurred should be expiated under the direction of the pontiffs. The temple of Juno Lucina, at Rome, was struck by lightning in such a manner, that the ceiling and the folding-doors were much damaged. At Puteoli several parts of the wall and a gate were struck by lightning, and two men killed. It was clearly proved that, at Nursia, in the midst of a calm, a tempest suddenly burst forth; and there also two men of free condition were killed. The Tusculans reported that a shower of earth fell in their country; and the Reatines, that a mule brought forth young in theirs. Expiations we

performed for all these, and the Latine festival was celebrated a second time, because the flesh-meat due to the Laurentians had not been given them. There was also a supplication made on account of those portents, the decemvirs giving directions from the books to which of the gods it should be performed. Ten freeborn youths, and ten virgins, all of whom had their fathers and mothers living, were employed in that ceremony; and the decemvirs sacrificed in the night young cattle not weaned from the dam. Publius Cornelius Scipio Africanus, before he left the city, erected an arch on the hill of the capitol, facing the road that leads up to the temple, adorned it with seven gilded statues, and two horses, and placed two marble cisterns in the front of the arch. About this time forty-three of the principal Ætolians, among whom was Damocritus and his brother, were brought to Rome by two cohorts, sent by Manius Acilius, and were thrown into the prison called Lautumiæ, or the quarry; the cohorts were ordered, by the consul Lucius Cornelius, to return to the army. Ambassadors came from Ptolemy and Cleopatra, king and queen of Egypt, congratulating the Romans on their consul Manius Acilius having driven King Antiochus out of Greece, and advising that he should carry over his army into Asia: "for all places, not only in Asia, but also in Syria, were filled with consternation; and that the king and queen of Egypt would hold themselves in readiness to act as the senate should direct." Thanks were returned to the king and queen, and presents were ordered to be made to the ambassadors, four thousand asses* to each.

4. The consul Lucius Cornelius, having finished what was necessary to be done at Rome, gave public notice, in an assembly of the people, that the soldiers, whom himself had enlisted for supplying deficiencies, and those who were in Bruttium with Aulus Cornelius, propretor, should all meet him at Brundusium on the ides of July. He likewise appointed three lieutenants-general, Sextus Digitius, Lucius Apustius, and Caius Fabricius Luscinus; who were to bring together ships from all parts of the sea-coast to Brundusium; and now, every thing being ready, he set out from the city in his military robe of state. No less than five thousand volunteers of the Romans and allies, who had served out the legal term, under the command of Publius Africanus, attended Cornelius at his departure, and offered their services. Lucius Æmilius Regillus, who commanded the fleet, set out likewise at the same time. Just at the time when the consul went to join the army during the celebration of the Apollinarian games, on the fifth of the ides of July, though the

* 12l. 18s. 4d.

sky was serene, the light was obscured in the middle of the day by the moon passing over the orb of the sun. Lucius Aurunculeius was commissioned by the senate to build thirty quinqueremes and twenty triremes, in consequence of a report prevailing that Antiochus, since the engagement at sea, was fitting out a much larger fleet. When the Ætolians learned from their ambassadors, who returned from Rome, that there was no prospect of peace, notwithstanding that their whole sea-coast, opposite to Peloponnesus, was ravaged by the Achæans, yet, regarding the danger impending more than their losses, they seized on Mount Corax, in order to shut up the pass against the Romans; for they had no doubt of their returning in the beginning of spring, and renewing the siege of Naupactum. Acilius, who knew that this was expected, judged it more advisable to undertake an enterprise that was not foreseen, and to lay siege to Lamia; for the garrison had been reduced by Philip almost to a state of desperation; and at present, from the very circumstance of their not apprehending any such attempt, they might probably be surprised and overpowered. Marching from Elatia, he formed his first encampment in the enemy's country, on the banks of the river Sperchius, and decamping thence in the night, he at break of day made a general assault on the town.

5. In consequence of the unexpectedness of the affair, great consternation and tumult ensued; yet the besieged fought with greater resolution than any one could suppose them capable of under such a sudden alarm, and the women brought weapons of every kind, and stones, to the walls; so that, although scaling ladders were raised in various places, yet for that day they maintained the defence of the place. About midday Acilius gave the signal of retreat, and drew off his men to their camp. After their strength was repaired by food and rest, before he dismissed the meeting in the pretorium, he gave them notice "to be ready, under arms, before day; and that they were not to return to their tents until the city should be taken." Next day, at the same hour as before, he began the assault again, in a greater number of places; and as not only the strength, but also the weapons, and above all the courage of the garrison began to fail, he made himself master of the town in the space of a few hours. One half of the spoil found there he sold: the other he gave to the soldiers; and then he held a council to determine what he should next undertake. No one approved of going against Naupactum, while the pass at Corax was occupied by the Ætolians. But not to lie in idleness, or, by his supineness, to allow the Ætolians that state of peace which they could not obtain from the senate, Acilius resolved to besiege Amphissa; and he led his army thither

from Heraclea by Œta. Having encamped under the walls, he proceeded against the place, not by general assault, as at Lamia, but by regular approaches. The ram was brought up to the walls in many places at once; and though these were shaken by it, yet the townsmen never endeavoured to provide or contrive any sort of defence against attacks of that kind; but placing all their hopes in their arms and daring courage, by frequent sallies they much annoyed not only the advanced guards of the Romans, but even those who were employed at the works and machines.

6. There were now many breaches made, when the consul received intelligence that his successor, having landed his army at Apollonia, was coming at the head of thirteen thousand foot and five hundred horse. He had lately arrived at the Malian bay, and sent a message to Hypata, demanding the surrender of the city; but the inhabitants answered, that they would do nothing without a decree of the general council of Ætolia: on which, unwilling to be detained in the siege of Hypata, while that of Amphissa was still unfinished, he sent on his brother Africanus before him, and marched himself towards Amphissa. A little before their arrival, the towns-people abandoned the city, for it was now for the most part stripped of its walls; and they, one and all, armed and unarmed, retired into the citadel, which they deemed an impregnable fortress. The consul pitched his camp at the distance of about six miles from the town; and thither came ambassadors from the Athenians, addressing, first, Publius Scipio, who preceded the main body as before mentioned, and afterward the consul, with earnest supplications in favour of the Ætolians. They received a milder answer from Africanus, who wished for an honourable pretext for relinquishing the Ætolian war, than they had from Rome. He was desirous of directing his views towards Asia and King Antiochus, and had recommended to the Athenians to persuade, not the Romans only, but the Ætolians likewise, to prefer peace to war. Pursuant to the advice of the Athenians, a numerous embassy of the Ætolians came speedily from Hypata, and the discourse of Africanus, whom they addressed first, augmented their hopes of peace; for he mentioned that "many nations and states, first in Spain, and afterward in Africa, had surrendered themselves to him; and that in all of them he had left greater monuments of clemency and kindness than of military prowess." The business seemed to be concluded, when the consul, on being applied to, repeated the very same answer with which they had been so much dismayed by the senate. The Ætolians, thunderstruck at this, as if they had never heard it before, (for they now perceived that no good was likely to arise, either from the

Athenian embassy, or the favourable reply of Africanus,) observed, that they wished to consult their countrymen on the affair.

7. They then returned to Hypata, where the council was utterly at a loss what course to take; for they had no means of paying the thousand talents; and, in case of an unconditional submission, they dreaded being subjected to bodily severities. They therefore ordered the same ambassadors to return to the consul and Africanus, and to request, that if they meant in reality to grant them peace, and not merely to amuse them with a prospect of it, frustrating the hopes of the wretched, they would either remit some part of the money required to be paid, or order that their persons might be exempted in the terms of the surrender. The consul could not be prevailed on to make any change; and that embassy also was dismissed without effect. The Athenian ambassadors accompanied them, with Echedemus, their principal. These, while the Ætolians, after so many repulses, were sunk into total dejection, and deplored with unavailing lamentations, the hard fate of their nation,—revived once more their hopes, by advising them to request a suspension of arms for six months, in order that they might send an embassy to Rome. He urged that "the delay could add nothing to their present calamities, which were already severe in the extreme; but that, if time were gained, many fortuitous events might occur, and lighten the distresses they then laboured under." Agreeably to this advice of Echedemus, the same ambassadors were sent again; who, making their first application to Publius Scipio, obtained through him, from the consul, a suspension of arms for the time they desired. The siege of Amphissa was then raised; Marcus Acilius gave up the command of the army to the consul, and left the province; and the consul returned from Amphissa into Thessaly, with intention to pass through Macedonia and Thrace into Asia. Here Africanus said to his brother, Lucius Scipio, "I agree with you in approving the route which you have chosen. But the whole matter rests on the inclinations of Philip; for if he is faithful to our government, he will afford us a passage, and provisions and every thing requisite to the maintenance and convenience of an army on a long march. But if he should fail in this, you will find no safety in any part of Thrace. In my opinion, therefore, the king's disposition ought in the first place to be discovered; and the best method to discover it will be to let the person sent approach him suddenly, and see how he is employed when not expecting any such visit." They chose for this purpose Tiberius Sempronius Gracchus, a young man, remarkable for his activity beyond all the youth

of the time: by means of relays of horses, and travelling with almost incredible expedition, he made good the journey from Amphissa, whence he was despatched, to Pella, on the third day. The king was sitting at a banquet, and had drank freely of wine; which circumstance, of his indulging such relaxation of mind, removed all suspicion of any intention of changing his measures. His guest was, for the present, kindly entertained; and next day, he saw plenty of provisions, already prepared for the army, bridges made over rivers, and roads formed where the ground was difficult to be passed. As he was bringing back this intelligence, with the same speed which he had used in coming, he met the consul at Thaumaci. The army, in high spirits at finding their hopes thus confirmed and augmented, advanced into Macedonia, where every thing was ready for their accommodation. On their arrival, the king received them with royal magnificence, and accompanied them on their march. He showed a great deal of pleasantry and good humour, which recommended him much to Africanus, who, with all the extraordinary endowments that he possessed, was not averse from mirth when confined within the bounds of decency. Philip then escorted them not only through Macedonia, but through Thrace also; furnishing them with every accommodation, until they arrived at the Hellespont.

8. Antiochus, after the sea-fight at Corycus, being left at liberty during the whole winter, to carry on his preparations by land and water, employed his principal attention on the refitting of his ships, lest he should be entirely excluded from the sea. He reflected that he had been defeated, when the Rhodian fleet was absent; if this fleet were present in an engagement, (and the Rhodians would certainly take care not to be dilatory a second time,) he required a vast number of ships to set him on an equality with the fleet of the enemy, considering the strength and size of their vessels; for this reason, he sent Hannibal into Syria, to bring in the Phœnician navy, and gave orders to Polyxenidas that, the more unsuccessful he had been before, the more diligence he should now exert in repairing the ships which he had, and procuring others. He himself passed the winter in Phrygia, calling in auxiliaries from every quarter. He even sent for that purpose to Gallogræcia. The people of that country were then more warlike than at present, retaining the Gallic spirit, as the generation which had emigrated thither was not yet extinct. He left his son Seleucus with an army in Ætolia to keep in obedience the maritime cities, which were solicited to revolt, on one side, by Eumenes, from Pergamus; on the other, by the Romans from Phocæa

and Erythræ. The Roman fleet, as mentioned before, wintered at Canæ: thither, about the middle of the season, came King Eumenes, with two thousand foot and one hundred horse. He affirmed that vast quantities of spoil might be brought off from the enemy's country round Thyatira; and, by his persuasions, prevailed on Livius to send with him five thousand soldiers. This party within a few days carried off an immense booty.

9. Meanwhile a sedition broke out at Phocæa, in consequence of the endeavours used by some to bring over the multitude to the party of Antiochus. The people were distressed by the ships wintering there; they were distressed by a tax imposed, for they were ordered to furnish five hundred gowns and five hundred tunics; and they were further distressed by a scarcity of corn, which obliged the Roman garrison and ships to leave the place. The faction, which laboured in their assemblies to draw the commonalty over to Antiochus, was now freed from all apprehension; the senate and higher ranks were disposed to adhere to the alliance with Rome, but the advisers of a revolt had greater influence with the multitude. The Rhodians, sensible of having been too tardy the year before, were therefore the earlier in their proceedings now; and, at the vernal equinox, they sent the same Pausistratus, commander of the fleet, with thirty-six ships. At this time Livius, with thirty ships, and seven quadriremes, which King Eumenes had brought with him, was on his passage from Canæ to the Hellespont, in order to prepare every thing necessary for the transportation of the army, which he expected to come by land. He first put into the harbour called the Achæan; whence going up to Ilium, he offered sacrifice to Minerva, and gave a kind reception to several embassies from the states in the neighbourhood: from Elæus, Dardanus, and Rhetæum, who came to surrender their respective states to him. Then he sailed to the entrance of the Hellespont; and, leaving ten ships stationed opposite to Abydos, he crossed over to Europe with the rest of the fleet, to attack Sestos. As the troops were advancing up to the walls, they were met, first, by a number of the priests of Cybele,* using extravagant gestures, and clad in the dress worn on their solemn processions. These said that, "by order of the mother of the gods, they, the immediate servants of the goddess, were come to pray the Roman commander to spare the walls and the city." No violence was offered to any of them; and, presently, the whole senate, and the magistrates, came out to surrender the place. The fleet then sailed over to Abydos; where, on sounding

* Called Galli, and Corybantes.

the temper of the inhabitants, in conferences, and finding no disposition to peaceful measures, they prepared themselves for a siege.

10. While these transactions passed at the Hellespont, Polyxenidas, the commander of the king's fleet, an exile from Rhodes, having heard that the ships of his countrymen had sailed from home, and that Pausistratus, who commanded them, had, in a public speech, uttered several haughty and contemptuous expressions respecting him, conceived the most violent jealousy against him in particular, and studied nothing else, night or day, but how, by deeds, to refute his arrogant words. He sent a person who was known to him, to say that, "if allowed, he was ready to perform an eminent service to Pausistratus, and to his native country; and that Pausistratus might restore him to the same." Pausistratus, in surprise, asked by what means such things could be effected; and, at the other's request, pledged his faith that he would either concur in the execution of the design, or bury it in silence. The emissary then told him that "Polyxenidas would deliver into his hands, either the whole of the king's fleet, or the greater part of it; and that in return for so great a service, he stipulated for nothing more than being allowed to return to his native country." The proposal was of such magnitude, as made him neither implicitly credit, nor at once reject it. He sailed to Panormus, in the Samian territory, and halted there, in order to examine thoroughly the business proposed to him. Several messengers passed between them, nor was Pausistratus satisfied of the other's sincerity until, in the presence of his messenger, Polyxenidas wrote with his own hand an engagement that he would perform all that he had promised, and sent the tablets sealed with his own seal. By such a pledge as this he thought he had acquired a kind of absolute dominion over the plotter; for that "he who lived under a king woul never act so absurdly, as to give evidence of guilt against himself, attested by his own signature." The method of conducting the pretended plot was then settled: Polyxenidas said that "he would neglect every kind of preparation; that he would not keep any considerable numbers on board, either of rowers or mariners; that he would haul up on land some of the ships, under pretence of refitting them; would send away others into the neighbouring ports, and keep a few at sea before the harbour of Ephesus; which, if circumstances made it necessary to come out, he would expose to a battle." The negligence which Pausistratus was told Polyxenidas would use in his fleet, he himself immediately practised. Part of his ships he sent to Halicarnassus to bring provisions, another part to the city of Samos, while he himself

waited at Panormus, that he might be ready to make an attack when he should receive the signal from the traitor. Polyxenidas continued to encourage his mistake by counterfeiting neglect; hauled up some ships, and, as if he intended to haul up others, put the docks in repair; he did not call the rowers from their winter-quarters to Ephesus, but assembled them secretly at Magnesia.

11. It happened that one of Antiochus's soldiers, having come to Samos on some business of his own, was seized as a spy, and brought to Panormus to Pausistratus. This man, moved either by fear or treachery towards his countrymen, on being asked what was doing at Ephesus, laid open every particular: that the fleet lay in harbour, fully equipped, and ready for sea: that all the rowers had been sent to Magnesia: that very few of the ships had been hauled on land: that the docks were shut: and that never was greater diligence employed in conducting the business of the fleet. But the mind of Pausistratus was so prepossessed, by misplaced confidence and vain hopes, that he gave no credit to this account. Polyxenidas, having fully adjusted all his measures, called in the rowers from Magnesia, launched hastily the ships that were in dock, and letting the next day pass, not so much because he had any preparations to make, as because he was unwilling that the fleet should be seen going to sea, set sail after sunset, with seventy decked ships; but the wind being contrary, put into the harbour of Pygelia before day appeared. After lying by there during the day, for the same reason as before, he passed over in the night to the nearest part of the Samian territory. From this place he detached one Nicander, an arch pirate, at the head of a squadron of five decked ships, with orders to sail to Palinurus, and thence to lead his armed men by the shortest road, through the fields towards Panormus, and so to come behind the enemy. In the mean time himself, with his fleet in two divisions, in order that it might command the mouth of the harbour on both sides, proceeded to Panormus. This event, so utterly unexpected, at first confounded Pausistratus; but being an experienced warrior, he quickly re-collected his spirits, and judging that it would be easier to repel the enemy from the land than on sea, he marched his armed forces in two bodies to the promontories, which, by their heads projecting into the deep, formed the harbour; for he thought that he should be able with ease to effect his purpose by the discharges of weapons from both sides. The sight of Nicander on the land quite disconcerted this design; he therefore suddenly changed his plan, and ordered all to go on board the ships. This produced the greatest dismay and confusion among both soldiers and sailors, who, seeing

themselves enclosed by the enemy, on land and sea at once, hurried on board like men running away. The only method of saving the fleet that occurred to Pausistratus was, to force through the narrow entrance of the port, and push out into the open sea. As soon therefore as he saw his men embarked, ordering the rest to follow, he himself led the way, and, with the utmost exertions of his oars, pressed to the mouth of the harbour. Just as his ship was clearing the entrance, Polyxenidas, with three quinqueremes, surrounded it. The vessel, shattered by their beaks, sunk; the crew were overwhelmed with weapons; and, among them, Pausistratus, fighting gallantly, was slain. Of the rest of the ships, some were taken outside of the harbour, some within, and others by Nicander, while they were putting off from the shore. Only five Rhodian and two Coan ships effected an escape; making a passage for themselves through the thick of the enemy by the terror of blazing flames, for they carried before them, on two poles projecting from their prows, a great quantity of fire contained in iron vessels. Some Erythræan triremes, which were coming to their assistance, met the Rhodian ships flying, not far from Samos, and therefore steered away to the Hellespont to join the Romans. About the same time Seleucus got possession of Phocæa, which was betrayed by the guards admitting him by one of the gates. Cyme, with the other cities on that coast, were induced by their fears to join him.

12. During these transactions in Ætolia, Abydos endured a siege of several days, a garrison of the king's troops defending the walls; but then, all growing weary, Philotas himself, the commander of the garrison, giving his permission, the magistrates entered into a treaty with Livius about the terms of a capitulation. The business was protracted for some time, as they could not agree whether the king's troops should march out with their arms or without them. While this negotiation was depending, news arrived of the defeat of the Rhodians; in consequence of which the whole matter was dropped, when on the point of being concluded: for Livius, fearing lest Polyxenidas, elated by his recent success in such an important enterprise, might surprise the fleet which lay at Canæ, instantly abandoned the siege of Abydos and the guard of the Hellespont, and drew out the ships that were in dock at Canæ. Eumenes came at this time to Elea. Livius, with the whole fleet, which had been joined by two triremes of Mitylene, sailed to Phocæa; but having learned that this place was held by a strong garrison of the king's troops, and that Seleucus was encamped at no great distance, he ravaged the sea-coast, hastily conveying on board the booty, which consisted chiefly of men, and

waiting only until Eumenes, with his fleet, came up, bent his course to Samos. Among the Rhodians, the news of their misfortune excited, at first, both consternation and the greatest grief at the same time: for, besides the loss of their ships and soldiers, the whole flower of their youth had perished, many young men of distinction having embarked in the expedition, led, among other motives, principally by the character of Pausistratus, which was deservedly very high among his countrymen. Afterward, when they reflected that they had been circumvented by treachery, and that, of all men, a countryman of their own had been the perpetrator, their grief was converted into anger. Immediately they sent out ten ships, and in a few days ten more, giving the command of the whole to Eudamus; who, though far inferior to Pausistratus in warlike qualifications, would yet, they supposed, prove a more cautious leader, as he was not of so high a spirit. The Romans and King Eumenes put in with their fleet, first, at Erythræa; and, staying there one night, they next day reached Corycus, a promontory in Teios. They intended to pass over hence to the nearest part of the Samian territory; but not waiting for the rising of the sun, from which the pilots could learn the state of the weather, they exposed themselves to a storm, which deprived them of the power of directing their course. About the middle of the passage the wind changed from northeast to north, and they found themselves tossed about on the sea, which rolled in very tremendous billows.

13. Polyxenidas, taking it for granted that the enemy would go to Samos to join the Rhodian fleet, set sail from Ephesus, and halted, first, at Myonnesus, from whence he crossed over to the island of Macris; in order that, when the enemy's fleet should sail by, he might attack with advantage either any ships that straggled from the main body, or the rear of the fleet itself. When he saw the same dispersed by the storm, he thought this a good opportunity to attack it; but, in a little time, the wind increased, and raised the waves to such a height, that he could not possibly come up with them: he therefore steered to the island of Æthalia, that from thence he might, next day, fall on the ships as they made for Samos from the main sea. A small number of Roman vessels, just as it grew dark, got into a desert harbour on the Samian coast; the rest, after being tossed about all night, ran into the same harbour in the morning. Having learned here, from the country people, that the enemy's fleet lay at Æthalia, they held a consultation whether they should attack them immediately, or wait for that of the Rhodians. Their determination was to postpone the attack, and they sailed away to Corycus, whence they had come. Polyxeni-

das, who, having kept his station for some time without effecting any thing, sailed home to Ephesus. On this the Roman ships, having the sea now clear of the enemy, sailed to Samos; where, a few days after, they were joined by the fleet from Rhodes; and, to show that they had only waited for this, they immediately sailed away to Ephesus, resolved either to fight the enemy, or, in case they should decline a battle, to extort from them a confession of fear, which would have the best effect on the minds of the states of Asia. They lay for some time opposite the entrance of the harbour, with the fleet formed in a line abreast, but none came out against them; on which they divided; and while one part lay at anchor, before the mouth of the harbour, the other landed a body of soldiers. These made depredations over a great extent of the country; and as they were conveying to the ships the great booty which they had seized, Andronicus, a Macedonian, who was in garrison at Ephesus, sallied out on them when they came near the walls, stripped them of the greatest part of their plunder, and drove them down to the shore to their ships. On the day following the Romans laid an ambuscade about the middle of the way, and marched in a body to the city, in order to entice the Macedonians out of the gates; but these were deterred from coming out, and the Romans returned to their ships. As the enemy thus avoided fighting, either on land or sea, the fleet sailed back to Samos, whence it came. The pretor then detached two Rhodian triremes, and two belonging to the Italian allies, under the command of Epicrates, a Rhodian, to guard the strait of Cephalenia, which was infested with pirates by Hybristas, a Lacedæmonian, at the head of a band of young Cephalenians, so that the passage was shut against the convoys from Italy.

14. Epicrates met at Piræus Lucius Æmilius Regillus, who was on his way to take the command of the fleet. On hearing of the defeat of the Rhodians, as he had only two quinqueremes, he carried back with him to Asia Epicrates and his four ships. He was attended also by some undecked vessels of the Athenians. He crossed the Ægean sea to Chios, to which place came, in the middle of the night, Timasicrates, a Rhodian, with two quadriremes from Samos; and being presented to Æmilius, he told him that he was despatched for the purpose of convoying him in safety, because the king's ships, by frequent excursions from the Hellespont and Abydos, rendered the sea on that coast dangerous to transports. In his passage from Chios to Samos, Æmilius was met by two Rhodian quadriremes, sent by Livius to attend him, and by King Eumenes with two quinqueremes. On his arrival at Samos, as soon as he had received the

command of the fleet from Livius, and duly performed the usual sacrifices, he called a council. Here Caius Livius, whose opinion was first asked, said, that "no one could give advice with more sincerity than he, who recommended to another what himself would do in the same case: that his intention had been to have sailed with the whole fleet to Ephesus; to have taken with him ships of burden, heavily laden with ballast, and to have sunk them in the entrance of the harbour: that the passage might be shut up, in this manner, with little difficulty; because the mouth of it was like a river, long and narrow, and full of shoals. By this expedient he would have cut off the enemy's communication with the sea, and rendered their fleet useless."

15. This plan was not approved by any of the council. King Eumenes asked, "whether when, by sinking the ships, they should have barred the pass to the sea, their own fleet would be at liberty to go away and succour their allies, and infuse terror into their enemies; or whether they might not, nevertheless, be obliged to block up the port with their whole force? for if they should withdraw, who could doubt that the enemy would weigh up the hulks that were sunk, and open the port with less labour than it had cost to shut it? But if, after all, they were to remain there, what advantage would accrue from the harbour being closed? Nay, on the contrary, the enemy enjoying a safe haven, and an opulent city, furnished at the same time with every thing from Asia, would pass the summer at their ease, while the Romans, exposed in the open sea to winds and waves, and in want of every accommodation, must continue on guard without intermission; and might more properly be said to be themselves tied down, and hindered from doing any thing that ought to be done, than to keep the enemy shut up." Eudamus, commander of the Rhodian fleet, rather showed his disapprobation of the plan proposed, than recommended any himself. Epicrates, the Rhodian, advised "not to think of Ephesus for the present, but to send a part of the fleet to Lycia, and bring Patara, the metropolis of that nation, into a treaty of alliance. This would conduce to two important purposes: first, the Rhodians, by peace being established in the countries opposite to their island, would be at liberty to apply the whole of their strength to the war against Antiochus; and then the fleet, which the enemy were fitting out in Lycia would be blocked up, and prevented from joining Polyxenidas." This plan was the most approved of. Nevertheless, it was determined that Regillus should sail, with the entire fleet, to the harbour of Ephesus, to strike terror into the enemy.

16. Caius Livius was sent to Lycia, with two Roman quinqueremes, four Rhodian quadriremes, and two open vessels

of Smyrna; being ordered to proceed first to Rhodes, and to communicate all his designs to the government there. The states which he passed in his way, Miletus, Myndus, Halicarnassus, Cnidus, and Cous, cheerfully obeyed his orders. When he came to Rhodes he explained to the persons in authority the business on which he was sent, and, at the same time, desired their opinion. They all approved the design; and gave him three quadriremes, in addition to his squadron; and with these he set sail for Patara. The wind being favourable at first, carried them very near the city, and they were in hopes of effecting something by surprise; but this suddenly veering, they had to labour in a very heavy sea. However, by dint of rowing they reached the land, but there was no safe anchorage there, nor could they ride in the road, as the sea was rough, and night was coming on. They therefore sailed past the city to the port of Phellus, which was not quite two miles distant, and which afforded shelter from the violence of the waves, but was overlooked by high cliffs; and these the townspeople, joined by the king's troops in garrison there, immediately seized. Livius, though the landing place was rugged and difficult, sent against them a party of the auxiliaries, composed of Issæans, and light infantry of Smyrna. These (as long as the business was carried on with missile weapons, and in slight attacks on the few who were there at first, and which was rather a skirmish than a battle) supported the contest sufficiently well. But greater numbers flocked thither from the city, and at length the whole multitude poured out, which made Livius fear, not only that the auxiliaries might be cut off, but that the ships would be in danger, lying so near the land. In consequence he led out to the engagement, not only the soldiers, but the marines, and even the crowd of rowers, armed with such weapons as each could find. After all, however, the fight was doubtful; and besides a considerable number of soldiers, Lucius Apustius fell in this disorderly combat. At last the Lycians were routed, and driven within their gates; and the Romans, victorious, but not without loss of blood, returned to their ships. They then proceeded to the gulf of Telonessus, which washes Caria on one side, and Lycia on the other, where all thoughts of any farther attempt on Patara were laid aside, the Rhodians were sent home, and Livius, sailing along the coast of Asia, crossed over to Greece, that he might have a meeting with the Scipios, who were at that time in Thessaly, and then take his passage to Italy.

17. Æmilius, although himself had been driven off from Ephesus by a storm, and had returned to Samos, without effecting any thing, yet hearing that the expedition to Lycia was dropped, and that Livius had gone to Italy, he thought

the miscarriage of the attempt on Patara disgraceful, and accordingly resolved to go thither, and attack the city with his utmost force. Having sailed past Miletus and the rest of the coast of the allies, he made a descent in the bay of Bargyllæ, with design to reduce Jassus. The city was held by a garrison of the king's troops, and the Romans made hostile depredations on all the country round. He then sent persons to confer with the magistrates, and principal inhabitants, and sound their dispositions; but, being told by them that nothing was in their power, he advanced to lay siege to the city. There were with the Romans some exiles from Jassus, who, in a body, earnestly importuned the Rhodians "not to suffer an unoffending city, which was both their neighbour, and connected with them in consanguinity, to be ruined. They themselves were banished for no other cause than their faithful attachment to the Romans; and those who remained in the place were held in subjection by the same force by which they had been expelled. The people of Jassus had all but one wish, to escape from a state of slavery under the king." The Rhodians, moved by their entreaties, and calling in the assistance of King Eumenes, represented, at the same time, their own connexions with them, and also the unfortunate condition of the city, which was kept in bondage by the king's garrison; and by these means prevailed on Æmilius to drop the siege. Departing hence, and coasting along the shore of Asia, where every other place was favourably disposed, he arrived at Loryma, a port opposite to Rhodes. Here the military tribunes, in their meeting at the pretorium, began, at first in private conversation, to make observations, which afterward reached the ears of Æmilius, that the fleet was going off to a distance from Ephesus, from the war which concerned themselves; so that the enemy, being left behind, without control, might safely make whatever attempts they pleased against so many states of the allies in their neighbourhood. Æmilius felt the justness of these remarks, and calling the Rhodians to him, asked them whether the whole fleet could lie in the harbour of Patara; to which they answered in the negative. Furnished with this excuse for laying aside the design, he sailed back to Samos.

18. In the mean time Seleucus, son of Antiochus, who had kept his army in Ætolia, through the whole of the winter, employing it, partly in succouring his allies, partly in ravaging the lands of those whom he could not seduce to his side, resolved to make an incursion on the territory of Eumenes, while he, at a great distance from home, was assisting the Romans and Rhodians in attacks on the maritime parts of Lycia. He advanced, as an enemy, first to Elæa, but so-

laid aside the design of besieging it; and, having wasted the country in a hostile manner, he led his army to lay siege to Pergamus, the capitol, and the principal fortress of the kingdom. Attalus, at first, placing advanced guards outside the city, and sending out parties of cavalry and light-infantry, acted an offensive, rather than a defensive part. But, after some time, having discovered in slight skirmishes that he was not a match for the enemy in any respect, he drew back his men within the fortifications, and then the siege was formed. About this time Antiochus, leaving Apamea, with a vast army compounded of various nations, encamped first at Sardis, and afterward took post at a small distance from the camp of Seleucus, at the head of the river Caicus. The most formidable part of his force was a body of four thousand Gauls, whom he had procured for hire: these, with a few others intermixed, he detached, with orders to waste utterly the country about Pergamus. When news of these transactions arrived at Samos, Eumenes being thus recalled by a war in his own dominions, sailed with his fleet to Elæa; and finding there in readiness some light troops of horse and foot, he took them for an escort, and proceeded directly to Pergamus, before the enemy could be apprized of his arrival, or take any steps to intercept him. The garrison now began again to sally out and skirmish; but Eumenes evidently avoided risking a decisive engagement. In a few days after the combined fleet of the Romans and Rhodians came from Samos to Elæa to support the king. When Antiochus was informed that these had landed troops at Elæa, and that so many fleets were assembled in one harbour, and at the same time heard that the consul, with his army, was already in Macedonia, and was making the necessary preparations for his passage over the Hellespont, he judged that now was the time for negotiation, before he should be pressed on sea and land at once; and with this view he chose for his camp a rising ground opposite to Elæa. Leaving there all the infantry, with his cavalry, amounting to six thousand, he went down into the plains, which lay under the walls of the town, having despatched a herald to Æmilius, to acquaint him that he wished to treat of peace.

19. Æmilius sent to Pergamus for Eumenes, and, desiring the Rhodians to be present, held a council on the message. The Rhodians were not averse from a pacification; but Eumenes affirmed that "they could not treat of peace at such a juncture; nor could a business of the kind be concluded. For," said he, "how can we, shut up as we are within our walls, and besieged, with honour accept terms of peace? Or who will deem such treaty valid, which we shall conclude, without the presence of the consul, without

a vote of the senate, and without an order of the Roman people? For, let me ask, supposing the matter concluded by you, would you immediately go home to Italy, and carry away your fleet and army, or would you wait to know the consul's determination on the case; what the senate should decree, or the people order? It is plain then that you must stay in Asia, that your troops must be led back to the quarters where they wintered, and, without having any thing to do against the enemy, exhaust the allies by their consumption of provisions: and then, if it seem fit to those who have the power of determining, we must begin the whole war anew. Whereas, if the present vigorous proceedings suffer no obstruction from delay, we may, with the will of the gods, bring it to a conclusion before the winter." His opinion was approved; and the answer giving to Antiochus was, that no treaty of peace could be admitted before the arrival of the consul. Antiochus, frustrated in this scheme for putting an end to the war, ravaged first the territory of Elæa, then that of Pergamus; and, leaving there his son Seleucus, marched in a hostile manner to Adramyttium, whence he proceeded to an opulent tract of country called the Plain of Thebes, a city celebrated in one of Homer's poems; and in no other place in Asia did the king's soldiers find such a plenty of booty. Æmilius and Eumenes also sailing round with the fleet, came to Adramyttium to protect the city.

20. It happened, just at this time, that ten thousand foot and one hundred horse, all under the command of Diophanes, arrived from Achaia at Elæa; who, on landing, were conducted in the night into Pergamus, by persons sent for the purpose by Attalus. They were all veterans, well skilled in war, and their commander was a disciple of Philopœmen's, the most consummate general among the Greeks in that age. They set apart two days to give rest to the men and horses, and, at the same time, to view the posts of the enemy, and to learn at what places, and what times, they advanced and retired. The king's troops generally approached to the foot of the hill on which the town stands; so that their detachments could plunder all the country behind at will, for not a man ever sallied out, even to throw darts from a distance, against their guards. When the garrison once became so dispirited as to confine themselves within the walls, the king's troops conceived a great contempt of them, and thence fell into a carelessness on their part. The greater number did not keep their horses either saddled or bridled; while few remained under arms and in the ranks; the rest, slipping away, were scattered all over the plain, some diverting themselves with youthful sports and tricks, others eating in the shade, and some even stretch

ed on the ground asleep. When Diophanes observed all these particulars, which the high situation of Pergamus enabled him to do fully, he ordered his men to take arms, and to be ready at a particular gate. He himself went to Attalus, and told him that he had a mind to try his fortune against the enemy's advanced guards. Attalus gave consent, but not without reluctance, as he saw that one hundred horse must fight against three hundred, one thousand foot against four thousand. Diophanes then marched by the gate, and took post at a small distance from the enemy's guard, waiting his opportunity. On one side, the people in Pergamus thought that he was actuated by madness rather than by courage; and, on the other, the enemy, after observing his party for a short time, and seeing no movement among them, were not in any degree roused from their supineness, but even ridiculed the smallness of the number. Diophanes for a long time kept his men quiet, as if they had been brought out merely for the purpose of looking about them; but as soon as he perceived that the enemy had quitted their ranks, ordering the infantry to follow as fast as they could, he himself, with his own troop, led the way at the head of the cavalry, and, pushing on with all possible speed, made a sudden charge on the enemy's party, while a shout was raised by every horseman and footman at once. Not the men only so attacked were terrified, but the horses also; insomuch that they broke their collars, and caused great confusion and tumult throughout. A few of the horses indeed stood unaffrighted; but even these the troopers could not easily saddle, or bridle, or mount; for the Achæans struck much greater terror than would be supposed from so small a party of horse. But now the infantry, in due order and preparation, assailed the enemy, dispersed through their own negligence, and almost half asleep; and slaughter and flight ensued in every part of the plain. Diophanes pursued the runaways as far as he could with safety, and then returned into garrison, after acquiring very great honour to the Achæan nation; for the whole affair had been seen from the walls of Pergamus, by the men and even by the women.

21. Next day the enemy's guard, in more regular and orderly condition, pitched their camp five hundred paces farther from the city, and the Achæans marched out at nearly the same time as before, and to the same place. During many hours both parties stood attentively watching each other, in continual expectation of an immediate attack. At the approach of sunset, the usual time of their returning to the main camp, the king's troops, forming together in a body, began to retire. Diophanes did not stir until they were out

of sight; and then he rushed on their rear guard with the same vehemence as before, and again excited such dismay and confusion, that, though the hindmost were put to the sword, not one of them halted, or thought of fighting; so that they were driven into their camp in confusion, and scarcely observing any order in their march. These daring exertions of the Achæans obliged Seleucus to decamp, and quit the territory of Pergamus. Antiochus, having learned that the Romans and Eumenes were come to protect Adramyttium, made no attempt on that city, but ravaged the country adjoining. He afterward reduced Peræa, a colony of Mityleneans; while Cotton, Corylenus, Aphrodisias, and Crene, were all taken at the first assault. He then returned through Thyatira to Sardis. Seleucus remained on the sea-coast, keeping the favourers of one party in fear, and protecting those of the other. The Roman fleet, with Eumenes and the Rhodians, retired first to Mitylene, and then to Elæa, whence they had set out. On their way to Phocæa they put in at an island called Bachius, near the city of Phocæa; and, though they had formerly spared the temples and statues, with which kind of decorations the island abounded in an extraordinary degree, yet they now pillaged them all, and then passed over to the city. They commenced the attack of it on three different sides, according to a plan concerted; but soon perceiving that it could not be taken by scalade and assault, without regular works, and learning that a reinforcement of three thousand soldiers, sent by Antiochus, had got into the city, they immediately broke up the siege, and the fleet retired to the island, without having effected any thing more than the devastation of the enemy's country in the neighbourhood.

22. Here it was resolved that Eumenes should return home, and make every necessary preparation for the passage of the consul and his army over the Hellespont; and that the Roman and Rhodian fleets should sail back to Samos, and remain stationed there, to prevent any attempt being made by Polyxenidas. Accordingly the king returned to Elæa, the Romans and Rhodians to Samos. There, Marcus Æmilius, brother to the pretor, died. When his obsequies were performed, the Rhodians, on a report that a fleet was on its way from Syria, sailed away with thirteen of their own ships, one Coan, and one Cnidian quinquereme, to Rhodes, where they were to lie. Two days before the arrival of Eudamus, and the fleet from Samos, another fleet of thirteen ships, under the command of Pamphilidas, had been sent out against the same Syrian fleet; and taking with them four ships, which had been left to protect Caria, they relieved Dædala and several other fortresses of Peræa, which were besieged by the

king's troops. It was determined that Eudamus should put to sea directly, and an addition of six undecked ships was made to his fleet. He accordingly set sail; and using all possible expedition, overtook the first squadron at a port called Magiste, from whence they proceeded in one body to Phaselis, resolving to wait there for the enemy.

23. Phaselis stands on the confines of Lycia and Pamphylia: it projects far into the sea, and is the first land seen by persons coming from Cilicia to Rhodes, and, from hence, ships can be seen at a great distance: for this reason, chiefly, this place was made choice of, that they might lie directly in the way of the enemy's fleet. But an event took place which they did not foresee; for, in consequence of the unwholesomeness of the place, and of the season of the year, it being now the middle of summer, diseases began to spread with violence, particularly among the rowers. The fear of this pestilential malady made them quit the place; and, sailing by the Pamphylian bay, they put into port at the river Eurymedon, where they learned from the people of Aspendæ that the enemy were then at Sida. The king's fleet had been the slower in its passage by reason of the unfavourable wind, called the Etesian; that being the time when it blows periodically from the northwest. The Rhodians had thirty-two quadriremes, and four triremes. In the king's fleet were thirty-seven ships of the larger rates; among which were three of seven, and four of six banks of oars; and besides these ten triremes. Both fleets, at the dawn of the next day, moved out of port, as resolved to come to an immediate engagement; and, as soon as the Rhodians passed the promontory that stretches into the deep from Sida, they descried the enemy, and were descried by them. The left squadron of the king's fleet, which was on the outside next the main sea, was commanded by Hannibal, the right by Apollonius, one of the nobles, and they had their ships already formed in a line, a-head. The Rhodians approached in a long line a-head also. Eudamus, in the commander's ship, led the van; Chariclitus brought up the rear; and Pamphilidas commanded the centre division. When Eudamus saw the enemy's line formed, and ready for battle, he pushed out towards the main, ordering the ships that followed to form, regularly, as they came up, in a line of battle. This caused some confusion at first; for he had not stretched out to the main far enough to give room for all the ships to come into a line between him and the land, while himself was so impatient, as, with only five ships, to engage with Hannibal; the rest, having received orders to form their line, did not come up. The rear division had no room left for it next to

the land; and, while they were in disorder, the fight was already begun, on the right against Hannibal.

24. But the goodness of their ships, and the expertness of their men in nautical business, quickly freed the Rhodians from all embarrassment. They pushed out hastily towards the main; by which means each made room, next the land, for the one immediately behind; and when any made a stroke with its beak against a ship of the enemy, it either shattered its prow, or swept off its oars; or, passing by it, in the clear space between the vessels, made an attack on its stern. One of the king's seven banked ships being sunk with one stroke by a Rhodian vessel of much smaller size, dispirited his fleet in a very great degree; insomuch, that their right squadron gave evident indications of an intention to fly. Hannibal, in the open sea, pressed Eudamus hard, by means chiefly of his superior number of ships; for, in every other respect, Eudamus had greatly the advantage; and he would have surrounded and overpowered him, had not the signal for a dispersed fleet collecting together again been displayed from the commander's ship. On which, all the ships which had been victorious in the left squadron hastened up to succour their friends. This made Hannibal himself, with all his division, betake themselves to flight; while the Rhodians could not pursue, because their rowers being most of them sick, were therefore the sooner wearied. While lying to take refreshment, Eudamus, observing the enemy towing, by means of their open vessels, several damaged and crippled ships, with more than twenty that were going off unhurt, commanded silence from the castle of the commander's ship, and then called out, "Arise, and feast your eyes with an extraordinary sight." They all started up, and, perceiving the disorderly flight of the enemy, cried out, almost with one voice, that they ought to pursue. Eudamus's ship was bulged in many places; he therefore ordered Pamphilidas and Chariclitus to pursue as far as they should think it safe. They accordingly pursued for a considerable time; but, seeing Hannibal make in close to the land, fearing to be wind-bound on an enemy's coast, they steered back to Eudamus, and with difficulty towed to Phaselis a captured seven banked ship, which had been damaged in the beginning of the engagement. They then sailed home to Rhodes, not so much exulting in their victory, as blaming one another for not, when it was in their power, having sunk or taken the whole of the enemy's fleet. Hannibal was so disheartened by the loss of this one battle, that, notwithstanding their departure, he durst not sail along the coast of Lycia, though he wished to join the king's main fleet as soon as possible. That he might not

effect this junction without opposition, the Rhodians sent Chariclitus with twenty ships to Patara, and the harbour of Magiste. They then ordered Eudamus, with seven of the largest vessels belonging to the fleet which he had commanded, to rejoin the Romans at Samos, and to endeavour, by every argument, and by all his influence, to prevail on the Romans to besiege Patara.

25. Great was the joy felt by the Romans; first, on receiving the news of the victory, and, afterward, on the arrival of the Rhodians; and there was abundant reason to believe that, if these were freed from care, they would render the seas in that part of the world safe. But, as Antiochus had marched out of Sardis, they could not allow them to quit the guard of Ionia and Æolia, lest the maritime cities should be crushed by his arms. However, they sent Pamphilidas, with four decked ships, to join the fleet which was at Patara. Antiochus not only collected aids from the circumjacent states, but also sent ambassadors to Prusias, king of Bithynia, with a letter in which he represented, in strong colours, the evil designs of the Romans in coming into Asia. "Their intentions were," he said, "to abolish all kingly governments, so that there should be no empire in any part of the world. They had already reduced Philip and Nabis; and they were now falling on him. Thus the conflagration would spread, without interruption, from one to another, as each lay nearest to the one last ruined, until it enveloped them all. From him there was but one step to Bithynia, now that Eumenes had submitted to voluntary servitude." This letter made a strong impression on Prusias; but he was convinced of such a suspicion being groundless, by a letter from the consul Scipio; and still more so, by one from his brother Africanus, who, besides urging the invariable practice of the Roman people, of augmenting, by every honourable addition, the grandeur of kings in alliance with them, demonstrated by instances taken from his own family, that it was the interest of Prusias to court their friendship. "The petty chieftains in Spain," he said, "and who had been received into alliance, he had left kings. Masinissa he had not only re-established in his father's kingdom, but had put him in possession of that of Syphax, by whom he had been formerly dethroned: so that he was at the present, not only by far the most powerful of all the kings in Africa, but equal, both in dignity and strength, to any monarch in any part of the world. Philip and Nabis, avowed enemies, were conquered in war by Titus Quintius; nevertheless, they were left in possession of their kingdoms. Philip even had the tribute remitted to him last year, and his son, who was a hostage, restored. Through

the indulgence of the Roman commanders, he had also got possession of several states beyond the boundaries of Macedonia. As to Nabis, he might have remained in the same honourable rank, had not, first, his own madness, and, afterward, the treachery of the Ætolians, brought him to ruin." But what contributed more than all to fix the king's resolution was, that Caius Livius, who had commanded the fleet as pretor, came to him ambassador from Rome. Livius showed him how much better reason the Romans had to expect success than Antiochus; and how much more scrupulously and constantly they would maintain a friendship once formed.

26. Antiochus having lost all prospect of an alliance with Prusias, went from Sardis to Ephesus, to review the fleet which was fitted out, and lay there ready for several months past; to which he now gave attention, rather because he saw it impossible, with his land forces, to make any stand against the Roman army and the two Scipios, its commanders, than that his naval force, by itself, had ever been successful, in any trial that he had made of it, or afforded at this juncture any great or well-grounded expectation. Yet there were at the time some circumstances which flattered his hopes; for he had heard that a large portion of the Rhodian fleet was at Patara, and that King Eumenes had gone to the Hellespont, with all his ships, to meet the consul. Besides, the destruction of the Rhodian fleet at Samos, under circumstances in which it had been artfully entangled, helped to inspire some degree of confidence. Buoyed up by these considerations, he sent Polyxenidas, with orders to try, at all events, the fortune of a naval engagement; while he himself marched his land forces to Notium. This town, which belongs to Colophon, stands close to the sea, at the distance of about two miles from Old Colophon. He wished to get this city into his power, because it was so near to Ephesus that nothing could be done there, on sea or land, that was not open to the view of the Colophonians, and, through them instantly known to the Romans; and he had no doubt that the latter, on hearing of the siege, would bring their fleet from Samos to the relief of an ally, which would give Polyxenidas an opportunity of coming to action. He therefore laid regular siege to the city, making his approaches at the same time on the two sides next the sea; in both places advancing his engines and mounds to the wall, and bringing up the rams under covered galleries. The Colophonians, terrified at the dangers threatening them, sent envoys to Lucius Æmilius, at Samos, imploring the protection of the pretor and people of Rome. Æmilius, thinking nothing more improbable than that Polyxenidas,

whom he had twice challenged, in vain, to fight, should ever offer him battle, was, for some time past, uneasy at lying so long inactive at Samos; and he considered it as dishonourable that the fleet of Eumenes should assist the consul in conveying the legions into Asia, while himself should be confined to one particular spot, and assisting Colophon under a siege, without knowing what would be the issue. Eudamus, the Rhodian, (who had before prevailed on him to stay at Samos, when he wished to go to the Hellespont,) with all the other officers, pressed him to comply, representing "how much more eligible it would be, either to relieve confederates from a siege, or to vanquish that fleet which he had vanquished before; in a word, to drive the enemy entirely away, than to abandon allies to destruction, leave Antiochus master of Asia, by sea and land, and, deserting that share of the war which properly belonged to him, to sail for the Hellespont, when the fleet of Eumenes was sufficient for that station."

27. They accordingly set sail from Samos in quest of provisions, their stock being consumed, with an intention to pass over to Chios. Samos served as a granary to the Romans, and thither all the store-ships sent from Rome directed their course. When they had sailed round from the city to the back of the island, which looks northward towards Chios and Erythræ, and were preparing to cross over, the pretor received a letter informing him that a vast quantity of corn had arrived at Chios from Italy; but that the vessels laden with wine were detained by storms. At the same time accounts were received that the people of Teos had furnished large supplies of provisions to the king's fleet, and had promised five thousand vessels of wine. On this the pretor immediately changed his course, and steered away to Teos, resolved either to make use of the provisions prepared for the enemy, with the consent of the inhabitants, or to treat them as foes. As the ships were making up to the land, about fifteen vessels appeared in sight near Myonnesus. The pretor at first thought that these belonged to the king's fleet, and sailed in pursuit of them; but it appeared afterward that they were a squadron of pirates. They had ravaged the sea-coast of Chios, and were returning with booty of every kind, when, on seeing the fleet approaching from the main sea, they betook themselves to flight. They had much the advantage both in point of swiftness, as being lighter, and constructed for the purpose, and also in being nearer the land; so that before Æmilius could overtake them they made their escape to Myonnesus, while he, unacquainted with the place, followed in expectation of forcing their ships out of the harbour. Myonnesus is a promontory

between Teos and Samos. It consists of a hill rising from a pretty large base to a sharp top, in shape of an obelisk. From the land, the access to it is by a narrow path; towards the sea it is terminated by cliffs undermined by the waves, so that in some places the superimpending rocks project beyond the vessels that lie at anchor. The ships not daring to approach lest they should be exposed to the weapons of the pirates, who stood above on the cliffs wasted the day to no purpose. At length, a little before nightfall, they gave over the attempt and retired, and next day reached Teos. Here the pretor, after mooring in the port at the back of the city, called by the inhabitants Geræsticum, sent out the soldiers to ravage the adjacent ports.

28. The Teians, as these ravages passed under their eyes, sent deputies to the Roman commander, carrying fillets, and other badges of suppliants, who assured him that their state was innocent of any hostile word or deed against the Romans. But he strongly charged them with "having assisted the enemy's fleet with provisions, and with having promised a supply of wine to Polyxenidas." He farther told them that if they would furnish the same supplies to the Roman fleet, he would recall his troops from plundering; otherwise, they should be treated as enemies." When the deputies carried back this distressing answer, the people were summoned to an assembly by the magistrates, to consult on the measures proper to be taken. It happened that Polyxenidas, who had sailed with the king's fleet from Colophon, having heard that the Romans had left Samos and pursued the pirates to Myonnesus; that they were ravaging the lands of the Teians, and that their fleet lay in the harbour of Geræsticum, cast anchor, just at this time, in a retired harbour of an island called Macris, opposite to Myonnesus. Lying so near, he easily discovered the motions of the enemy; and, at first, entertained strong hopes of vanquishing the Roman fleet here, in like manner as he had vanquished the Rhodian at Samos: by securing, with a proper force, both sides of the harbour's mouth. Nor was the place in its nature unlike to that of Samos: by the promontories advancing their points towards each other, the harbour is enclosed in such a manner, that two ships can scarcely go out together. Polyxenidas intended to seize this narrow pass in the night; and, while ten ships stood at each of the promontories, to attack from the right and left both sides of the enemy's fleet sailing out, to land the armed men out of the rest of the fleet, as he had done at Panormus, and by that means to overpower the Roman on land and sea at once. His plan would probably have succeeded to his wish, had not the Romans, on the Teians promising to comply with their demands, judged it

more convenient for receiving the provisions, to remove the fleet into the inner port in front of the city. It is said also that Eudamus the Rhodian had pointed out the fault of the outer harbour, on occasion of two ships happening to entangle their oars together, so as to break them, in the narrow entrance. Among other motives, the consideration of the danger to be apprehended from the land, as Antiochus lay encamped at no great distance, inclined the pretor to change his station.

29. When the fleet was brought round to the city, as they had not the least notion of the enemy being so near, both soldiers and sailors went on shore to divide the provisions, and the wine particularly, among the ships; when, about midday, a peasant happened to be brought before the pretor, who told him that the enemy's fleet was lying at the island of Macris these two days; and that a little while ago, some of them were observed to be in motion, as if preparing to sail. Greatly alarmed at this unexpected event, the pretor ordered the trumpets to sound, to call in such as might have straggled into the country, and sent the tribunes into the city to hasten the soldiers and sailors on board. The confusion was not less than if the place were on fire, or taken by an enemy; some running to call out the men; others hurrying to the ships, while the orders of the officers were confounded by irregular shouts, intermixed and heightened by the clangour of the trumpets, until at length the crowd collected at the ships. Here scarcely could each know his own ship, or make his way through the tumult; and the disorder would probably have been productive of much mischief on land and sea, if the commanders had not exerted themselves quickly. Æmilius, in the commander's ship, sailed out first into the main; where, receiving the rest, he put each into his own place, so as to form a line abreast; and Eudamus, with the Rhodian fleet, waited at the shore, that the men might be embarked without confusion, and that every ship, as soon as ready, might leave the harbour. By these means the foremost division formed under the eye of the pretor, while the rear was brought up by the Rhodians; and then the whole line in as regular order as if within sight of the foe, advanced into the open sea. They were between Myonnesus and the promontory of Corycus, when they first got sight of the enemy. The king's fleet, which was coming in a long line, with only two vessels abreast, then formed themselves in order of battle, stretching out their left division so far, as that it might enclose the right of the Romans. When Eudamus, who commanded in the rear, perceived that the Romans could not form an equal front, but were just on the point of being surrounded, he pushed up his ships. They

were Rhodians, by far the fastest sailors of any of the fleet; and having filled up the deficiency in the extent of the line, he opposed his own ship to the commander's, on board of which was Polyxenidas.

30. The fleets were by this time engaged in every part. The Romans fought eighty ships, of which twenty-two were Rhodians. The enemy's fleet consisted of eighty ships, and they had of the largest rates three of six and two of seven banks. In the strength of the vessels, and valour of the soldiers, the Romans had greatly the advantage of the king's party, as had the Rhodians in the activity of their vessels, the skill of the pilots, and the dexterity of the rowers: yet the enemy was chiefly terrified by those who carried fires before them; and what was the sole cause of their preservation, when they were surrounded at Panormus, proved here the principal means of victory to the Romans: for the king's ships, through fear of the fire, turned aside, and to avoid at the same time encountering the enemy's prow with their own; so that they could not strike their antagonist with the beaks, but exposed the side of their ships to his strokes; and if any did venture an encounter, it was immediately overspread with the fire that was poured in; while the men were more hurried and disordered by their efforts to quench the flames than by fighting. However, the bravery of the soldiers, as is generally the case, was what chiefly availed in deciding the fate of the battle: for the Romans having broke through the centre of the enemy's line, tacked about and fell on the rear of the division which was engaged with the Rhodians; and, in an instant of time, both Antiochus's centre division, and the ships on the left, were sunk. The squadron on the right, which was still entire, was terrified, rather by the disaster of their friends, than any immediate danger threatening themselves; but when they saw the others surrounded, and Polyxenidas's ship deserting its associates, and sailing away, they quickly hoisted their topsails and betook themselves to flight, having a favourable wind making for Ephesus. They lost in that battle forty-two ships; of which thirteen struck, and fell into the hands of the Romans; the rest were burned or sunk. Two Roman ships were so shattered that they foundered, and several were much damaged. One Rhodian vessel was taken by an extraordinary casualty: for, on its striking a Sidonian ship with its beak, its anchor, thrown out by the force of the shock, caught fast hold of the other's prow with its fluke, as if it were a grappling iron thrown in. Great confusion ensuing, the Rhodians, who wished to disengage themselves, pulled back; by which means its cable being dragged forcibly, and at the same time entangled with the oars, swept off the whole set

on one side. The vessel, thus crippled, became the prize of the very ship which it had wounded with its beak and grappled. Such was the issue of the sea-fight at Myonnesus.

31. Antiochus was much dismayed at this defeat, and on finding himself driven from the sea; despairing therefore of being able to defend distant posts, he commanded the garrison to be withdrawn from Lysimachia, lest it should be overpowered by the Romans. This was ill-judged, as events afterward proved; for it would have been easy for him, not only to defend Lysimachia from the first attack of the Romans, but to have protracted the siege through the whole winter; and by thus prolonging the time, to have reduced the besiegers to the extremity of want; while he might, in the mean time, have tried every opportunity that offered for effecting an accommodation. But, after the defeat at sea, he not only gave up Lysimachia, but even raised the siege of Colophon, and retired to Sardis. Here, bending all his thoughts to one single object, that of meeting the enemy in the field, he sent into Cappadocia to Ariarathes to request assistance, and to every other place within his power to collect forces. Æmilius Regillus, after his victory at sea, proceeded to Ephesus, drew up his ships before the harbour, and, having extorted from the enemy a final acknowledgment of their having surrendered the dominion of the sea, sailed to Chios, whither he intended to have gone before the sea-fight happened. As soon as he had refitted the ships that had been damaged in the battle, he sent off Lucius Æmilius Scaurus, with thirty others, to the Hellespont to carry over the army; and decorating the Rhodian vessels with naval spoils, and allowing them a part of the booty, he ordered them to return home. The Rhodians spiritedly resolved to do business first. They therefore proceeded to assist in transporting the consul's forces, and when they had completed that service they returned to Rhodes. The Roman fleet sailed from Chios to Phocæa. This city stands at the bottom of a bay, and is of an oblong shape. The wall encompasses a space of two miles and a half in length, and then contracts on both sides into a narrow wedge-like form, which place they call Lampter, or the light-house. The breadth here is one thousand two hundred paces; and a tongue of land stretching out about a mile towards the sea divides the bay nearly in the middle, as if with a line, and where it is connected with the main land by a narrow isthmus, so as to form two very safe harbours, one on each side. The one that fronts the south is called Naustathmos, the station for ships, from the circumstance of its being capable of containing a vast number; the other is close to Lampter.

32. The Roman fleet, having taken possession of these harbours, where they rode in perfect safety, the pretor thought proper before he attempted the fortifications, either by scalade or works, to send persons to sound the disposition of the magistrates and principal people in the place; but finding them obstinate, he formed two attacks, which he carried on at the same time. In the part against which one attack was directed, the houses were few, the temples of the gods occupying a great deal of the ground. In this place he first brought up his rams, and began to batter the wall and towers; and when the multitude within ran thither to defend that spot, the battering rams were applied in the other quarter. The walls now began to fall in both places; on which the Romans made an assault, scrambling over the ruins as they fell, while others of them attempted to scale the parts that were standing; but the townsmen made such an obstinate resistance, as plainly showed that they had a firmer dependance on their arms and courage than on their fortifications. The pretor, therefore, seeing the danger which awaited his men, was obliged to sound a retreat; the more especially as they were now become so furious through rage and despair, as to expose themselves rashly. Although the fighting ceased, yet the besieged did not even then think of rest; but all hastened from every quarter to strengthen the walls, and to raise new ones in the place of those that had been demolished. While they were busily employed in this manner, Quintus Antonius came to them with a message from the pretor. After blaming them for their obstinacy, he assured them, that "the Romans were more anxious than they were themselves to prevent the siege being carried to the ruin of the city. If they would desist from their madness, Æmilius would allow them to capitulate on the same terms on which they formerly surrendered to Caius Livius." On hearing this, they desired five days' time to deliberate; during which they sent to learn whether they might hope for succour from Antiochus; and having received an answer by their deputies, that it was not in his power to relieve them, they opened their gates on the single condition of not being ill-treated. When the troops were marching into the city, and the pretor had proclaimed that it was his pleasure that the surrendered townsmen should be spared, there arose a universal clamour, that it was shameful "to suffer the Phocæans, who had never been faithful to any alliance, and had always been bitter in enmity, to escape with impunity." After which words, as if a signal had been given by the pretor, they ran, in parties, every way to plunder the city. Æmilius, at first, endeavoured to stop them; calling them back, and telling them,

that "towns taken by storm, and not such as surrendered, were to be plundered; and that even with regard to the former, the determination lay with the commander, not with the soldiers." But rage and avarice were too strong for his authority; wherefore, despatching heralds through all parts of the city, he ordered that all persons of free condition should come to him in the forum, to avoid ill treatment; and in every particular, as far as he was able, he fulfilled his promise to them. He restored to them their city, their lands, and their laws; and, as the winter now approached, he chose the harbour of Phocæa for the station of his fleet until spring.

33. About the same time, as the consul was marching along the frontiers of the Ænians and Maronites, he received the news of the victory over the king's fleet at Myonnesus, and of Lysimachia being evacuated by the garrison. This latter event gave much more satisfaction than even the success at sea; especially when, arriving at that city, which was replenished with stores of every kind, as if purposely laid in for the reception of the army, the troops found comfortable accommodation; a place in the besieging of which they had expected to meet with extreme want and hardship. There they halted a few days, to give time for the coming up of the baggage, and of the sick; for many, overcome by diseases, or the length of the way, had been left behind in all the forts of Thrace. When all had joined, they began again their march through the Chersonese, and arrived at the Hellespont; where, every thing requisite for their passage having been previously got ready by the care of King Eumenes, they crossed over, without opposition or confusion, as if to friendly shores, and the ships put in at several different places. This raised to a high degree the spirit of the Romans, who saw the passage into Asia left open to them; for they had always supposed that they could not accomplish it without a violent contest. They afterward remained encamped a considerable time at the Hellespont; this happening to be the time of the festival wherein the sacred bucklers are carried about, during which it is not allowed to march. The same festival had occasioned Publius Scipio's being separated from the army; for he was bound by a duty more particularly incumbent on him, as being one of the Salian priests: himself therefore caused some farther delay.

34. In the mean time an ambassador came from Antiochus to the camp,—Heraclides, a Byzantian, with a commission to treat of peace. His hopes of obtaining it were greatly encouraged by the dilatory proceeding of the Romans; for he had imagined that, as soon as they set foot in Asia, they

would have advanced rapidly against the king. He resolved, however, not to address himself to the consul until he had first applied to Publius Scipio, having received instructions to that purpose from the king. Indeed, his highest expectations were from Scipio, because his greatness of soul, and the fulness of his glory, naturally tended to produce a placable temper. Besides, all the world knew how he had behaved during a flow of success, both in Spain and afterward in Africa; and also, and more especially, because his son was then a prisoner with Antiochus. Where, and when, and by what accident he became a prisoner, are points, like very many others, not ascertained among writers. Some say that in the beginning of the war, as he was going from Chalcis to Oreum, he was intercepted by some of the king's ships; others, that after the army came into Asia, he was sent with a troop of Fregellans to Antiochus's camp, to gain intelligence; that, on the cavalry sallying out against him, he retreated; and having fallen from his horse, in the confusion, he was, together with two horsemen, overpowered, and thus conducted to the king. In one particular all are agreed; that, if peace had still subsisted with the Romans, and likewise a personal friendship between the king and the Scipios, the young man could not have been treated and distinguished with greater generosity and kindness than he met with. The ambassador, for these reasons, waited the arrival of Publius Scipio; and, as soon as he came, applied to the consul, requesting his permission to lay before him the business with which he was charged.

35. A full council being assembled, audience was given to the ambassador; who said, that "notwithstanding many embassies about peace had already been sent, backwards and forwards, without producing any effect, yet he conceived strong hopes of obtaining it from the very circumstance of the former delegates having obtained nothing; for the objects of contention in those discussions were Smyrna and Lampsacus, the Trojan Alexandria, and Lysimachia in Europe. Of these the king had already ceded Lysimachia, that it might not be said that he possessed any thing in Europe; and those cities which lay in Asia he was now ready to deliver up, as well as any others which the Romans, in consideration of having joined their party, might wish to render independent of the king's government. The king was also willing to pay to the Roman people half of the charges of the war." These were the conditions proposed. In the rest of his discourse he exhorted them to "consider the instability of human affairs; to use with moderation the advantages afforded by their own situation, and not to bear too hard on that of others; to be content with the empire of Europe;

that, in itself, was immense. It was an easier matter to make acquisitions, one after another, than to retain them when acquired. But if their wishes were so unbounded as not to be satisfied without taking away part of Asia also; if they would define it by indisputable limits, the king, for the sake of peace and harmony, would willingly suffer his own moderate temper to be overcome by the insatiableness of the Romans." These concessions, which appeared to the ambassador of great moment towards obtaining a peace, the Romans deemed trifling. They thought it reasonable that "the king should defray the whole expense occasioned by the war, because it was through his fault that it was begun: and that not only Ionia and Æolia ought to be evacuated by the king's troops, but as all Greece had been set free, so all the cities of that nation in Asia should also be free; which could no other way be effected than by Antiochus relinquishing the possession of that part of Asia on the hither side of Mount Taurus.

36. The ambassador, perceiving that no reasonable terms were to be obtained from the council, made a separate application to Publius Scipio, as he had been ordered, and, to prevail on him to favour his cause, told him, first, that the king would restore him his son without a ransom; and then, as ignorant of the disposition of Scipio as he was of the Roman manners, he promised an immense weight of gold, and, excepting the title of king, an absolute partnership in the sovereignty, if, through his means, he should obtain a peace. To this Scipio answered, "I am the less surprised at your ignorance of the Roman character in general, and of mine, to whom you have been sent, when I see that you are unacquainted with the situation even of the person from whom you come. You ought to have kept Lysimachia, to prevent our entering the Chersonese, or to have opposed us at the Hellespont, to hinder our passing into Asia, if you meant to ask peace from us as from people solicitous about the issue of the war. But, after leaving the passage into Asia open, and receiving not only a bridle but also a yoke, how can you pretend to negotiate on a footing of equality, and when you know that you must submit to orders? I shall consider my son as the greatest gift that the king's munificence can confer; any other instances of it, I trust in the gods, my circumstances will never need,—my mind certainly never will. For such an act of generosity to me he shall find me grateful, if, for a personal favour, he will accept a personal return of gratitude. In my public capacity I will neither accept from him nor give him any thing. All that is in my power, at present, to give him, is sincere advice. Go, then, and desire him, in my name, to cease hostilities,

and to refuse no terms of peace." This counsel had no effect on the king, who thought that no chance of war could make his condition worse, since terms were dictated to him already, as if he were totally vanquished. Laying aside, therefore, for the present, all farther mention of peace, he turned his whole attention to the preparations for war.

37. The consul, having made the necessary preparations for the execution of his designs, quitted the post where he lay, and marched, first, to Dardanus, and then to Rhœteum; from both which places the people came out in crowds to meet him. He then advanced to Troy; and having pitched his camp in the plain under the walls, went up to the city, and into the citadel, where he offered sacrifices to Minerva, the tutelar deity of the place. The Trojans, by every act and expression of respect, showed themselves proud of the Romans being descended from them, while the Romans testified their happiness in having sprung from that origin. The army, marching thence, arrived on the sixth day at the source of the river Caicus. Here they were joined by King Eumenes. He had at first endeavoured to bring back his fleet from the Hellespont to Elæa, for the winter; but being prevented during many days by contrary winds, from passing the promontory of Lectos, and unwilling to be absent at the commencement of operations, he landed, and came with a small body of men by the shortest road to the Roman camp. From the camp he was sent home to Pergamus, to hasten supplies of provisions; and, as soon as he had delivered the corn to the persons appointed by the consul, he returned to the camp, which remained on the same spot. The plan now adopted was, to have provisions prepared sufficient for a great many days, and to march directly against the enemy before the winter should come on to stop them. The king's camp was near Thyatira; and Antiochus, hearing there that Publius Scipio had fallen sick, and was conveyed to Elæa, sent ambassadors to conduct his son to him. As this present was highly grateful to the mind of the father, so was the satisfaction which it gave no less salutary to his body. After long indulging his rapture in the embraces of his son, at length he said to the ambassadors, "Tell the king that I return him thanks; that, at present, I can make him no other requital than my advice; which is, not to come to an engagement until he shall have heard that I have rejoined the army." Although an army of seventy thousand foot, and more than twelve thousand horse, inspired Antiochus at times with confidence to hope for a favourable issue of a battle, yet moved by the advice of so great a man as Scipio, in whom, when he considered the uncertainty of the events of war, he placed his greatest hopes for safety in any kind of

fortune that might befall him, he retired beyond the river Phrigius, and pitched his camp near Magnesia of Sipylus. However, and lest, while he wished to prolong the time, the Romans might attempt his works, he drew round it a fosse six cubits deep and twelve broad, and on the outside a double rampart; raising on the inside bank a wall flanked with towers at small distances, by means of which it was easy to hinder the enemy from passing the moat.

38. The consul, thinking that the king was still in the neighbourhood of Thyatira, marched five days without halting, until he came down into the Hyrcanian plains. Then, hearing of his departure, he followed his tracts, and encamped on the hither side of the river Phrigius, at the distance of four miles from his post. Here a body of about one thousand horse, the greatest part of whom were Gallogræcians, the rest Dahans, and archers on horseback of other nations intermixed, passing the river with great fury, made an attack on the advanced Roman guards, who, being unprepared, were at first thrown into disorder. But as the dispute was maintained, notwithstanding, and as the Romans (who could easily be reinforced, from their camp lying so near) increased in strength, the king's troops becoming weary and unable to withstand superior numbers, endeavoured to retreat; but before they could reach the river, very many were killed on the bank by the enemy pressing on their rear. For two days after all remained quiet, neither party passing the river. On the third the Romans passed it with their whole force, and encamped at the distance of about two miles and a half from the enemy. While they were laying out and fortifying the camp, a body of the king's troops, consisting of three thousand chosen horse and foot, approached with great rapidity and violence. The party on guard, though much inferior in number, (being only two thousand,) without calling off any of the soldiers from the fortifying of the camp, sustained the combat with equal success at first, and, in the progress of it, repulsed the enemy, killing one hundred, and taking about the same number. For the four ensuing days both armies stood in order of battle before their respective camps. On the fifth, the Romans advanced into the middle of the plain, but Antiochus did not stir; so that his rear was not so far as one thousand feet from his rampart.

39. Æmilius, seeing him unwilling to fight, called a council next day, and asked their opinion, "how he ought to act if Antiochus would not give him an opportunity of engaging: for the winter was at hand, and he must either keep the soldiers in camp, or, if they chose to retire to winter-quarters, defer the business of the war until summer." The Romans

never entertained a more contemptuous opinion of any people. The whole assembly therefore called on him to lead on immediately, and make use of the present ardour of the troops; who, as if the business were not to fight against so many thousands, but to slaughter an equal number of cattle, were ready to force their way, through trenches and ramparts, into the camp, if the enemy would not come out to battle. Cneius Domitius was then sent to discover the nature of the ground by which they were to march, and on what side they could best approach the enemy's rampart. On his returning, with a full account of every particular, it was resolved that the camp should next day be moved nearer to the enemy. On the third day the standards were carried forward into the middle of the plain, and the troops began to form their line. Antiochus now thought it would be wrong to defer matters longer, lest, by declining a battle, he should damp the courage of his men, and add to the confidence of the enemy. He therefore drew out his forces, advancing only so far as to show that he was willing to come to an engagement. The Roman line was nearly uniform throughout, in respect both of men and armour. There were two Roman legions, and two brigades of allies and Latines, each containing five thousand four hundred men. The Romans formed the centre, the Latines the wings. The spearmen composed the first line, the first-rank men the second, and the veterans closed the rear. Besides this regular body, the consul formed on the right of it, and in a straight line with it, the auxiliary troops of Eumenes, intermixed with Achæan targeteers, making about three thousand foot; beyond these he posted somewhat less than three thousand horse, of which eight hundred belonged to Eumenes; all the rest of the cavalry was Roman: and, in the extremity of the line, he placed bodies of Trallians and Cretans, equal in number, each making up five hundred men. His left wing did not need such supports, because it was flanked by a river with steep banks. However, four troops of horse were posted there. This was the whole amount of the Roman force. Two thousand Macedonians and Thracians, who had of their own accord accompanied the army, were left to guard the camp. Sixteen elephants were placed behind the veterans in reserve; for, besides that they were not supposed capable of withstanding the great number of the king's elephants, no less than fifty-four,—the African elephants are not able to cope with an equal number of Indian, being inferior to them both in size and in steadiness of courage.

40. The king's line was more checkered with troops of many nations, dissimilar both in their persons and armour. There was a body of sixteen thousand men armed after the

manner of the Macedonians, which they called a phalanx. This formed the centre, had five hundred men in front, and was divided into ten parts, which parts were separated by two elephants placed between each two; its depth from the front, was thirty-two ranks. This was the main strength of the king's army, and it exhibited a formidable sight, both in the other particulars of its appearance, and in the elephants, towering so high above the heads of the soldiers. They were of huge bulk, and were rendered more terrific by the caparisons of their foreheads and crests, and the towers fixed on their backs; four armed men stood on each tower, besides the managers of the beasts. On the right of the phalanx were placed five hundred Gallogræcian horsemen, to whom were joined three thousand horsemen clad in complete armour, whom they call cataphracti, or mailed. To these were added a brigade of near a thousand horse, which body they called agema. They were Medes, all picked men, with a mixture of horsemen from many other nations in that part of the world. Adjoining these a body of sixteen elephants was placed in reserve. On the same side, a little farther on towards the wing, was the royal cohort; these were called argyraspides,* from the kind of armour which they wore. Next to these stood one thousand two hundred Dahan bowmen on horseback; then three thousand light infantry, nearly half Cretans and half Trallians; adjoining these, two thousand five hundred Mysian archers; and the flank of the whole was covered by four thousand Cyrtæan slingers and Elymæan archers intermixed. Next to the left flank of the phalanx stood one thousand five hundred Gallogræcian horse, and two thousand Cappadocians, sent by King Ariarathes, wearing the same kind of armour; then auxiliaries of all kinds mixed together, two thousand seven hundred; then three thousand mailed horsemen; then one thousand other horsemen, being a royal cohort, equipped with lighter coverings for themselves and their horses, but in other respects not unlike the rest: they were mostly Syrians, with a mixture of Phrygians and Lydians. In the front of this body of cavalry were the chariots, armed with scythes, and a kind of camels called dromedaries. These were ridden by Arabian archers, who carried thin swords four cubits long, that they might be able to reach the enemy from so great a height. Then followed another multitude, like that in the right wing; first, Tarentines; then two thousand five hundred Gallogræcian horsemen; then one thousand new Cretans, and one thousand five hundred Carians and Cilicians, armed in the same manner; then an equal number of

* Silver shield-bearers.

Trallians, with three thousand targeteers, Pisidians, Pamphylians, and Lycians; then came brigades of Cyrtæans and Elymæans, equal to those posted in the right wing, and sixteen elephants, standing at a small distance. The king himself took post in the right wing; the command of the left he gave to his son Seleucus, and Antipater, the son of his brother; that of the centre to Minio, Zeuxis, and Philip, the master of the elephants.

41. A morning fog, which as the day advanced rose up in clouds, spread a general darkness; and the moisture, issuing from it, and coming from the southward, wetted every thing. This circumstance, which was scarcely any inconvenience to the Romans, was of extreme prejudice to the king's troops: for the line of the Romans was of a moderate length, and the obscuring of the light did not hinder their seeing every part of it; they were, besides, mostly heavy-armed troops, so that the fog had no tendency to blunt their swords and javelins. But the king's line was so very extensive that from the centre of it the wings could not be seen, much less could those at the extremities see one another; and then the moisture relaxed the strings of their bows, their slings, and the thongs of their javelins. Besides, the armed chariots, by means of which Antiochus had trusted utterly to disorder the enemy's line, turned the terror of their operations on their owners. The manner in which they were armed was this: from the yoke, on both sides of the pole, they had ten scythes, each of a cubit in length, standing out like horns, to transfix any thing that they met; at each extremity of the yoke two scythes projected, one on a line with the yoke, the other on its lower side, pointing to the ground; the former to cut through any thing that might come within its reach on the side, the other to catch such as fell, or endeavoured to go under it. At each extremity of the axle of the wheels two knives were fastened in the same manner. The chariots, thus armed, if they had been placed in the rear, or between the ranks, must have been driven through his own ranks; the king therefore, as already mentioned, placed them in front. Eumenes, seeing this, and being not unexperienced in such kind of fight; knowing, likewise, that those machines might prove as dangerous to their employers, as to their antagonists, if means were used to frighten the horses, rather than a regular attack; ordered the Cretan bowmen, and slingers, and javelin bearers, with some troops of horse, not in a body, but scattering themselves as widely as possible, to rush forward, and pour weapons on them from all sides at once. This storm, as it were, partly by the wounds made by the missile weapons thrown from every quarter, and partly by the discordant shouts raised, so terrified the horses,

that immediately, as if unbridled, they galloped about at random. The light infantry, the lightly-accoutred slingers, and the active Cretans, quickly evaded their encounter. The horsemen, following them, increased the tumult and the terror of the horses and camels at the same time, while the crowd of followers redoubled their shouts. By these means the chariots were driven out of the ground between the two lines. When this empty piece of parade was removed, both parties gave the signal, and advanced to a regular engagement.

42. But these chariots, thus ineffective against the enemy, soon proved the cause of great mischief to the army of the king: for the troops, posted next behind, being terrified at the wild disorder of the horses, betook themselves to flight, leaving all exposed as far as to the post of the mailed horsemen; and even these, when the Romans, after dispersing the reserves, approached, did not sustain their first onset. Some fled, and others, being delayed by the weight of their coverings and armour, were put to the sword. The whole left wing then gave way, and the auxiliaries, posted between the cavalry and the phalanx, being thrown into confusion, the terror spread even to the centre. Here the ranks were broken by the flying soldiers rushing in between them, while the same cause deprived the men of the use of their long spears, called by the Macedonians sarissas. While they were in this disorder, the Roman legions, advancing, discharged their javelins among them. Even the elephants, standing in the way, did not deter the Roman soldiers, who had learned by experience in the African wars, both to evade the onset of the animal, and getting at one side of it, either to ply it with darts, or, if they could come near enough, to wound its sinews with their swords. The front of the centre was now almost cut to pieces, and the reserve, being surrounded, was attacked on the rear, when the Romans perceived their troops in another quarter flying, and heard shouts of dismay almost close to their camp: for Antiochus, who commanded the right wing, having observed that the enemy, relying on the river for security, had placed no reserve there, except four troops of horse, and that these, keeping close to the infantry, left an open space on the bank of the river, made a charge on them with a body of auxiliaries and mailed horsemen. He not only attacked them in front, but going round the extremity of their line, near the river, pressed them in flank also; until having routed the cavalry first, and then the infantry, he made them fly with precipitation to their camp.

43. The camp was commanded by Marcus Æmilius, a military tribune, son of Marcus Lepidus, who, in a few

years after, became chief pontiff. On seeing the troops flying he went out, with his whole guard, to meet them. He ordered them first to halt, and then to return to the fight; at the same time upbraiding them with cowardice. He then proceeded to threats,—that if they did not obey his orders, they would rush blindly on their own destruction. At last he gave orders to his own men to kill the foremost of the runaways, and with their swords to drive the crowd that followed back to their station. The greater fear now overcame the less. Compelled by the danger on either side, they first halted, and then marched, as commanded, to meet the enemy. Æmilius, with his guard, consisting of two thousand men of distinguished valour, gave a vigorous check to the furious pursuit of Antiochus. At the same time Attalus, the brother of Eumenes, having, from the right wing, where the left of the enemy had been routed at the beginning of the engagement, observed the flight of his friends on the left, and the tumult near the camp, came up seasonably with two hundred horse. When Antiochus saw those men renewing the fight, whom but just before he had seen running away, and another large body advancing from the camp, with a third from the line, he turned about his horse and fled. The Romans, thus victorious in both wings, advanced over heaps of slain, which were most numerous in the centre, where the strength of the bravest men and the heavy armour had prevented flight, and proceeded to rifle the camp. The horsemen of Eumenes first, and then the rest of the cavalry, pursued the enemy through all parts of the plain, and killed the hindmost as they overtook them. But the fugitives were exposed to more severe distress by the chariots, elephants, and camels intermixed, and by their own disorderly haste; for, after they once broke their ranks, they rushed, as if blind, one on another, and were trodden to death by their numerous beasts. In the camp also there was great slaughter committed, rather greater than even in the field; for the first that quitted it, in general, directed their flight to the camp. The guard, encouraged by the great number of these, defended their works with the more obstinacy. The Romans having been stopped at the gates and rampart, which they had expected to master at the first push, when they did at length break through, were led by rage to make the more dreadful carnage.

44. According to accounts given by historians, there were killed, on that day, fifty thousand foot and four thousand horse; taken one thousand four hundred, with fifteen elephants and their managers. Of the Romans many were wounded, but no more than three hundred foot and twenty-four horsemen killed; and of the troops of Eumenes twenty-

five. That day the victors, after plundering the enemy's camp, returned with great store of booty to their own. On the day following they stripped the bodies of the slain, and collected the prisoners. Ambassadors came from Thyatira and Magnesia, near Sipylus, with a surrender of those cities. Antiochus fled with very few attendants; but greater numbers collecting about him on the road, he arrived at Sardis, with a numerous body of soldiers, about the middle of the night, and hearing there that his son Seleucus, and several of his friends, had gone on to Apamea, he likewise, at the fourth watch, set out for that city with his wife and daughter, having committed to Zeno the command of the city, and the government of Lydia to Timon; but the townspeople, disregarding both these and the soldiers who were in the citadel, agreed to send deputies to the consul.

45. About this time deputies came from Tralles, from Magnesia, on the Mæander, and from Ephesus, to surrender those cities. Polyxenidas had quitted Ephesus as soon as he heard of the battle; and, sailing with the fleet as far as Patara in Lycia, where, through fear of the Rhodian fleet stationed at Megiste, he landed, and with a small retinue, pursued his journey by land into Syria. The several states of Asia submitted themselves to the disposal of the consul, and to the dominion of the Roman people. He was now at Sardis, whither Publius Scipio came from Elæa, as soon as he was able to endure the fatigue of travelling. Shortly after arrived a herald from Antiochus, who solicited, through Publius Scipio, and obtained from the consul, permission for the king to send ambassadors. In a few days' time, Zeuxis, who had been governor of Lydia, and Antipater, the king's nephew, arrived in that character. These, having first had a meeting with Eumenes, whom they expected to find most averse from peace, on account of old disputes, and seeing him better disposed to a reconciliation than either they or the king had hoped, addressed themselves then to Publius Scipio, and, through him, to the consul. At their request a full council was assembled to hear the business of their commission, when Zeuxis spoke to this effect: "Romans, we are not prepared to make any proposal from ourselves; but rather desire to know, from you, by what atonements we can expiate the error of our king, and obtain pardon and peace from our conquerors. You have ever displayed the greatest magnanimity, in pardoning vanquished kings and nations, and ought you not to show a much greater and more placable spirit, after your late victory, which has made you masters of the whole world? You ought now, like deities, laying aside all disputes with mortal beings, to protect and spare the human race." It had been determined,

before the ambassadors came, what answer should be given them; and it was agreed that Africanus should deliver it. He is said to have spoken thus: "Of those things that are in the gift of the immortal gods, we Romans possess as much as the gods have been pleased to bestow. Our spirit, which is in the direction of our own mind, is the same to-day that it has always been in every state of fortune: prosperity has never elated, nor adversity depressed it. Of the truth of this, (to omit other instances,) I might produce your friend Hannibal as a convincing proof; but I can appeal to yourselves. After we had passed the Hellespont; before we saw the king's camp or his army; when the chance of war was open to both, and the issue uncertain; on your proposing to treat of peace, we offered you terms, at a time when we were both of us on a footing of equality; and the very same terms we offer you now, when we are victorious, and you vanquished. Resign all pretensions in Europe, and cede that part of Asia which lies on this side of Mount Taurus. Then towards the expenses of the war, you shall pay fifteen thousand talents of Eubœa;* five hundred immediately, two thousand five hundred when the senate and people of Rome shall have ratified the peace, and one thousand annually for twelve years after. It is likewise thought fit that four hundred talents be paid to Eumenes, and the quantity of corn remaining unpaid of what was due to his father. When we shall have settled these articles, it will be a kind of assurance to us of your performance of them, if you give twenty hostages, such as we shall choose. But never can we be properly satisfied that the Roman people will enjoy peace on the side of that country in which Hannibal shall be. Him therefore we demand above all. You shall also deliver up Thoas, the Ætolian, the fomenter of the Ætolian war, who armed you against us by the assurances of their support, and them by assurances of yours; and, together with him, Mnesilochus, the Acarnanian, and Philo and Eubulias, of Chalcis. The king will now make peace under worse circumstances, on his side, because he makes it later than he might have done. If he now causes any delay, let him consider that it is more difficult to pull down the majesty of kings, from the highest to the middle stage, than it is to precipitate it from the middle to the lowest." The king's instructions to his ambassadors were to accede to any terms of peace. It was settled, therefore, that ambassadors should be sent to Rome. The consul distributed his army in winter-quarters at Magnesia, on the Mæander, Tralles, and Ephesus. In a few days after the king brought the hostages to Ephesus to the consul; and

* About 2,900,000*l.*

also the ambassadors who were to go to Rome arrived. Eumenes set out for Rome at the same time with the king's ambassadors, and they were followed by embassies from all the states of Asia.

46. During the time of these transactions in Asia, two proconsuls arrived, almost together, at Rome, from their provinces, with hopes of triumphing; Quintus Minucius, from Liguria, and Manius Acilius, from Ætolia. After hearing recitals of their services, the senate refused a triumph to Minucius, but, with great cheerfulness, decreed one to Acilius, and he rode through the city in triumph over King Antiochus and the Ætolians. In the procession were carried two hundred and thirty military ensigns; of unwrought silver, three thousand pounds weight; of coin, one hundred and thirteen thousand Attic tetradrachms;* and two hundred and forty-eight thousand cistophoruses;† of chased silver vessels a great number, and of great weight. He bore also the king's plate, furniture, and splendid wardrobe; golden crowns, presents from the allied states, forty-five; with spoils of all kinds. He led thirty-six prisoners of distinction, officers in the armies of the king and of the Ætolians. Damocritus, the Ætolian general, a short time before, escaped out of prison in the night; but, being overtaken by the guards on the bank of the Tiber, he stabbed himself with a sword before he was seized. Nothing was wanted but the soldiers to follow the general's chariot; in every other respect the triumph was magnificent, both in the grandeur of the procession, and the splendour of his exploits. The joy, however, was much damped by melancholy news from Spain:—that the army under the command of Lucius Æmilius, proconsul, had been defeated in a battle with the Lacitanians, at the town of Lycon, in the country of the Vastitans; that six thousand of the Romans were killed; and that the rest, being driven in a panic within their rampart, found it difficult to defend the camp, and had retreated, by long marches, as if flying into a friendly country. Such were the accounts from Spain. From Gaul, Lucius Aurunculeius, pretor, introduced to the senate deputies from Placentia and Cremona, who represented those colonies as distressed by the want of inhabitants; some having been carried off by the casualties of war, others by sickness; and several weary of the neighbourhood of the Gauls, having removed from them. On this the senate decreed that "Caius Lælius, the consul, if

* 14,596*l.* 16*s.* 8*d.*

† 4270*l.* 19*s.* 9*d.* A cistophorus was a coin so called, from its bearing the image of a priest carrying in a box (cistus) the consecrated things used in the mysteries of Ceres, and of other deities. In value 7 1-2*d.* were equal to four drachmas.

he thought proper, should enrol six thousand families, to be distributed and settled at the before-mentioned places; and that Lucius Aurunculeius, pretor, should appoint commissioners to conduct them." Accordingly, Marcus Atilius Serranus, Lucius Valerius Flaccus, son of Publius, and Lucius Valerius Tappus, son of Caius, were named to that office.

47. Not long after, as the time of the consular elections drew nigh, the consul, Caius Lælius, came home to Rome from Gaul. He not only enrolled the colonists, ordered by the decree of the senate passed in his absence, as a supplement to Cremona and Placentia, but proposed,—and, on his recommendation, the senate voted,—that two new colonies should be established in the lands which had belonged to the Boians. At the same time arrived a letter from the pretor, Lucius Æmilius, containing an account of the sea-fight at Myonnesus, and of the consul, Lucius Scipio, having transported his army into Asia. A supplication for one day was decreed, on account of the naval victory, and another, for a second day, to implore the gods, that, as the Roman army had then for the first time pitched a camp in Asia, that event might in the issue prove prosperous and happy. The consul was ordered to sacrifice twenty of the greater victims, on occasion of each supplication. The election of consuls was then held, and was attended with a strong contest. One of the candidates, Marcus Æmilius Lepidus, lay under general censure, for having, in order to sue for the office, left his province of Sicily without asking leave of the senate. The other candidates were Marcus Fulvius Nobilior, Cneius Manlius Vulso, and Marcus Valerius Messala. Fulvius alone was elected consul, the rest not having gained a majority of the centuries; and, the next day, rejecting Lepidus, (for Messala had declined,) he declared Cneius Manlius his colleague. Then were chosen pretors, two of the name of Quintus Fabius Labeo, and Pictor; the latter of whom had, in that year, been inaugurated flamen quirinalis; Marcus Sempronius Tuditanus, Spurius Postumius Albinus, Lucius Plautius Hypsæus, and Lucius Bæbius Dives.

48. Valerius Antias says that at the time when Marcus Fulvius Nobilior and Cneius Manlius Vulso came into the consulship, [A. U. C. 563. B. C. 189,] a rumour prevailed strongly at Rome, and was received as almost certain, that the consul, Lucius Scipio, and, with him, Publius Africanus, had been invited by the king to a conference, under pretence of restoring young Scipio; that they were both seized, and that, when the leaders were thus made prisoners, the enemy's army was immediately led up to the Roman camp; that this was stormed, and the forces entirely cut off; that, in conse-

quence of thi
to obey order
gone into M
liaries; tha
Lepidus, hac
Ætolia, to c
he adds, tha
senate, amo
ed the accou
in Asia by
answered, t
bassadors,
any other v
self to affi
groundless

49. Whe
audience o
cumstance
humbly se
began witl
and, in an
bravery, ir
offence by
their thus
been forgo
injuries th
they stood
hatred. T
mitted then
by another
enemies
on whic
ate ther
lians w
were
Whe
enem
cum
nate
the
mar
of
Æ
to
A

province, and without being accompanied by a Roman deputy, all such would be treated as enemies."—In this manner were the Ætolians dismissed.

50. The consuls then consulted the senate on the distribution of the provinces; and it was resolved that they should cast lots for Ætolia and Asia. To him, to whose lot Asia should fall, was assigned the army, then under Lucius Scipio; and, to recruit its numbers, four thousand Roman foot, and two hundred horse, and, of the allies and Latines, eight thousand foot, and four hundred horse; with which force he was to carry on the war with Antiochus. To the other consul was decreed the army in Ætolia; and he was allowed to raise, for a reinforcement, the same number of natives and allies allotted to his colleague. He was likewise ordered to equip and take with him the ships that had been fitted out the year before; and not only to wage war with the Ætolians, but also to pass over into the island of Cephalenia. He was farther directed, if he could do it without injury to the public service, to come home to Rome to hold the elections; for, besides replacing the annual magistrates, it was resolved that censors also should be created; and if any particular business should detain him, he was then to acquaint the senate that he could not attend at the time of the elections. Ætolia fell by lot to Marcus Fulvius; Asia to Cneius Manlius. The pretor then cast lots, and Spurius Postumius Albinus obtained the city and foreign jurisdiction; Marcus Sempronius Tuditanus, Sicily; Quintus Fabius Pictor, the flamen quirinalis, Sardinia; Quintus Fabius Labeo, the fleet; Lucius Plautius Hypsæus, Hither Spain; Lucius Bæbius Dives, Farther Spain. For Sicily was allotted one legion, with the squadron then in the province; and the pretor was ordered to levy on the Sicilians two tenths of the corn; one of which he was to send into Asia, the other into Ætolia. It was also ordered that the same impost should be collected in Sardinia, and the corn sent to the same armies as the Sicilian corn. A reinforcement was given to Lucius Bæbius, for Spain, of one thousand Roman foot, and fifty horse, with six thousand Latine foot, and two hundred horse. To Plautius Hypsæus, for the Hither Spain, were assigned one thousand Roman foot, and two thousand Latines, with two hundred horse; so that, with these supplies, each of the two Spains should have a legion. Of the magistrates of the preceding year, Caius Lælius was continued in command for a year, with his present army, as was Publius Junius, propretor in Etruria, with the forces then in the province, and Marcus Tuccius, pretor in Bruttium and Apulia.

51. Before the pretors went into their provinces, a dispute arose between Publius Licinius, chief pontiff, and Quintus

Fabius Pictor, flamen quirinalis; such as had happened in the time of their fathers, between Lucius Metellus and Postumius Albinus. Metellus, who was chief pontiff at the time, had detained, for the performance of the business of religion, Albinus, who was consul, and was setting out with his colleague, Caius Lutatius, to the fleet at Sicily; and now Publius Licinius detained the pretor Fabius from going to Sardinia. The matter was agitated in very warm debates, both in the senate and before the commons: authoritative commands were issued on both sides; pledges seized to secure appearance, fines imposed, applications made to the tribunes, and appeals to the people. At last, considerations of religion prevailed, and the flamen obeyed the order of the pontiff; whereon the fines were remitted, by order of the people. The pretor, thus bereft of his province, resolved to abdicate his office, but was deterred by the authority of the senate, who decreed that he should hold the civil jurisdiction between natives and foreigners. The levies being finished in a few days, (for the soldiers to be enlisted were not many,) the consuls and pretors repaired to their provinces. There was spread at this time an unauthenticated report, the author of which no one knew, of the transactions that had passed in Asia; and, in a few days after, certain information, and a letter from the general, arrived at Rome. The satisfaction which this occasioned was great, not so much because of any apprehensions entertained of late,—(for Antiochus, since his defeat in Ætolia, was no longer an object of dread,) as because of the opinion which had been formerly conceived; for when this war was first begun he was considered as a very formidable enemy, both on account of his own strength, and of his having Hannibal to direct the business of the war. The senate however made no change in the plan of sending the consul into Asia; nor did they lessen the force intended for that province, because they feared that they might be engaged in a war with the Gauls settled in that country.

52. In a short time after Marcus Aurelius Cotta, deputy from Lucius Scipio, also ambassadors from King Eumenes, Antiochus, with others from Rhodes, arrived at Rome. Cotta, first in the senate, and then, by their order, in the assembly of the people, gave a narrative of the services performed in Asia. On which a decree was passed, ordering a supplication of three days' continuance, and that forty victims of the greater kinds should be offered on the occasion. Then audience was given, first, to Eumenes. After briefly returning thanks to the senate for having relieved him and his brother from a siege, and protected his kingdom from the unjust attacks of Antiochus; and then, congratulating them on the success of their arms, by sea and

land, whereby they had utterly routed Antiochus, driven him out of his camp, and expelled him, first, from Europe, and then from all Asia, on this side of Mount Taurus; he added, that with respect to his services, he wished them to be learned from their own generals and their own deputies, rather than from his mouth. All were pleased with his discourse, and desired him to lay aside his modesty so far as to tell frankly what recompense he thought himself deserving of from the senate and people of Rome: assuring him that "the senate were inclined to act with greater zeal, and more abundant liberality, if possible, than even his deserts demanded." To this the king answered, that "had others offered him a choice of rewards, and allowed him the privilege of consulting the Roman senate, he would have applied to that most august body for their advice; that he might not appear to have wanted either moderation in his wishes, or modesty in his requests. But now, when they themselves were the donors, it was much more proper that their munificence towards him and his brothers should be regulated by their own judgment." The senate, not discouraged by this answer, still urged him to speak; and, after a long contest of kindness on one side, and reservation on the other, Eumenes, with a degree of complaisance as insuperable as it was equal in both parties, withdrew from the senate-house. The senate persisted in their resolution, and said, that "it was idle to suppose that the king was unable to inform them of the objects of his hopes, and of his views in coming. He best knew what would be suitable to his own dominions. He was much better acquainted with Asia than were the senate. They ought therefore to call him back, and insist on his explaining his wishes and sentiments."

53. The king being brought back by the pretor, and desired to speak freely, began thus: "Conscript fathers, I should have persevered in declining to speak, but that I knew you would presently call in the Rhodian ambassadors, and that when they had been heard, I must of necessity have spoken. And my task therein will be the more difficult, as their demands will be of such a nature that, so far from appearing to contain any thing detrimental to me, they will not even seem to have any immediate connexion with their own interest: for they will plead the cause of the Grecian states, and allege that they ought to be set free; which point being gained, is it not plain to every one that they will alienate from us not only those states which shall be liberated, but likewise those that have been tributary to us since the earliest times; and that, after having bound them under so great an obligation, they will keep them under the de-

nomination of allies, in reality subject to their government, and entirely at their disposal? Now, while they are aspiring to such a height of power, they will pretend that the business no way concerns themselves; they will only say that it is becoming of you, and conformable to your past conduct. It will be proper therefore to be on your guard, lest you be deceived by such specious arguments; and lest by an unfair distribution, you not only depress some of your allies too much, while you exalt others beyond measure, but also, put those who bore arms against you in a better state than your friends. As to what regards myself, in other cases, I should rather wish it to be thought I had yielded somewhat of the full extent of my right, than that I had kept up too obstinate a struggle to maintain it; but in a contest of friendship and good-will towards you, and of the respect to be paid to you, I cannot with any patience bear to be outdone. Friendship with you was the principal inheritance that I received from my father; who, of all the inhabitants of Asia and Greece, was the first who formed a league of amity with you; and this he maintained with constant and invariable fidelity to the last hour of his life. Nor did he demonstrate, merely, a faithful and kind inclination towards you, but took an active part in all the wars which you waged in Greece, whether on land or sea: he supplied you with all kinds of provisions in such a manner, that not one of your allies could vie with him in any respect; and, finally, while he was exhorting the Bœotians to alliance with you, in the middle of his discourse, he was struck by a fit, and expired soon after. In his steps I have trod; and though I could not surpass the warmth of his wishes, and the zeal with which he cultivated your friendship,—for these could not be exceeded,—yet fortune, the times, Antiochus, and the war waged in Asia, afforded me occasion of outdoing him in real acts, in meritorious and expensive services. Antiochus, king of Asia, and a part of Europe, offered me his daughter in marriage; offered to restore immediately the states that had revolted from us, and gave great hopes of enlarging my dominions, if I would have joined him in the war against Rome. I will not boast, as a matter of merit, that I was guilty of no trespass against you; but I will rather mention those instances of conduct which are worthy of the very early friendship between our house and you. I gave your commanders such succours of land and sea forces, that not one of your allies can stand in competition with me. I supplied them with provisions for both services; in all the naval engagements, fought in various places, I took my share, and I never was sparing of my labour and danger. What, among all the calamities of war, is the most grievous, I underwent a siege; being shut up in Pergamus, in the utmost danger both of my kingdom and of my life. When this was raised, notwithstanding that Antiochus was encamped on one side of the capital of my dominions, and Seleucus on another, regardless of my own affairs, I went with my whole fleet to the Hellespont, to meet your consul Lucius Scipio, and to assist in transporting his army. From the time that the army came over into Asia I never quitted the consul; no Roman soldier was more regular in his attendance in your camp, than I and my brothers. No expedition, no battle of cavalry, was undertaken without me. In the field I took that post, and I maintained that ground, which the consul's pleasure allotted to me. I do not intend, conscript fathers, to say who can compare his services during that war to mine. There is not one of all those nations, or kings, you hold in high esteem, with whom I do not set myself on a level. Masinissa was your enemy before he became your ally; nor did he, while his kingdom flourished, come to your aid at the head of his troops; but dethroned, exiled, and stripped of all his forces, he fled for refuge to your camp with one troop of horse. Nevertheless, because he faithfully and diligently adhered to your cause in Africa, against Syphax and the Carthaginians, you not only restored him to the throne of his father, but, by adding to his domain the most opulent part of the kingdom of Syphax, rendered him the most potent of all the kings in Africa. What reward then, and what honour do we deserve at your hands, who have never been foes, but always allies? My father, myself, my brothers, have carried arms in your cause by sea and land, not only in Asia, but in countries remote from our home; in Peloponnesus, in Bœotia, in Ætolia, during the wars with Philip, and Antiochus, and the Ætolians. It may be asked me, what then are your demands? Conscript fathers, since I must comply with what I perceive is your desire, and explain my wishes; if you have removed Antiochus beyond the mountains of Taurus with the intention of holding those countries yourselves, I wish for no other people to settle near me, no other neighbours than you; nor do I expect that any other event could give greater safety and stability to my government. But if your purpose is to retire hence, and withdraw your armies, I may venture to affirm that not one of your allies is more deserving than I am of possessing what you have acquired. But then it will be a glorious act to liberate states from bondage. I agree that it will, provided they have committed nothing hostile against you. But, if they took part with Antiochus, is it not much more becoming your wisdom and equity, to consult the interest of your well-deserving friends, than that of your enemies?"

54. The senate was well pleased with the king's discourse, and plainly manifested a disposition to act, in every particular, with liberality, and an earnest desire to gratify him. An embassy from Smyrna was next introduced, because some of the Rhodian ambassadors were not present; but this was quickly despatched. The Smyrnæans were very highly commended for having resolved to endure the last extremities rather than surrender to the king. The Rhodians were next introduced. The chief of their embassy, after taking a view of the early periods of their friendship with the Roman people, and displaying the merits of the Rhodians in the war with Philip, and, afterward, in that with Antiochus, proceeded thus: "Conscript fathers, there is nothing in the whole course of our business that gives us more trouble and uneasiness than having a debate with Eumenes; with whom alone, of all the kings in the world, each of us, as individuals, and what weighs more with us, our state, as a community, is closely connected in friendship. But, conscript fathers, not our own inclinations disunite us, but the nature of things, whose sway is all-powerful, according to which, we being free ourselves, plead the cause of other men's freedom; while kings wish to have all things subservient and subject to their will. Yet, however that matter may be, we are more embarrassed by our respect towards the king, than either by any intricacy in the subject of debate, or any perplexity which it seems likely to occasion in your deliberations: for if you could make no honourable requital to the king, your friend and ally, who has merited highly in this very war, and the rewarding of whose services is now under your consideration, by any other means than by delivering free states into his power, you might then, indeed, find it hard to determine between the sending away your friend, the king, without an honourable requital, and the departing from your own established practice; tarnishing, now, by the servitude of so many states, the glory which you acquired in the war with Philip. But, from this necessity of retrenching either from your grateful intentions towards your friend, or from your own glory, fortune completely frees you; for through the bounty of the gods, your victory is not more glorious than it is rich, so that it can easily acquit you of that debt. Lycaonia, and both the Phrygias, with Pisidia, the Chersonese, and the adjoining parts of Europe, are all in your power; and any one of these, added to Eumenes' possessions, would more than double his dominions; but, if they were all conferred on him, they would set him on a level with the greatest of kings. You have it, therefore, in your

power to enrich your allies with the prizes of the war; and at the same time to adhere to your established mode of conduct, by keeping in mind what motive you assigned as your cause of war, first against Philip, now against Antiochus; what line of conduct you pursued after your conquest of Philip; what is now desired and expected from you, not so much because you have done it before, as because it is suitable to your character to do it: for, what to some is both a specious and an honourable incitement for taking arms, is not so to others. Some go to war to get possession of land, some of villages, some of towns, some of ports, and some of the sea-coast. Such things you never coveted, when you had them not; and you cannot covet them now, when the whole world is under your dominion. You ever fought for the exaltation of your dignity and glory, in the sight of the whole human race, who, for a long time past, have revered your name and empire next to that of the immortal gods. What was arduous in the pursuit and acquisition, may, perhaps, prove more difficult to be maintained. You have undertaken to deliver out of bondage under kings a nation the most ancient and most highly distinguished, both by the fame of its exploits, and by universal praise for politeness and learning; and the whole of it having been received under your care and protection, has a claim on you for your patronage for ever. The cities, standing on the original soil, are not more Grecian than their colonies, which formerly migrated thence into Asia; nor has change of country changed either their race or manners. Every state among us has ventured to maintain a doubtful contest with its parents and founders, vying with them in every virtue and valuable qualification. Most of you have visited the cities in Greece, and those in Asia. We acknowledge an inferiority in no other respect, than in our being farther distant from you. The Massilians, (whom, if the nature implanted, as it were, in the disposition of their country, could have been overcome, the many barbarous tribes surrounding them would, by this time, have rendered as savage as themselves,) are, as we hear, deservedly held in as high esteem by you as if they were inhabitants of the very heart of Greece: for they have preserved, not only the sound of the language, the mode of dress, and the habit; but what is more material than any thing else, the manners, the laws, and a mind pure and untainted by contagion from their neighbours. The boundary of your empire, at present, is Mount Taurus. Nothing within that line ought to be thought remote. To whatever extent your arms have reached, let the emanations of your justice, from this centre, reach to the same length. Let barbarians, with whom the commands of masters have always served instead of laws, have kings, as it is their wish; but Greeks, in whatever condition fortune assigns them, carry spirits like your own. They too, in former times, supported empire by their internal strength. They now pray that empire may remain to eternity, where it is lodged at present. They are well pleased at their liberty being protected by your arms, since they are unable to protect it by their own. But it is objected that some of their states sided with Antiochus. So did others before with Philip; so did the Tarentines with Pyrrhus. Not to enumerate other nations, Carthage enjoys liberty and its own laws. Consider, conscript fathers, how much you owe to this precedent, set by yourselves. You will surely be disposed to refuse to the ambition of Eumenes, what you refused to your own most just resentment. With what brave and faithful exertions we, Rhodians, have assisted you, both in this late war, and in all the wars that you have waged in that part of the world, we leave to your own judgment. We, now, in peace, offer you such advice, that if you conform to it, all the world will judge that your use of the victory redounds more to the splendour of your glory than the victory itself." Their arguments seemed well adapted to the Roman grandeur.

55. After the Rhodians, the ambassadors of Antiochus were called. These, after the common practice of petitioners for pardon, acknowledged the king's error, and besought the conscript fathers to let their deliberations be directed rather by their own clemency, than by the misconduct of the king, who had suffered punishment fully sufficient; in fine, to ratify, by their authority, the terms of the peace granted by their general Lucius Scipio." The senate voted that the peace should be observed; and the people, a few days after, passed an order to the same purpose. The treaty was concluded in the capitol with Antipater, chief of the embassy, and nephew of King Antiochus. Then audience was given to the other embassies from Asia, to all of whom was returned the same answer, that "the senate, in conformity to the usage of their ancestors, would send ten ambassadors to examine and adjust the affairs of Asia. That the outline of the arrangement was to be this: that the places on the hither side of Mount Taurus, which had been within the limits of the realm of Antiochus, should be assigned to Eumenes, excepting Lycia and Caria, as far as the river Mæander; and that these last mentioned should become the property of the Rhodians. The other states of Asia, which had been tributary to Attalus, should likewise pay tribute to Eumenes; and such as had been tributary to Antiochus, should be free and independent." The ten ambassadors appointed were, Quintus Minucius Rufus, Lucius

Furius Purpureo, Quintus Minucius Thermus, Appius Claudius Nero, Cneius Cornelius Merula, Marcus Junius Brutus, Lucius Aurunculeius, Lucius Æmilius Paulus, Publius Cornelius Lentulus, and Publius Ælius Tubero.

56. These were commissioned with full powers to determine all points that required investigation on the spot. The general plan the senate settled thus: that "all Lycaonia, both the Phrygias, and Mysia, the royal forests, and Lydia, and Ionia, excepting those towns which had been free on the day whereon the battle was fought with Antiochus, and excepting, by name, Magnesia at Sipylus; then the city Caria, called also Hydrela, and the territory of Hydrela, stretching towards Phrygia, and the forts and villages on the river Mæander, and likewise the towns, excepting such as had been free before the war, and excepting, by name, Telmissus, and the fort of Telmissium, and the lands which had belonged to Ptolemy of Telmissus; all those should be given to King Eumenes. Lycia was assigned to the Rhodians, excepting the same Telmissus, and the fort of Telmissium, with the lands which had belonged to Ptolemy of Telmissus; these were withheld from both Eumenes and the Rhodians. To the latter was given also that part of Caria which lies beyond the river Mæander nearest to the island of Rhodes, with its towns, villages, forts, and lands, extending to Pisidia, excepting those towns which had been in a state of freedom on the day before that of the battle with Antiochus." The Rhodians, after returning thanks for these favours, mentioned the city of Soli, in Cilicia, "the inhabitants of which," they said, "as well as themselves, derived their origin from Argos: and, in consequence of this relation, a brotherly affection subsisted between the two states. They therefore requested the senate, as an extraordinary favour, to exempt that city from subjection to the king." The ambassadors of Antiochus were called in, and the matter was proposed to them, but their consent could not be obtained; Antipater appealing to the treaty, in opposition to which the Rhodians were striving to become masters, not only of the city of Soli, but of all Cilicia, and to pass beyond the summits of Taurus. The Rhodians were called again before the senate, and the fathers, after acquainting them how earnestly the king's ambassadors opposed the measure, added, that "if the Rhodians were of opinion that the affair was particularly interesting to the dignity of their state, they would use every means to overcome the obstinacy of the ambassadors." Hereon the Rhodians, with greater warmth than before, testified their gratitude, and declared that they would rather give way to the arrogance of Antipater, than afford any reason for disturbing the peace. So no change was made with respect to Soli.

57. During the time of these transactions, intelligence was brought, by messengers from Marseilles, that Lucius Bæbius, the pretor, on his way into his province of Spain, had been surrounded by the Ligurians, great part of his retinue slain, and himself wounded; that he had made his escape, without his lictors, and with but few attendants, to Marseilles, and in three days after expired. The senate, on hearing of this misfortune, decreed that Publius Junius Brutus, who was propretor in Etruria, should leave the command of the province and army to a lieutenant-general, and go himself into Farther Spain, which must be his province. This decree, accompanied with a letter, the pretor Spurius Postumius sent into Etruria, and Publius Junius Brutus, the propretor, set out accordingly. But long before the new governor's arrival in that province, Lucius Æmilius Paulus, who afterward, with great glory, conquered King Perseus, though his efforts had been unsuccessful the year before, hastily collected a body of troops, and fought a pitched battle with the Lucitanians. The enemy were routed, and put to flight; eighteen thousand were killed, three thousand three hundred taken, and their camp stormed. This victory contributed much to tranquillize affairs in Spain. During the same year, on the third day before the calends of January, Lucius Valerius Flaccus, Marcus Atilius Serranus, and Lucius Valerius Tappus, triumvirs, pursuant to a decree of senate, settled a Latine colony at Bononia. The number of the settlers was three thousand men. Seventy acres were given to each horseman, fifty to each of the other colonists. The land had been taken from the Boian Gauls, who had formerly expelled the Tuscans.

58. There were many candidates for the censorship this year, all of them men of illustrious characters; and this business, as if it were not in itself sufficient to excite dispute, gave rise to another contest of a much more violent nature. The candidates were, Titus Quintius Flaminius, Publius Cornelius Scipio, son of Cneius, Lucius Valerius Flaccus, Marcus Porcius Cato, Marcus Claudius Marcellus, and Manius Acilius Glabrio, who had defeated Antiochus and the Ætolians at Thermopylæ. The general favour inclined chiefly to this last; because he had been liberal of his largesses, and had thereby attached great numbers to his interest. As it was a severe mortification to so many of the nobility to see a new man preferred so far before them, Publius Sempronius Gracchus, and Caius Sempronius Rutilus, plebeian tribunes, commenced a prosecution against him, on a charge, that he had neither exhibited in his triumph, nor lodged in the treasury, a large part of the royal treasure, and of the booty taken in the camp of Antiochus. The de-

positions of the lieutenants-general and military tribunes varied. Beyond all the other witnesses Marcus Cato was remarkable; but the deference due to his assertions, from the constant tenor of his life, was greatly impaired by the circumstance of his being himself a candidate. On being examined, he affirmed that he had not observed, in the triumph, the gold and silver vessels which, on the taking of the camp, he had seen among the other spoils of the king. At last, Glabrio declared, that he declined the election, and that chiefly with the view of reflecting discredit on Cato. Men of noble families resented the matter in silence, but he, a competitor, (whose pretensions to nobility were no higher than his own,) endeavoured to counterwork him by perjury, so atrocious, that no fine could be adequate to his guilt. The penalty which his prosecutors proposed to have inflicted was a hundred thousand asses;* and this point was twice argued, but, at a third hearing, as the accused had declined the election, and the people were unwilling to vote about the fine, the tribunes also dropped the business. The censors elected were, Titus Quintius Flaminius and Marcus Claudius Marcellus.

59. At the same time, Lucius Æmilius Regillus, who, at the head of the Roman fleet, had defeated that of King Antiochus, had audience of the senate in the temple of Apollo, outside the city; and, after hearing the recital of his services; his numerous engagements with the enemy; how many of their ships he had sunk and taken, they unanimously voted him a naval triumph. He triumphed on the calends of February. In this procession were carried forty-nine golden crowns; but the quantity of money was not near so great as might be expected in a triumph over a king, being only thirty-four thousand seven hundred Attic tetradrachms,† and one hundred and thirty-one thousand three hundred cistophoruses.‡ Supplications were then performed by order of the senate, in consideration of the successful services to the state achieved in Spain by Lucius Æmilius Paulus. Not long after, Lucius Scipio arrived at the city; and, that he might be equal to his brother in point of a surname, he chose to be called Asiaticus. He recited his services before both the senate and a general assembly. There were some who imagined that the war he had conducted was magnified in the representation beyond its real importance; for it was terminated entirely by one memorable engagement; and that, of the glory acquired there, a share was due to those who conquered before at Thermopylæ. But, to any person judging impartially, it must appear, that the fight at Thermo-

* 322*l.* 18*s.* 4*d.* † 4,482*l.* 1*s.* 8*d.* ‡ About 2,2[illegible]0*l.*

pylæ was with the Ætolians, rather than with the king; for how small a portion of his own strength did Antiochus employ in that battle! whereas, in the other, in Asia, the strength of the whole Asiatic continent stood combined; for he had collected auxiliaries of all nations from the remotest quarters of the east. With good reason, therefore, the greatest possible honours were paid to the immortal gods, for having rendered a most important victory easy in the acquisition; and a triumph was decreed to the commander. He triumphed in the intercalary month, the day before the calends of March; but his triumph, though, in the magnificence of the procession, superior to that of his brother Africanus, yet when we recollect the exploits on which they were grounded, and estimate the dangers and difficulties surmounted, it was no more to be compared to it, than one general to the other, or Antiochus, as a captain, to Hannibal. He carried in his triumph military standards, two hundred and thirty-four; elephants' teeth, one thousand two hundred and twenty; crowns of gold, two hundred and twenty-four; pounds weight of silver, one hundred and thirty-seven thousand four hundred and twenty; Attic tetradrachms, two hundred and twenty-four thousand;* cistophoruses, three hundred and thirty-one thousand and seventy;† gold pieces called Philippics, one hundred and forty thousand;‡ silver vases, all engraved, to the amount of one thousand four hundred and twenty four pounds weight; of golden vases, one thousand and twenty-four pounds weight; and of the king' [illegible] generals, governors, and principal courtiers, thirty-two we[illegible] led before his chariot. He gave to his soldiers twenty-f[illegible] denariuses§ each; double to a centurion, triple to a ho[illegible] man: and after the triumph, their pay and allowance [illegible] corn were doubled. He had already doubled them after [illegible] battle in Asia. His triumph was celebrated about a ye[illegible] after the expiration of his consulship.

60. Cneius Manlius, consul, arrived in Asia, and Quintus Fabius Labeo, pretor, at the fleet, nearly at the same time. The consul did not want reasons for employing his arms against the Gauls; but, at sea, since the final defeat of Antiochus, all was quiet. Fabius, therefore, turned his thoughts to consider what employment he should undertake, that he might not appear to have held a province where nothing was to be done; and he could discover no better plan than to sail over to the island of Crete. The Cydonians were engaged in war against the Gortynians and Gnossians; and it was reported that there were a great number of Roman and other Italian captives in slavery, in various parts of the island.

* 28,984l. 6s. 8d. † 5,699l. 8s. 5d. ‡ 77,629l. 3s. 4d. § 16s. 1 1-2d.

Having sailed with the fleet from Ephesus, as soon as he touched the shore of Crete, he despatched orders to all the states to cease from hostilities, and each of them to search for the captives, in its own cities and territory, and bring them to him; also to send ambassadors to him to treat of matters which equally concerned the Romans and Cretans. The Cretans took little notice of his message: excepting the Gortynians, none of them restored the captives. Valerius Antias writes, that there were restored out of the whole island no less than four thousand captives, in consequence of the fears excited by his threats of a war; and that this was deemed a sufficient reason for Fabius obtaining from the senate a naval triumph, although he performed no other business. From Crete he returned to Ephesus, and despatched thence three ships to the coast of Thrace, with orders to remove the garrison of Antiochus from Ænos and Maronea, that these cities might be left at liberty.

---

## BOOK XXXVIII.

CHAP. 1. WHILE the war raged in Asia, Ætolia was not free from commotions, which took their rise from the nation of the Athamanians. At that period, since the expulsion of Amynander, Athamania was kept in subjection by royal garrisons, under governors appointed by Philip, who by their haughty and overbearing conduct in command had made the people regret the loss of Amynander. Amynander, then in exile in Ætolia, from the letters of his friends, which discovered the condition of Athamania, conceived hopes of recovering his throne, and sent persons to Argithea, the metropolis, to inform the principal men that, if they were sufficiently assured of the inclinations of their countrymen, he would obtain succours from the Ætolians, and come into Athamania with the select council of that nation, and their pretor, Nicander. Finding that they were ready for any undertaking, he gave them notice, from time to time, of the day on which he would enter Athamania at the head of an army. Four persons, at first, conspired against the Macedonian garrison; then each of these associated with himself six assistants for the execution of the business; but afterward thinking it unsafe to rely on so small a number, which was rather calculated for the concealment than for the execution of the design, they took in a number of associates equal to the former. Being thus increased to fifty-two, they divided themselves into four parties; one of which repaired to Heraclea, another to Tetraphylia, where the royal treasure used to be kept, a third to Theudoria, and the fourth to Argithea. It was agreed that they should at first appear in the forum publicly, without any bustle, as if they had come about their own ordinary concerns; and then, on a certain day, raise the whole populace, so as to dislodge the Macedonian garrisons from the citadels. At the appointed time Amynander appeared on the frontiers with a thousand Ætolians; when, as had been concerted, the Macedonian garrisons were driven from the four places at once; while letters were despatched to the other cities, calling on them to rescue themselves from the exorbitant tyranny of Philip, and to reinstate their hereditary and lawful prince. Accordingly, the Macedonians were everywhere expelled. The town of Theium, (in consequence of the letters being intercepted by Teno, commander of the garrison, and of the citadel being occupied by the king's troops,) stood a siege of a few days, and then surrendered, as the rest had done, to Amynander; who had now all Athamania in his power, except the fort of Athenæum, on the borders of Macedonia.

2. When Philip heard of the defection of Athamania he set out at the head of six thousand men, and proceeded with the utmost speed to Gomphi. There he left the greater part of his force, as they would not have been equal to such long marches, and went forward with two thousand, to Athenæum, the only place of which his troops had kept the possession. From some trials, which he made on the nearest places, he clearly perceived that all the rest of the country was hostile to him: returning therefore to Gomphi, he brought the whole of his army into Athamania. He then sent Zeno at the head of one thousand foot, with orders to seize on Ethopia, which stands advantageously for commanding Argithea; and, as soon as he understood that his party were in possession of that post, he himself followed, and encamped near the temple of Acræan Jupiter. Here he was detained one whole day by a tremendous storm; and on the next marched on towards Argithea. The troops had but just begun to move when they immediately descried the Athamanians hastening to the hills which overlooked the road. On the sight of these the foremost battalions halted, fear and confusion spread through the whole army, and every one began to consider what might have been the consequence, if the troops had gone down into the valleys commanded by those cliffs. The king, who wished, if his men would follow him, to push on rapidly through the defile, was obliged, by the confusion that prevailed among them,

to call back the foremost, and return by the same road by which he came. The Athamanians, for some time, followed at a distance, without making any attempt; but being joined by the Ætolians, they left these to harass the rear, while themselves pressed forward on both flanks. Some of them, by taking a shorter way, through known paths, got before the enemy, and seized the passes; and with such dismay were the Macedonians struck, that they repassed the river in a manner more like a hasty flight than a regular march, leaving behind many of their men and arms. Here the pursuit ended; and the Macedonians, without farther injury, returned to Gomphi, and from thence into Macedonia. The Athamanians and Ætolians ran together, from all sides, to Ethopia, to crush Zeno and his thousand Macedonians; who, having little dependance on that post, removed to a hill, which was higher and steeper on all sides. But the Athamanians, making their way up in several places, soon dislodged them; and while they were dispersed, and unable to find the road through a pathless and unknown country, covered with rocks, slew many, and made many prisoners. Great numbers, in their panic, tumbled down the precipices; and a very few, with Zeno, effected their escape to the king. They were afterward allowed liberty to bury the dead; for which purpose a suspension of arms was agreed to.

3. Amynander, on recovering possession of his kingdom, sent ambassadors, both to the senate at Rome and to the Scipios in Asia, who, since the grand battle with Antiochus, resided at Ephesus. He requested a treaty of amity, apologized for having had recourse to the Ætolians for the recovery of his hereditary dominions, and made many charges against Philip. The Ætolians from Athamania proceeded into Amphilochia, and, with the consent of the greater part of the inhabitants, reduced that nation under their power and dominion. After the recovery of Amphilochia, for it had formerly belonged to the Ætolians, they passed on, with hopes of equal success, into Aperantia, which, for the most part, surrendered likewise to the Ætolians without a contest. The Dolopians had never been subject to the Ætolians, but they were to Philip. These, at first, ran to arms; but when they were informed of the Amphilochians taking part with the Ætolians, of Philip's flight out of Athamania, and the destruction of his detachment, they also revolted from Philip to the Ætolians. While these latter flattered themselves with being sufficiently secured against the Macedonians, as being screened on all sides by those states, they received the news of Antiochus being defeated in Asia by the Romans; and in a short time after-

their ambassadors came home from Rome, not only without any prospect of peace, but also with intelligence that the consul Fulvius, with his army, had already crossed the sea. Dismayed at these accounts, they first sent ambassadors to solicit Rhodes and Athens; hoping, through the influence of those states, that their petitions, lately rejected, might meet with a more favourable reception from the senate. They then despatched some of the chief men of their nation to Rome, to try the issue of their last hope, as they had taken no kind of precaution to avert the war until the enemy was almost within sight. Marcus Fulvius, having brought over his army to Apollonia, was at this time consulting with the Epirot chiefs where he should commence his operations. These recommended it to him to attack Ambracia, which had lately united itself to Ætolia; alleging that, "in case the Ætolians should come to its relief, there were open plains around it to fight in; and that if they should avoid a battle, there would be no great difficulty in the siege, as there were at hand abundant materials for raising mounds and other works, while the Aretho, a navigable river, affording an easy conveyance of every thing requisite, flowed by the walls; besides, the summer was just approaching, the fittest season for the enterprise." By these arguments they persuaded him to march on through Epirus.

4. When the consul came to Ambracia he perceived that the siege would be a work of no small difficulty. Ambracia stands at the foot of a rocky hill, called by the natives Perranthe: the city, where the wall faces the plain and the river, is situated towards the west; the citadel, which is seated on the hill, towards the east. The river Aretho, which rises in Acarnania, falls here into a gulf of the sea called the Ambracian, from the name of the adjacent city. Besides, the place being strengthened on one side by the river, and on another by hills, it was defended by a firm wall, extending in circuit somewhat more than three miles, on the side opposite the plain. Fulvius formed two camps, at a short distance from each other, with one fort on the high ground opposite the citadel; all which he intended to join together by a rampart and trench, in such a manner as to leave no passage for the besieged to go out of the city, or for any reinforcement to get in. The Ætolians, on the report of Ambracia being besieged, were by this time assembled at Stratum, in obedience to an edict of their pretor, Nicander. At first they intended to have marched hence with their whole force to raise the siege, but when they heard that the place was already in a great measure surrounded with works, and that the Epirots were encamped on level ground, on the other side of the river, they resolved to divide their forces. Eu-

polemus, with one thousand light troops, marching to Ambracia, made his way into the city through openings where the works were not yet joined. Nicander's first plan was, to have attacked the camp of the Epirots in the night with the rest of the troops, as it would not be easy for them to receive succour from the Romans, the river running between. This enterprise he afterward judged too hazardous, lest the Romans might happen to discover it and cut off his retreat. Being deterred by these considerations from the prosecution of that design, he marched away to ravage the country of Acarnania.

5. The consul having completed his works for the circumvallation of the city, and likewise those which were to be brought forward to the walls, formed five attacks at once against the place: three, at equal distances from each other, he directed against the quarter which they called Pyrrheum; to which, as it lay next the plain, the approach was the easier; one opposite to the temple of Æsculapius, and one against the citadel. The battlements were at one post battered with rams, and at another torn down with poles, armed at the end with hooks. At first the formidable appearance of the works, and the shocks given to the walls, attended with a dreadful noise, filled the townsmen with terror and dismay: but as, beyond their hopes, these still stood, they again resumed courage, and, by means of cranes, threw down on the battering-rams weighty masses of lead, or stone, or beams of timber. Catching, likewise, the armed poles with iron grapples, they drew them within the walls, and broke off the hooks: while by sallies, both in the night against the watch-guards, and in the day against the advanced posts, they kept the besiegers in a state of continual alarm. While affairs at Ambracia were in this state, the Ætolians, having returned from ravaging Acarnania to Stratum, their pretor, Nicander, conceived hopes of raising the siege by a bold effort. He sent a person called Nicodamus, accompanied by five hundred Ætolians, with orders to get into Ambracia; having fixed on a certain night, and even on the hour when, from within the city, they were to assault the works of the enemy, opposite to the Pyrrheum, while himself should alarm the Roman camp. His opinion was, that in consequence of the tumult in both places at once, and of darkness augmenting the enemy's fears, he might be able to effect something of importance. Nicodamus, during the dead of the night, (having escaped the notice of some of the parties on watch, and broken through others,) without halting, passed the intrenchment, and made his way into the city; which gave the besieged new hopes, and courage for any enterprise. As soon as the ap-

pointed time arrived, according to concert, he made a sudden assault on the works; but the attempt, though formidable at first, produced no great effect, there being no attack made from without: for the pretor of the Ætolians had either been deterred by fear, or had judged it more advisable to carry succours to Amphilochia, which had been lately reduced, and was now very vigorously besieged by Philip's son Perseus, sent by his father to recover both that and Dolopia.

6. The Romans, as has been mentioned, carried on their works against the Pyrrheum in three different places, all which works the Ætolians assaulted at once, but not with like weapons or like force. Some advanced with burning torches, others carrying tow and pitch, and firebrands, so that their whole band appeared in a blaze of fire. Their first assault cut off many of the men on guard; but when the shout and uproar reached the camp, and the signal was given by the consul, the troops took arms, and poured out of all the gates to succour their friends. In one place the contest was carried on with fire and sword; from the other two the Ætolians retired with disappointment, after essaying rather than supporting a fight; while the whole brunt of the battle fell on the one quarter with great fury. Here the two commanders, Eupolemus and Nicodamus, in their different posts, encouraged their men, and animated them with hope nearly certain, that Nicander would, according to his agreement, come up speedily, and attack the enemy's rear. This expectation for some time supported their courage in the fight; but at last, as they did not receive the concerted signal from their friends, and saw the number of their enemies continually increasing, they slackened their efforts, considering themselves as deserted; and, in a short time, finally abandoned the attempt, when they could scarcely retreat with safety. They were obliged to fly into the city, after having burned a part of the works, however, and killed a much greater number than they lost. If the affair had been conducted according to the plan concerted, there was no reason to doubt but one part, at least, of the works, might have been stormed with great havoc of the Romans. The Ambracians, and the Ætolians who were within, not only renounced the enterprise of that night, but, supposing themselves betrayed by their friends, became much less spirited. None of them any longer sallied out, as before, against the enemy's posts; and, standing on the walls and towers, fought without danger.

7. Perseus, on hearing of the approach of the Ætolians, raised the siege of the city in which he was employed; and, having done nothing more than ravaged the country, quitted

Amphilochia, and returned into Macedonia. The Ætolians too were called away by devastations committed on their coasts. Pleuratus, king of the Illyrians, entered the Corinthian gulf with sixty barks, and being joined by the ships of the Achæans lying at Patræ, wasted the maritime parts of Ætolia. Against these were sent one thousand Ætolians, who, to whatever place the fleet steered round, by taking shorter roads across the windings of the coasts, were ready there to oppose them. The Romans at Ambracia, by the battering of their rams in many places at once, laid open a great part of the city; but, nevertheless, were unable to penetrate into the heart of it: for no sooner was a part of the wall demolished, than a new one was raised in its place, while the armed men, standing on the ruins, formed a kind of bulwark. The consul, therefore, finding that he made no progress by open force, resolved to form a secret mine, covering the ground first with his machines. For a long time his workmen, though employed both night and day, not only in digging, but also in carrying away the earth, escaped the observation of the enemy. A heap of it, however, rising suddenly, gave the townsmen the first intimation of what was going on, and, terrified lest the wall should be already undermined, and a passage opened into the city, they drew a trench within, opposite to the work that was covered with machines. This they sunk as deep as the bottom of the mine could well be; then, keeping profound silence, they applied their ears to several different places to catch the sound of the miners employed. No sooner was this heard, than they opened a way directly towards them, which did not require much labour, for they came in a short time to where the wall was supported with props by the enemy. The works joining here, and the passage being open from the trench to the mine, the parties began to fight in the dark under ground; the miners with the tools which they had used in the works, but they were soon supported by armed men. The warmth however of this contest soon abated; for the besieged had it in their power, whenever they pleased, to stop the passage, sometimes by stretching strong hair cloths across it, sometimes by hastily placing doors in the way of their antagonists. They also played off against those in the mine a contrivance of an unusual kind, which required no great labour. They took a large vessel, and bored a hole in its bottom of a moderate size; in this they fixed an iron pipe, and put over the vessel a cover also of iron, perforated in many places: this vessel they filled with small feathers; and, turning the mouth of it towards the mine, through the holes in the covering, projected those long spears which they call sarissas to keep off the enemy. They then put a small spark of fire among the feathers, which they kindled by blowing with a smith's bellows inserted into the end of the pipe, and by this means filled the whole mine with smoke, which was not only thick, but so offensive, from the nauseous stench of the burnt feathers, that it was scarcely possible for any one to remain in the way of it.

8. While such was the situation of affairs at Ambracia, Phæneas and Damoteles came to the consul as ambassadors from the Ætolians, invested with full powers by a decree of the general assembly of that nation: for when their pretor saw, on one side, Ambracia besieged; on another, the sea-coast infested by the enemy's ships; on a third, Amphilochia and Dolopia ravaged by the Macedonians, and that the Ætolians were incapable of resisting the three enemies at once, he summoned a council, and demanded the judgment of the chiefs on the measures to be pursued. The opinions of all tended to one point: that peace must be obtained on as easy terms as possible. Having undertaken the war, relying on the support of Antiochus, now that Antiochus had been vanquished on land and sea, and driven beyond the mountains of Taurus, indeed, almost out of the world, what hope remained of their being able to support it? Let Phæneas and Damoteles act to the best of their judgment, for the service of the Ætolians, in their present circumstances. But what room for counsel, what option had fortune left them?" The ambassadors despatched with these instructions besought the consul to "have mercy on the city, and to take compassion on a nation, once acknowledged as an ally; and since driven to desperation, they would not say by ill treatment, but undoubtedly by their sufferings. The Ætolians," they said, "had not in Antiochus's war deserved a larger share of punishment than they had of reward in that against Philip; and as, in the last-mentioned case, the compensation made to them was not very liberal, neither ought their penalties now to be excessive." To this the consul answered that "the Ætolians had often, indeed, sued for peace, but never with sincere intentions. Let them, in soliciting peace, imitate Antiochus, whom they had drawn into the war. He had ceded, not the few cities whose liberty was the ground of the dispute, but an opulent kingdom, all Asia, on this side Mount Taurus. That he, the consul, would not listen to any overtures whatever from the Ætolians until they laid down their arms. They must, in the first place, deliver up these, and all their horses; and then pay one thousand talents* to the Roman people; half of which sum

* 193,750*l*.

must be laid down immediately, if they wished for peace. To these articles he would add, in the treaty, that they must have the same allies and the same enemies as the Roman people."

9. The ambassadors, considering these terms as very unreasonable, and knowing the changeful tempers of their countrymen, made no reply, but returned home, that they might again, before any thing was concluded, receive the instructions of the pretor and council. They were received with clamour and reproaches for protracting the business, and commanded to bring with them a peace of some kind or other. But as they were going back to Ambracia they were caught in an ambuscade, laid near the road by the Acarnanians, with whom they were at war, and carried to Tyrrheum into confinement. This accident delayed the conclusion of the peace. The ambassadors of the Athenians and Rhodians, who had come to mediate in their favour, were now with the consul; and Amynander also, king of Athamania, having obtained a safe conduct, came into the Roman camp, being more concerned for the city of Ambracia, where he had spent the greatest part of his exile, than for the nation of the Ætolians. When the consul was informed by them of the accident which had befallen the ambassadors, he ordered them to be brought from Tyrrheum; and, on their arrival, the negotiations for peace were opened. Amynander, as that was his principal object, laboured assiduously to persuade the Ambracians to a capitulation. But, finding that he could not accomplish this by coming under the walls and conferring with their chiefs, he at last, with the consul's permission, went into the city; where, partly by arguments, partly by entreaties, he prevailed on them to surrender themselves to the Romans. The Ætolians received also great assistance from the consul's uterine brother, Caius Valerius, the son of Lævinus, the first who had made a treaty of alliance with that nation. The Ambracians, having first stipulated that they might send away the auxiliary Ætolians in safety, opened their gates. The conditions then prescribed to the Ætolians were, that "they should pay five hundred Euboic talents,* two hundred at present, and three hundred at six equal annual payments; that they should deliver up to the Romans the prisoners and deserters; that they should not claim jurisdiction over any city which, since the first coming of Titus Quintius into Greece, had either been taken by the arms of the Romans, or voluntarily entered into alliance with them; and that the island of Cephalenia should not be included in the treaty." Although these terms were

* About 96,000l.

more moderate than they themselves had expected, yet the Ætolians begged permission to lay them before the council, and their request was granted. The council spent some time in debating about the cities which, having been once members of their state, they could not without pain bear to have torn off, as it were, from their body. However, they unanimously voted that the terms of peace should be accepted. The Ambracians presented the consul with a golden crown of one hundred and fifty pounds weight. The brazen and marble statues with which Ambracia was more richly decorated than any other city in that country, as having been the royal residence of Pyrrhus, were all removed and carried away; but nothing else was injured, or even touched.

10. The consul, marching into the interior parts of Ætolia, encamped at Amphilochian Argos, twenty-two miles from Ambracia. Here, at length, the Ætolian ambassadors, whose delay had surprised the consul, arrived. When they informed him that the council had approved the terms of peace, he ordered them to go to Rome to the senate; gave permission for the Athenian and Rhodian mediators to go with them; appointed his brother, Caius Valerius, to accompany them, and then himself passed over to Cephalenia. The ambassadors found the ears and minds of all the principal people at Rome prepossessed by charges made against them by Philip, who had complained, both by ambassadors and by letters, that Dolopia, Amphilochia, and Athamania, had been forcibly taken from him; that his garrison, and, at last, even his son Perseus, had been driven out of Amphilochia; and these accusations had predisposed the senate to refuse to listen to their entreaties. The Athamanians and Rhodians were, nevertheless, heard with attention. One of the Athenian ambassadors, Leon, son of Icesias, is said to have even affected them much by his eloquence. Making use of a common simile, and comparing the multitude of Ætolians to a calm sea, when it comes to be ruffled by the winds, he said, that "as long as they faithfully adhered to the alliance with Rome, they rested in the calm state natural to the nations; but that, when Thoas and Dicæarchus began to blow from Asia, Menetas and Damocrites from Europe, then was raised that storm which dashed them on Antiochus as on a rock."

11. The Ætolians, after long suspense and uncertainty, at length prevailed to have articles of peace concluded. They were these: "The Ætolian nation, without fraud or deceit, shall maintain the empire and majesty of the Roman people; they shall not suffer to pass through their territories, nor, in any manner whatever, aid nor assist any army that shall march against the allies and friends of the Romans; they

shall have the same enemies as the Roman people; and they shall bear arms against them, and take a share in their wars; they shall deliver up the deserters, fugitives, and prisoners, to the Romans and their allies, excepting such as, having been prisoners before, and returned home, were afterward captured; and also such as at the time of their being taken were enemies to Rome, while the Ætolians acted in conjunction with the Romans. The others shall be delivered up without reserve to the magistrates of Corcyra, within one hundred days; and such as cannot now be found, as soon as they shall be discovered. They shall give forty hostages to be chosen by the Roman consul, none younger than twelve years, nor older than forty; neither the pretor, nor the general of the horse, nor the public secretary, shall be a hostage; nor any person who has been before a hostage in the hands of the Romans. Cephalenia not to be included in these articles." With respect to the sum of money which they were to pay, and the mode of payment, no alteration was made in the arrangement settled by the consul. If they chose to give gold instead of silver, it was agreed that they might do so, provided that one piece of gold should be deemed equivalent to ten of silver of the same weight. "Whatever cities, whatever lands, whatever men have been formerly under the jurisdiction of the Ætolians, and have, either in the consulate of Titus Quintius and Publius Ælius, or since their consulate, either been subdued by the arms of the Roman people, or that made a voluntary submission to them, the Ætolians are not to reclaim. The Œnians, with their city and lands, are to belong to the Acarnanians." On these conditions was the treaty concluded with the Ætolians.

12. During the same summer, and even at the very time, when the consul, Marcus Fulvius, was thus employed in Ætolia, the other consul, Cneius Manlius, carried on war in Gallogræcia; the progress of which I shall now relate. At the first opening of spring he came to Ephesus, and having received the command of the army from Lucius Scipio, and purified the troops, he made an harangue to the soldiers, in which he praised their bravery in having completely conquered Antiochus in a single battle. He then encouraged them to undertake, with spirit, a new war against the Gauls, who had supported him as auxiliaries; and were, besides, of such untractable tempers, that the removing of that monarch beyond the mountains of Taurus would answer no purpose, unless the power of the Gauls were reduced. He then spoke briefly of himself, in terms neither ill-grounded nor extravagant. They listened to his discourse with much satisfaction, and universally applauded it: for, considering the Gauls as having been a part of the strength

of Antiochus, they thought that, since that king had been vanquished, the forces of that people, by themselves, would be an easy conquest. The absence of Eumenes, who was then at Rome, seemed to the consul an unseasonable circumstance, as he was well acquainted with the nature of the country and of the inhabitants; and also, as his own interest must make him wish to crush the power of the Gauls. He therefore sent for his brother Attalus from Pergamus whom he persuaded to join in undertaking the war; and who, having promised his assistance, and that of his countrymen, was sent home to make the necessary preparations. A few days after the consul began his march from Ephesus, and at Magnesia Attalus met him with one thousand foot and two hundred horse, having ordered his brother Athenæus to follow with the rest of his troops, committing the care of Pergamus to persons whom he knew to be faithful to his brother, and to his government. The consul highly commended the young prince, and, advancing with all his forces, encamped on the bank of the Mæander, for that river not being fordable, it was necessary to collect shipping for carrying over the army.

13. Having passed the Mæander, they came to Hiera Come.* In this place there is a magnificent temple and oracle of Apollo, where responses are said to be given in not in elegant verses. From hence, in two days' march, they reached the river Harpasus; whither came ambassadors from the Alabandians, entreating the consul, either by his authority or his arms, to compel a fort which had lately revolted from them, to return to its former allegiance. At the same place he was joined by Athenæus, the brother of Eumenes, and Attalus, with Leusus, a Cretan, and Corragos, a Macedonian commander. They brought with them of various nations, one thousand foot and three hundred horse. The consul detached a military tribune, with a small party, who retook the fort by assault, and restored it to the Alabandians. He did not himself quit his route, but went on to Antiochia, on the Mæander, where he pitched his camp. The source of this river rises in Celænæ, which city was formerly the metropolis of Phrygia. The inhabitants afterward removed to a spot not far distant from Old Celænæ, which new city they called Apamea, the name of the wife of King Seleucus. The river Marsyas also rising at a little distance from the head of the Mæander, falls into the latter river, and the general opinion is, that at Celænæ happened the contest between Marsyas and Apollo in playing on the flute. The Mæander, springing up in the highest part of the cit-

* Holy Town.

adel of Cælenæ, runs down through the middle of the city, then through Caria, afterward through Ionia, and empties itself into a bay which lies between Priene and Miletus. Seleucus, son of Antiochus, came into the consul's camp at Antiochia, to furnish corn for the troops, in conformity to the treaty with Scipio. Here a small dispute arose concerning the auxiliary troops of Attalus; for Seleucus affirmed that the engagement of Antiochus went no farther than the supplying of corn to the Roman soldiers. This difference was soon terminated by the firmness of the consul, who sent a tribune with orders that the Roman soldiers should receive none, until the auxiliaries, under Attalus, should have received their share. From hence the army advanced to Gordiutichos,* as it is called: from which place it marched in three days to Tabæ. This city stands on the confines of Pisidia, on the side opposite the Pamphylian sea. Before the strength of their country was reduced, its inhabitants had been remarkable as valiant warriors; and even on this occasion their horsemen, sallying out on the Roman troops, caused, by their first onset, no small confusion; but soon finding themselves overmatched both in number and bravery, they fled into the city, on which the townsmen, begging pardon for their transgressions, offered to surrender the place. They were ordered to pay twenty-five talents of silver,† and ten thousand bushels of wheat; and on these terms their surrender was accepted.

14. On the third day after their leaving this place the army reached the river Chaos, and proceeding thence, took the city of Eriza at the first assault. They then came to Thabusios, a fort standing on the bank of the river Indus, so called from an Indian thrown into it from an elephant. They were now not far from Cibyra, yet no embassy appeared from Moagetes, the tyrant of that state; a man whose conduct in every circumstance was branded with infidelity and injustice. The consul, in order to learn his intentions, sent forward Caius Helvius, with four thousand foot and five hundred horse. When this party entered his frontiers, they were met by ambassadors, who declared that Moagetes was willing to submit to their orders; entreated Helvius to pass through the country without hostilities, and to restrain his soldiers from plundering it; bringing with them in lieu of a golden crown fifteen talents. Helvius promised to protect their territory, and ordered the ambassadors to go on to the consul, who, on the same message being delivered by them, answered, "We Romans see no signs of the tyrant having any good-will towards us; and we are decidedly of

* The Gordian wall. † 4,843*l.* 15*s.*

opinion, that such is his character, that we ought rather to think of punishing than of contracting friendship with him." Struck with astonishment at such a reception, the ambassadors confined their request to his acceptance of the fifteen talents, with permission for their master to come before him, and vindicate his conduct. Having obtained the consul's leave, the tyrant came next day into the camp. His dress and retinue were in a style scarcely becoming a private person of moderate fortune; while his discourse was humble and incoherent, tending to diminish the idea of his wealth, being filled with complaints of his own poverty, and that of the cities in his state. He had under his dominion, besides Cibyra, Syleum, and the city called Alimne. Out of these he promised, (but in such a manner as if he were diffident of his ability to accomplish it, by stripping himself and his subjects,) to raise twenty-five talents. "This," said the consul, "is not to be endured. Was it not enough that you should endeavour to impose on us by your ambassadors, but you must now come in person to persist in the falsehood? What! twenty-five talents will exhaust your dominions! If, within three days, you do not pay down five hundred talents,* expect to see your lands wasted, and your city besieged." Although terrified by this menace, yet he persisted obstinately in his plea of poverty; gradually advancing, however, with sordid reluctance, (sometimes cavilling, sometimes recurring to prayers and counterfeit tears,) he was brought to agree to the payment of one hundred talents,† to which were added ten thousand bushels of corn; all this was done within six days.

15. From Cibyra the army was led through the territory of the Sendians, and after crossing the river Caular, encamped. Next day they marched along the side of the lake of Caralis, and passed the night at Mandropolis. As they advanced to the next city, Lagos, the inhabitants fled through fear. The place being deserted, yet filled with abundance of every thing, was pillaged by the soldiers. They next day proceeded by the head of the river Lysis, to the river Cobulatus. At this time the Termessians were besieging the citadel of the Isiondians, after having taken the city. The besieged, destitute of every other hope of relief, sent ambassadors to the consul, imploring succour; adding that, "being shut up in the citadel with their wives and children, they were in daily expectation of perishing, either by the sword or famine." The consul was well pleased at an occasion offering for turning aside to Pamphylia. His approach raised the siege of Isionda. He granted peace to

* 96,875l. † 19,375l.

Termessus on receiving fifty talents;* and, likewise, to the Aspendians and other states of Pamphylia. In his return out of that country he pitched his camp the first day at the river Taurus, and the second at Come Xyline,† as they call it. Departing from which, he proceeded by uninterrupted marches to the city of Cormasa. The next city was Darsa, which he found abandoned by the inhabitants through fear, but plentifully stored with every thing useful. As he marched thence along the morasses, he was met by ambassadors from Lysinoe, with the surrender of that state. He then came into the Sagalassenian territory, rich and abounding in every kind of production. The inhabitants are Pisidians, the best soldiers by far of any in that part of the world. This circumstance, together with the fertility of their soil, the multitude of their people, and the situation of their city, which is stronger than most others, gave them boldness. Manlius, as no embassy attended him on the frontiers, sent a party to ravage the country; which overcame their obstinacy, as they saw their effects carried and driven away. They then sent ambassadors; and on their agreeing to pay fifty talents, with twenty thousand bushels of wheat and twenty thousand of barley, they obtained peace. The consul then marched to the source of the Obrima, and encamped at the village called Comi Aporidos. Hither Seleucus came next day from Apamea; to which place the sick and the useless baggage were sent; and the army being furnished with guides by Seleucus, and marching that day into the plain of Metropolis, advanced on the day following to Diniæ in Phrygia, and thence to Synnas, all the towns on every side being deserted by the inhabitants through fear. The spoil of these overloaded the army, and retarded its motion so much, that it scarcely marched five miles in a whole day; when it reached the town called Old Beudi. Next day it encamped at Anabura; on the following, at the source of the Alander, and on the third at Abassus, where it lay for several days, being now arrived at the borders of the Tolistoboians.

16. These Gauls, in a very numerous body, quitting their native country, under the conduct of Brennus, either through hopes of plunder, or in consequence of a scarcity of land; and thinking that no nation through which they were to pass would be a match for them in arms, made their way into Dardania. There a dissension arose, and twenty thousand of them, under the chieftains Leonorius and Lutarius, separating from Brennus, turned their route to Thrace. As they went along, they fought with such as resisted them, imposed a tribute on such as sued for peace, and arriving at Byzantium, held possession for a long time of the cities in

* 9,687l. 10s. † The wood town.

that quarter, laying the coast of the Propontis under contribution. They were afterward seized by a desire of passing over into Asia, from the accounts which they heard in its neighbourhood of the great fruitfulness of its lands; and, having taken Lysimachia by treachery, and possessed themselves of the whole Chersonesus by force of arms, they went down to the Hellespont. When they there beheld Asia on the other side of a narrow strait, their wishes to pass into it were much more highly inflamed, and they despatched envoys to Antipater, governor of that coast, to adjust matters relating to their passage. But this business being protracted to a greater length than they expected, a new quarrel broke out between their chieftains; in consequence of which, Leonorius, with the greater part of the people, went back to Byzantium, whence they came; and Lutarius, having taken from some Macedonians (sent by Antipater as spies, under the pretext of an embassy) two decked ships and three barks, employed these in carrying over one division after another, by day or by night, until, within a few days, he had transported his whole army. Not long after Leonorius, with the assistance of Nicomedes, king of Bithynia, passed over from Byzantium. The Gauls then reunited their forces, and assisted Nicomedes in a war which he was carrying on against Zybœa, who held possession of a part of Bithynia. By their assistance chiefly, Zybœa was subdued, and the whole of Bithynia reduced under the dominion of Nicomedes. Then leaving Bithynia, they advanced into Asia; and although, of their twenty thousand men, not more than ten carried arms, yet such a degree of terror did they strike into all the natives dwelling on this side of Taurus, that those which they visited, and those which they did not visit, the remotest as well as the nearest, submitted to their authority. At length, as there were three tribes of them, the Tolistoboians, the Trocmians, and the Tectosagians, they made a division of Asia into three provinces, according to which the contributions imposed on them were to be paid to each of their states respectively. The coast of the Hellespont was assigned to the Trocmians; Ionia and Æolia were allotted to the Tolistoboians, and the inland parts of Asia to the Tectosagians. They levied tribute throughout every part of Asia, but chose their own residence on the banks of the river Halys; and so great was the terror of their name, their numbers, too, increasing by a rapid population, that at last even the kings of Syria did not refuse to pay them tribute. The first of all the inhabitants of Asia, who ventured a refusal was Attalus, the father of King Eumenes; and beyond the expectation of all, fortune favoured his bold resolution. He defeated them in a pitched battle; yet he did not so effectually break their spirits as to make them give up their pretensions to empire. Their power continued the same until the war between Antiochus and the Romans; and, even then, after Antiochus was expelled the country, they still entertained a hope that, as they lived remote from sea, the Roman army would not come so far.

17. As the troops were about to act against this enemy, so terrible to all in that part of the world, the consul, calling them to an assembly, spoke to this effect: "It is not unknown to me that, of all the nations inhabiting Asia, the Gauls have the highest reputation as soldiers. A fierce nation, after overrunning the face of the earth with its arms, has fixed its abode in the midst of a race of men the gentlest in the world. Their tall persons, their long red hair, their vast shields, and swords of enormous length; their songs also, when they are advancing to action, their yells and dances, and the horrid clashing of their armour, while they brandish their shields in a peculiar manner, practised in their original country; all these are circumstances calculated to strike terror. But let Greeks, and Phrygians, and Carians, who are unaccustomed to, and unacquainted with these things, be frightened by such; the Romans, long acquainted with Gallic tumults, have learned the emptiness of their parade. Once, indeed, in an early period, they defeated our ancestors at the Allia. Ever since that time, for, now, two hundred years, the Romans drive them before them in dismay, and kill them like cattle; there have, indeed, been more triumphs celebrated over the Gauls than over almost all the rest of the world. It is now well known by experience, that if you sustain their first onset, which they make with fiery eagerness, and blind fury, their limbs are unnerved with sweat and fatigue; their arms flag; and, though you should not employ a weapon on them, the sun, dust, and thirst, sink their enervate bodies, and their no less enervate minds. We have tried them, not only with our legions against theirs, but in single combat, man to man. Titus Manlius and Marcus Valerius have demonstrated how far Roman valour surpasses Gallic fury. Marcus Manlius, singly, thrust back the Gauls who were mounting the capitol in a body. Our forefathers had to deal with genuine native Gauls; but they are now degenerate, a mongrel race, and, in reality, what they are named, Gallogræcians; just as is the case of vegetables; the seeds not being so efficacious for preserving their original constitution, as the properties of the soil and climate in which they may be reared, when changed, are towards altering it. The Macedonians who settled at Alexandria in Egypt, or in Seleucia, or Babylonia, or in any other of their colonies scattered over the world, have sunk

into Syrians, Parthians, or Egyptians. Marseilles, by being situated in the midst of Gauls, has contracted somewhat of the disposition of its adjoining neighbours. What trace do the Tarentines retain of the hardy rugged discipline of Sparta? Every thing that grows in its own natural soil attains the greater perfection; whatever is planted in a foreign land, by a gradual change in its nature, degenerates into a similitude to that which affords it nurture. You will therefore fight with men of the like description as those whom you have already vanquished and cut to pieces; those Phrygians, encumbered with Gallic armour, in the battle with Antiochus. I fear that they will not oppose us sufficiently, so as that we may acquire honour from our victory. King Attalus often routed and put them to flight. Brutes retain for a time, when taken, their natural ferocity: but, after being long fed by the hands of men, they grow tame. Think you, then, that nature does not act in the same manner, in softening the savage tempers of men? Do you believe these to be of the same kind that their fathers and grandfathers were? Driven from home by want of land, they marched along the craggy coast of Illyricum; then fought their way, against the fiercest nations, through the whole length of Pæonia and Thrace, and took possession of these countries. After being hardened, yet soured, by so great hardships, they gained admittance here; a territory capable of glutting them with an abundance of every thing desirable. By the very great fertility of the soil, the very great mildness of the climate, and the gentle dispositions of the neighbouring nations, all that barbarous fierceness which they brought with them has been quite mollified. As for you, who are sons of Mars, believe me, you ought, from the very beginning, to guard against, and shun, above all things, the enticing delights of Asia; so great is the power of those foreign pleasures in extinguishing the vigour of the mind, so strong the contagion from the relaxed discipline and manners of the people about you. One thing has happened fortunately; that though they will not bring against you a degree of strength by any means equal to what they formerly possessed; yet they still retain a character among the Greeks equal to what they had at their first coming; consequently, you will acquire, by subduing them, as high renown among the allies for military prowess, as if they had kept up to their ancient standard of courage."

18. He then dismissed the assembly; and, having despatched ambassadors to Eposognatus, (who alone, of all the petty princes, had remained in friendship with Eumenes, and refused to assist Antiochus against the Romans,) proceeded on his march. He came, the first day, to the river

Alander, and the next to a village called Tyscos. Here he was met by ambassadors from the Oroandians, begging to be admitted into friendship. He ordered them to pay two hundred talents;* and, on their requesting liberty to report that matter at home, gave them permission. He then led the army to Plitendos, and, proceeding thence, encamped at Alyatti. The persons sent to Epossognatus returned to him here, and with them ambassadors from that chieftain, who entreated him not to make war on the Tolistoboians, for that Epossognatus himself would go among that people and persuade them to submission. This request of the prince was complied with. The army then marched through the country called Axylos,† which name was given from the nature of the place, being entirely destitute not only of timber, but even of brambles, or any other species of fire-wood. The inhabitants, instead of wood, use cow dung. While the Romans were encamped at Cuballum, a fort of Gallogræcia, a party of the enemy's cavalry appeared advancing with great fury. And they not only disordered by their sudden charge the advanced guards of the Romans, but killed several of the men. No sooner, however, did the uproar reach the camp, than the Roman cavalry, pouring out hastily by all the gates, routed and dispersed the Gauls, killing many as they fled. The consul, now, perceiving that he had reached the enemy's country, took care for the future to explore the ground through which his route led, and to keep a proper guard on his rear. Having by continued marches arrived at the river Sangarius, he set about constructing a bridge, no passable ford being anywhere found. The Sangarius, running from the mountain of Adoreos, through Phrygia, joins the river Thymbris at the confines of Bithynia. After doubling its quantity of water by this junction, it proceeds, in a more copious stream, through Bithynia, and empties itself into the Euxine sea. Yet it is not so remarkable for the size of its current, as for the vast quantity of fish which it supplies to the people in its vicinity. When the bridge was finished, and the army had passed the river, as they were marching along the bank, they were met by the Gallic priests of the Great Mother, from Pessinus, with the symbols of their office; who, in rhymes, which they chanted as if they were inspired, foretold that the goddess would grant the Romans a safe passage, success in the war, and the empire over that country. The consul, saying that he embraced the omen, pitched his camp on that very spot. On the following day he arrived at Gordium. This town, though not very large, is a celebrated and well-frequented

* 38,750*l.*    † Woodless.

mart, exceeding, in that respect, most other inland places. It has the advantage of three seas, nearly equidistant from it, that at Hellespontus, that at Sinope, and that on the opposite coast of Cilicia. It is also contiguous to the borders of many and great nations, the commerce of which, mutual convenience caused to centre principally in this place. The Romans found the town deserted by the inhabitants through fear, yet at the same time filled with plenty of every thing. While they halted here, ambassadors came from Eposognatus, with information, that "he had applied to the petty princes of the Gauls, but could not bring them to reason; that they were removing in crowds from the villages and lands in the open country; and, with their wives and children, carrying and driving whatever could be carried or driven, were going to Mount Olympus, where they hoped to defend themselves by their arms and the nature of the ground."

19. Deputies from the Oroandians brought, afterward, more particular intelligence; that "the state of the Tolistoboians had seized Mount Olympus, but that the Tectosagians, taking a different route, were gone to another mountain called Magaba; and that the Trocmians, leaving their wives and children in charge with the Tectosagians, had resolved to carry their armed force to the assistance of the Tolistoboians." The chieftains of the three states, at that time, were Ortiagon, Combolomarus, and Gaulotus; and their principal reason for choosing this mode of conducting the war was, that as they had possession of the highest mountains in that part of the world, and had conveyed thither stores of every kind, sufficient for their consumption during a long time, they thought that the enemy would be wearied out by the tediousness of the enterprise: being fully persuaded, that "they would never venture to climb over places so steep and uneven; that if such an attempt should be made, a small number would be able to repulse and drive them down; and that they never could bring themselves to sit inactive, at the foot of black mountains, exposed to cold and hunger." Although the height of their posts was, in itself, a strong defence, yet they drew, besides, a trench and other fortifications round the summits which they occupied. The least part of their care was employed in providing a stock of missile weapons; for they trusted that the rocky ground itself would furnish stones in abundance.

20. The consul, having foreseen that his men could not come to a close engagement, in the attack of the enemy's post, had prepared an immense quantity of javelins, light infantry, spears, arrows, balls of lead, and small stones, fit to be thrown with slings. Furnished with this stock of missile weapons,

he marched towards Mount Olympus, and encamped within five miles of it. Next day, accompanied by Attalus, he advanced, with an escort of four hundred horse, to examine the nature of the mountain, and situation of the camp of the Gauls; but a party of the enemy's cavalry, double in number to his, sallying out, obliged them to retire. He even lost some men in the retreat, and had more wounded. On the third day he went to make his observations, at the head of all his cavalry; and none of the enemy coming out beyond their fortifications, he rode round the mountain with safety. He saw that, on the south side, the hills were composed of earth, and rose to a certain height, with a gentle slope, but that, on the north, there was nothing but steep and almost perpendicular cliffs. He found, too, that there were but three ways by which the troops could ascend; one at the middle of the mountain, where the ground was earthy, and two others, both very difficult, one on the southeast, and the other on the northwest. After taking a full view of all these places, he pitched his camp, that day, close to the foot of the mountain. On the day following, after offering sacrifice, in which the first victims afforded the desired omens, he advanced against the enemy with his army in three divisions. He himself, with the greatest part of the forces, marched up where the mountain afforded the easiest ascent. He ordered his brother, Lucius Manlius, to mount on the southeast side, as far as the ground allowed him to ascend with safety; but if he should meet such precipices as he could not surmount without danger, then, not to contend with the unfavourable nature of the place, or attempt to conquer obstacles insuperable, but to come sloping across the mountain towards him, and join the body under his command; and he directed Caius Helvius, with the third division, to march round leisurely by the foot of the mountain, and to climb the hill on the northeast. The auxiliary troops of Attalus he distributed equally among the three divisions, ordering the young prince to accompany them himself. The cavalry and elephants he left in the plain, at the foot of the hills, charging the commanding officers to watch attentively every thing that should happen, and to be expeditious in bringing succour wherever circumstances should require.

21. The Gauls, (thoroughly satisfied that the ground on their two flanks was impassable,) in order to secure, by arms, the ascent on the south side, sent about four thousand soldiers to keep possession of a hill which hung over the road, at the distance of near a mile from their camp; hoping that this would serve as a fortress to stop the enemy's progress. On seeing this, the Romans prepared for the fight. The light infantry advanced, at a small distance, in

the front of the line; and, of Attalus's troops, the Cretan archers and slingers, the Trallians and Thracians. The battalions of infantry, as the ground was steep, marched at a slow pace, holding their shields before them, merely to ward off missile weapons, for there was no likelihood of a close engagement. As soon as they came within reach, the fight commenced with the missile weapons, and continued for a short time equal; the Gauls having the advantage in situation, the Romans in variety and plenty of weapons. But, as the contest advanced, this equality was soon lost: the Gauls carried long shields, but too narrow for the breadth of their bodies; and even these were flat, and therefore afforded but a bad defence. Besides, in a little time they had nothing left but swords, which, as the enemy did not come close, were useless. They had only stones to throw, and those not of a proper size, as they had laid in no store of such, but used whatever each, in his hurry and confusion, found next at hand; and then being unused to this manner of fighting, they did not know how to aid the blow with either skill or strength. At the same time every part was assailed with arrows, leaden balls, and darts; the approach of which they could not perceive, and scarcely conscious, indeed, of what they were doing, so blinded were they by rage and fear together; while they found themselves engaged in a kind of fight, for which they were utterly unqualified. When close with an enemy, and where they can receive and give wounds in turn, rage inflames their courage; but when they are wounded at a distance, with light weapons from unknown hands, and have no object on which they can vent their intemperate fury, like wounded wild beasts, they rush forward at random, and often on their own party. Their wounds made the greater show, because they always fight naked. Their bodies are plump, —consequently the blood flowed in greater quantity,—and their skins white, being never stripped except in battle. Thus the cuts appeared the more shocking, while the whiteness of their skins made the black stains of the blood more conspicuous. But they were not much affected by open wounds. Sometimes they even cut off the skin, when the wound was more broad than deep, thinking that in this condition they fought with the greater glory. But when the point of an arrow, or a ball, sinking deep in the flesh, tormented them, and while, notwithstanding all their endeavours to extract it, the weapon could not be got out, then they fell into fits of phrensy and shame, at being destroyed by so small a hurt; and dashing themselves on the ground, lay scattered over the place. Some rushing against the enemy, were overwhelmed with darts; and, when any of them came near, they were cut to pieces by the light infantry. A soldier of this description carries a shield three feet long, and, in his right hand, javelins, which he throws at a distance. He has at his side a Spanish sword, which, when he has occasion to fight close, he draws, and shifts the spears into his left hand. There were few of the Gauls now left; and these, seeing themselves overpowered by the light infantry, and the battalions of the legions advancing, fled in confusion to the camp; which, by this time, was full of tumult and dismay, as the women, children, and others unfit to bear arms, were all crowded together there. The hills, thus abandoned by the enemy, were seized by the victorious Romans.

22. At this juncture, Lucius Manlius and Caius Helvius, having marched up as high as the sloping hills allowed them to do, and, indeed, to insuperable steeps, turned towards that side of the mountain where, only, the ascent was practicable; and began, as if by concert, to follow the consul's party at moderate distances; being driven by necessity to adopt the plan, now, which would have been the best at the beginning: for in such disadvantageous ground reserves have often been of the utmost use; as, should the first line happen to be repulsed, the second may both cover their retreat, and succeed to their place in the fight. The consul, as soon as the vanguard of the legions reached the hills taken by the light infantry, ordered the troops to halt and take breath; at the same time he showed them the bodies of the Gauls spread about the hills, asking them, "Since the light troops had fought such a battle, what might be expected from the legions, from a regular army, and from the spirit of the bravest soldiers? They ought certainly to take the camp into which the enemy had been driven, especially now that they were in dismay." He then sent forward the light infantry, who, while the army halted, had employed even that time to good purpose in collecting missiles from about the hills, that they might have a sufficient stock for the occasion. They now approached the camp. The Gauls, not confiding in the strength of their works, had posted themselves, in arms, on the outside of the rampart. The Romans assailed them with a shower of weapons of every sort; and, as they stood

ithout effect. They were

trenches, leaving only

strong guards at the entrances of the gates. Against the crowd that fled into the camp a vast quantity of missile weapons were discharged, and the shouts, intermixed with lamentations of the women and children, showed that great numbers were wounded. The first line of the legions hurled their javelins against the guards posted at the gates; however, these, in general, were not wounded, but most of them having their shields pierced through, were entangled and fastened together, nor did they longer withstand the attack.

23. The gates being now open, the Gauls, in order to escape the conquerors, fled out of the camp to all quarters. They rushed on, without looking before them, where there were roads and where there were none: no craggy cliffs, nor even perpendicular rocks, stopped them, for they now feared nothing but the enemy. Great numbers, therefore, falling down precipices of vast height, were either maimed or killed. The consul, taking possession of the camp, restrained the soldiers from plundering it; ordering all to pursue with their utmost speed, to press on the enemy, and to increase their present panic. The other party, under Lucius Manlius, now came up. These he did not suffer to enter the camp, but sent them forward in the pursuit, and whom he followed shortly after, committing the guard of the prisoners to some military tribunes; for he hoped, from their present consternation, that he might, by exertion, put an entire end to the war. After the consul's departure, Caius Helvius arrived with the third division. It was not in his power to prevent their sacking the camp; and, by one of fortune's most unjust dispensations, the booty fell into the hands of men who had not had any concern in the action. The cavalry stood for a long time ignorant of the fight, and of the success of their army. At last they also, as far as their horses could climb up the hills, pursued the Gauls, (who were now dispersed round the foot of the mountain,) killing and taking many. The number of the slain could not easily be ascertained, on account of the windings of the hills among which they were pursued. Many likewise fell from impassable cliffs into cavities of prodigious depth; others were killed in the woods and thickets. Claudius, who mentions two battles on Mount Olympus, asserts that forty thousand fell in them; yet Valerius Antias, who is generally addicted to great exaggeration in point of numbers, says not more than ten thousand. That the number of prisoners amounted to forty thousand there is no doubt, because the Gauls had dragged along with them a crowd of people of all descriptions and of all ages, like men removing to another country rather than going out to war. The consul collected in one heap, and burned, the arms of the enemy; he then ordered all to bring together the rest of the booty, and selling that portion which was to be applied to the use of the public, distributed the remainder among the soldiers, taking care that the shares should be as just as possible. He likewise commended them in public assemblies, and conferred presents according to the deserts of each; distinguishing Attalus above all others, with the gen-

eral approbation of all: for not only by his courage and activity in undergoing dangers and fatigue, but also by the modesty of his deportment, that young prince had rendered himself eminently conspicuous.

24. The war with the Tectosagians remained still to be begun. The consul, marching against them, arrived on the third day at Ancyra, a city remarkable in those parts, from which the enemy were but a little more than ten miles distant. While he lay encamped here a memorable action was performed by a female. Among many other captives was the wife of the Gallic chieftain Ortiagon, a woman of exquisite beauty. The commander of the guards was a centurion, avaricious and amorous, as soldiers often are. He first endeavoured to learn her sentiments, but finding that she abhorred the thought of voluntary dishonour, he employed violence. Afterward, in order to make some atonement for the injury and insult, he gave her hopes of liberty to return to her friends; but even this he would not grant without a compensation. He stipulated for a certain weight of gold; but, being unwilling that his countrymen should be privy to the business, gave her leave to send any one of the prisoners whom she chose with a message to her friends. He appointed a spot near the river, to which two of this woman's friends, and not more, were to come with the gold in the night following, and to receive her from his hands. It happened that, among the prisoners, under the same guard, was a servant of her own: he was employed as the messenger; and the centurion, as soon as it grew dark, conveyed him beyond the advanced posts. Her friends came to the place at the appointed time, as did the centurion with his prisoner. Here, on their producing the gold, which amounted to an Attic talent, for that was the sum demanded, in her own language, she ordered them to draw their swords and kill the centurion, while he was weighing the gold. After he was slain she caused his head to be cut off, and, wrapping it up in her garment, carried it to her husband Ortiagon, who had fled home from Olympus. Before she would embrace him she threw down the centurion's head at his feet; and on his asking, with astonishment, whose head it was, and what was the meaning of such a proceeding, so unaccountable in a female, she acknowledged to her husband the injury committed on her person, and the vengeance she had taken for the forcible violation of her chastity. It is said that she maintained to the last, by the purity and strictness of her life, the glory of this achievement, so honourable to her sex.

25. The Tectosagians sent envoys to the consul at Ancyra, entreating him not to decamp until he had held a confer-

ence with their kings; adding, that they preferred peace on any conditions to war. The time was fixed for the next day; and the place, a spot which seemed the most central between the camp of the Gauls and Ancyra. The consul came thither at the appointed hour, with a guard of five hundred horse; but seeing none of the Gauls there, he returned into his camp: after which the same envoys came again, with an apology, that their kings could not come, being prevented by religious considerations, but that the principal men of the nation would attend, and that the business might be as well transacted by them. To which the consul answered, that he would send Attalus on his part. To this meeting both parties came, Attalus attended by an escort of three hundred horse, when a conversation ensued respecting the terms of peace; but as this could not be finally concluded without the presence of the commanders-in-chief, it was agreed that the consul and the kings should meet in the same place on the following day. The intention of the Gauls in postponing matters was, first, to waste time, that they might remove their effects, so as not to be encumbered in case of danger, and also their wives and children, to the other side of the river Halys; and secondly, to favour a plot which they were forming against the consul, while he should harbour no suspicion of treachery during the conference. They chose for this purpose one thousand horsemen of approved intrepidity; and their plan would have taken effect had not fortune exerted herself in favour of the law of nations, which they plotted to violate. The Roman parties who went out for forage and wood were led towards that quarter where the conference was to be held; for the tribunes judged that to be the safest course, as they would have the consul's escort and himself, as a guard between them and the enemy. However, they posted another guard of their own, of six hundred horse, nearer to the camp. The consul, being assured by Attalus that the kings would come, and that the business might be concluded, set out from his camp with the same attendants as before. When he had advanced about five miles, and was near the place appointed, he saw, on a sudden, the Gauls coming on with hostile fury, as fast as their horses could gallop. He halted, and ordering his horsemen to make ready their arms and their courage, received the enemy's first charge with firmness, and kept his ground. At length, overpowered by numbers, he began to retreat leisurely, without disturbing the order of the troops; but at last, the danger of delay appearing greater than any advantage to be derived from keeping their ranks, they all fled in hurry and disorder. The Gauls, seeing them disperse, pursued eagerly, and killed several; and a great part of them would have been cut off, had not the six hundred horse, the guard of the foragers, come up to meet them. These, on hearing at a distance the shout of dismay raised by their friends, made ready their weapons and horses, and, with their vigour fresh, renewed the fight after it had become desperate. The fortune of the battle therefore was instantly reversed, and dismay retorted on the victors. At the first charge the Gauls were routed: at the same time the foragers from the fields ran together towards the spot, so that wherever the fugitives turned they met an enemy. Thus they could not retreat with either ease or safety, especially as the Romans pursued on fresh horses, while theirs were fatigued. Few therefore escaped; yet not one was taken: the far greater part paid their lives as a forfeit for having violated the faith of a conference. The whole army of the Romans, with minds burning with rage, marched up next day close to the enemy.

26. The consul, resolved that no particular should escape his knowledge, spent two days in examining the nature of the mountain with his own eyes. On the third day, after taking the auspices, and then offering sacrifice, he formed his troops in four divisions; that two might go with him up the middle of the mountain, while the other two should march, one on each side, against the wings of the Gauls. The main strength of the enemy, the Tectosagians and Trocmians, amounting to fifty thousand men, formed the centre of their line. The cavalry, about ten thousand men, being dismounted, (their horses being useless among the uneven rocks,) were placed on the right wing, and the Cappadocians of Ariarathes, with the auxiliary troops of Morzes, making up near four thousand, on the left. The consul, as he had done before at Mount Olympus, placed his light troops in the van, taking care that they should have ready at hand the same abundance of weapons of every sort. When they approached the enemy, all circumstances, on both sides, were the same as in the former battle, excepting that the spirits of the Romans were elated by their success, and those of the Gauls depressed; because, though themselves had not been defeated, yet they considered as their own the overthrow of people of there own race. The battle, therefore, commencing under like circumstances, had the same issue. The cloud, as it were, of light weapons that were thrown, overwhelmed the army of the enemy; and as none of them dared to come forward, for fear of exposing all parts of their bodies open to the blows, so, while they stood still, the closer they were together the more wounds they received, as the assailants had the better mark to aim at. The consul now judged, that as they were already disordered, if he should once let

them see the standards of the legions, they would all instantly turn about and fly; receiving, therefore, the light infantry and the rest of the irregulars between the ranks, he ordered the line to advance.

27. The Gauls, discouraged by reflecting on the defeat of the Tolistoboians, and distressed by carrying weapons sticking in their flesh, fatigued also by long standing, were not able to support even the first shout and onset of the Romans. Their flight was directed towards their camp, but a few of them entered within the trenches; the greater part, passing by on the right and left, fled whichever way each man's giddy haste carried him. The conquerors followed, cutting off the hindmost; but then, through greediness for booty, they stopped in the camp, and not one of them continued the pursuit. The Gauls in the wings stood some time longer, because it was later when the Romans reached them, but fled at the first discharge of weapons. The consul, as he could not draw off the men who had got into the camp for plunder, sent forward those who had been in the wings to pursue the enemy. They accordingly followed them a considerable way, yet in the pursuit, for there was no fight, they killed not more than eight thousand men: the rest crossed the river Halys. A great part of the Romans lodged that night in the enemy's camp; the rest the consul led back to his own. Next day he took a review of the prisoners, and of the booty; the quantity of which was as great as might be expected to have been heaped together by a nation most greedy of rapine, after holding possession, by force of arms, of all the country on this side Mount Taurus, during a space of many years. The Gauls, after this dispersion, reassembled in one place, a great part of them being wounded or unarmed; and as all were destitute of every kind of property, they sent deputies to the consul to supplicate for peace. Manlius ordered them to attend him at Ephesus; and, being in haste to quit those cold regions, in the vicinity of Mount Taurus, it being now the middle of autumn, he led back his victorious army into winter-quarters on the sea-coast.

28. During the time of those transactions in Asia, the other provinces were in a state of tranquillity. At Rome the censors, Titus Quintius Flamininus and Marcus Claudius Marcellus, read over the roll of the senate; Publius Scipio Africanus was a third time declared prince of the senate, and only four members were struck out, none of whom had held any curule office. In their review of the knights also the censors acted with great mildness. They contracted for the erection of a building in the Æquimælium, on the capitoline mount, and for paving with flint a road from the Capuan gate to the temple of Mars. The Campanians, having re-

quested the direction of the senate, respecting the place where their census should be held, an order passed, that it should be performed at Rome. Extraordinary quantities of rain fell this year; twelve times the Tiber overflowed the field of Mars and the lower parts of the city. The war with the Gauls in Asia having been brought to a conclusion by the consul, Cneius Manlius, the other consul, Marcus Fulvius, as the Ætolians were now completely reduced, passed over to Cephalenia, and sent messengers round the states of the island to inquire whether they chose to submit to the Romans, or to try the fortune of war. Fear operated so strongly on them all, that they did not refuse to surrender. They gave the number of hostages demanded, which was proportioned to the abilities of a weak people, the Nesians, Cranians, Pallenians, and Samæans, giving twenty each. Peace had now, beyond what could have been hoped for, begun to diffuse its benign influence through Cephalenia, when one state, the Samæans, from what motive is uncertain, suddenly broke out in opposition. They said, that as their city was commodiously situated, they were afraid that the Romans would compel them to remove from it. But whether they conceived this in their own minds, and under the impulse of a groundless fear, disturbed the general quiet, or whether such a project had been mentioned in conversation among the Romans, and reported to them, has not been discovered: thus much is certain, that after having given hostages they suddenly shut their gates, and could not be prevailed on to relinquish their design, even by the prayers of their friends, whom the consul sent to the walls to try how far they might be influenced by compassion for their parents and countrymen. As their answers showed nothing of a pacific disposition, siege was laid to the city. The consul had a sufficient store of engines and machines which had been brought over from Ambracia; and the works necessary to be performed were executed by the soldiers with great diligence. The rams were therefore brought forward in two places, and began to batter the walls.

29. The townsmen omitted nothing that could serve to obstruct the works or the motions of the besiegers. But the two methods of defence which they found most effectual were, first the raising always, instead of a part of the wall that was demolished, a new wall of equal strength on the inside; and the other, making sudden sallies at one time against the enemy's works, at another against his advanced guards; and in those attacks they generally got the better. The only means of confining them that could be contrived seems of no great consequence; it was however this,—the bringing one hundred slingers from Ægium, Patræ, and Dy

mæ. These men, according to the customary practice of that nation, were exercised from their childhood in throwing with a sling, into the open sea, the round pebbles which, mixed with sand, generally cover the shores; and by this means they acquired such a degree of dexterity, as to cast weapons of that sort to a greater distance, with surer aim, and more powerful effect, than even the Balearian slingers. Besides, their sling does not consist merely of a single strap, like the Balearic, and that of other nations, but the receptacle of the bullet is three-fold, and made firm by several seams, that it may not, by the yielding of the strap in the act of throwing, be let fly at random, but that lying here steady, while whirled about, it may be discharged as if sent from the string of a bow. Being accustomed to drive their bullets through circular marks of small circumference, placed at a great distance, they not only hit the enemy's heads, but any part of their face that they aimed at. These slings checked the Samæans from sallying either so frequently or so boldly; insomuch that they would sometimes, from the walls, beseech the Achæans to retire for a while, and be quiet spectators of their fight with the Roman guards. Same supported a siege of four months. At last, as some of their small number were daily killed or wounded, and the survivors were, through continual fatigues, greatly reduced both in strength and spirits, the Romans one night, scaling the wall of the citadel, which they call Cyatides, made their way into the forum. The Samæans, on discovering that a part of the city was taken, fled with their wives and children into the greater citadel; but submitting next day, they were all sold as slaves, and their city was plundered.

30. As soon as he had settled the affairs of Cephalenia, the consul, leaving a garrison in Same, sailed over to Peloponnesus, where his presence had been often solicited for a long time past, chiefly by the Ægians and Lacedæmonians. From the first institution of the Achæan council, the assemblies of the nation had been held at Ægium, whether out of respect to the dignity of the city, or on account of the commodiousness of its situation. This usage Philopœmen first attempted to subvert in that year, and determined to introduce an ordinance, that these should be held in every one of the cities, which were members of the Achæan union, in rotation; and a little before the arrival of the consul, when the demiurguses, who are the chief magistrates in the states, summoned the representatives to Ægium, Philopœmen, then pretor, by proclamation, appointed their meeting at Argos. As it was apparent that, in general, all would repair to the latter place, the consul likewise, though he favoured the cause of the Ægians, went thither, but, after

the matter had been debated, seeing that the opposite party was likely to succeed, he declined being farther concerned. The Lacedæmonians then drew his attention to their disputes. Their state was kept in constant uneasiness, principally by the exiles, of whom great numbers resided in the maritime forts on the coast of Laconia, all which had been taken from the Lacedæmonians. At this the latter were deeply chagrined, as they wished to enjoy free access to the sea, if they should have occasion to send ambassadors to Rome, or any other place; and at the same time to possess some mart and repository for foreign merchandise for their necessary demands. They therefore attacked in the night a maritime village called Las, and seized it by surprise. The inhabitants, and the exiles residing in the place, were terrified at first by the sudden assault; but afterward collecting in a body, before day, after a slight contest, they drove back the Lacedæmonians. A general alarm, nevertheless, spread over the whole coast, and all the forts and villages, with the exiles resident there, united in sending a common embassy to the Achæans.

31. The pretor, Philopœmen,—(who, from the beginning, had ever been a friend to the cause of the exiles, and had always advised the Achæans to reduce the power and influence of the Lacedæmonians,)—on the request of the ambassadors, gave them an audience of the council. There, on a motion made by him, a decree was passed, that "whereas Titus Quintius and the Romans had committed their forts and villages, on the coast of Laconia, to the protection and guardianship of the Achæans; and whereas, according to treaty, the Lacedæmonians ought to leave them unmolested: notwithstanding which, the village of Las had been attacked by them, and bloodshed committed therein; therefore, unless the authors and abetters of this outrage were delivered up to the Achæans, they would consider it as a violation of the treaty." To demand those persons, ambassadors were instantly despatched to Lacedæmon. This authoritative injunction appeared to the Lacedæmonians so haughty and insolent, that if their state had been in its ancient condition they would undoubtedly have flown to arms. What distracted them most of all was the fear lest, if by obeying the first mandates they once received the yoke, Philopœmen, pursuant to a scheme which he had long had in contemplation, should put the exiles in possession of Lacedæmon. Enraged therefore to madness, they put to death thirty men of the faction which had held some correspondence with Philopœmen and the exiles, passed a decree, renouncing all alliance with the Achæans, ordering ambassadors to be sent immediately to Cephalenia, to surrender Lacedæmon to the consul, Marcus

Fulvius, beseeching him to come into Peloponnesus, and to receive Lacedæmon under the protection and dominion of the Roman people.

32. When the Achæan ambassadors returned with an account of these proceedings, war was declared against the Lacedæmonians, by a unanimous vote of all the states of the confederacy; and nothing but the winter prevented its being commenced immediately. However, they detached several small parties, not only by land, but by sea, which, making incursions more like freebooters than regular troops, laid waste the Lacedæmonian frontiers. This commotion brought the consul into Peloponnesus, and, by his order, a council was summoned at Elis; the Lacedæmonians being called on to attend, and to plead their own cause. The debates there were violent, and proceeded even to altercation. But the consul, who, in other respects, acted in a very conciliatory manner, and who gave no explicit opinion, put an end to the dispute by one decisive order, that they should desist from hostilities until they sent ambassadors to Rome, to the senate. Both parties sent ambassadors accordingly. The Lacedæmonian exiles, also, authorized the Achæans to act in their cause, and negotiate on their behalf. Diophanes and Lycortas, both of them Megalopolitans, were at the head of the Achæan embassy; and, as they were of different sentiments with regard to public affairs at home, so their discourses on the occasion were of quite different tendencies. Diophanes proposed to leave the determination of every point entirely to the senate, "who," he said, "would best decide the controversies between the Achæans and Lacedæmonians;" while Lycortas, according to the instructions of Philopœmen, required that the senate should permit the Achæans to execute their own decrees, made conformable to treaty and their own laws; and to possess, uninfringed, the liberty which themselves had bestowed. The Achæan nation was at that time in high esteem with the Romans; yet it was resolved that no alteration should be made respecting the Lacedæmonians; but the answer given was so obscure, that, while the Achæans understood that they were left at liberty to act as they pleased towards Lacedæmon, the Lacedæmonians construed it, as not conveying any such license.

33. The use which the Achæans made of this power was immoderate and tyrannical. They continued Philopœmen in office, who in the beginning of spring, collecting an army, encamped in the territory of the Lacedæmonians, and thence sent ambassadors to insist on their delivering up the authors of the insurrection; promising, that if they complied, their state should remain in peace, and that those persons should not suffer any punishment, without a previous

trial. The rest were held silent by their fears; but the persons demanded by name declared, that they would voluntarily go, provided they received assurance from the ambassadors that they should be safe from violence until their cause were heard. Several other men of illustrious characters went along with them; both from a wish to aid those private individuals, and because they thought their cause concerned the public interest. The Achæans had never before brought the Lacedæmonian exiles into the country, because they knew that nothing would so much disgust the people; but now, the vanguard of almost their whole army was composed of them. When the Lacedæmonians came to the gate of the camp, these met them in a body, and, first, began to provoke them with ill language; a wrangle then ensuing, and their passions being inflamed, the most furious of the exiles made an attack on the Lacedæmonians. While these appealed to the gods and the faith of the ambassadors; and while the ambassadors and the pretor, driving back the crowd, protected the Lacedæmonians, and kept off some who were already binding them in chains,—the multitude, roused by the tumult, gathered about them in prodigious numbers. The Achæans, at first, ran thither to see what was doing; but then, the exiles, with loud clamours, complained of the sufferings that they had undergone, implored assistance, and at the same time insisted that "such another opportunity, if they neglected this, could never be hoped for; that these men had been the means of rendering useless the treaties, solemnly ratified in the capitol at Olympia, and in the citadel of Athens; and that before their hands should be tied up by a new treaty they ought to punish the guilty." By these expressions all were inflamed, so that on one man calling out, to fall on, the whole crowd attacked them with stones; and seventeen persons, who, during the disturbance, had been put in chains, were killed. The next day sixty-three, whom the pretor had protected from violence, not because he wished them safe, but because he was unwilling that they should perish before they were tried, were taken into custody, brought before an enraged multitude, and, after addressing a few words to such prejudiced ears, they were all condemned and executed.

34. After this terrible example had been made, to humble the Lacedæmonians, orders were sent to them, first, that they should demolish their walls; then, that all the foreign auxiliaries, who had served for pay under the tyrants, should quit the Laconian territories; then, that the slaves, whom the tyrants had set free, who amounted to a great multitude, should depart before a certain day, after which, should any remain in the country, the Achæans were authorized to seize, sell, and

carry them away. That they should abrogate the laws and institutions of Lycurgus, and adopt those of the Achæans, by which all would become one body, and concord would be established among them. They obeyed none of these injunctions more willingly than that of demolishing the walls; nor suffered any with more reluctance, than the giving up of the exiles. A decree for their restoration was made at Tegea, in a general council of the Achæans; where, an account being brought, that the foreign auxiliaries had been sent away, and that the newly registered Lacedæmonians (so they called the slaves enfranchised by the tyrants) had left the city and dispersed through the country, it was resolved, that before the army was disbanded, the pretor should go with some light troops, and, seizing that description of people, sell them as spoil. Great numbers were accordingly seized and sold; and with the money arising from the sale a portico at Megalopolis, which the Lacedæmonians had demolished, was rebuilt, with the approbation of the Achæans. The lands of Belbinis, of which the Lacedæmonian tyrants had unjustly kept possession, were also restored to that state, according to an old decree of the Achæans, made in the reign of Philip, son of Amyntas. The state of Lacedæmon having, by these means, lost the sinews of its strength, remained long in subjection to the Achæans; but nothing hurt it so materially as the abolition of the discipline of Lycurgus, in the practice of which they had continued during seven hundred years.

35. After the sitting of the council, wherein the debate between the Achæans and Lacedæmonians was held in presence of the consul, as the year was near expiring, Marcus Fulvius went home to Rome to hold the elections. The consuls elected were Marcus Valerius Messala, and Caius Livius Salinator, having, this year, procured the rejection of his enemy, Marcus Æmilius Lepidus. Then were elected pretors, Quintus Marcius Philippus, Marcus Claudius Marcellus, Caius Stertinius, Caius Atinius, Publius Claudius Pulcher, and Lucius Manlius Acidinus. When the elections were finished, it was resolved that the consul, Marcus Fulvius, should return into his province to the army, and that he and his colleague, Cneius Manlius, should be continued in command for a year. In this year, in pursuance of directions from the decemvirs, a statue of Hercules was set up in his temple, and a gilded chariot with six horses, in the capitol, by Publius Cornelius. The inscription mentioned, that Publius Cornelius, consul, made the offering.* The curule

* This does not prove that he was in the office of consul at the time of his making it; for it was usual to mention in such inscriptions the highest office that the person ever held.

ediles, also, Publius Claudius and Servius Sulpicius Galba, dedicated twelve gilded shields, out of money raised by fines on corn-merchants, for raising the market by hoarding the grain. And Quintus Fulvius Flaccus, plebeian edile, having prosecuted to conviction one malefactor, (for the ediles prosecuted separately,) dedicated two gilded statues. His colleague, Aulus Cæcilius, did not convict any one. The Roman games were exhibited entire, thrice; the plebeian, five times. Marcus Valerius Messala, and Caius Livius Salinator, entering into office on the ides of March, proposed to the senate's consideration the state of the commonwealth, the provinces, and the armies. With respect to Ætolia and Asia no alteration was made. The provinces assigned to the consuls were, to one, Pisæ, where he was to act against the Ligurians; to the other, Gaul. They were ordered to cast lots for these, or to settle the matter between themselves, to levy new armies, two legions for each; and to raise, of the Latine allies, fifteen thousand foot, and one thousand two hundred horse. Liguria fell, by lot, to Messala; Gaul, to Salinator. The pretors then cast lots, and the city jurisdiction fell to Marcus Claudius; the foreign to Publius Claudius; Sicily, to Quintus Marcius; Sardinia, to Caius Stertinius; Hither Spain, to Lucius Manlius; Farther Spain, to Caius Atinius.

36. The dispositions made respecting the armies were these. It was ordered that the legions which had served under Caius Lælius should be removed out of Gaul into Bruttium, and put under the command of Marcus Tuccius, propretor; that the army which was in Sicily should be disbanded, and the fleet which was there brought home to Rome by Marcus Sempronius, propretor. For the Spains were decreed the legions then in those provinces, one for each; with orders, that each of the two pretors should levy, from among the allies, to recruit their numbers, three thousand foot and two hundred horse, which they were to carry with them. Before the new magistrates set out for their provinces a supplication of three days' continuance was ordered by the college of decemvirs, to be performed in every street, on account of a darkness having overspread the sky, between the third and fourth hours of the day; and the nine days' solemnity was proclaimed, on account of a shower of stones having fallen on the Aventine. As the censors obliged the Campanians, pursuant to the decree of the senate, made last year, to pass the general survey at Rome, (for, before that, it had not been fixed where they should be surveyed,) they petitioned, that they might be allowed to take in marriage women who were citizens of Rome, and that any who had heretofore married such might retain them;

and, likewise, that children born of such marriages before that day might be deemed legitimate, and entitled to inherit; both which requests were complied with. Caius Valerius Tappus, a plebeian tribune, proposed an order of the people concerning the towns of Formiæ, Fundi, and Arpinum, that they should be invested with the right of voting, for hitherto they had been members of the state without that right. Against this proposal four plebeian tribunes entered a protest, because it was not made under the direction of the senate; but being informed that the power of imparting that privilege to any persons belonged to the people, and not to the senate, they desisted from their opposition. An order was passed, that the Formians and Fundans should vote in the Æmilian tribe, and the Arpinians in the Cornelian; and in these tribes they were then, for the first time, rated in the census, in pursuance of the order of the people proposed by Valerius. Marcus Claudius Marcellus, censor, having got the better of Titus Quintius in the lots, closed the lustrum. The number of citizens rated was two hundred and fifty-eight thousand three hundred and eight. When the survey was finished, the consuls set out for their provinces.

37. During the winter wherein this passed at Rome, Cneius Manlius, at first, while consul, and afterward, when proconsul, was attended, in his winter-quarters in Asia, by embassies from all the nations and states on this side of Mount Taurus; and although the conquest of Antiochus was more splendid and glorious to the Romans than that of the Gauls, yet the latter gave greater joy to the allies than the former. Subjection to the king had been more tolerable to them than the neighbourhood of these fierce and savage barbarians; of whom they were in daily apprehension, added to the uncertainty where the storm of their depredations might fall. Having therefore obtained liberty by the expulsion of Antiochus, and permanent peace by the conquest of the Gauls, they brought, not only congratulations, but also golden crowns, in proportion to the ability of each. Ambassadors also came from Antiochus, and from the Gauls themselves, to receive the conditions of peace; and from Ariarathes, king of Cappadocia, to solicit pardon, and make atonement by money for his crime, in assisting Antiochus with troops. He was fined two hundred talents.* The Gauls were answered, that when King Eumenes arrived, he would settle the conditions. The embassies of the several states were dismissed with kind answers, and with their minds much more at ease than when they arrived. The ambassadors of Antiochus were ordered to bring the money

* 38,750l.

and the corn due by the treaty concluded with Lucius Scipio into Pamphylia, whither the consul intended to go with his forces. In the beginning of the next spring, after performing the ceremony of purifying the army, he began his march, and on the eighth day arrived at Apamea. There he rested three days; and, on the third day after his departure from that place, arrived in Pamphylia, whither he had ordered the king's ambassadors to repair with stipulated supplies. Here he received two thousand five hundred talents of silver,* which he sent to Apamea; the corn he distributed to the army. Thence he marched to Perga, the only place in the country still held by a garrison of the king's troops. On his approach the governor of the town went out to meet him, and requested thirty days' time, that he might consult Antiochus about the surrender of the city. The time was granted, and, on the expiration of it, the city was surrendered. From Perga he detached his brother, Lucius Manlius, with four thousand men, to exact from the Oroandians the remainder of the money which they had promised; and, ordering the ambassadors of Antiochus to follow, he led back his army to Apamea, having heard that King Eumenes and the ten ambassadors from Rome were arrived at Ephesus.

38. Here, with the concurrence of the ten ambassadors, a treaty was concluded with Antiochus, and written in nearly the following words: "There shall be friendship between King Antiochus and the Roman people, on these terms and conditions. He shall not suffer any army, intended to act against the Roman people, or their allies, to pass through his own kingdom, or the territory of any state under his dominion, nor supply it with provisions, nor give any other assistance. The Romans and their allies are to observe the same conduct towards Antiochus, and those under his government. It shall not be lawful for Antiochus to wage war with the inhabitants of the islands, or to pass over into Europe. He shall evacuate the cities, lands, villages, and forts, on this side of Mount Taurus, as far as the river Halys; and from the foot of Taurus to the summit, where are the confines of Lycaonia. He shall not remove any arms out of any of the evacuated towns, lands, or forts; and if any have been removed, he shall replace them as before. He shall not receive any soldier, or other person, from King Eumenes. If any natives of those cities, which are hereby separated from his kingdom, are now with Antiochus, or within the bounds of his realms, they shall all return to Apamea before a certain day, hereafter to be ap-

* 484,275*l*.

pointed. Such of the natives of Antiochus's kingdom as are now with the Romans and their allies, shall have liberty to depart, or to stay. All their slaves, whether fugitives or taken in war, likewise all free-born persons, whether prisoners or deserters, he shall deliver to the Romans and their allies. He shall give up all his elephants, and not procure others. He shall also surrender his ships of war, and their stores; and shall not keep more than ten light trading vessels, none of which are to be worked with more than thirty oars, nor a galley of one tier of oars, for the purpose of an offensive war; nor shall any ship of his come on this side of the promontories Calycadnus and Sarpedon, except it shall be a ship carrying money, tribute, ambassadors, or hostages. King Antiochus shall not hire soldiers out of those nations which are under the dominion of the Roman people, nor even receive volunteers. All houses and buildings, within the limits of Antiochus's kingdom, and which were belonging to the Rhodians and their allies, shall hold on the same footing as they did before the war. If any sums of money are due to them, they shall have a right to enforce payment; likewise, if any of their property has been taken away, they shall have a right to search for, discover, and reclaim it. If any of the cities which ought to be surrendered are held by people to whom Antiochus gave them, he shall remove the garrisons, and take care that the surrender be properly executed. He shall pay, within twelve years, by equal annual payments, twelve thousand talents of silver,* of the proper Attic standard, the talent to weigh not less than eighty Roman pounds; and five hundred and forty thousand pecks of wheat. He shall pay to King Eumenes, within five years, three hundred and fifty talents;† and, for the corn due, according to his own valuation, one hundred and twenty-seven talents.‡ He shall deliver to the Romans twenty hostages, and change them every third year; none of which are to be younger than eighteen, or older than forty-five years. If any of the allies of the Roman people shall make war on Antiochus, he shall be at liberty to repel force by force, provided he does not keep possession of any city, either by right of arms, or by admitting it into a treaty of amity. Whatever controversies may arise between him and them shall be decided by arbitration, according to the rules of equity; or, if it shall be the choice of both parties, by arms." A clause was added to this treaty about delivering up Hannibal, the Carthaginian; Thoas, the Ætolian; Mnasimachus, the Acarnanian; and the Chalcidians, Eubolis and Philo; and another, that if the parties should

* 2,235,000*l.* † 67,812*l.* ‡ 24,609*l.*

afterward agree to add, to expunge, or alter any of the above articles, it might be done without impeachment to the validity of the treaty.

39. The consul swore to the observance of this treaty, and sent Quintus Minucius Thermus and Lucius Manlius, who happened to return just at that time from Oroanda, to require the oath of the king. At the same time he wrote to Quintus Fabius Labeo, commander of the fleet, to sail without delay to Patara, to burn and destroy the king's ships that lay there. Sailing accordingly from Ephesus, he burned, or otherwise destroyed, fifty decked ships; and, in the same voyage, took Talmessus, the inhabitants being terrified by his sudden appearance. Then, having ordered those whom he left at Ephesus to follow him, he passed on from Lycia, through the islands to Greece. At Athens he waited a few days, until the ships from Ephesus came to Piræus, and then he brought home the whole fleet to Italy. Cneius Manlius having, among other matters to be given up by Antiochus, received his elephants, gave them all as a present to Eumenes. He then admitted to a hearing the representatives of the several states, many of which were in an unsettled condition, in consequence of the changes that had taken place. King Ariarathes, through the mediation of Eumenes, to whom he had lately betrothed his daughter, obtained a remission of half the fine imposed on him, and was received into friendship. After hearing what the respective nations had to say on their own behalf, the ten ambassadors made different arrangements with respect to the difference of their cases. Such as had been tributary to King Antiochus, and had sided with the Romans, they rendered independent; and such as had taken part with Antiochus, or had been tributary to King Attalus, all these they ordered to pay tribute to Eumenes. To the Colophonians, living in Notium, the Cymæans, and Milasenians, whom they specified by name, they granted independence, to the Clazomenians the same, besides bestowing on them the island of Drymusa. To the Milesians they restored what was called the sacred lands. They added to the territory of the Trojans Rhœteum and Gergithus, not so much in consideration of any recent merit of theirs, as out of respect to their own origin. The same motive procured liberty to Dardanus. To the Chians also, the Smyrnæans and Erythræans, they granted lands, in consideration of the singular fidelity which they had shown during the war, treating them in every instance with particular distinction. To the Phocæans they restored the territory which they had enjoyed before the war, and the privilege of being governed by their own ancient laws. They confirmed to the Rhodian

the grants mentioned in the former decree. Lycia and Caria were assigned to them as far as the river Mæander, excepting Telmessus. To King Eumenes they gave, in Europe, the Chersonese and Lysimachia, with the forts, towns, and lands thereof, bounded as when held by Antiochus; and, in Asia, both the Phrygias, the one on the Hellespont, and the other called the Greater, restoring to him Mysia, which had been taken by King Prusias, and also Lycaonia, and Milyas, and Lydia, and, by express mention, the cities of Tralles and Ephesus and Telmessus. A dispute arising between Eumenes and Antiochus's ambassadors concerning Pamphylia, because part of it lay on the hither side, and part beyond Taurus, the matter was referred wholly to the senate.

40. When these treaties and grants were concluded, Manlius, with the ten ambassadors, and all his army, marched to the Hellespont, whither he had ordered the petty princes of the Gauls to come; and there he prescribed the terms on which they should maintain peace with Eumenes, and warned them to put an end to the practice of rambling in arms, and to confine themselves within the bounds of their own territories. Then, having collected ships from all parts of the coast, and Eumenes' fleet also being brought thither from Elæ by Athenæus, that king's brother, he transported all his forces into Europe. Proceeding through the Chersonese, by short marches, the army being heavily encumbered with booty of every sort, he halted at Lysimachia, in order that he might have the beasts of burden as fresh and vigorous as might be, when he should enter Thrace, the march through which was generally considered with terror. On the day of his leaving Lysimachia, he came to the river called Melas,* and thence, next day, to Cypsela. The road, about ten miles from Cypsela, he found obstructed by woods, narrow and broken. On account of these difficulties he divided the army into two parts; and, ordering one to advance in front, and the other at a considerable distance, to cover the rear, he placed between them the baggage, consisting of wagons with the public money, and other booty of great value. As they marched in this order through the defile, a body of Thracians, not more in number than ten thousand, composed of four states, the Astians, Cænians, Maduatians, and Cœleans, posted themselves on both sides of the road at the narrowest part. Many were of opinion that this was done at the treacherous instigation of Philip, king of Macedonia, as he knew that the Romans were to return through Thrace, and that they carried with them a large quantity of

* Black.

money. The general himself was in the van, anxious about the disadvantages to which his men were exposed from the nature of the place. The Thracians did not stir until the troops passed by; but, when they saw that the foremost division had got clear of the narrow pass, and that the rear division was not yet drawing near, they rushed on the baggage, and having killed the guards, some rifled the wagons, while others led off the horses under their loads. When the shout reached those on the rear, who just then entered the pass, and, afterward those in the van, they ran together from both extremities to the centre, and an irregular sort of fight commenced in many different places at once. The booty was the great occasion of slaughter to the Thracians; for, besides being encumbered with burdens, most of them had thrown away their arms, that they might be at liberty to seize the prey; while, on the other side, the Romans laboured under great disadvantages from the nature of the place, as the barbarians, acquainted with every path, made their attacks with advantage, and sometimes came, unperceived, through the hollow glens. The loads too, and the wagons, lying incommodiously for one party or the other, as chance directed, were great obstructions to their movements; and, here the plunderer, there, the defender of the booty fell. The fortune of the fight was variable, according as the ground was favourable to this party or that, and according to the spirit of the combatants, and their numbers; on both sides, however, great numbers fell. The night, at length, approaching, the Thracians retired from the fight, not for the purpose of avoiding wounds or death, but because they had gotten enough of booty.

41. The first division of the Romans encamped beyond the pass, in open ground, round the temple of Bendis;* the other division remained in the middle of the defile, to guard the baggage, which they surrounded with a double rampart. Next day, having carefully examined the ground, they rejoined the first. In that battle, although part of the baggage was lost, while a great part of the attendants, and many of the soldiers, perished, (the fight having been carried on through almost the whole extent of the defile,) yet the heaviest loss sustained was in the death of Quintus Minucius Thermus, a brave and gallant officer. The army arrived that day at the Hebrus, and thence passed through the country of the Ænians, by the temple of Apollo, which the natives call Zerynthium. At a place called Tempyra they came to another defile, as rugged and uneven as the former; but, as there were no woods near, it afforded no means for an am-

---

* Diana, so called in the Thracian language.

buscade. Hither assembled another tribe of Thracians, called Thrausians, with the same hope of plunder; but, as the Romans were enabled, by the nakedness of the valleys, to descry them at a distance, posted on each side of the road, they were less alarmed and confused; for, although they were obliged to fight on disadvantageous ground, yet it was in a regular battle, in the open field, and a fair encounter. Advancing in close order, with the war shout, and falling on the enemy, they soon drove them off the ground: and the sequel was flight and slaughter; for the narrow passes, in which the enemy had trusted for safety, actually impeded their escape. The Romans, after this success, encamped at a village of the Maronites called Sare. Next day, marching through an open country, they reached the plain of Priate, where they halted three days, to receive supplies of corn, partly from the country of the Maronites, who made a voluntary contribution, and partly from their own ships, which attended them with stores of every kind. From this post they had one day's march to Apollonia, whence they proceeded through the territory of Abdera to Neapolis. This march through the Grecian colonies the troops performed in security. During the remainder, and in the midst of the Thracians, they were all free from attacks, yet never free from apprehensions, night or day, until they arrived in Macedonia. This same army, when it proceeded by the same route under Scipio, had found the Thracians more peaceable, for no other reason, than because it had not then such a quantity of booty to tempt them: although Claudius writes that, even on that occasion, a body of fifteen thousand Thracians opposed Mutines, the Numidian, who had advanced to explore the country. He had with him four hundred Numidian horsemen, and a few elephants. Mutines' son, with one hundred and fifty chosen horsemen, broke through the middle of the enemy; and, presently, when Mutines, placing his elephants in the centre, and the horse on the wings, had begun to engage the enemy, he fell furiously on their rear, which attack of the cavalry so disordered the Thracians, that they did not come near the main body of infantry. Cneius Manlius conducted his army through Macedonia into Thessaly; and, having proceeded through Epirus to Apollonia, passed the winter there, for the people had not yet learned so far to despise the sea of that season, as to venture on the passage.

42. The year had almost expired when the consul, Marcus Valerius, came from Liguria to Rome to elect new magistrates; although he had not performed in his province any important business that could afford a reasonable excuse for coming later than usual to the elections. The assembly for

choosing consuls was held on the twelfth day before the calends of March, and the two elected were Marcus Æmilius Lepidus and Caius Flaminius. The following day were elected pretors, Appius Claudius Pulcher, Servius Sulpicius Galba, Quintus Terentius Culleo, Lucius Terentius Massa, Quintus Fulvius Flaccus, and Marcus Furius Crassipes. When the elections were concluded the consul proposed to the senate the appointment of the provinces for the pretors: two were decreed to the administration of justice in Rome; two out of Italy—Sicily and Sardinia; and two in Italy—Tarentum and Gaul; with orders that the pretors should immediately cast lots, before their commencement in office. To Servius Sulpicius fell the city jurisdiction; to Quintus Terentius the foreign: Lucius Terentius obtained Sicily; Quintus Fulvius, Sardinia; Appius Claudius, Tarentum; and Marcus Furius, Gaul. In that year, Lucius Minucius Myrtilus, and Lucius Manlius, being charged with having beaten the Carthaginian ambassadors, were, by order of Marcus Claudius, city pretor, delivered up by heralds to the ambassadors, and carried to Carthage. Reports prevailed of great preparations for war being made in Liguria, and of their growing every day more formidable. When therefore the new consuls proposed to the consideration of the senate the state of the commonwealth, and the appointing of their provinces, the senate voted that Liguria should be the province of both the consuls. To this vote the consul Lepidus objected, asserting that "it would be highly indecorous to shut up the consuls among the valleys of Liguria, while Marcus Fulvius and Cneius Manlius reigned, a second year, one in Europe, the other in Asia, as if substituted in the room of Philip and Antiochus. If it was resolved to keep armies in those countries, it was more fitting that they should be commanded by consuls, than by private persons, who made their circuits, with all the terrors of war, among nations against whom war had not been declared; trafficking peace for money. If armies were necessary for the security of those provinces, in the same manner as Lucius Scipio, consul, had succeeded Marcus Acilius, consul; and as Marcus Fulvius and Cneius Manlius succeeded Lucius Scipio, so ought Caius Livius and Marcus Valerius, consuls, to have succeeded Fulvius and Manlius. But, unquestionably, at this time, after the Ætolian war had been concluded, Asia taken from Antiochus, and the Gauls subdued,—either the consuls ought to be sent to the consular armies, or the legions ought to be brought home, and restored to the commonwealth." Notwithstanding these arguments, the senate persisted in their vote, that Liguria should be the province of both the consuls; but they ordered that Manlius and Fulvius should leave their provinces, withdraw the troops, and come home to Rome.

43. There subsisted a quarrel between Marcus Fulvius and the consul Æmilius; the latter complaining particularly that, through the intrigues of Fulvius, he had been kept back from obtaining the consulship two years. In order therefore to exasperate the minds of the public against him, he introduced to the senate ambassadors from Ambracia, whom he had previously instructed in the charges they were to make against him. These complained that "when they were in a state of peace, after they had obeyed the commands of former consuls, and were ready to show the same obedience to Marcus Fulvius, war had been made on them. That first their lands were ravaged; and then their city terrified by denunciations of plundering and slaughter, that their fears might compel them to shut their gates. They were then besieged and assaulted, while all the severities ever practised in war, were inflicted on them, in murders, burnings, the sacking and demolishing of their city. Their wives and children were dragged away into slavery; their goods taken from them; and, what shocked them more than all, their temples were despoiled of their ornaments, the images of their gods, nay, the gods themselves, were torn from their mansions, and carried away; so that the Ambracians had no object of worship left, nothing to which they could address their prayers and supplications, but naked walls and pillars." While they were making these complaints, the consul, as had been agreed, by asking questions leading to farther charges, drew them on, as if against their inclinations, to the mention of other matters. Their representations moved the senators, but the other consul, Caius Flaminius, took up the cause of Marcus Fulvius. "The Ambracians," he said, "had set out in an old course, now long out of use. In this manner Marcus Marcellus had been accused by the Syracusans; and Quintus Fulvius by the Campanians. Why might not the senate as well allow accusations to be so brought against Titus Quintius by King Philip; against Manius Acilius and Lucius Scipio, by Antiochus; against Cneius Manlius, by the Gauls; and against Fulvius himself, by the Ætolians and the states of Cephalenia? Do you think, conscript fathers, that the besieging and taking Ambracia, the removing thence the statues and ornaments, and the other proceedings, usual on the capture of cities, will be denied, either by me, on behalf of Marcus Fulvius, or by Marcus Fulvius himself, who intends to demand a triumph from you for those very services, and to carry before his chariot those statues, the removal of which is charged as criminal, together with other spoils of that city,

at the same time inscribing on the pillars of his house, Ambracia captured? There is no kind of pretence for their separating themselves from the Ætolians; the cause of the Ambracians and of the Ætolians is the same. Let, therefore, my colleague either vent his malice in some other case; or, if he is determined to proceed in this, let him detain his Ambracians until Fulvius comes home. I will not suffer any determination, concerning either the Ambracians or Ætolians, to pass in the absence of Marcus Fulvius."

44. Æmilius, inveighing against the artful malignity of his adversary as being notorious to all, affirmed that he would spin out the time by affected delays, so as not to return to Rome during the present consulate. Two days were wasted in this dispute, and it was apparent that while Flaminius was present no decision of the cause could be procured. Æmilius, therefore, laid hold of an opportunity, when Flaminius, happening to fall sick, was absent, and on his proposing the motion, the senate decreed, that "the Ambracians should have all their effects restored, should enjoy liberty, and the benefit of their own laws, and should levy what duties they might think proper on goods conveyed by land or sea, provided that the Romans and the Latine confederates should be exempted therefrom. That with respect to the statues and other ornaments carried away from their sacred buildings, as alleged in their complaint, their order was, that immediately on the return of Marcus Fulvius to Rome the business should be laid before the college of pontiffs, and their directions obeyed." Nor was the consul content with this; but afterward, in a thin meeting, he procured a clause to be added to the decree, "that it did not appear that Ambracia was taken by force." A supplication of three days' continuance was then performed for the health of the people, on account of a grievous pestilence which desolated the city and country. The Latine festival was afterward celebrated; when the consuls, being acquitted of these religious duties, and having finished their levies, (for both of them chose to employ new soldiers,) set out for their provinces, where they disbanded all the old troops.

45. Shortly after the departure of the consuls, Cneius Manlius, proconsul, arrived at Rome. Servius Sulpicius, pretor, assembled the senate in the temple of Bellona, to give him audience; when, after enumerating the services which he had performed, he demanded that, in consideration thereof, public thanks should be offered to the immortal gods, and permission be granted to himself to ride through the city in triumph. This was opposed by the greater number of the ten ambassadors who had been in the province along with him; and particularly by Lucius Furius Purpureo an

Lucius Æmilius Paulus. They represented that "they had been appointed plenipotentiaries, in conjunction with Manlius, to make peace with Antiochus, and to conclude a treaty on the preliminary articles settled with Lucius Scipio: that Cneius Manlius laboured, to the utmost of his power, to obstruct the conclusion of this peace, and to draw Antiochus into an ambuscade; but that he (Antiochus) having discovered the treacherous designs of the consul, though frequently tempted by proposals of a conference, was so far from consenting to the meeting, that he avoided even the sight of him. So eager was the wish of Manlius to cross Taurus, that he was with difficulty restrained by the ten ambassadors, who besought him not to expose himself voluntarily to the curse denounced in the Sibylline verses against such as should pass those fatal limits. Nevertheless, he marched his army thither, and encamped almost on the very summit where the waters take opposite directions. As he could find no sort of pretence for hostilities, the king's subjects being perfectly quiet, he led round his army to the Gallogræcians, and, without any decree of the senate, or order of the people, commenced a war against that nation. Did ever any general before presume to act, in like manner, on his own judgment? The latest wars were those with Antiochus, with Philip, and with Hannibal and the Carthaginians; concerning all these the senate had passed its decrees, the people their orders; several embassies were previously sent; restitution demanded; and, finally, heralds were sent to proclaim war. Now, Cneius Manlius," said they, "has any one of these proceedings been observed in the present case? Has it been a war of the Roman people, or a predatory expedition of your own contrivance? But, did even thus much content you? Did you lead your army against those whom you had chosen to consider as enemies by the direct course, or did you ramble through every deflection of the roads, stopping wherever they were divided, in order that, to whatever side Eumenes' brother, Attalus, should turn his route, the consul, as an auxiliary in his pay, might follow with a Roman army? In a word, did you not ransack every recess and corner of Pisidia, Lycaonia, and Phrygia, levying contributions from the tyrants and peasants in those remote regions? for, what had you to do with the Oroandians, what with other states equally inoffensive?

46. "But, to consider in itself this war, on the merit of which you ask a triumph; in what manner did you conduct it? Did you fight on equal ground, and at the time of your own choosing? Indeed there is some propriety in your requiring that thanks be returned to the immortal gods: first, because they did not ordain that the army should undergo

the penalty deserved by the temerity of its commander, in commencing a war unjustifiable by any law of nations; and next, because they gave us for antagonists brutes, and not men. Do not suppose that the name only of the Gallogræcians is corrupted; their bodies, and their minds, have been long so. Had they been such Gauls as those whom we have a thousand times encountered in Italy, with various success, do you think it probable, from the conduct of our commander, that one of us would have returned to tell the story? Two battles were fought: twice he advanced against them by most dangerous paths, bringing his army into a valley beneath, and almost under the feet of the enemy; so that, if they had never discharged a weapon, they might, from the advantage of the higher ground, have overwhelmed us. What, then, was the consequence? Great is the fortune of the Roman people; great and terrible its name! By the recent downfall of Hannibal, Philip, and Antiochus, the Gauls were in a manner thunderstruck. Bulky as their bodies were, they were dismayed, and put to flight by slings and arrows; not a sword was blooded in battle during the Gallic war. Like flocks of birds, they flew away at the very sound of our missile weapons. But, indeed, when we, the same army, were on our return, and happened to fall in with a party of Thracian Robbers, (as if fortune meant to teach us what the issue would have been, had we been opposed by men,) we, I say, were beaten, routed, and stripped of our baggage. Among many brave soldiers fell Quintus Minucius Thermus, whose death was a much greater loss than if Cneius Manlius, to whose rashness the misfortune was owing, had perished. An army, carrying home the spoils of King Antiochus, being scattered in three places; the vanguard in one, the rear in another, and the baggage in a third, hid itself for a night among bushes, in the retirements of wild beasts. Is a triumph demanded for such exploits as these? Although no disaster and disgrace had been suffered in Thrace, over what enemies would you triumph? Is it over those against whom the Roman senate or people had commissioned you to fight? On this ground, indeed, a triumph was granted to Lucius Scipio; to Manius Acilius, over King Antiochus; to Titus Quintius, over King Philip; and to Publius Africanus, over Hannibal, the Carthaginians, and Syphax. Now, after the senate had voted a declaration of war, the following points, trifling as they appear, were nevertheless attended to:—To whom the declaration ought to be made; whether to the kings in person, or whether making it at some of their garrisons were sufficient. Do you wish, then, that all these rites should be disregar and profaned? That the laws of the heralds be abrogat that there should be no heralds? Let religion (the gods pardon the expression) be thrown aside; retain not a thought of the gods. Do you, also, judge it fit that the senate should not be consulted concerning war? That the people should not be asked whether they choose and order war to be made on the Gauls? On a late occasion the consuls certainly wished for the provinces of Greece and Asia, yet when the senate persisted in assigning Liguria as their province, they obeyed its commands. They will, therefore, if successful in the war, justly demand a triumph from you, conscript fathers, under whose authority they carried it on."

47. Such were the arguments of Furius; and Æmilius Manlius, as we are told, replied in nearly the following manner: "Conscript fathers, formerly the tribunes of the people were accustomed to oppose generals demanding a triumph. I am thankful to the present tribunes for paying so much regard either to me, or to the greatness of my services, as not only to show, by their silence, their approbation of my pretensions to that honour, but likewise for having declared themselves ready, if there were occasion, to make a motion to that purpose. It is my lot, it seems, to be opposed by some of the ten ambassadors, the actual council which our ancestors assigned to generals for the purpose of arranging their conquests and proclaiming their victories. They who forbid me to mount the triumphal chariot, who would pluck from my head the crown of glory, are Lucius Furius and Lucius Æmilius, the persons whom, if the tribunes had opposed my triumph, I should have cited as witnesses to bear testimony to my services. Conscript fathers, be assured I envy no man's honours; but, on a late occasion, when the tribunes of the people, brave and active men, objected to the triumph of Quintus Fabius Labeo, you interposed your authority, and forced them to desist. Fabius enjoyed a triumph; although, if his adversaries were to be believed, he never even saw an enemy: whereas I, who fought so many pitched battles with one hundred thousand of your fiercest enemies; who killed or made prisoners more than forty thousand; who stormed two of their camps; who left all the countries on this side of the summits of Taurus in greater tranquillity than is enjoyed by the country of Italy,—am not only defrauded of a triumph, but obliged, like a criminal, to plead my cause before you, conscript fathers, against charges advanced by my own council of ambassadors. Conscript fathers, their charge, as you perceive, is twofold: for they assert that I ought not to have waged war with the Gauls, and that my conduct in the war was rash and imprudent. The Gauls were not enemies; but, though they were peaceable and obedient to orders, you committed hostilities against

them. You are well acquainted with the savage fierceness of the Gallic nation in general, and with their most inveterate hatred to the Roman name, but you are not to apply the same character to that part of them who reside in those countries. Exclude the infamous and odious character of the whole nation, and judge of these Gauls separately and by themselves. I wish King Eumenes, I wish all the states of Asia, were present, and that you heard their complaints rather than my charges against them. Send ambassadors round all the cities of Asia, and ask whether they were relieved from more grievous servitude by the removal of Antiochus beyond the summits of Taurus, or by the conquest of the Gauls. Let them tell you how often their territories were ravaged, how often their property and their people were carried off as prey, while, scarcely ever allowed to ransom any prisoners, they heard of nothing but human victims slain, and their children offered up in sacrifice. Let me inform you, that your allies paid tribute to these Gauls; and, though delivered now by you from the yoke of Antiochus, must still have continued to pay it, if I had lain inactive. The farther Antiochus was removed, the more licentiously would the Gauls have domineered in Asia; and all the countries on this side of Taurus you would have annexed to their empire, not to your own.

48. "But, allowing all this to be true, say they, the Gauls formerly sacked Delphi, the common oracle to which all mankind resort, and the central point of the globe of the earth; yet the Roman people did not, on that account, make war against them. I really thought that there was some distinction to be made between that period when Greece and Asia were not yet under your jurisdiction and dominion, and the present, when you have made Mount Taurus the boundary of the Roman empire; when you grant liberty and independence to the states of that country; when you augment the territories of some; amerce others in a part of their lands; impose tribute; add to, diminish, give, and take away kingdoms; and deem it your business to take care that they enjoy peace both on land and sea. You thought the liberty of Asia incomplete unless Antiochus withdrew his garrisons, which lay quiet in their citadels; and can you think that, if the armies of the Gauls roamed about without control, the grants which you made to King Eumenes would be secure, or the liberty of the states entire? But why do I reason thus? as if I had not found the Gauls enemies, but made them such! I appeal to you, Lucius Scipio, whose bravery and good fortune I prayed to the immortal gods to grant me, when I succeeded you in the command; and I prayed not in vain: and to you, Publius Scipio, who held, both with you

brother the consul and with the army, the commission of a lieutenant-general, and the dignity of a colleague,—were the legions of the Gauls, to your knowledge, in the army of Antiochus? Did you see them in his line of battle, posted in both wings; for there was his main strength? Did you fight them as declared enemies? Did you kill them? Did you carry off their spoils? Yet the senate had decreed, and the people ordered, war against Antiochus, not against the Gauls. But I take for granted that their decree and order included, at the same time, all those who should fight under his banner; so that, excepting Antiochus, with whom Scipio had negotiated a peace, and with whom, specifying him by name, you had directed a treaty to be concluded, every one who had borne arms on the side of Antiochus, against us, were our enemies. In this light I was to consider all the Gauls, as well as several petty princes and tyrants; nevertheless, I made peace with the rest, after compelling them to atone for their transgressions as the dignity of your empire required. I made trial, at the same time, of the temper of the Gauls, whether they could be reclaimed from their natural ferocity; but, perceiving them untractable and implacable, I then judged it necessary to chastise them by force of arms.

49. "Having fully refuted the charge respecting the undertaking of the war, I am now to account for my conduct in the prosecution of it. On this head, indeed, I should perfectly confide in the merits of my cause, though I were pleading, not before a Roman, but before a Carthaginian senate, who are said to crucify their commanders if they act, even with success, on wrong plans. But in such a state as this, which, in the commencement and progress of every undertaking, makes application to the gods to prompt them rightly, so that malicious calumnies may not prevail; and which, in the established form, when it decrees a supplication or triumph, uses these words,—'For having conducted the business of the public successfully and fortunately;'—if I should be unwilling, if I should think it presumptuous and arrogant to boast of my own bravery, and if I should demand, in consideration of my own good fortune, and that of my army, in having vanquished so great a nation without any loss of men, that thanks should be given to the immortal gods, and that I should ascend the capitol in triumph, from whence I took my departure, with vows duly offered,—would you refuse this to me,—would you refuse acknowledgments to the immortal gods? Yes; for I fought on unfavourable ground. Tell me, then, on what more favourable ground could I have fought, when the enemy had seized on a mountain, and kept themselves in a strong spot? Surely, if I wished to con-

Lightning Source UK Ltd.
Milton Keynes UK
UKHW020757220119
335989UK00010B/915/P